Elements of Causal Inference

Foundations and Learning Algorithms

A complete list of books published in The Adaptive Computation and Machine Learning series appears at the back of this book.

Elements of Causal Inference

Foundations and Learning Algorithms

Jonas Peters, Dominik Janzing, and Bernhard Schölkopf

The MIT Press
Cambridge, Massachusetts
London, England

This book was set in LaTeX by the authors.

Printed and bound in the United States of America.

Library of Congress Cataloging-in-Publication Data
Names: Peters, Jonas. | Janzing, Dominik. | Schölkopf, Bernhard.
Title: Elements of causal inference : foundations and learning algorithms / Jonas Peters, Dominik Janzing, and Bernhard Schölkopf.
Description: Cambridge, MA : MIT Press, 2017. | Series: Adaptive computation and machine learning series | Includes bibliographical references and index.
Identifiers: LCCN 2017020087 | ISBN 9780262037310 (hardcover : alk. paper)
Subjects: LCSH: Machine learning. | Logic, Symbolic and mathematical. | Causation. | Inference. | Computer algorithms.
Classification: LCC Q325.5 .P48 2017 | DDC 006.3/1–dc23
LC record available at https://lccn.loc.gov/2017020087

10 9 8 7 6 5 4 3

To all those who enjoy the pursuit of causal insight

Contents

Preface

Causality is a fascinating topic of research. Its mathematization has only relatively recently started, and many conceptual problems are still being debated — often with considerable intensity.

While this book summarizes the results of spending a decade assaying causality, others have studied this problem much longer than we have, and there already exist books about causality, including the comprehensive treatments of Pearl [2009], Spirtes et al. [2000], and Imbens and Rubin [2015]. We hope that our book is able to complement existing work in two ways.

First, the present book represents a bias toward a subproblem of causality that may be considered both the most fundamental and the least realistic. This is the cause-effect problem, where the system under analysis contains only two observables. We have studied this problem in some detail during the last decade. We report much of this work, and try to embed it into a larger context of what we consider fundamental for gaining a selective but profound understanding of the issues of causality. Although it might be instructive to study the bivariate case first, following the sequential chapter order, it is also possible to directly start reading the multivariate chapters; see Figure I.

And second, our treatment is motivated and influenced by the fields of machine learning and computational statistics. We are interested in how methods thereof can help with the inference of causal structures, and even more so whether causal reasoning can inform the way we should be doing machine learning. Indeed, we feel that some of the most profound open issues of machine learning are best understood if we do not take a random experiment described by a probability distribution as our starting point, but instead we consider causal structures underlying the distribution.

We try to provide a systematic introduction into the topic that is accessible to readers familiar with the basics of probability theory and statistics or machine learning (for completeness, the most important concepts are summarized in Appendices A.1 and A.2).

While we build on the graphical approach to causality as represented by the work of Pearl [2009] and Spirtes et al. [2000], our personal taste influenced the choice of topics. To keep the book accessible and focus on the conceptual issues, we were forced to devote regrettably little space to a number of significant issues in causality, be it advanced theoretical insights for particular settings or various methods of practical importance. We have tried to include references to the literature for some of the most glaring omissions, but we may have missed important topics.

Our book has a number of shortcomings. Some of them are inherited from the field, such as the tendency that theoretical results are often restricted to the case where we have infinite amounts of data. Although we do provide algorithms and methodology for the finite data case, we do not discuss statistical properties of such methods. Additionally, at some places we neglect measure theoretic issues, often by assuming the existence of densities. We find all of these questions both relevant and interesting but made these choices to keep the book short and accessible to a broad audience.

Another disclaimer is in order. Computational causality methods are still in their infancy, and in particular, learning causal structures from data is only doable in rather limited situations. We have tried to include concrete algorithms wherever possible, but we are acutely aware that many of the problems of causal inference are harder than typical machine learning problems, and we thus make no promises as to whether the algorithms will work on the reader's problems. Please do not feel discouraged by this remark — causal learning is a fascinating topic and we hope that reading this book may convince you to start working on it.

We would have not been able to finish this book without the support of various people.

We gratefully acknowledge support for a Research in Pairs stay of the three authors at the Mathematisches Forschungsinstitut Oberwolfach, during which a substantial part of this book was written.

We thank Michel Besserve, Peter Bühlmann, Rune Christiansen, Frederick Eberhardt, Jan Ernest, Philipp Geiger, Niels Richard Hansen, Alain Hauser, Biwei Huang, Marek Kaluba, Hansruedi Künsch, Steffen Lauritzen, Jan Lemeire, David Lopez-Paz, Marloes Maathuis, Nicolai Meinshausen, Søren Wengel Mogensen, Joris Mooij, Krikamol Muandet, Judea Pearl, Niklas Pfister, Thomas Richardson, Mateo Rojas-Carulla, Eleni Sgouritsa, Carl Johann Simon-Gabriel, Xiaohai Sun, Ilya Tolstikhin, Kun Zhang, and Jakob Zscheischler for many helpful comments and interesting discussions during the time this book was written. In particular,

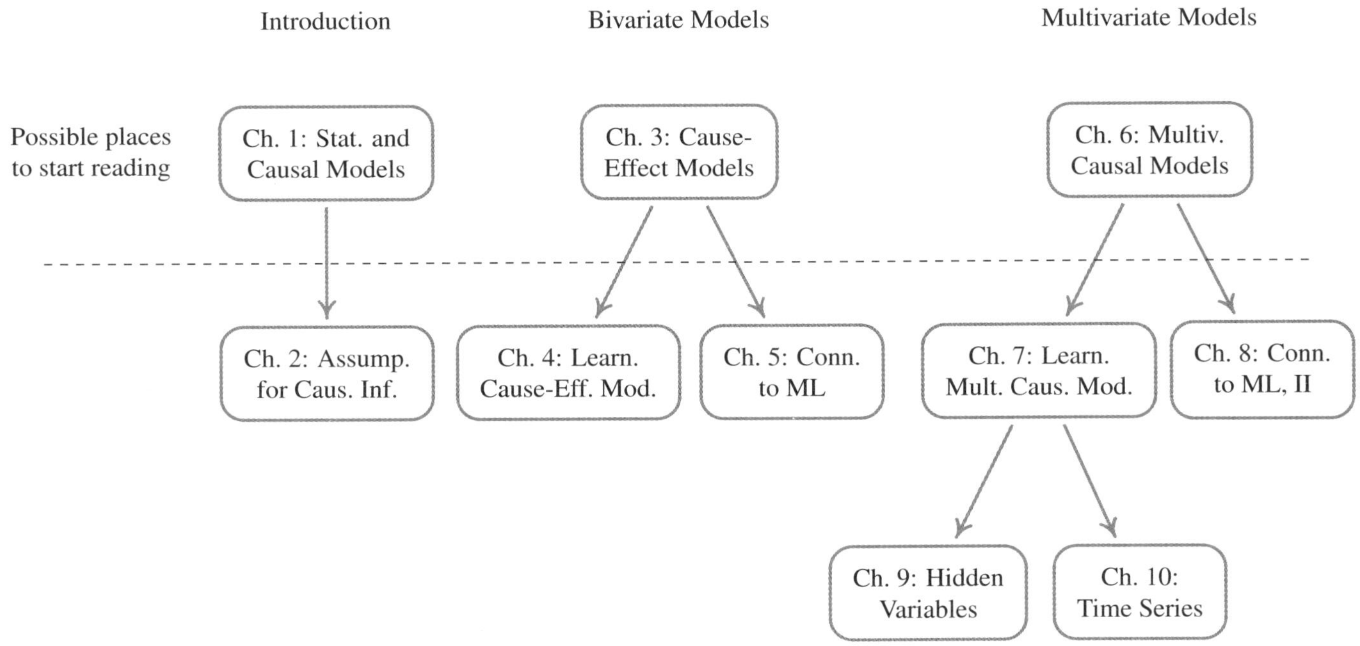

Figure I: This figure depicts the stronger dependences among the chapters (there exist many more less-pronounced relations). We suggest that the reader begins with Chapter 1, 3, or 6.

Joris and Kun were involved in much of the research that is presented here.

We thank various students at Karlsruhe Institute of Technology, Eidgenössische Technische Hochschule Zürich, and University of Tübingen for proofreading early versions of this book and for asking many inspiring questions.

Finally, we thank the anonymous reviewers and the copyediting team from Westchester Publishing Services for their helpful comments, and the staff from MIT Press, in particular Marie Lufkin Lee and Christine Bridget Savage, for providing kind support during the whole process.

København and Tübingen, August 2017

Jonas Peters
Dominik Janzing
Bernhard Schölkopf

Notation and Terminology

X,Y,Z	random variable; for noise variables, we use N, N_X, $N_j, \ldots$
x	value of a random variable X
P	probability measure
P_X	probability distribution of X
$X^1,\ldots,X^n \overset{\text{iid}}{\sim} P_X$	an i.i.d. sample of size n; sample index is usually i
$P_{Y\|X=x}$	conditional distribution of Y given $X = x$
$P_{Y\|X}$	collection of $P_{Y\|X=x}$ for all x; for short: conditional of Y given X
p	density (either probability mass function or probability density function)
p_X	density of P_X
$p(x)$	density of P_X evaluated at the point x
$p(y\|x)$	(conditional) density of $P_{Y\|X=x}$ evaluated at y
$\mathbb{E}[X]$	expectation of X
$\text{var}[X]$	variance of X
$\text{cov}[X,Y]$	covariance of X,Y
$X \perp\!\!\!\perp Y$	independence between random variables X and Y
$X \perp\!\!\!\perp Y \mid Z$	conditional independence
$\mathbf{X} = (X_1,\ldots,X_d)$	random vector of length d; dimension index is usually j
$\mathfrak{C}$	structural causal model
$P_Y^{\mathfrak{C};do(X:=3)}$	intervention distribution
$P_Y^{\mathfrak{C}\|Z=2,X=1;do(X:=3)}$	counterfactual distribution
$\mathcal{G}$	graph
$\mathbf{PA}_X^{\mathcal{G}}$, $\mathbf{DE}_X^{\mathcal{G}}$, $\mathbf{AN}_X^{\mathcal{G}}$	parents, descendants, and ancestors of node X in graph $\mathcal{G}$

1

Statistical and Causal Models

Using statistical learning, we try to infer properties of the dependence among random variables from observational data. For instance, based on a joint sample of observations of two random variables, we might build a predictor that, given new values of only one of them, will provide a good estimate of the other one. The theory underlying such predictions is well developed, and — although it applies to simple settings — already provides profound insights into learning from data. For two reasons, we will describe some of these insights in the present chapter. First, this will help us appreciate how much harder the problems of *causal* inference are, where the underlying model is no longer a fixed joint distribution of random variables, but a structure that implies multiple such distributions. Second, although finite sample results for causal estimation are scarce, it is important to keep in mind that the basic statistical estimation problems do not go away when moving to the more complex causal setting, even if they seem small compared to the causal problems that do not appear in purely statistical learning. Building on the preceding groundwork, the chapter also provides a gentle introduction to the basic notions of causality, using two examples, one of which is well known from machine learning.

1.1 Probability Theory and Statistics

Probability theory and statistics are based on the model of a random experiment or probability space $(\Omega, \mathcal{F}, P)$. Here, Ω is a set (containing all possible outcomes), $\mathcal{F}$ is a collection of events $A \subseteq \Omega$, and P is a measure assigning a probability to each event. Probability theory allows us to reason about the outcomes of random experiments, given the preceding mathematical structure. Statistical learning, on the other hand, essentially deals with the inverse problem: We are given the outcomes of experiments, and from this we want to infer properties of the underlying mathematical structure. For instance, suppose that we have observed data

$$(x_1, y_1), \dots, (x_n, y_n), \tag{1.1}$$

where $x_i \in \mathcal{X}$ are **inputs** (sometimes called **covariates** or **cases**) and $y_i \in \mathcal{Y}$ are **outputs** (sometimes called **targets** or **labels**). We may now assume that each (x_i, y_i), $i = 1, \dots, n$, has been generated independently by the same unknown random experiment. More precisely, such a model assumes that the observations $(x_1, y_1), \dots, (x_n, y_n)$ are realizations of random variables $(X_1, Y_1), \dots, (X_n, Y_n)$ that are **i.i.d. (independent and identically distributed)** with joint distribution $P_{X,Y}$. Here, X and Y are random variables taking values in metric spaces $\mathcal{X}$ and $\mathcal{Y}$.[1] Almost all of statistics and machine learning builds on i.i.d. data. In practice, the i.i.d. assumption can be violated in various ways, for instance if distributions shift or interventions in a system occur. As we shall see later, some of these are intricately linked to causality.

We may now be interested in certain properties of $P_{X,Y}$, such as:

(i) the expectation of the output given the input, $f(x) = \mathbb{E}[Y \mid X = x]$, called **regression**, where often $\mathcal{Y} = \mathbb{R}$,

(ii) a binary **classifier** assigning each x to the class that is more likely, $f(x) = \operatorname{argmax}_{y \in \mathcal{Y}} P(Y = y \mid X = x)$, where $\mathcal{Y} = \{\pm 1\}$,

(iii) the density $p_{X,Y}$ of $P_{X,Y}$ (assuming it exists).

In practice, we seek to estimate these properties from finite data sets, that is, based on the sample (1.1), or equivalently an empirical distribution $P^n_{X,Y}$ that puts a point mass of equal weight on each observation.

This constitutes an **inverse problem**: We want to estimate a property of an object we cannot observe (the underlying distribution), based on observations that are obtained by applying an operation (in the present case: sampling from the unknown distribution) to the underlying object.

[1] A random variable X is a measurable function $\Omega \to \mathcal{X}$, where the metric space $\mathcal{X}$ is equipped with the Borel σ-algebra. Its distribution P_X on $\mathcal{X}$ can be obtained from the measure P of the underlying probability space $(\Omega, \mathcal{F}, P)$. We need not worry about this underlying space, and instead we generally start directly with the distribution of the random variables, assuming the random experiment directly provides us with values sampled from that distribution.

1.2 Learning Theory

Now suppose that just like we can obtain f from $P_{X,Y}$, we use the empirical distribution to infer empirical estimates f^n. This turns out to be an **ill-posed problem** [e.g., Vapnik, 1998], since for any values of x that we have not seen in the sample $(x_1, y_1), \ldots, (x_n, y_n)$, the conditional expectation is undefined. We may, however, define the function f on the observed sample and extend it according to any fixed rule (e.g., setting f to $+1$ outside the sample or by choosing a continuous piecewise linear f). But for any such choice, small changes in the input, that is, in the empirical distribution, can lead to large changes in the output. No matter how many observations we have, the empirical distribution will usually not perfectly approximate the true distribution, and small errors in this approximation can then lead to large errors in the estimates. This implies that without additional assumptions about the class of functions from which we choose our empirical estimates f^n, we cannot guarantee that the estimates will approximate the optimal quantities f in a suitable sense. In statistical learning theory, these assumptions are formalized in terms of **capacity** measures. If we work with a function class that is so rich that it can fit most conceivable data sets, then it is not surprising if we can fit the data at hand. If, however, the function class is a priori restricted to have small capacity, then there are only a few data sets (out of the space of all possible data sets) that we can explain using a function from that class. If it turns out that nevertheless we can explain the data at hand, then we have reason to believe that we have found a regularity underlying the data. In that case, we can give probabilistic guarantees for the solution's accuracy on future data sampled from the same distribution $P_{X,Y}$.

Another way to think of this is that our function class has incorporated **a priori knowledge** (such as smoothness of functions) consistent with the regularity underlying the observed data. Such knowledge can be incorporated in various ways, and different approaches to machine learning differ in how they handle the issue. In Bayesian approaches, we specify prior distributions over function classes and noise models. In regularization theory, we construct suitable regularizers and incorporate them into optimization problems to bias our solutions.

The complexity of statistical learning arises primarily from the fact that we are trying to solve an inverse problem based on empirical data — if we were given the full probabilistic model, then all these problems go away. When we discuss causal models, we will see that in a sense, the causal learning problem is harder in that it is ill-posed *on two levels*. In addition to the statistical ill-posed-ness, which is essentially because a finite sample of arbitrary size will never contain all information about the underlying distribution, there is an ill-posed-ness due to the fact that even complete knowledge of an observational distribution usually does not determine the underlying causal model.

Let us look at the statistical learning problem in more detail, focusing on the case of **binary pattern recognition** or classification [e.g., Vapnik, 1998], where $\mathcal{Y} = \{\pm 1\}$. We seek to learn $f : \mathcal{X} \to \mathcal{Y}$ based on observations (1.1), generated i.i.d. from an unknown $P_{X,Y}$. Our goal is to minimize the expected error or **risk**[2]

$$R[f] = \int \frac{1}{2}|f(x) - y| \, dP_{X,Y}(x,y) \tag{1.2}$$

over some class of functions $\mathcal{F}$. Note that this is an integral with respect to the measure $P_{X,Y}$; however, if $P_{X,Y}$ allows for a density $p(x,y)$ with respect to Lebesgue measure, the integral reduces to $\int \frac{1}{2}|f(x) - y| \, p(x,y) \, dxdy$.

Since $P_{X,Y}$ is unknown, we cannot compute (1.2), let alone minimize it. Instead, we appeal to an **induction principle**, such as **empirical risk minimization**. We return the function minimizing the training error or empirical risk

$$R^n_{\text{emp}}[f] = \frac{1}{n} \sum_{i=1}^{n} \frac{1}{2}|f(x_i) - y_i| \tag{1.3}$$

over $f \in \mathcal{F}$. From the asymptotic point of view, it is important to ask whether such a procedure is **consistent**, which essentially means that it produces a sequence of functions whose risk converges towards the minimal possible within the given function class $\mathcal{F}$ (in probability) as n tends to infinity. In Appendix A.3, we show that this can only be the case if the function class is "small." The Vapnik-Chervonenkis (VC) dimension [Vapnik, 1998] is one possibility of measuring the **capacity** or **size** of a function class. It also allows us to derive finite sample guarantees, stating that with high probability, the risk (1.2) is not larger than the empirical risk plus a term that grows with the size of the function class $\mathcal{F}$.

Such a theory does not contradict the existing results on **universal consistency**, which refers to convergence of a learning algorithm to the lowest achievable risk with *any* function. There are learning algorithms that are universally consistent, for instance nearest neighbor classifiers and Support Vector Machines [Devroye et al., 1996, Vapnik, 1998, Schölkopf and Smola, 2002, Steinwart and Christmann, 2008]. While universal consistency essentially tells us everything can be learned in

---

[2]This notion of risk, which does not always coincide with its colloquial use, is taken from statistical learning theory [Vapnik, 1998] and has its roots in statistical decision theory [Wald, 1950, Ferguson, 1967, Berger, 1985]. In that context, $f(x)$ is thought of as an action taken upon observing x, and the loss function measures the loss incurred when the state of nature is y.

the limit of infinite data, it does not imply that every problem is well learnable from finite data, due to the phenomenon of **slow rates**. For any learning algorithm, there exist problems for which the learning rates are arbitrarily slow [Devroye et al., 1996]. It does tell us, however, that if we fix the distribution, and gather enough data, then we can get arbitrarily close to the lowest risk eventually.

In practice, recent successes of machine learning systems seem to suggest that we are indeed sometimes already in this asymptotic regime, often with spectacular results. A lot of thought has gone into designing the most data-efficient methods to obtain the best possible results from a given data set, and a lot of effort goes into building large data sets that enable us to train these methods. However, in all these settings, it is crucial that the underlying distribution does not differ between training and testing, be it by interventions or other changes. As we shall argue in this book, describing the underlying regularity as a probability distribution, without additional structure, does not provide us with the right means to describe what might change.

1.3 Causal Modeling and Learning

Causal modeling starts from another, arguably more fundamental, structure. A causal structure *entails* a probability model, but it contains additional information *not* contained in the latter (see the examples in Section 1.4). **Causal reasoning**, according to the terminology used in this book, denotes the process of drawing conclusions from a causal model, similar to the way probability theory allows us to reason about the outcomes of random experiments. However, since causal models contain more information than probabilistic ones do, causal reasoning is more powerful than probabilistic reasoning, because causal reasoning allows us to analyze the effect of interventions or distribution changes.

Just like statistical learning denotes the inverse problem to probability theory, we can think about how to infer causal structures from its empirical implications. The empirical implications can be purely observational, but they can also include data under interventions (e.g., randomized trials) or distribution changes. Researchers use various terms to refer to these problems, including **structure learning** and **causal discovery**. We refer to the closely related question of which parts of the causal structure can in principle be inferred from the joint distribution as **structure identifiability**. Unlike the standard problems of statistical learning described in Section 1.2, even full knowledge of P does not make the solution trivial, and we need additional assumptions (see Chapters 2, 4, and 7). This difficulty should

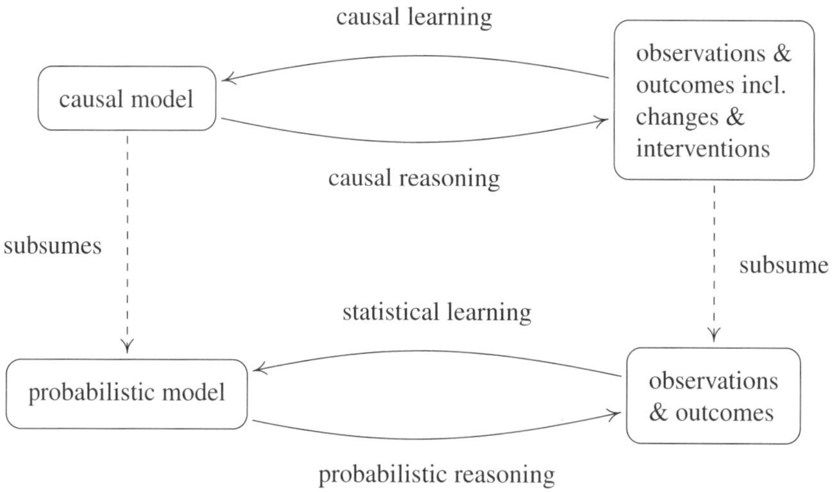

Figure 1.1: Terminology used by the present book for various **probabilistic inference** problems (bottom) and **causal inference** problems (top); see Section 1.3. Note that we use the term "inference" to include both learning and reasoning.

not distract us from the fact, however, that the ill-posed-ness of the usual statistical problems is still there (and thus it is important to worry about the capacity of function classes also in causality, such as by using additive noise models — see Section 4.1.4 below), only confounded by an additional difficulty arising from the fact that we are trying to estimate a richer structure than just a probabilistic one. We will refer to this overall problem as **causal learning**. Figure 1.1 summarizes the relationships between the preceding problems and models.

To learn causal structures from observational distributions, we need to understand how causal models and statistical models relate to each other. We will come back to this issue in Chapters 4 and 7 but provide an example now. A well-known topos holds that *correlation does not imply causation*; in other words, statistical properties alone do not determine causal structures. It is less well known that one may postulate that while we cannot infer a concrete causal structure, we may at least infer the existence of causal links from statistical dependences. This was first understood by Reichenbach [1956]; we now formulate his insight (see also Figure 1.2).[3]

[3]For clarity, we formulate some important assumptions as *principles*. We do not take them for granted throughout the book; in this sense, they are not axioms.

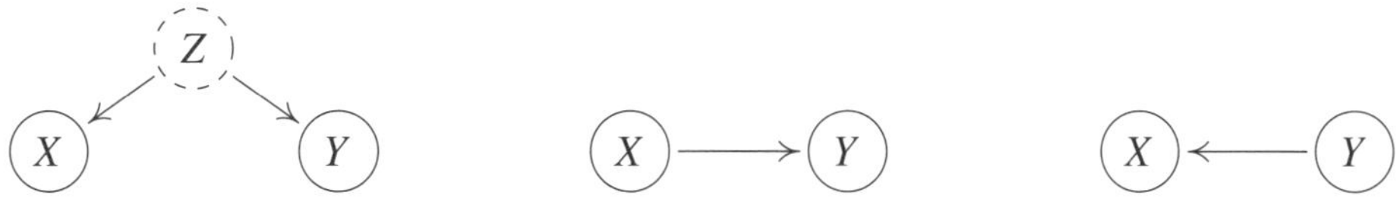

Figure 1.2: Reichenbach's common cause principle establishes a link between statistical properties and causal structures. A *statistical* dependence between two observables X and Y indicates that they are *caused* by a variable Z, often referred to as a **confounder** (left). Here, Z may coincide with either X or Y, in which case the figure simplifies (middle/right). The principle further argues that X and Y are statistically independent, conditional on Z. In this figure, direct causation is indicated by arrows; see Chapters 3 and 6.

Principle 1.1 (Reichenbach's common cause principle) *If two random variables X and Y are statistically dependent ($X \not\perp\!\!\!\perp Y$), then there exists a third variable Z that* causally *influences both. (As a special case, Z may coincide with either X or Y.) Furthermore, this variable Z screens X and Y from each other in the sense that given Z, they become independent, $X \perp\!\!\!\perp Y \,|\, Z$.*

In practice, dependences may also arise for a reason different from the ones mentioned in the common cause principle, for instance: (1) The random variables we observe are conditioned on others (often implicitly by a selection bias). We shall return to this issue; see Remark 6.29. (2) The random variables only *appear* to be dependent. For example, they may be the result of a search procedure over a large number of pairs of random variables that was run without a multiple testing correction. In this case, inferring a dependence between the variables does not satisfy the desired type I error control; see Appendix A.2. (3) Similarly, both random variables may inherit a time dependence and follow a simple physical law, such as exponential growth. The variables then *look* as if they depend on each other, but because the i.i.d. assumption is violated, there is no justification of applying a standard independence test. In particular, arguments (2) and (3) should be kept in mind when reporting "spurious correlations" between random variables, as it is done on many popular websites.

1.4 Two Examples

1.4.1 Pattern Recognition

As the first example, we consider *optical character recognition*, a well-studied problem in machine learning. This is not a run-of-the-mill example of a causal structure, but it may be instructive for readers familiar with machine learning. We describe two causal models giving rise to a dependence between two random variables, which we will assume to be handwritten digits X and class labels Y. The two models will lead to the same statistical structure, using distinct underlying causal structures.

Model (i) assumes we generate each pair of observations by providing a sequence of class labels y to a human writer, with the instruction to always produce a corresponding handwritten digit image x. We assume that the writer tries to do a good job, but there may be noise in perceiving the class label and executing the motor program to draw the image. We can model this process by writing the image X as a function (or mechanism) f of the class label Y (modeled as a random variable) and some independent noise N_X (see Figure 1.3, left). We can then compute $P_{X,Y}$ from P_Y, P_{N_X}, and f. This is referred to as the **observational distribution**, where the word "observational" refers to the fact that we are passively observing the system without intervening. X and Y will be dependent random variables, and we will be able to learn the mapping from x to y from observations and predict the correct label y from an image x better than chance.

There are two possible interventions in this causal structure, which lead to **intervention distributions**.[4] If we intervene on the resulting image X (by manipulating it, or exchanging it for another image after it has been produced), then this has no effect on the class labels that were provided to the writer and recorded in the data set. Formally, changing X has no effect on Y since $Y := N_Y$. Intervening on Y, on the other hand, amounts to changing the class labels provided to the writer. This will obviously have a strong effect on the produced images. Formally, changing Y has an effect on X since $X := f(Y, N_X)$. This directionality is visible in the arrow in the figure, and we think of this arrow as representing direct causation.

In alternative **model (ii)**, we assume that we *do not* provide class labels to the writer. Rather, the writer is asked to decide himself or herself which digits to write, and to record the class labels alongside. In this case, both the image X and the recorded class label Y are functions of the writer's intention (call it Z and think of it as a random variable). For generality, we assume that not only the process generating the image is noisy but also the one recording the class label, again with independent noise terms (see Figure 1.3, right). Note that if the functions and noise terms are chosen suitably, we can ensure that this model entails an observational distribution $P_{X,Y}$ that is identical to the one entailed by model (i).[5]

---

[4]We shall see in Section 6.3 that a more general way to think of interventions is that they change functions and random variables.

[5]Indeed, Proposition 4.1 implies that *any* joint distribution $P_{X,Y}$ can be entailed by both models.

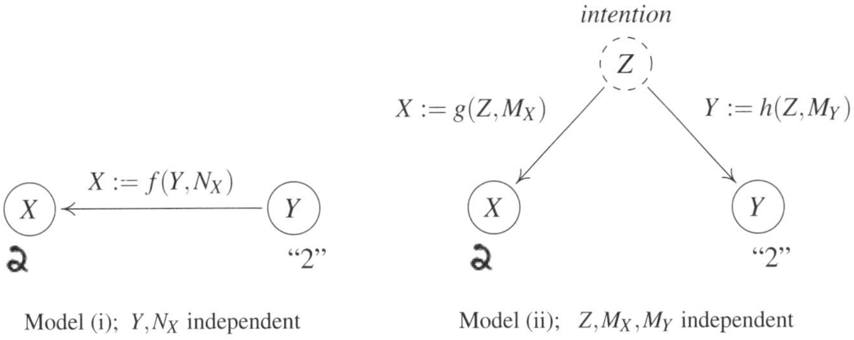

Figure 1.3: Two structural causal models of handwritten digit data sets. In the left model (i), a human is provided with class labels Y and produces images X. In the right model (ii), the human decides which class to write (Z) and produces both images and class labels. For suitable functions f, g, h and noise variables N_X, M_X, M_Y, Z, the two models produce the same observable distribution $P_{X,Y}$, yet they are interventionally different; see Section 1.4.1.

Let us now discuss possible interventions in model (ii). If we intervene on the image X, then things are as we just discussed and the class label Y is not affected. However, if we intervene on the class label Y (i.e., we change what the writer has recorded as the class label), then unlike before this will *not* affect the image.

In summary, without restricting the class of involved functions and distributions, the causal models described in (i) and (ii) induce the same observational distribution over X and Y, but different intervention distributions. This difference is not visible in a purely probabilistic description (where everything derives from $P_{X,Y}$). However, we were able to discuss it by incorporating structural knowledge about how $P_{X,Y}$ comes about, in particular graph structure, functions, and noise terms.

Models (i) and (ii) are examples of **structural causal models (SCMs)**, sometimes referred to as **structural equation models** [e.g., Aldrich, 1989, Hoover, 2008, Pearl, 2009, Pearl et al., 2016]. In an SCM, all dependences are generated by functions that compute variables from other variables. Crucially, these functions are to be read as assignments, that is, as functions as in computer science rather than as mathematical equations. We usually think of them as modeling physical mechanisms. An SCM entails a joint distribution over all observables. We have seen that the same distribution can be generated by different SCMs, and thus information about the effect of interventions (and, as we shall see in Section 6.4, information about counterfactuals) may be lost when we make the transition from an SCM to the corresponding probability model. In this book, we take SCMs as our starting point and try to develop everything from there.

We conclude with two points connected to our example:

First, Figure 1.3 nicely illustrates Reichenbach's common cause principle. The dependence between X and Y admits several causal explanations, and X and Y become independent if we condition on Z in the right-hand figure: The image and the label share no information that is not contained in the intention.

Second, it is sometimes said that causality can only be discussed when taking into account the notion of **time**. Indeed, time does play a role in the preceding example, for instance by ruling out that an intervention on X will affect the class label. However, this is perfectly fine, and indeed it is quite common that a statistical data set is generated by a process taking place in time. For instance, in model (i), the underlying reason for the statistical dependence between X and Y is a dynamical process. The writer reads the label and plans a movement, entailing complicated processes in the brain, and finally executes the movement using muscles and a pen. This process is only partly understood, but it is a physical, dynamical process taking place in time whose end result leads to a non-trivial joint distribution of X and Y. When we perform statistical learning, we only care about the end result. Thus, not only causal structures, but also purely probabilistic structures may arise through processes taking place in time — indeed, one could hold that this is ultimately the only way they can come about. However, in both cases, it is often instructive to disregard time. In statistics, time is often not necessary to discuss concepts such as statistical dependence. In causal models, time is often not necessary to discuss the effect of interventions. But both levels of description can be thought of as abstractions of an underlying more accurate physical model that describes reality more fully than either; see Table 1.1. Moreover, note that variables in a model may not necessarily refer to well-defined time instances. If, for instance, a psychologist investigates the statistical or causal relation between the motivation and the performance of students, both variables cannot easily be assigned to specific time instances. Measurements that refer to well-defined time instances are rather typical for "hard" sciences like physics and chemistry.

1.4.2 Gene Perturbation

We have seen in Section 1.4.1 that different causal structures lead to different intervention distributions. Sometimes, we are indeed interested in predicting the outcome of a random variable under such an intervention. Consider the following, in some ways oversimplified, example from genetics. Assume that we are given activity data from gene A and, correspondingly, measurements of a phenotype; see

Model	Predict in i.i.d. setting	Predict under changing distr. or intervention	Answer counterfactual questions	Obtain physical insight	Learn from data
Mechanistic/ physical, e.g., Sec. 2.3	yes	yes	yes	yes	?
Structural causal model, e.g., Sec. 6.2	yes	yes	yes	?	?
Causal graphical model, e.g., Sec. 6.5.2	yes	yes	no	?	?
Statistical model, e.g., Sec. 1.2	yes	no	no	no	yes

Table 1.1: A simple taxonomy of models. The most detailed model (top) is a mechanistic or physical one, usually involving sets of differential equations. At the other end of the spectrum (bottom), we have a purely statistical model; this model can be learned from data, but it often provides little insight beyond modeling associations between epiphenomena. Causal models can be seen as descriptions that lie in between, abstracting away from physical realism while retaining the power to answer certain interventional or counterfactual questions. See Mooij et al. [2013] for a discussion of the link between physical models and structural causal models, and Section 6.3 for a discussion of interventions.

Figure 1.4 (top left) for a toy data set. Clearly, both variables are strongly correlated. This correlation can be exploited for classical prediction: If we *observe* that the activity of gene A lies around 6, we expect the phenotype to lie between 12 and 16 with high probability. Similarly, for a gene B (bottom left). On the other hand, we may also be interested in predicting the phenotype after *deleting* gene A, that is, after setting its activity to 0.[6] Without any knowledge of the causal structure, however, it is impossible to provide a non-trivial answer. If gene A has a causal influence on the phenotype, we expect to see a drastic change after the intervention (see top right). In fact, we may still be able to use the same linear model that we have learned from the observational data. If, alternatively, there is a common cause, possibly a third gene C, influencing both the activity of gene B and the phenotype, the intervention on gene B will have no effect on the phenotype (see bottom right).

[6]Let us for simplicity assume that we have access to the true activity of the gene without measurement noise.

As in the pattern recognition example, the models are again chosen such that the joint distribution over gene A and the phenotype equals the joint distribution over gene B and the phenotype. Therefore, there is no way of telling between the top and bottom situation from just observational data, even if sample size goes to infinity. Summarizing, if we are not willing to employ concepts from causality, we have to answer "I do not know" to the question of predicting a phenotype after deletion of a gene.

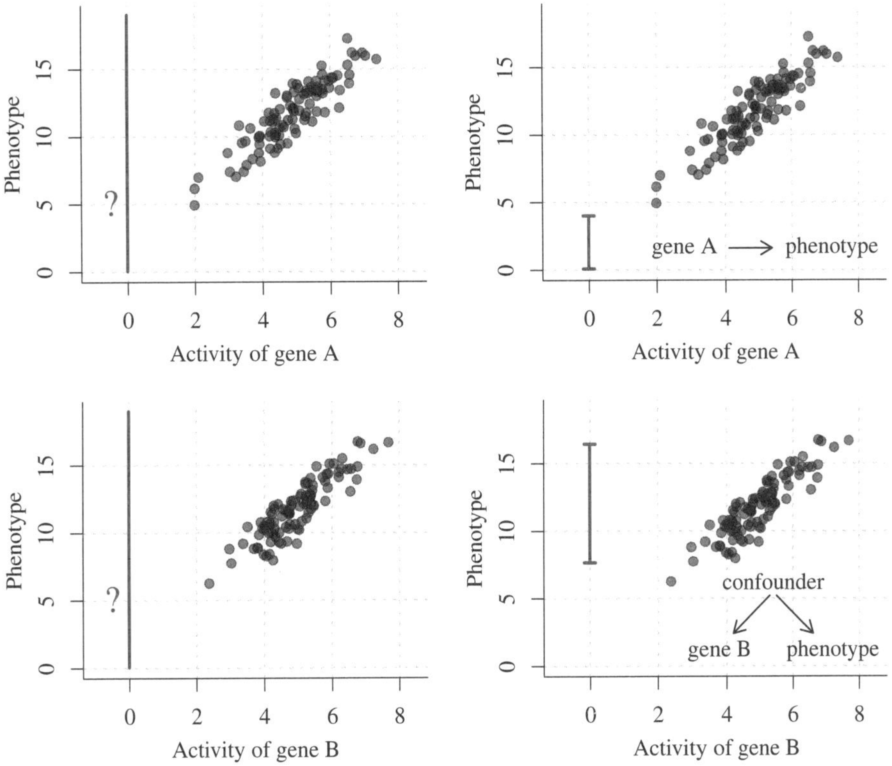

Figure 1.4: The activity of two genes (top: gene A; bottom: gene B) is strongly correlated with the phenotype (black dots). However, the best prediction for the phenotype when *deleting the gene*, that is, setting its activity to 0 (left), depends on the causal structure (right). If a common cause is responsible for the correlation between gene and phenotype, we expect the phenotype to behave under the intervention as it usually does (bottom right), whereas the intervention clearly changes the value of the phenotype if it is causally influenced by the gene (top right). The idea of this figure is based on Peters et al. [2016].

2

Assumptions for Causal Inference

Now that we have encountered the basic components of SCMs, it is a good time to pause and consider some of the assumptions we have seen, as well as what these assumptions imply for the purpose of causal reasoning and learning.

A crucial notion in our discussion will be a form of **independence**, and we can informally introduce it using an optical illusion known as the Beuchet chair. When we see an object such as the one on the left of Figure 2.1, our brain makes the assumption that the object and the mechanism by which the information contained in its light reaches our brain are independent. We can violate this assumption by looking at the object from a very specific viewpoint. If we do that, perception goes wrong: We perceive the three-dimensional structure of a chair, which in reality is not there. Most of the time, however, the independence assumption does hold. If we look at an object, our brain assumes that the object is independent from our vantage point and the illumination. So there should be no unlikely coincidences, no separate 3D structures lining up in two dimensions, or shadow boundaries coinciding with texture boundaries. This is called the *generic viewpoint assumption* in vision [Freeman, 1994].

The independence assumption is more general than this, though. We will see in Section 2.1 below that the causal generative process is composed of autonomous modules that do not inform or influence each other. As we shall describe below, this means that while one module's output may influence another module's input, the modules themselves are independent of each other.

In the preceding example, while the overall percept is a function of object, lighting, and viewpoint, the object and the lighting are not affected by us moving about — in other words, some components of the overall causal generative model remain *invariant*, and we can infer three-dimensional information from this invariance.

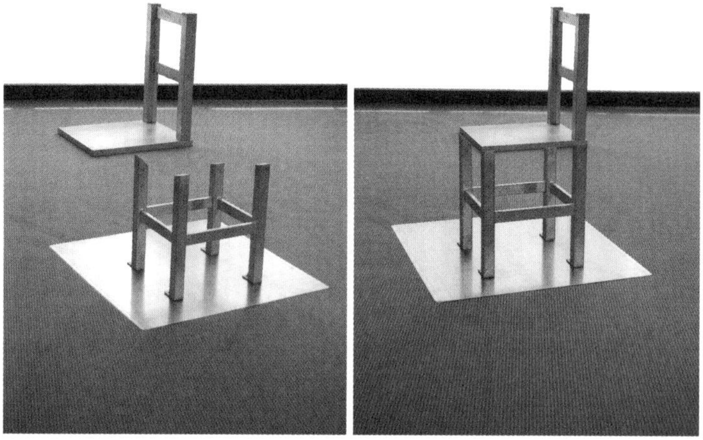

Figure 2.1: The left panel shows a generic view of the (separate) parts comprising a *Beuchet chair*. The right panel shows the illusory percept of a chair if the parts are viewed from a single, very special vantage point. From this *accidental viewpoint*, we perceive a chair. (Image courtesy of Markus Elsholz.)

This is the basic idea of *structure from motion* [Ullman, 1979], which plays a central role in both biological vision and computer vision.

2.1 The Principle of Independent Mechanisms

We now describe a simple cause-effect problem and point out several observations. Subsequently, we shall try to provide a unified view of how these observation relate to each other, arguing that they derive from a common independence principle.

Suppose we have estimated the joint density $p(a,t)$ of the altitude A and the average annual temperature T of a sample of cities in some country (see Figure 4.6 on page 65). Consider the following ways of expressing $p(a,t)$:

$$\begin{aligned} p(a,t) &= p(a|t)\, p(t) \\ &= p(t|a)\, p(a) \end{aligned} \tag{2.1}$$

The first decomposition describes T and the conditional $A|T$. It corresponds to a factorization of $p(a,t)$ according to the graph $T \to A$.[1] The second decomposition corresponds to a factorization according to $A \to T$ (cf. Definition 6.21). Can we

[1] Note that the conditional density $p(a|t)$ allows us to compute $p(a,t)$ (and thus also $p(a)$) from

decide which of the two structures is the *causal* one (i.e., in which case would we be able to think of the arrow as causal)?

A first idea (see Figure 2.2, left) is to consider the **effect of interventions**. Imagine we could change the altitude A of a city by some hypothetical mechanism that raises the grounds on which the city is built. Suppose that we find that the average temperature decreases. Let us next imagine that we devise another intervention experiment. This time, we do not change the altitude, but instead we build a massive heating system around the city that raises the average temperature by a few degrees. Suppose we find that the altitude of the city is unaffected. Intervening on A has changed T, but intervening on T has not changed A. We would thus reasonably prefer $A \to T$ as a description of the causal structure.

Why do we find this description of the effect of interventions plausible, even though the hypothetical intervention is hard or impossible to carry out in practice?

If we change the altitude A, then we assume that the *physical mechanism* $p(t|a)$ responsible for producing an average temperature (e.g., the chemical composition of the atmosphere, the physics of how pressure decreases with altitude, the meteorological mechanisms of winds) is still in place and leads to a changed T. This would hold true independent of the distribution from which we have sampled the cities, and thus independent of $p(a)$. Austrians may have founded their cities in locations subtly different from those of the Swiss, but the mechanism $p(t|a)$ would apply in both cases.[2]

If, on the other hand, we change T, then we have a hard time thinking of $p(a|t)$ as a mechanism that is still in place — we probably do not believe that such a mechanism exists in the first place. Given a set of different city distributions $p(a,t)$, while we could write them all as $p(a|t)\,p(t)$, we would find that it is impossible to explain them all using an invariant $p(a|t)$.

Our intuition can be rephrased and postulated in two ways: If $A \to T$ is the correct causal structure, then

(i) it is in principle **possible to perform a localized intervention** on A, in other words, to change $p(a)$ without changing $p(t|a)$, and

(ii) $p(a)$ and $p(t|a)$ are **autonomous**, **modular**, or **invariant** mechanisms or objects in the world.

$p(t)$, which may serve to motivate the direction of the arrow in $T \to A$ for the time being. This will be made precise in Definition 6.21.

[2]This is an idealized setting — no doubt counterexamples to these general remarks can be constructed.

Interestingly, while we started off with a hypothetical intervention experiment to arrive at the causal structure, our reasoning ends up suggesting that actual interventions may not be the only way to arrive at causal structures. We may also be able to identify the causal structure by checking, for data sources $p(a,t)$, which of the two decompositions (2.1) leads to autonomous or invariant terms. Sticking with the preceding example, let us denote the joint distributions of altitude and temperature in Austria and Switzerland by $p^{\ddot{\mathrm{O}}}(a,t)$ and $p^{\mathrm{S}}(a,t)$, respectively. These may be distinct since Austrians and Swiss founded their cities in different places (i.e., $p^{\ddot{\mathrm{O}}}(a)$ and $p^{\mathrm{S}}(a)$ are distinct). The causal factorizations, however, may still use the same conditional, i.e. $p^{\ddot{\mathrm{O}}}(a,t) = p(t|a)\, p^{\ddot{\mathrm{O}}}(a)$ and $p^{\mathrm{S}}(a,t) = p(t|a)\, p^{\mathrm{S}}(a)$.

We next describe an idea (see Figure 2.2, middle), closely related to the previous example, but different in that it also applies for *individual* distributions. In the causal factorization $p(a,t) = p(t|a)\, p(a)$, we would expect that the conditional density $p(t|a)$ (viewed as a function of t and a) provides no information about the marginal density function $p(a)$. This holds true if $p(t|a)$ is a model of a physical mechanism that does not care about what distribution $p(a)$ we feed into it. In other words, the mechanism is not influenced by the ensemble of cities to which we apply it.

If, on the other hand, we write $p(a,t) = p(a|t)p(t)$, then the preceding **independence of cause and mechanism** does not apply. Instead, we will notice that to connect the observed $p(t)$ and $p(a,t)$, the mechanism $p(a|t)$ would need to take a rather peculiar shape constrained by the equation $p(a,t) = p(a|t)p(t)$. This could be empirically checked, given an ensemble of cities and temperatures.[3]

We have already seen several ideas connected to independence, autonomy, and invariance, all of which can inform causal inference. We now turn to a final one (see Figure 2.2, right), related to the independence of noise terms and thus best explained when rewriting (2.1) as a distribution entailed by an SCM with graph $A \to T$, realizing the effect T as a noisy function of the cause A,

$$
\begin{aligned}
A &:= N_A, \\
T &:= f_T(A, N_T),
\end{aligned}
$$

where N_T and N_A are statistically **independent noises** $N_T \perp\!\!\!\perp N_A$. Making suitable restrictions on the functional form of f_T (see Sections 4.1.3–4.1.6 and 7.1.2) allows us to identify which of two causal structures ($A \to T$ or $T \to A$) has entailed the observed $p(a,t)$ (without such restrictions though, we can always realize both

[3]We shall formalize this idea in Section 4.1.7.

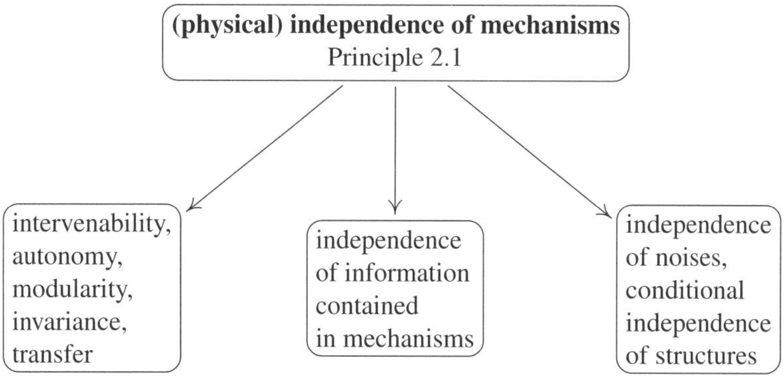

Figure 2.2: The principle of independent mechanisms and its implications for causal inference (Principle 2.1).

decompositions (2.1)). Furthermore, in the multivariate setting and under suitable conditions, the assumption of jointly independent noises allows the identification of causal structures by conditional independence testing (see Section 7.1.1).

We like to view all these observations as closely connected instantiations of a general *principle of (physically) independent mechanisms*.

Principle 2.1 (Independent mechanisms) *The causal generative process of a system's variables is composed of autonomous modules that do not inform or influence each other.*

In the probabilistic case, this means that the conditional distribution of each variable given its causes (i.e., its mechanism) does not inform or influence the other conditional distributions. In case we have only two variables, this reduces to an independence between the cause distribution and the mechanism producing the effect distribution.

The principle is plausible if we conceive our system as being composed of modules comprising (sets of) variables such that the modules represent physically independent mechanisms of the world. The special case of two variables has been referred to as *independence of cause and mechanism* (ICM) [Daniušis et al., 2010, Shajarisales et al., 2015]. It is obtained by thinking of the input as the result of a *preparation* that is done by a mechanism that is independent of the mechanism that turns the input into the output.

Before we discuss the principle in depth, we should state that not all systems will satisfy it. For instance, if the mechanisms that an overall system is composed of have been tuned to each other by design or evolution, this independence may be violated.

We will presently argue that the principle is sufficiently broad to cover the main aspects of causal reasoning and causal learning (see Figure 2.2). Let us address three aspects, corresponding, from left to right, to the three branches of the tree in Figure 2.2.

1. One way to think of these modules is as physical machines that incorporate an input-output behavior. This assumption implies that we can **change one mechanism without affecting the others** — or, in causal terminology, we can *intervene* on one mechanism without affecting the others. Changing a mechanism will change its input-output behavior, and thus the inputs other mechanisms downstream might receive, but we are assuming that the physical mechanisms themselves are unaffected by this change. An assumption such as this one is often implicit to justify the possibility of interventions in the first place, but one can also view it as a more general basis for causal reasoning and causal learning. If a system allows such localized interventions, there is no physical pathway that would connect the mechanisms to each other in a directed way by "meta-mechanisms." The latter makes it plausible that we can also expect a tendency for mechanisms to remain *invariant* with respect to changes within the system under consideration and possibly also to some changes stemming from outside the system (see Section 7.1.6). This kind of *autonomy* of mechanisms can be expected to help with *transfer* of knowledge learned in one domain to a related one where some of the *modules* coincide with the source domain (see Sections 5.2 and 8.3).

2. While the discussion of the first aspect focused on the physical aspect of independence and its ramifications, there is also an information theoretic aspect that is implied by the above. A time evolution involving several coupled objects and mechanisms can generate statistical dependence. This is related to our discussion from page 10, where we considered the dependence between the class label and the image of a handwritten digit. Similarly, mechanisms that are physically coupled will tend to generate information that can be quantified in terms of statistical or algorithmic information measures (see Sections 4.1.9 and 6.10 below).

   Here, it is important to distinguish between two levels of information: obviously, an effect contains information about its cause, but — according to the independence principle — the mechanism that generates the effect from its cause contains no information about the mechanism generating the cause. For a causal structure with more than two nodes, the independence principle states that the mechanism generating every node from its direct causes contain no information about each other.[4]

3. Finally, we should discuss how the assumption of independent noise terms, commonly made in structural equation modeling, is connected to the principle of independent mechanism. This connection is less obvious. To this end, consider a variable $E := f(C,N)$ where the noise N is discrete. For each value s taken by N, the assignment $E := f(C,N)$ reduces to a deterministic mechanism $E := f^s(C)$ that turns an input C into an output E. Effectively, this means that the noise randomly chooses between a number of mechanisms f^s (where the number equals the cardinality of the range of the noise variable N). Now suppose the noise variables for two mechanisms at the vertices X_j and X_k were statistically dependent.[5] Such a dependence could ensure, for instance, that whenever one mechanism f_j^s is active at node j, we know which mechanism f_k^t is active at node k. This would violate our principle of independent mechanisms.

   The preceding paragraph uses the somewhat extreme view of noise variables as selectors between mechanisms (see also Section 3.4). In practice, the role of the noise might be less pronounced. For instance, if the noise is additive (i.e., $E := f(C) + N$), then its influence on the mechanism is restricted. In this case, it can only *shift* the output of the mechanism up or down, so it selects between a set of mechanisms that are very similar to each other. This is consistent with a view of the noise variables as variables outside the system that we are trying to describe, representing the fact that a system can never be totally isolated from its environment. In such a view, one would think that a weak dependence of noises may be possible without invalidating the principle of independent mechanisms.

All of the above-mentioned aspects of Principle 2.1 may help for the problem of causal learning, in other words, they may provide information about causal structures. It is conceivable, however, that this information may in cases be conflicting, depending on which assumptions hold true in any given situation.

---

[4]There is an intuitive relation between this aspect of independence and the one described under 1.: whenever the mechanisms change independently, the change of one mechanism does not provide information on how the others have changed. Despite this overlap, the second independence contains an aspect that is not strictly contained in the first one because it is also applicable to a scenario in which none of the mechanisms has changed; for example, it refers also to homogeneous data sets.

[5]Although we have so far focused on the two-variable case, we phrase this argument such that it also applies for causal structures with more than two variables.

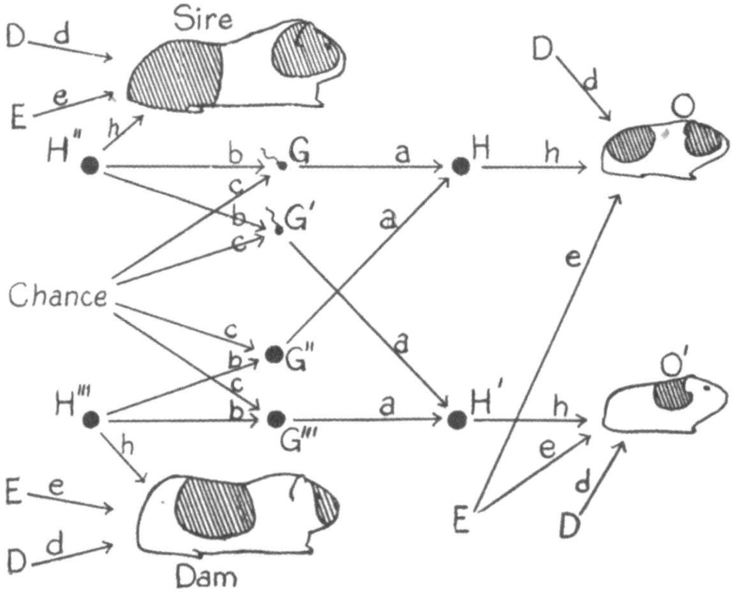

FIG. 5.

Diagram illustrating the casual relations between litter mates (O, O′) and between each of them and their parents. H, H′, H″, H,‴ represent the genetic constitutions of the four individuals, G, G′, G″, and G‴ that of four germ cells. E represents such environmental factors as are common to litter mates. D represents other factors, largely ontogenetic irregularity. The small letters stand for the various path coefficients.

Figure 2.3: Early path diagram; dam and sire are the female and male parents of a guinea pig, respectively. The path coefficients capture the importance of a given path, defined as *the ratio of the variability of the effect to be found when all causes are constant except the one in question, the variability of which is kept unchanged, to the total variability.* (Reproduced from Wright [1920].)

2.2 Historical Notes

The idea of autonomy and invariance is deeply engrained in the concept of structural equation models (SEMs) or SCMs. We prefer the latter term, since the term SEM has been used in a number of contexts where the structural assignments are used as algebraic equations rather than assignments. The literature is wide ranging, with overviews provided by Aldrich [1989], Hoover [2008], and Pearl [2009].

An intellectual antecedent to SEMs is the concept of a path model pioneered by Wright [1918, 1920, 1921] (see Figure 2.3). Although Wright was a biologist, SEMs are nowadays most strongly associated with econometrics. Following Hoover [2008], pioneering work on structural econometric models was done in the

1930s by Jan Tinbergen, and the conceptual foundations of probabilistic econometrics were laid in Trgyve Haavelmo's work [Haavelmo, 1944]. Early economists were trying to conceptualize the fact that unlike correlation, regression has a natural direction. The regression of Y on X leads to a solution that usually is *not* the inverse of the regression of X on Y.[6] But how would the data then tell us in which direction we should perform the regression? This is a problem of *observational equivalence*, and it is closely related to a problem econometricians call *identification*.

A number of early works saw a connection between what made a set of equations or relations *structural* [Frisch and Waugh, 1933], and properties of *invariance* and *autonomy* — according to Aldrich [1989], indeed the central notion in the pioneering work of Frisch et al. [1948]. Here, a *structural* relation was aiming for more than merely modeling an observed distribution of data — it was trying to capture an underlying structure connecting the variables of the model.

At the time, the Cowles Commission was a major economic research institute, instrumental in creating the field of econometrics. Its work related causality to the invariance properties of the structural econometric model [Hoover, 2008]. Pearl [2009] credits Marschak's opening chapter of a 1950 Cowles monograph with the idea that structural equations remain invariant to certain changes in the system [Marschak, 1950]. A crucial distinction emphasized by the Cowles work was the one between *endogenous* and *exogenous variables*. Endogeneous variables are those that the modeler tries to understand, while exogenous ones are determined by factors outside the model, and are taken as given. Koopmans [1950] assayed two principles for determining what should be treated as exogeneous. The *departmental principle* considers variables outside of the scope of the discipline as exogeneous (e.g., weather is exogeneous to economics). The (preferred) *causal principle* calls those variables exogenous that influence the remaining (endogeneous) variables, but are (almost) not influenced thereby.

Haavelmo [1943] interpreted structural equations as statements about hypothetical controlled experiments. He considered cyclic stochastic equation models and discussed the role of invariance as well as policy interventions. Pearl [2015] gives an appraisal of Haavelmo's role in the study of policy intervention questions and the development of the field of causal inference. In an account of causality in

[6] As an aside, while most of the early works were using linear equations only, there have also been attempts to generalize to nonlinear SEMs [Hoover, 2008].

economics and econometrics, Hoover [2008] discusses a system of the form

$$X^i := N_X^i$$
$$Y^i := \theta X^i + N_Y^i,$$

where the errors N_X^i, N_Y^i are i.i.d., and θ is a parameter. He attributes to Simon [1953] the view (which does not require any temporal order) that X^i may be referred to as causing Y^i since one knows all about X^i without knowing about Y^i, but not vice versa. The equations also allow us to predict the effect of interventions. Hoover goes on to argue that one can rewrite the system reversing the roles of X^i and Y^i while retaining the property that the error terms are uncorrelated.[7] He thus points out that we cannot infer the correct causal direction on the basis of a single set of data ("observational equivalence"). Experiments, either controlled or natural, could help us decide. If, for example, an experiment can change the conditional distribution of Y^i given X^i, without altering the marginal distribution of X^i, then it must be that X^i causes Y^i. Hoover refers to this as *Simon's invariance criterion*: the true causal order is the one that is invariant under the right sort of intervention.[8] Hurwicz [1962] argues that an equation system becomes *structural* by virtue of invariance to a domain of modifications. Such a system then bears resemblance to a natural law. Hurwicz recognized that one can use such modifications to determine structure, and that while structure is necessary for causality, it is not for prediction.

Aldrich [1989] provides an account of the role of autonomy in structural equation modeling. He argues that autonomous relations are likely to be more stable than others. He equates Haavelmo's *autonomous variables* with what subsequently became known as exogeneous variables. Autonomous variables are parameters fixed by external forces, or treated as stochastically independent.[9] Following Aldrich [1989, page 30], "the use of the qualifier *autonomous* and the phrase *forces external to the sector under consideration* suggest that ... the parameters of that model would be invariant to changes in the sectoral parameters." He also relates invariance to a notion termed *super-exogeneity* [Engle et al., 1983].

While the early proponents of structural equation modeling already had some profound insights in their causal underpinnings, the developments in computer sci-

---

[7]We shall revisit this topic in more detail in Section 4.1.3.

[8]We would argue that this may not hold true if interventions are coupled to each other, for example, to keep the *anticausal* conditional (which describes the cause, given its effect) invariant. This could be seen as a violation of Principle 2.1 *on the level of interventions*. We return to this point in Section 2.3.4.

[9]This is akin to the independence of noise terms we use in SCMs.

ence initially happened separately. Pearl [2009, p. 104] relates how he and his coworkers started connecting Bayesian networks and structural equation modeling: "It suddenly hit me that the century-old tension between economists and statisticians stems from simple semantic confusion: statisticians read structural equations as statements about $\mathbb{E}[Y|x]$ while economists read them as $\mathbb{E}[Y|do(x)]$. This would explain why statisticians claim that structural equations have no meaning and economists retort that statistics has no substance." Pearl [2009, p. 22] formulates the independence principle as follows: "that each parent-child relationship in the network represents a stable and autonomous physical mechanism — in other words, that it is conceivable to change one such relationship *without* changing the others."

It is noteworthy, and indeed a motivation for writing the present book, that among the different implications of Principle 2.1, shown in Figure 2.2, most of the work using causal Bayesian networks only exploits the independence of noise terms.[10] It leads to a rich structure of conditional independences [Pearl, 2009, Spirtes et al., 2000, Dawid, 1979, Spohn, 1980], ultimately deriving from Reichenbach's Principle 1.1. The other aspects of independence received significantly less attention [Hausman and Woodward, 1999, Lemeire and Dirkx, 2006], but there is a recent thread of work aiming at formalizing and using them. A major motivation for this has been the cause-effect problem where conditional independence is useless since we have only two variables (see Sections 4.1.2 and 6.10). Janzing and Schölkopf [2010] formalize independence of mechanism in terms of algorithmic information theory (Section 4.1.9). They view the functions in an SCM as representing independent causal mechanisms that persist after manipulating the distribution of inputs or other mechanisms. More specifically, in the context of causal Bayesian networks, they postulate that the conditional distributions of all nodes given their parents are algorithmically independent. In particular, for the causal Bayesian network $X \to Y$, P_X and $P_{Y|X}$ contain no algorithmic information about each other — meaning that knowledge of one does not admit a shorter description of the other. The idea that unrelated mechanisms are *algorithmically* independent follows from the generalization of SCMs from random variables to individual objects where *statistical* dependences are replaced with *algorithmic* dependences.

Schölkopf et al. [2012, e.g., Section 2.1.1.] discuss the question of robustness with respect to changes in the distribution of the cause (in the two-variable set-

[10] Certain Bayesian structure learning methods [Heckerman et al., 1999] can be viewed as implementing the independence principle by assigning *independent* priors to the conditional probabilities of each variable given its causes.

ting), and connect it to problems of **machine learning**; see also Chapter 5. Within an SCM, they analyze invariance of either the function or of the noises, for different learning scenarios (e.g., transfer learning, concept drift). They employ a notion of independence of mechanism and input that subsumes both independence under changes and information-theoretic independence (we called this the "overlap" between the first and second independence in Figure 2.2 in the discussion of the boxes): "$P_{E|C}$ contains no information about P_C and vice versa; in particular, if $P_{E|C}$ changes at some point in time, there is no reason to believe that P_C changes at the same time."

Further links to transfer and related machine learning problems are discussed by Bareinboim and Pearl [2016], Rojas-Carulla et al. [2016], Zhang et al. [2013] and Zhang et al. [2015]. Peters et al. [2016] exploited invariance across environments for learning parts of the graph structure underlying a multivariate SCM (Section 7.1.6).

2.3 Physical Structure Underlying Causal Models

We conclude this chapter with some notes on connections to physics. Readers whose interests are limited to mathematical and statistical structures may prefer to skip this part.

2.3.1 The Role of Time

An aspect that is conspicuously missing in Section 2.1 is the role of time. Indeed, physics incorporates causality into its basic laws by excluding causation from future to past.[11] This does not do away with all problems of causal inference, though. Already Simon [1953] recognized that while time ordering can provide a useful asymmetry, it is asymmetry that is important, not the temporal sequence.

Microscopically, the time evolution of both classical systems and quantum mechanical systems is widely believed to be invertible. This seems to contradict our intuition that the world evolves in a directed way — we believe we would be able to tell if time were to flow backward. The contradiction can be resolved in two ways. In one of them, suppose we have a complexity measure for states [Bennett, 1982, Zurek, 1989], and we start with a state whose complexity is very low. In that

[11]More precisely, an event can only influence events lying in its light cone since no signal can travel faster than the speed of light in a vacuum, according to the theory of relativity.

case, time evolution (assuming it is sufficiently ergodic) will tend to increase complexity. In the other way, we assume that we are considering open systems. Even if the time evolution for a closed system is invertible (e.g., in quantum mechanics, a unitary time evolution), the time evolution of an open subsystem (which interacts with its environment) in the generic case need not be invertible.

2.3.2 Physical Laws

An often discussed causal question can be addressed with the following example. The ideal gas law stipulates that pressure p, volume V, amount of substance n, and absolute temperature T satisfy the equation

$$p \cdot V = n \cdot R \cdot T, \tag{2.2}$$

where R is the ideal gas constant. If we, for instance, change the volume V allocated to a given amount of gas, then pressure p and/or temperature T will change, and the specifics will depend on the exact setup of the intervention. If, on the other hand, we change T, then V and/or p will change. If we keep p constant, then we can, at least approximately, construct a cycle involving T and V. So what causes what? It is sometimes argued that such laws show that it does not make sense to talk about causality unless the system is temporal. In the next paragraph, we argue that this is misleading. The gas law (2.2) refers to an *equilibrium state* of an underlying dynamical system, and writing it as a simple equation does not provide enough information about what interventions are in principle possible and what is their effect. SCMs and their corresponding directed acyclic graphs do provide us with this information, but in the general case of non-equilibrium systems, it is a hard problem whether and how a given dynamical systems leads to an SCM.

2.3.3 Cyclic Assignments

We think of SCMs as abstractions of underlying processes that take place in time. For these underlying processes, there is no problem with feedback loops, since at a sufficiently fast time scale, those loops will be unfolded in time, assuming there are no instantaneous interactions, which are arguably excluded by the finiteness of the speed of light.

Even though the time-dependent processes do not have cycles, it is possible that an SCM derived from such processes (for instance, by methods mentioned below in Remarks 6.5 and 6.7), involving only quantities that no longer depend on time, does have cycles. It becomes a little harder to define general interventions in such systems, but certain types of interventions should still be doable. For instance, a hard intervention where we set the value of one variable to a fixed value may be possible (and realizable physically by a forcing term in an underlying set of differential equations; see Remark 6.7). This cuts the cycle, and we can then derive the entailed *intervention* distribution.

However, it may be impossible to derive an entailed *observational* distribution from a cyclic set of structural assignments. Let us consider the two assignments

$$
\begin{aligned}
X &:= f_X(Y, N_X) \\
Y &:= f_Y(X, N_Y)
\end{aligned}
$$

and noise variables $N_X \perp\!\!\!\perp N_Y$. Just like in the case of acyclic models, we consider the noises and functions as given and seek to compute the entailed joint distribution of X and Y. To this end, let us start with the first assignment $X := f_X(Y, N_X)$, and substitute some initial Y into it. This yields an X, which we can then substitute into the other assignment. Suppose we iterate the two assignments and converge to some fixed point. This point would then correspond to a joint distribution of X, Y simultaneously satisfying both structural assignments as equalities of random variables.[12] Note that we have here assumed that the same N_X, N_Y are used at every step, rather than independent copies thereof.

However, such an equilibrium for X, Y need not always exist, and even if it does, it need not be the case that it can be found using the iteration. In the linear case, this has been analyzed by Lacerda et al. [2008] and Hyttinen et al. [2012]; see also Lauritzen and Richardson [2002]. For further details see Remark 6.5.

This observation that one may not always be able to get an entailed distribution satisfying two cyclic structural assignments is consistent with the view of SCMs as *abstractions* of underlying physical processes — abstractions whose domain of validity as causal models is limited. If we want to understand general cyclic systems, it may be unavoidable to study systems of differential equations rather than SCMs. For certain restricted settings, on the other hand, it can still make sense to stay on the phenomenologically more superficial level of SCMs; see, for example, Mooij et al. [2013]. One may speculate that this difficulty inherent to SCMs (or SEMs) is part of the reason why the econometrics community started off viewing SEMs as

[12] The fact that the assignments are satisfied as equalities of random variables means that we are considering an ensemble of systems that differ in the realizations of the noise variables. Each realization leads to a (possibly different) realization for X, Y, and thus the distribution of the noises implies a distribution over X, Y.

causal models, but later on parts of the community decided to forgo this interpretation in favor of a view of structural equations as purely algebraic equations.

2.3.4 Feasibility of Interventions

We have used the principle of independent mechanisms to motivate interventions that only affect one mechanism (or structural assignment) at a time. While real systems may admit such kind of interventions, there will also be interventions that replace several assignments at the same time. The former type of interventions may be considered more elementary in an intuitive physical sense. If multiple elementary interventions are combined, then this may in principle happen in a way such that they tuned to each other, and we would view this as violating a form of our independence Principle 2.1; see footnote 8 on page 24. One may hope that combined interventions that are "natural" will not violate independence. However, to tell whether an intervention is "natural" in this sense requires knowledge of the causal structure, which we do not have when trying to use such principles to perform causal learning in the first place. Ultimately, one can try to resort to physics to assay what is elementary or natural.

The questions of which operations on a physical system are elementary plays a crucial role in modern quantum information theory. There, the question is closely related to analyzing the structure of physical interactions.[13] Likewise, we believe that understanding physical mechanisms underlying causal relations may sometimes explain why some interventions are natural and others are complex, which essentially defines the "modules" given by the different structural equations.

2.3.5 Independence of Cause and Mechanism and the Thermodynamic Arrow of Time

We provide a discussion as well as a toy model illustrating how the principle of independent mechanisms can be viewed as a principle of physics. To this end, we

[13] For the interested reader: A system consisting of n two-level quantum systems is described by the 2^n-dimensional Hilbert space $\mathbb{C}^2 \otimes \cdots \otimes \mathbb{C}^2$. Unitary operators acting on this Hilbert space correspond to physical processes. For several such systems, researchers have shown how to implement "basic" unitaries that act on at most two of the n tensor components [Nielsen and Chuang, 2000] and act trivially on the remaining $n-2$ ones. Then one can generate any other unitary [DiVincenzo, 1995] approximately by concatenation. Although this is by no means the only possible choice for the set of "basic" unitary operations, the choice seems natural given the structure of physical interactions.

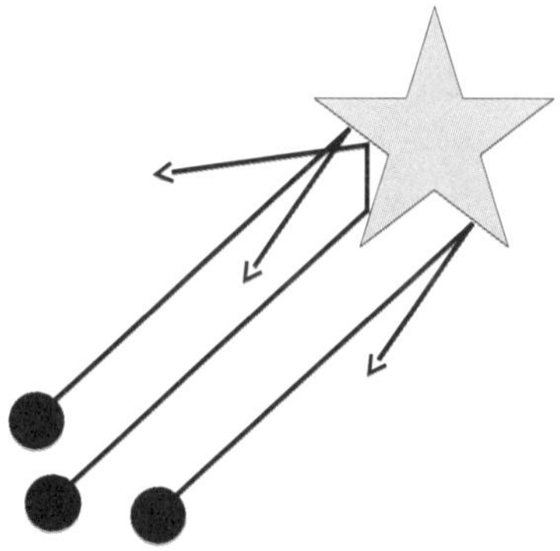

Figure 2.4: Simple example of the independence of initial state and dynamical law: beam of particles that are scattered at an object. The outgoing particles contain information about the object while the incoming do not.

consider the special case of two variables and postulate the following as a specialization of Principle 2.1:

Principle 2.2 (Initial state and dynamical law) *If s is the initial state of a physical system and M a map describing the effect of applying the system dynamics for some fixed time, then s and M are independent. Here, we assume that the initial state, by definition, is a state that has not interacted with the dynamics before.*

Here, the "initial" state s and "final" state $M(s)$ are considered as "cause" and "effect." Accordingly, M is the mechanism relating cause and effect. The last sentence of Principle 2.2 requires some explanation to avoid erroneous conclusions. We now discuss its meaning for an intuitive example.

Figure 2.4 shows a scenario where the independence of initial state and dynamics is so natural that we take it for granted: a beam of n particles propagating in exactly the same direction are approaching some object, where they are scattered in various directions. The directions of the outgoing particles contain information about the object, while the beam of *incoming* particles does not contain information about it. The assumption that the particles initially propagate exactly in the same direction can certainly be weakened. Even if there is some disorder in the incoming beam, the outgoing beam can still contain information about the object. Indeed, vision and photography are only possible because photons contain information about the objects at which they were scattered.

We can easily time-reverse the scenario by "hand-designing" an incoming beam for which all particles propagate in the same direction *after* the scattering process. We now argue how to make sense of Principle 2.2 in this case. Certainly, such a beam can only be prepared by a machine or a subject that is aware of the object's shape and then directs the particles accordingly. As a matter of fact, particles that have never been in contact with the object cannot a priori contain information about it. Then, Principle 2.2 can be maintained if we consider the process of directing the particles as part of the mechanism and reject the idea of calling the state of the hand-designed beam an *initial* state. Instead, the initial state then refers to the time instant before the particles have been given the fine-tuned momenta.

The fact that photographic images show what has happened in the past and not what will happen in the future is among the most evident asymmetries between past and future. The preceding discussion shows that this asymmetry can be seen as an implication of Principle 2.2. The principle thus links asymmetries between cause and effect with asymmetries between past and future that we take for granted.

After having explained the relation between Principle 2.1 and the asymmetry between past and future in physics on an informal level, we briefly mention that this link has been made more formally by Janzing et al. [2016] using algorithmic information theory. In the same way as Principle 4.13 formalizes independence of P_C and $P_{E|C}$ as algorithmic independence, Principle 2.2 can also be interpreted as algorithmic independence of s and M. Janzing et al. [2016, Theorem 1] show that for any bijective M, Principle 2.2 then implies that the physical entropy of $M(s)$ cannot be smaller than the entropy of s (up to an additive constant) provided that one is willing to accept Kolmogorov complexity (see Section 4.1.9) as the right formalization of physical entropy, as proposed by Bennett [1982] and Zurek [1989]. Principle 2.2 thus implies non-decrease of entropy in the sense of the standard arrow of time in physics.

3

Cause-Effect Models

The present chapter formalizes some basic concepts of causality for the case where the causal models contain only two variables. Assuming, these two variables are non-trivially related and their dependence is not solely due to a common cause, this constitutes a cause-effect model. We briefly introduce SCMs, interventions, and counterfactuals. All of these concepts are defined again in the context of multivariate causal models (Chapter 6) and we hope that encountering them for two variables first makes the ideas more easily accessible.

3.1 Structural Causal Models

SCMs constitute an important tool to relate causal and probabilistic statements.

Definition 3.1 (Structural causal models) *An SCM $\mathfrak{C}$ with graph $C \to E$ consists of two **assignments***

$$C := N_C, \tag{3.1}$$

$$E := f_E(C, N_E), \tag{3.2}$$

where $N_E \perp\!\!\!\perp N_C$, that is, N_E is independent of N_C.

In this model, we call the random variables C the **cause** and E the **effect**. Furthermore, we call C a **direct cause of** E, and we refer to $C \to E$ as a **causal graph**. This notation hopefully clarifies and coincides with the reader's intuition when we talk about interventions, for example, in Example 3.2.

If we are given both the function f_E and the noise distributions P_{N_C} and P_{N_E}, we can sample data from such a model in the following way: We sample noise values

N_E, N_C and then evaluate (3.1) followed by (3.2). The SCM thus entails a joint distribution $P_{C,E}$ over C and E (for a formal proof see Proposition 6.3).

3.2 Interventions

As discussed in Section 1.4.2, we are often interested in the system's behavior under an intervention. The intervened system induces another distribution, which usually differs from the observational distribution. If any type of intervention can lead to an arbitrary change of the system, these two distributions become unrelated and instead of studying the two systems jointly we may consider them as two separate systems. This motivates the idea that after an intervention only parts of the data-generating process change. For example, we may be interested in a situation in which variable E is set to the value 4 (irrespective of the value of C) without changing the mechanism (3.1) that generates C. That is, we replace the assignment (3.2) by $E := 4$. This is called a **(hard) intervention** and is denoted by $do(E := 4)$. The modified SCM, where (3.2) is replaced, entails a distribution over C that we denote by $P_C^{do(E:=4)}$ or $P_C^{\mathfrak{C};do(E:=4)}$, where the latter makes explicit that the SCM $\mathfrak{C}$ was our starting point. The corresponding density is denoted by $c \mapsto p^{do(E:=4)}(c)$ or, in slight abuse of notation, $p^{do(E:=4)}(c)$.[1] However, manipulations can be much more general. For example, the intervention $do\left(E := g_E(C) + \tilde{N}_E\right)$ keeps a functional dependence on C but changes the noise distribution. This is an example of a **soft intervention**. We can replace either of the two equations.

The following example motivates the namings "cause" and "effect":

Example 3.2 (Cause-effect interventions) Suppose that the distribution $P_{C,E}$ is entailed by an SCM $\mathfrak{C}$

$$\begin{aligned} C &:= N_C \\ E &:= 4 \cdot C + N_E, \end{aligned} \tag{3.3}$$

with $N_C, N_E \overset{\text{iid}}{\sim} \mathcal{N}(0,1)$, and graph $C \to E$. Then,

$$\begin{aligned} P_E^{\mathfrak{C}} = \mathcal{N}(0,17) \neq \mathcal{N}(8,1) &= P_E^{\mathfrak{C};do(C:=2)} = P_{E|C=2}^{\mathfrak{C}} \\ \neq \mathcal{N}(12,1) &= P_E^{\mathfrak{C};do(C:=3)} = P_{E|C=3}^{\mathfrak{C}}. \end{aligned}$$

[1] In the literature, the notation $p(c \,|\, do(E := 4))$ is also commonly used. We prefer $p^{do(E:=4)}$ since interventions are conceptually different from conditioning, and $p(c \,|\, do(E := 4))$ resembles the usual notation for the latter, $p(c \,|\, E = 4)$.

Intervening on C changes the distribution of E. But on the other hand,

$$P_C^{\mathfrak{C};do(E:=2)} = \mathcal{N}(0,1) = P_C^{\mathfrak{C}} = P_C^{\mathfrak{C};do(E:=314159265)} \left(\neq P_{C|E=2}^{\mathfrak{C}} \right). \tag{3.4}$$

No matter how strongly we intervene on E, the distribution of C remains what it was before. This model behavior corresponds well to our intuition of C "causing" E: for example, no matter how much we whiten someone's teeth, this will not have any effect on this person's smoking habits. (Importantly, the conditional distribution of C given $E = 2$ is different from the distribution of C after intervening and setting E to 2.) → This makes intuitive sense, but mathematically not sure ?

The asymmetry between cause and effect can also be formulated as an independence statement. When we replace the assignment (3.3) with $E := \tilde{N}_E$ (think about randomizing E), we break the dependence between C and E. In

$$P_{C,E}^{\mathfrak{C};do\left(E:=\tilde{N}_E\right)}$$

we find $C \perp\!\!\!\perp E$. This independence does not hold when randomizing C. As long as $\text{var}[\tilde{N}_C] \neq 0$, we find $C \not\perp\!\!\!\perp E$ in

$$P_{C,E}^{\mathfrak{C};do\left(C:=\tilde{N}_C\right)};$$

the correlation between C and E remains non-zero. □

Code Snippet 3.3 The code samples from the SCM described in Example 3.2.

```
set.seed(1)
# generates a sample from the distribution entailed by the SCM
C <- rnorm(300)
E <- 4*C + rnorm(300)
c(mean(E), var(E))
# [1] 0.1236532 16.1386767
#
# generates a sample from the intervention distribution do(C:=2);
# this changes the distribution of E
C <- rep(2,300)
E <- 4*C + rnorm(300)
c(mean(E), var(E))
# [1] 7.936917 1.187035
#
# generates a sample from the intervention distribution do(E:=N~);
# this breaks the dependence between C and E
C <- rnorm(300)
E <- rnorm(300)
cor.test(C,E)$p.value
# [1] 0.2114492
```

Summary of 3.2: Given SCM, intervening on the cause changes effect, but intervening on effect does not change cause.

3.3 Counterfactuals

Another possible modification of an SCM changes all of its noise distributions. Such a change can be induced by observations and allows us to answer **counterfactual** questions. To illustrate this, imagine the following hypothetical scenario:

Example 3.4 (Eye disease) There exists a rather effective treatment for an eye disease. For 99% of all patients, the treatment works and the patient gets cured ($B = 0$); if untreated, these patients turn blind within a day ($B = 1$). For the remaining 1%, the treatment has the opposite effect and they turn blind ($B = 1$) within a day. If untreated, they regain normal vision ($B = 0$).

Which category a patient belongs to is controlled by a rare condition ($N_B = 1$) that is unknown to the doctor, whose decision whether to administer the treatment ($T = 1$) is thus independent of N_B. We write it as a noise variable N_T.

Assume the underlying SCM

$$\mathfrak{C}: \begin{array}{rcl} T & := & N_T \\ B & := & T \cdot N_B + (1-T)\cdot(1-N_B) \end{array} \tag{3.5}$$

with Bernoulli distributed $N_B \sim \text{Ber}(0.01)$; note that the corresponding causal graph is $T \to B$.

Now imagine a specific patient with poor eyesight comes to the hospital and goes blind ($B = 1$) after the doctor administers the treatment ($T = 1$). We can now ask the counterfactual question "*What would have happened had the doctor administered treatment $T = 0$?*" Surprisingly, this can be answered. The observation $B = T = 1$ implies with (3.5) that for the given patient, we had $N_B = 1$. This, in turn, lets us calculate the effect of $do\,(T := 0)$.

To this end, we first condition on our observation to update the distribution over the noise variables. As we have seen, conditioned on $B = T = 1$, the distribution for N_B and the one for N_T collapses to a point mass on 1, that is, δ_1. This leads to a modified SCM:

$$\mathfrak{C}|B = 1, T = 1: \begin{array}{rcl} T & := & 1 \\ B & := & T \cdot 1 + (1-T)\cdot(1-1) = T \end{array} \tag{3.6}$$

Note that we only update the noise distributions; conditioning does not change the structure of the assignments themselves. The idea is that the physical mechanisms are unchanged (in our case, what leads to a cure and what leads to blindness), but we have gleaned knowledge about the previously unknown noise variables *for the given patient*.

Next, we calculate the effect of $do(T = 0)$ for this patient:

$$\mathfrak{C}|B=1,T=1;do(T:=0): \begin{array}{rcl} T & := & 0 \\ B & := & T \end{array} \tag{3.7}$$

Clearly, the entailed distribution puts all mass on $(0,0)$, and hence

$$P^{\mathfrak{C}|B=1,T=1;do(T:=0)}(B=0)=1\,.$$

This means that the patient would thus have been cured ($B = 0$) if the doctor had not given him treatment, in other words, $do(T := 0)$. Because of

$$P^{\mathfrak{C};do(T:=1)}(B=0)=0.99 \quad \text{and}$$
$$P^{\mathfrak{C};do(T:=0)}(B=0)=0.01\,,$$

however, we can still argue that the doctor acted optimally (according to the available knowledge). □

Interestingly, Example 3.4 shows that we can use counterfactual statements to falsify the underlying causal model (see Section 6.8). Imagine that the rare condition N_B can be tested, but the test results take longer than a day. In this case, it is possible that we observe a counterfactual statement that contradicts the measurement result for N_B. The same argument is given by Pearl [2009, p.220, point (2)]. Since the scientific content of counterfactuals has been debated extensively, it should be emphasized that the counterfactual statement here is falsifiable because the noise variable is not unobservable in principle but only at the moment when the decision of the doctor has to be made.

3.4 Canonical Representation of Structural Causal Models

We have discussed two types of causal statements both entailed by SCMs: first, the behavior of the system under potential interventions, and second, counterfactual statements. To further understand the difference between them, we introduce the following "canonical representation" of an SCM.[2] According to the structural assignment

$$E = f_E(C, N_E),$$

[2]This representation has been used in the literature in various places, for example, [Pearl, 2009] although we have not found the term "canonical representation."

for each fixed value n_E of the noise N_E, E is a deterministic function of C:

$$E = f_E(C, n_E). \tag{3.8}$$

In order words, if C and E attain values in $\mathcal{C}$ and $\mathcal{E}$, respectively, then the noise N_E switches between different functions from $\mathcal{C}$ to $\mathcal{E}$. Without loss of generality, we may therefore assume that N_E attains values in the set of functions from $\mathcal{C}$ to $\mathcal{E}$, denoted by $\mathcal{E}^{\mathcal{C}}$. Using this convention, we can also rewrite (3.8) as

$$E = n_E(C), \tag{3.9}$$

and call this the canonical representation of the structural equation relating C and E.

Let us now explain why two SCMs with different canonical representations may induce the same interventional probabilities, although they differ in their counterfactual statements. To this end, we restrict the attention to the case where C attains values in the finite set $\mathcal{C} = \{1, \ldots, k\}$. Then the set of functions from $\mathcal{C}$ to $\mathcal{E}$ is given by the k-fold Cartesian product

$$\mathcal{E}^k := \underbrace{\mathcal{E} \times \cdots \times \mathcal{E}}_{k \text{ times}},$$

where the jth component describes which value E attains for $C = j$. Accordingly, the distribution P_{N_E} is given by a joint distribution on $\mathcal{E}^k$ whose marginal distribution of the jth component determines the conditional $P_{E|C=j}$. Since C is the cause and E the effect, we have $P_E^{do(C:=j)} = P_{E|C=j}$; in other words, here interventional probabilities and observational conditional probabilities coincide. Thus, the interventional causal implications of the SCM are completely determined by the marginal distributions of each component of the vector-valued noise variable N_E even though the SCM includes a precise specification of P_{N_E}, that is, the joint distribution of all components. While the statistical dependences between the components of the noise variable N_E referring to the effect are irrelevant for interventional causal statements, they do matter for *counterfactual* statements. To see this, let C and E be binary, that is, $\mathcal{C} = \mathcal{E} = \{0, 1\}$. The set of functions from $\{0, 1\}$ to $\{0, 1\}$ reads $\mathcal{E}^{\mathcal{C}} = \{\mathbf{0}, \mathbf{1}, \text{ID}, \text{NOT}\}$ where $\mathbf{0}, \mathbf{1}$ denote the constant functions attaining 0 and 1, respectively, and ID and NOT denote identity and negation, respectively. To construct two different distributions $P^1_{N_E}$ and $P^2_{N_E}$ inducing the same conditional $P_{E|C=0}$, $P_{E|C=1}$, first choose the uniform mixture of $\mathbf{0}$ and $\mathbf{1}$ and second the uniform mixture of ID and NOT. In both cases, C and E are statistically independent and the distribution of E is unaffected by interventions on C because E remains an unbiased coin toss regardless of C. In the Cartesian product representation, the four functions read $\mathcal{E}^C = \{(0,0),(1,1),(0,1),(1,0)\}$, the first and the second component denote the images of $C = 0$ and $C = 1$, respectively. Obviously, the uniform mixture of $(0,0)$ and $(1,1)$ and the uniform mixture of $(0,1)$ and $(1,0)$ both induce the same marginal distributions on the first and the second component of the Cartesian product — in agreement with our remark that they induce the same intervention distributions. The counterfactual statement "E would have attained a different value if C had been set to a different one," however, is true only for the mixture of ID and NOT, but not for the mixture of **0** and **1**. Hence, counterfactual statements depend not only on the marginal distributions of the components of the noise variable N_E, but also on the statistical dependences between the Cartesian product components.

Note that two formally different SCMs may induce not only the same interventional distribution but even imply the same counterfactual statements: Given the assignment

$$E := f_E(C, N_E),$$

reparameterizations of N_E are obviously irrelevant. More explicitly, we may set

$$E := \tilde{f}_E(C, \tilde{N}_E) = f_E(C, g^{-1}(\tilde{N}_E)),$$

for some bijection g on the range of N_E and redefine the noise variable by $\tilde{N}_E := g(N_E)$. Using the canonical representation (3.9), we got rid of this additional degree of freedom that would have confused this discussion of counterfactuals.

3.5 Problems

Problem 3.5 (Sampling from an SCM) *Consider the SCM*

$$X := Y^2 + N_X \tag{3.10}$$

$$Y := N_Y \tag{3.11}$$

with $N_X, N_Y \overset{iid}{\sim} \mathcal{N}(0,1)$. *Generate an i.i.d. sample of size* 200 *from the joint distribution* (X,Y).

Problem 3.6 (Conditional distributions) *Show that* $P^{\mathfrak{C}}_{C|E=2}$ *in Equation* (3.4) *is a Gaussian distribution:*

$$C \,|\, E = 2 \sim \mathcal{N}\left(\frac{8}{17}, \sigma^2 = \frac{1}{17}\right).$$

Problem 3.7 (Interventions) *Assume that we know that a process either follows the SCM*

$$
\begin{aligned}
X &:= Y + N_X \\
Y &:= N_Y,
\end{aligned}
$$

where $N_X \sim \mathcal{N}(\mu_X, \sigma_X^2)$ *and* $N_Y \sim \mathcal{N}(\mu_X, \sigma_Y^2)$ *with unknown* μ_X, μ_Y *and* $\sigma_X, \sigma_Y > 0$*, or it follows the SCM*

$$
\begin{aligned}
X &:= M_X \\
Y &:= X + M_Y,
\end{aligned}
$$

where $M_X \sim \mathcal{N}(\nu_X, \tau_X^2)$ *and* $M_Y \sim \mathcal{N}(\nu_Y, \tau_Y^2)$ *with unknown* ν_X, ν_Y *and* $\tau_X, \tau_Y > 0$*. Is there a single intervention distribution that lets you distinguish between the two SCMs?*

Problem 3.8 (Cyclic SCMs) *We have mentioned that if the assignments inherit a cyclic structure, the SCM does not necessarily induce a unique distribution over the observed variables. Sometimes there is no solution and sometimes it is not unique.*

a) We first look at an example that induces a unique solution. Consider the SCM

$$X := 2 \cdot Y + N_X \tag{3.12}$$

$$Y := 2 \cdot X + N_Y \tag{3.13}$$

with $(N_X, N_Y) \sim P$ *for an arbitrary distribution P. Compute* $\alpha, \beta, \gamma, \delta$ *such that*

$$
\begin{aligned}
X &:= \alpha N_X + \beta N_Y \\
Y &:= \gamma N_X + \delta N_Y
\end{aligned}
$$

yields a solution (X, Y, N_X, N_Y) *of the SCM; that is, the vector satisfies Equations* (3.12) *and* (3.13)*. The solution can be seen as a special case of Equation* (6.2).

b) Consider the SCM

$$
\begin{aligned}
X &:= Y + N_X \\
Y &:= X + N_Y
\end{aligned}
$$

with $(N_X, N_Y) \sim P$. *Show that if P allows for a density with respect to Lebesgue measure and factorizes, that is,* $N_X \perp\!\!\!\perp N_Y$, *then there is no solution* (X, Y, N_X, N_Y) *of the SCM.*

Furthermore, construct a distribution P, and a vector (X, Y, N_X, N_Y) *that solves the SCM.*

4

Learning Cause-Effect Models

Readers who are familiar with the conditional statistical independence-based approach to causal discovery from observational data [Pearl, 2009, Spirtes et al., 2000] may be surprised by a chapter discussing causal inference for the case of only two observed variables, that is, a case where no non-trivial conditional independences can hold. This chapter introduces assumptions under which causal inference with just two observed variables is possible.

Some of these assumptions may seem too strong to be realistic, but one should keep in mind that empirical inference, even if it is not concerned with causal problems, requires strong assumptions. This is true in particular when it deals with high-dimensional data and low sample sizes. Therefore, oversimplified models are ubiquitous and they have been proven helpful in many learning scenarios.

The list of assumptions is diverse and we are certain that it is incomplete, too. Current research is still in a phase of exploring the enormous space of assumptions that yield identifiability between cause and effect. We hope that this chapter inspires the reader who may then add other — hopefully realistic — assumptions that can be used for learning causal structures.

We provide the assumptions and theoretical identifiability results in Section 4.1; Section 4.2 shows how these results can be used for structure identification in the case of a finite amount of data.

1) look out for assumptions that might be realized in the setting!

4.1 Structure Identifiability

4.1.1 Why Additional Assumptions Are Required

In Chapter 3, we introduced SCMs where the effect E is computed from the cause C using a function assignment. One may wonder whether this asymmetry of the data-generating process (i.e., that E is computed from C and not vice versa) becomes apparent from looking at $P_{C,E}$ alone. That is, does the joint distribution $P_{X,Y}$ of two variables X,Y tell us whether it has been induced by an SCM from X to Y or from Y to X? In other words, is the structure **identifiable** from the joint distribution? The following known result shows that the answer is "no" if one allows for general SCMs.

Proposition 4.1 (Non-uniqueness of graph structures) *For every joint distribution $P_{X,Y}$ of two real-valued variables, there is an SCM*

$$Y = f_Y(X, N_Y), \quad X \perp\!\!\!\perp N_Y,$$

where f_Y is a measurable function and N_Y is a real-valued noise variable.

Proof. Analogously to Peters [2012, Proof of Proposition 2.6], define the conditional cumulative distribution function

$$F_{Y|x}(y) := P(Y \leq y \,|\, X = x).$$

Then define

$$f_Y(x, n_Y) := F_{Y|x}^{-1}(n_Y),$$

where $F_{Y|x}^{-1}(n_Y) := \inf\{x \in \mathbb{R} : F_{Y|x}(x) \geq n_Y\}$. Then, let N_Y be uniformly distributed on $[0,1]$ and independent of X. □

The result can be applied to the case $X = C$ and $Y = E$ as well as to the case $X = E$ and $Y = C$, thus every joint distribution $P_{X,Y}$ admits SCMs in both directions. For this reason, it is often thought that the causal direction between just two observed variables cannot be inferred from passive observations alone. We will see in Chapter 7 that this claim fits into a framework in which causal inference is based on (conditional) statistical independences only [Spirtes et al., 2000, Pearl, 2009]. Then, the causal structures $X \to Y$ and $Y \to X$ are indistinguishable. For just two variables, the only possible (conditional) independence would condition on the empty set, which does not render X and Y independent unless the causal influence is non-generic.[1] More recently, this perspective has been challenged by approaches that also use information about the joint distribution other than conditional independences. These approaches rely on additional assumptions about the relations between probability distributions and causality.

The remaining part of Section 4.1 discusses under which assumptions the graph structure can be recovered from the joint distribution (structure identifiability). Section 4.2 then describes methods that estimate the graph from a finite data set (structure identification). These statistical methods do not need to be motivated by the proofs of the identifiability results. Methods that follow the proofs closely are often inefficient in making use of the data.

4.1.2 Overview of the Type of Assumptions

A Priori Restriction of the Model Class One possible approach to distinguish cause and effect is to define a class of "particularly natural" conditionals[2] $P_{E|C}$ and marginals P_C. For several such classes, there are theoretical results showing that "generic" combinations of marginals P_X and conditionals $P_{Y|X}$ induce joint distributions that cannot be described by the same class when X and Y are swapped. Statements of this kind are also called *identifiability* results and we will see such examples in the remainder of Section 4.1.

For example, one may define classes of conditionals $P_{E|C}$ and marginals P_C by restricting the class of functions f_E; see (3.2), and/or the class of noise distributions in (3.1) and (3.2), as will be discussed in Sections 4.1.3–4.1.6. This approach seems particularly natural from a machine learning perspective, where restricting the complexity of functions appears everywhere in standard tasks such as regression and classification. Note that inferring causal directions via restricted function classes implicitly assumes that the noise variables are still independent, in agreement with the definition of an SCM (see Definition 3.1). In this sense, one could say that these methods employ the independence of noise according to Figure 2.2, but keep in mind that independence of noise renders causal directions only identifiable after restricting the function class (see Proposition 4.1).

Another option of classes can be found in Sun et al. [2006], Janzing et al. [2009b],

[1] Note that this non-generic case should not be called "trivial" because non-trivial counterfactual influence can be consistent with $X \perp\!\!\!\perp Y$ (see Section 3.4).

[2] We use the notation $P_{E|C}$ as a shorthand for the collection $(P_{E|C=c})_c$ of conditional distributions and implicitly assume the existence of a density, in other words, that $P_{E,C}$ is absolutely continuous with respect to a product measure.

and Comley and Dowe [2003]. Sun et al. [2006] and Janzing et al. [2009b], for instance, consider second-order exponential models, for which the logarithmic densities of $P_{E|C}$ and P_C are second order polynomials in e and c (up to a partition function), or in c, respectively.

We conclude this part with two questions: First, how should one define model classes that describe a reasonable fraction of empirical data in real life? Second, given that an empirical distribution admits such a model in exactly one direction, why should this be the causal one? The first question is actually not specific to the problem of causal inference; constructing functions that describe relations between observed variables always requires us to fit functions from a "reasonable" class. The second question appears to be among the deepest problems concerning the relation between probability and causality. We are only able to give some intuitive and vague ideas, which now follow.

We start by providing an intuitive motivation that is related to the reason why usual machine learning relies on restricted model classes. Whenever we find a model from a small function class that fits our limited number of data, we expect that the model will also fit future observations, as argued in Chapter 1. Hence, finding models from a small class that fit data is crucial for the ability to generalize to future observations. Formally, learning *causal* models is substantially different from the usual learning scenario because it aims at inferring a model that describes the behavior of the system under interventions and not just observations taken from the same distribution. Therefore, there is no straightforward way to adopt arguments from statistical learning theory, to obtain a learning theory for causal relations. Nevertheless, we believe that finding a model from a small class suggests — up to some error probability — that the model will also hold under different background conditions. We further believe that models that hold under many different background conditions are more likely to be causal than models that just fit observations from a single data set (see "Different Environments" in Section 7.1.6). This way, cause-effect inference via restricting the model class is vaguely related to ideas from statistical learning theory although drawing the exact link has to be left to the future. The preceding informal arguments for using causal models from small classes should not be mistaken as stating that causal relations in nature are indeed simple. The question whether or not we will often succeed in fitting data with *simple* functions, is a completely different question. We only argue for the belief that *if* there is a simple function that fits the data, it is more likely to also describe a *causal* relation. Furthermore, we will draw one connection between restricted model classes and the independence of cause and mechanism in Section 4.1.9. To be prepared for those quite formal derivations, we first provide a rather unrealistic toy model that we consider more a metaphor than a serious example.

Independence of Cause and Mechanism Section 2.1 describes the idea that P_C and $P_{E|C}$ correspond to two independent mechanisms of nature. Therefore, they typically contain no information about each other (cf. Principle 2.1 and the middle box in Figure 2.2). Naturally, postulating that P_C and $P_{E|C}$ are independent in the sense that they do not contain information about each other raises the question of what type of information is meant. There is no obvious sense in which the postulate can be formalized by a condition that could be checked by a *statistical* independence test. This is because we are talking about a scenario where one fixed joint distribution $P_{C,E}$ is visible and not a collection of distributions in which we could check whether the distribution of the hypothetical cause and the distribution of the hypothetical effect, given the cause, change in a dependent way (this is essentially the difference between the left and the middle boxes in Figure 2.2). To translate the independence of cause and mechanism into the language of SCMs, we assume that the distribution of the cause should be independent of the function and the noise distribution representing the causal mechanism. Note that this is, again, a priori, not a statement about *statistical* independence. Instead, it states that f_E and P_{N_E} contain no information about P_C and vice versa. This fact can only be used for causal inference if the independence is violated for all structural models that describe $P_{C,E}$ from E to C.

Sections 4.1.7 and 4.1.8 describe two toy scenarios for which well-defined notions of independence versus dependence can be given. Finally, in Section 4.1.9, we describe a formalization of independence of P_C and $P_{E|C}$ that is applicable to more general scenarios rather than being restricted to the simple toy scenarios in Sections 4.1.7 and 4.1.8. Here, dependence is measured by means of *algorithmic* mutual information, a concept that is based on description length in the sense of Kolmogorov complexity. Since the latter is uncomputable, it should be considered as a philosophical principle rather than a *method*. Its practical relevance is two-fold. First, it may inspire the development of new methods and, second, justifications of existing methods can be based on it. For instance, the independence principle can justify inference methods based on an a priori restriction of the model class; see Section 4.1.9 for a specific example. To get a rough intuition about how independence is related to restricted model classes, consider a thought experiment where P_C is randomly chosen from a class of k different marginal distributions. Likewise, assume that $P_{E|C}$ is chosen from another class of ℓ different conditional distributions. This induces $k \cdot \ell$ different joint distributions $P_{C,E}$. In the generic case (unless the classes are defined in a rather special way), this yields $k \cdot \ell > k$ different marginals P_E and $k \cdot \ell > \ell$ different conditionals $P_{C|E}$. Hence, *typical* combinations of P_C and $P_{E|C}$ induce joint distributions $P_{E,C}$ for which the "backward marginal and conditional" P_E and $P_{C|E}$ will not be in the original classes and would require larger model classes instead. In other words, no matter how large one chooses the set of possible P_C and $P_{E|C}$, the set of induced $P_{C|E}$ and P_E is even larger. This thought experiment is more like a metaphor because it is based on the naive picture of randomly choosing from a finite set. Nevertheless, it motivates the belief that in the *causal* direction, marginals and conditionals are more likely to admit a description from an a priori chosen small set provided that the latter has been constructed in a reasonable way.

Sections 4.1.3 to 4.1.6 describe model assumptions with a priori restriction of the model class, while Sections 4.1.7 to 4.1.9 formalize an independence assumption. Section 4.1.9, however, plays a special role because it should be considered a foundational principle rather than an inference method in its own right.

4.1.3 Linear Models with Non-Gaussian Additive Noise

While linear structural equations with Gaussian noise have been extensively studied, it has been observed more recently [Kano and Shimizu, 2003, Shimizu et al., 2006, Hoyer et al., 2008a] that linear *non-Gaussian* acyclic models (LiNGAMs) allow for new approaches to causal inference. In particular, the distinction between X causes Y and Y causes X from observational data becomes feasible. The assumption is that the effect E is a linear function of the cause C up to an additive noise term:

$$E = \alpha C + N_E, \quad N_E \perp\!\!\!\perp C,$$

with $\alpha \in \mathbb{R}$ (which is a special case of additive noise models introduced in Section 4.1.4). The following result shows that this assumption is sufficient for identifying cause and effect.

Theorem 4.2 (Identifiability of linear non-Gaussian models) *Assume that $P_{X,Y}$ admits the linear model*

$$Y = \alpha X + N_Y, \quad N_Y \perp\!\!\!\perp X, \tag{4.1}$$

with continuous random variables X, N_Y, and Y. Then there exist $\beta \in \mathbb{R}$ and a random variable N_X such that

$$X = \beta Y + N_X, \quad N_X \perp\!\!\!\perp Y, \tag{4.2}$$

if and only if N_Y and X are Gaussian.

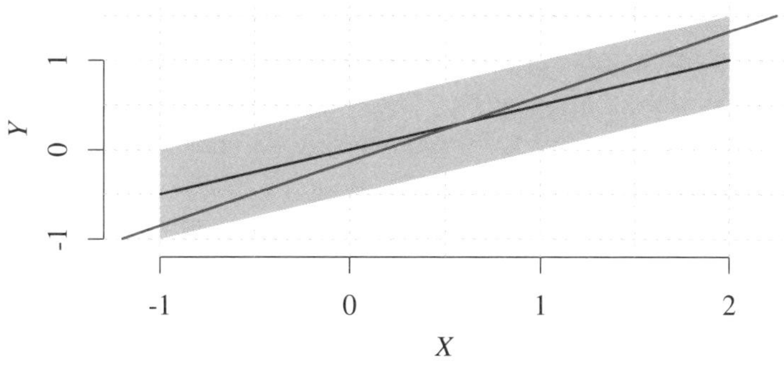

Figure 4.1: Joint density over X and Y for an identifiable example. The blue line is the function corresponding to the forward model $Y := 0.5 \cdot X + N_Y$, with uniformly distributed X and N_Y; the gray area indicates the support of the density of (X,Y). Theorem 4.2 states that there cannot be any valid backward model since the distribution of (X,N_Y) is non-Gaussian. The red line characterized by (b,c) is the least square fit minimizing $\mathbb{E}[X - bY - c]^2$. This is not a valid backward model $X = bY + c + N_X$ since the resulting noise N_X would not be independent of Y (the size of the support of N_X would differ for different values of Y).

Hence, it is sufficient that C or N_E are non-Gaussian to render the causal direction identifiable; see Figure 4.1 for an example.

Let us look into slightly more details on how this result is proved. Theorem 4.2 is the bivariate case of the model class LiNGAM introduced by Shimizu et al. [2006], who prove a multivariate version of Theorem 4.2 using independent component analysis (ICA) [Comon, 1994, Theorem 11]. The proof of ICA is based on a characterization of the Gaussian distribution that was proved independently by Skitovič and Darmois [Skitovič, 1954, 1962, Darmois, 1953] and that we now state.

Theorem 4.3 (Darmois-Skitovič) *Let $X_1,\dots,X_d$ be independent, non-degenerate random variables (see Appendix A.1). If there exist non-vanishing coefficients $a_1,\dots,a_d$ and $b_1,\dots,b_d$ (that is, for all i, $a_i \neq 0 \neq b_i$) such that the two linear combinations*

$$l_1 = a_1X_1 + \ldots + a_dX_d,$$
$$l_2 = b_1X_1 + \ldots + b_dX_d$$

are independent, then each X_i is normally distributed.

It turns out that one can prove the bivariate version stated in Theorem 4.2 as a short and direct consequence from the theorem of Darmois-Skitovič; for illustration purposes we attach this proof in Appendix C.1. Furthermore, it can be shown that the identifiability of bivariate SCMs generalizes to identifiability of multivariate SCMs [Peters et al., 2011b]. With this result, the multivariate identifiability of LiNGAM then follows from Theorem 4.2.

Linear models with non-Gaussian additive noise can also be applied to a problem that sounds uncommon from the perspective of machine learning but that is interesting from the perspective of theoretical physics: estimating the arrow of time from data. Peters et al. [2009b] show that autoregressive models are time-reversible if and only if the noise variables are normally distributed. To explore asymmetries of empirical time series, they infer the time direction by fitting two autoregressive models, one from the past to the future, as standard, and one from the future to the past. In their experiments, the noise variables for the former direction indeed tend to be more independent than in the inverted time direction (cf. Section 4.2.1). Bauer et al. [2016] extend the idea to multivariate time series. Janzing [2010] links this observed asymmetry to the thermodynamic arrow of time, which suggests that asymmetries between cause and effect discussed in this book are also related to fundamental questions in statistical physics.

4.1.4 Nonlinear Additive Noise Models

We now describe additive noise models (ANMs), a less extreme restriction of the class of SCMs that is still strong enough to render cause-effect inference feasible.

Definition 4.4 (ANMs) *The joint distribution $P_{X,Y}$ is said to admit an ANM from X to Y if there is a measurable function f_Y and a noise variable N_Y such that*

$$Y = f_Y(X) + N_Y, \quad N_Y \perp\!\!\!\perp X. \tag{4.3}$$

By overloading terminology, we say that $P_{Y|X}$ admits an ANM if (4.3) *holds.*

The following theorem shows that "generically," a distribution does not admit an ANM in both directions at the same time.

Theorem 4.5 (Identifiability of ANMs) *For the purpose of this theorem, let us call the ANM* (4.3) *smooth if N_Y and X have strictly positive densities p_{N_Y} and p_X, and f_Y, p_{N_Y}, and p_X are three times differentiable.*

Assume that $P_{Y|X}$ admits a smooth ANM from X to Y, and there exists a $y \in \mathbb{R}$ such that

$$(\log p_{N_Y})''(y - f_Y(x)) f_Y'(x) \neq 0 \tag{4.4}$$

for all but countably many values x. Then, the set of log densities $\log p_X$ *for which the obtained joint distribution* $P_{X,Y}$ *admits a smooth ANM from Y to X is contained in a 3-dimensional affine space.*

Proof. (Sketch of the idea. For details, see Hoyer et al. [2009]) The ANM from Y to X, given by

$$p(x,y) = p_Y(y) p_{N_X}(x - f_X(y)), \tag{4.5}$$

implies

$$\log p(x,y) = \log p_Y(y) + \log p_{N_X}(x - f_X(y)).$$

One can show that $\log p(x,y)$ then satisfies the following differential equation:

$$\frac{\partial}{\partial x}\left(\frac{\partial^2 \log p(x,y)/\partial x^2}{\partial^2 \log p(x,y)/(\partial x \partial y)}\right) = 0. \tag{4.6}$$

On the other hand, the ANM from X to Y reads

$$p(x,y) = p_{N_X}(x) p_{N_Y}(y - f_Y(x)). \tag{4.7}$$

Taking the logarithm of (4.7) yields

$$\log p(x,y) = \log p_X(x) + \log p_{N_Y}(y - f_Y(x)). \tag{4.8}$$

Applying (4.6) to (4.8) yields a differential equation for the third derivative of $\log p_X$ in terms of (first, second, and third) derivatives of f_X and $\log p_{N_Y}$. Thus, f_X and p_{N_E} (which are properties of the conditional $P_{Y|X}$) determine $\log p_X$ up to the three free parameters $\log p_{N_X}(\nu)$, $(\log p_{N_X})'(\nu)$, and $(\log p_{N_X})''(\nu)$ for an arbitrary point ν. □

Theorem 4.5 states identifiability in the "generic" case, where "generic" is characterized by complicated conditions such as (4.4) and the three-dimensional subspace. For the case where p_X and p_{N_Y} is Gaussian, there is a much simpler identifiability statement saying that only linear functions f generate distributions that admit an ANM in backward direction [see Hoyer et al., 2009, Corollary 1]. Figure 4.2 visualizes two "non-generic" examples of bivariate distributions that admit additive noise models in both directions. First, the obvious case of a bivariate Gaussian and, second, a sophisticated one that requires fine-tuning between p_X and N_X [Mooij et al., 2016].

To relate Theorem 4.5 to causal semantics, assume first that we know a priori that the joint distribution $P_{X,Y}$ of cause and effect admits an ANM from C to E, but we

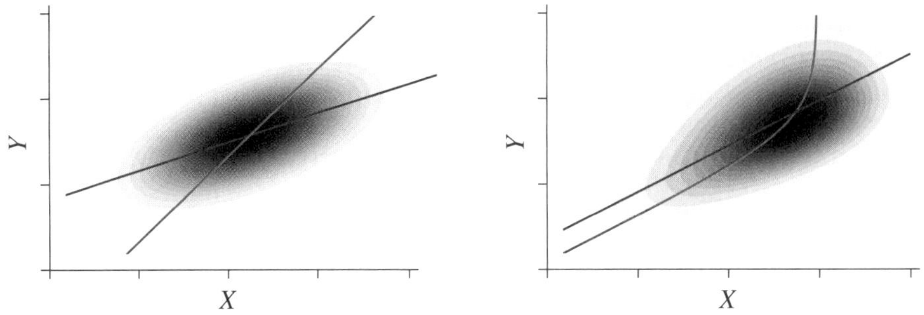

Figure 4.2: Joint density over X and Y for two non-identifiable examples. The left panel shows the linear Gaussian case and the right panel shows a slightly more complicated example, with "fine-tuned" parameters for function, input, and noise distribution (the latter plot is based on kernel density estimation). The blue function f_Y corresponds to the forward model $Y := f_Y(X) + N_Y$, and the red function f_X to the backward model $X := f_X(Y) + N_X$.

do not know whether $X = C$ and $Y = E$ or vice versa. Theorem 4.5 then states that generically there will not be an ANM from E to C, and we can thus easily decide which one of the variables is the cause C.

In general, however, conditionals $P_{E|C}$ in nature are not so strongly restricted that they necessarily admit an ANM. But is it possible that P_C and $P_{E|C}$ then induce a joint distribution $P_{C,E}$ that admits an ANM from E to C? (In this case, we would infer the wrong causal direction.) We argue in Section 4.1.9 that this is unlikely if P_C and $P_{E|C}$ are independently chosen.

4.1.5 Discrete Additive Noise Models

Additive noise can be defined not solely for real-valued variables, but for any variable that attains values in a ring. Peters et al. [2010, 2011a] introduce ANMs for the rings[3] $\mathbb{Z}$ and $\mathbb{Z}/m\mathbb{Z}$. That is, the set of integers and the set of integers modulo $m \in \mathbb{Z}$. In the latter ring, we identify numbers that have the same remainder after division by m. For example, both integers 132 and 4 have the remainder (namely 4) after dividing by 8 and we write $132 \equiv 4 \mod 8$. Such a modular arithmetic may be appropriate when one of the domains inherits a cyclic structure. If we consider the day of the year, for example, we may want the days December 31 and January 1 to have the same distance as August 25 and August 26.

[3] In a ring, we can perform addition and multiplication. The latter operation does not necessarily have an inverse, though.

As in the continuous case, we can show that in the generic case, a joint distribution admits an ANM in at most one direction. The following result considers the example of the ring $\mathbb{Z}$.

Theorem 4.6 (Identifiability of discrete ANMs) *Assume that a distribution $P_{X,Y}$ allows for an ANM $Y = f(X) + N_Y$ from X to Y and that either X or Y has finite support. $P_{X,Y}$ allows for an ANM from Y to X if and only if there exists a disjoint decomposition $\bigcup_{i=0}^{l} C_i = \operatorname{supp} X$, such that the following conditions a), b), and c) are satisfied:*

a) The C_i's are shifted versions of each other

$$\forall i \exists d_i \geq 0 : C_i = C_0 + d_i$$

and f is piecewise constant: $f|_{C_i} \equiv c_i \ \forall i$.

b) The probability distributions on the C_is are shifted and scaled versions of each other with the same shift constant as above: For $x \in C_i$, $P(X = x)$ satisfies

$$P(X = x) = P(X = x - d_i) \cdot \frac{P(X \in C_i)}{P(X \in C_0)}.$$

c) The sets $c_i + \operatorname{supp} N_Y := \{c_i + h : P(N_Y = h) > 0\}$ are disjoint sets.

(By symmetry, such a decomposition satisfying the same criteria also exists for the support of Y.) Figure 4.3 shows an example that allows an ANM in both directions [Peters et al., 2011a].

There are similar results available for discrete ANMs modulo m. We refer to Peters et al. [2011a] for all details; we would like to mention, however, that the uniform noise distribution plays a special role: $Y \equiv f(X) + N_Y \mod m$ with a noise variable that is uniformly distributed on $\{0, \ldots, m-1\}$ leads to independent X and Y and therefore allows an ANM from Y to X, too.

A discrete ANM imposes strong assumptions on the underlying process that are often violated in practice. As in the continuous case, we want to argue that *if* the process allows for a discrete ANM in one direction, it might be reasonable to infer that direction as causal (see also Section 4.1.9).

4.1.6 Post-nonlinear Models

A more general model class than the one presented in Section 4.1.4 has been analyzed by Zhang and Hyvärinen [2009]; see also Zhang and Chan [2006] for an early reference.

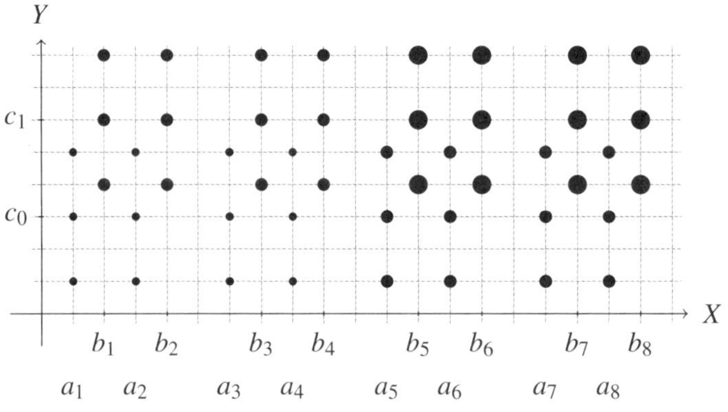

Figure 4.3: Only carefully chosen parameters allow ANMs in both directions (radii correspond to probability values); see Theorem 4.6. The sets described by the theorem are $C_0 = \{a_1, a_2, \ldots, a_8\}$ and $C_1 = \{b_1, b_2, \ldots, b_8\}$. The function f takes the values c_0 and c_1 on C_0 and C_1, respectively.

Definition 4.7 (Post-nonlinear models) *The distribution $P_{X,Y}$ is said to admit a post-nonlinear model if there are functions f_Y, g_Y and a noise variable N_Y such that*

$$Y = g_Y(f_Y(X) + N_Y), \quad N_Y \perp\!\!\!\perp X. \tag{4.9}$$

The following result essentially shows that a post-nonlinear model exists at most in one direction except for some "rare" non-generic cases.[4]

Theorem 4.8 (Identifiability of post-nonlinear models) *Let $P_{X,Y}$ admit a post-nonlinear model from X to Y as in* (4.9) *such that p_X, f_Y, g_Y are three-times differentiable. Then it admits a post-nonlinear model from Y to X only if p_X, f_Y, g_Y are adjusted to each other in the sense that they satisfy a differential equation described in Zhang and Hyvärinen [2009].*

4.1.7 Information-Geometric Causal Inference

To provide an idea of how independence between $P_{E|C}$ and P_C can be formalized, this section describes information-geometric causal inference (IGCI). IGCI, in particular the simple version described here, is a highly idealized toy scenario that nicely illustrates how independence in one direction implies dependence in the

[4]Here, "rare" should not be mistaken as saying that there are only finitely many exceptions.

other direction [Daniušis et al., 2010, Janzing et al., 2012]. It relies on the (admittedly strong) assumption of a deterministic relation between X and Y in both directions; that is,

$$Y = f(X) \quad \text{and} \quad X = f^{-1}(Y).$$

In other words, the noise variable in (3.2) is constant. Then the principle of independence of cause and mechanism described in Section 4.1.2 reduces to the independence of P_X and f. Remarkably, this independence implies dependence between P_Y and f^{-1}. To show this, we consider the following special case of the more general setting of Daniušis et al. [2010].

Definition 4.9 (IGCI model) *Here, $P_{X,Y}$ is said to satisfy an IGCI model from X to Y if the following conditions hold: $Y = f(X)$ for some diffeomorphism[5] f of $[0,1]$ that is strictly monotonic and satisfies $f(0) = 0$ and $f(1) = 1$. Moreover, P_X has the strictly positive continuous density p_X, such that the following "independence condition" holds:*

$$\operatorname{cov}[\log f', p_X] = 0, \tag{4.10}$$

where $\log f'$ and p_X are considered as random variables on the probability space $[0,1]$ endowed with the uniform distribution.[6]

Note that the covariance in (4.10) is explicitly given by

$$\begin{aligned}\operatorname{cov}[\log f', p_X] &= \int_0^1 \log f'(x) p_X(x) dx - \int_0^1 \log f'(x) dx \int_0^1 p_X(x) dx \\ &= \int_0^1 \log f'(x) p_X(x) dx - \int_0^1 \log f'(x) dx.\end{aligned}$$

The following result is shown in Daniušis et al. [2010] and Janzing et al. [2012].

Theorem 4.10 (Identifiability of IGCI models) *Assume the distribution $P_{X,Y}$ admits an IGCI model from X to Y. Then the inverse function f^{-1} satisfies*

$$\operatorname{cov}[\log f^{-1'}, p_Y] \geq 0, \tag{4.11}$$

with equality if and only if f is the identity.

---

[5] A function is called a diffeomorphism if it is differentiable and bijective and it has a differentiable inverse.

[6] This view may be unexpected, but recall that random variables are defined as measurable functions on a probability space. Here, both $\log f'$ and p_X are functions of $x \in [0,1]$, thus they are random variables on the common probability space $[0,1]$. Therefore, any distribution on $[0,1]$ defines a joint distribution of these random variables.

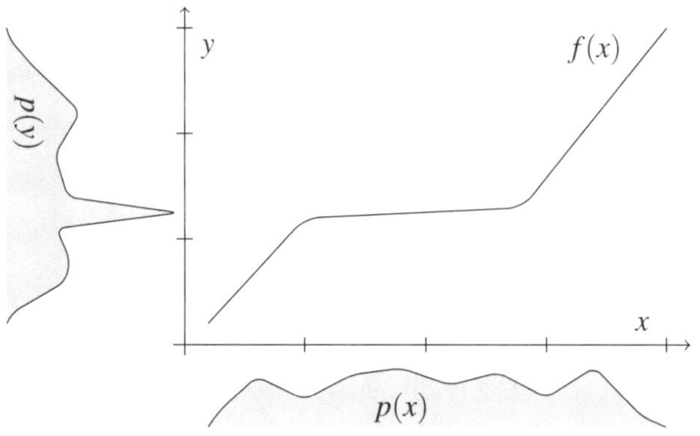

Figure 4.4: Visualization of the idea of IGCI: Peaks of p_Y tend to occur in regions where f has small slope and f^{-1} has large slope (provided that p_X has been chosen independently of f). Thus p_Y contains information about f^{-1}. IGCI can be generalized to non-differentiable functions f [Janzing et al., 2015].

In other words, uncorrelatedness of $\log f'$ and p_X implies positive correlation between $\log f^{-1'}$ and p_Y except for the trivial case $f = id$. This is illustrated in Figure 4.4. It can be shown [Janzing and Schölkopf, 2015] that uncorrelatedness of f' and p_X (i.e., the analogue of (4.10) without logarithm) implies positive correlations between $f^{-1'}$ and p_Y, but IGCI uses logarithmic derivatives because this admits various information-theoretic interpretations [Janzing et al., 2012]. As justification of (4.10), Janzing et al. [2012] describe a model where f is randomly generated independently of P_X and shows that (4.10) then holds approximately with high probability. It should be emphasized, however, that such justifications always refer to oversimplified models that are unlikely to describe realistic situations. Note that IGCI can easily be extended to bijective relations between vector-valued variables (as already described by Daniušis et al. [2010, Section 3]), but bijective deterministic relations are rare for empirical data. Therefore, IGCI only provides a toy scenario for which cause-effect inference is possible by virtue of an approximate independence assumption. The assumptions of IGCI have also been used [Janzing and Schölkopf, 2015] to explain why the performance of semi-supervised learning depends on the causal direction as stated in Section 5.1. By no means, is (4.10) meant to be *the* correct formalization of independence of cause and mechanism, nor do we believe that a unique formalization exists. Sgouritsa et al. [2015], for instance, propose an "unsupervised inverse regression" technique that tries to predict $P_{Y|X}$ from P_X and $P_{X|Y}$ from P_Y; they then suggest that the direction with the poorer performance is the causal one. Hence, this approach interprets "independence" as making such kind of unsupervised prediction impossible.

4.1.8 Trace Method

Janzing et al. [2010] and Zscheischler et al. [2011] describe an IGCI-related independence between P_C and $P_{E|C}$ for the case where C and E are high-dimensional variables coupled by a linear SCM:

Definition 4.11 (Trace condition) *Let* $\mathbf{X}$ *and* $\mathbf{Y}$ *be variables with values in* $\mathbb{R}^d$ *and* $\mathbb{R}^e$*, respectively, satisfying the linear model*

$$\mathbf{Y} = A\mathbf{X} + N_{\mathbf{X}}, \quad N_{\mathbf{X}} \perp\!\!\!\perp \mathbf{X}, \tag{4.12}$$

where A *is an* $e \times d$ *matrix of structure coefficients. Then* $P_{\mathbf{X},\mathbf{Y}}$ *is said to satisfy the trace condition from* $\mathbf{X}$ *to* $\mathbf{Y}$ *if the covariance matrix* $\Sigma_{\mathbf{XX}}$ *and* A *are "independent" in the sense that*

$$\tau_e(A\Sigma_{\mathbf{XX}}A^T) = \tau_d(\Sigma_{\mathbf{XX}})\tau_e(AA^T), \tag{4.13}$$

where $\tau_k(B) := \mathrm{tr}(B)/k$ *denotes the renormalized trace of a matrix* B.

A simple case that violates the trace condition would be given by a matrix A that shrinks all eigenvectors of $\Sigma_{\mathbf{XX}}$ corresponding to large eigenvalues and stretches those with small eigenvalues. This would certainly suggest that A has not been chosen independently of $\Sigma_{\mathbf{XX}}$. Roughly speaking, (4.13) describes an uncorrelatedness between the eigenvalues of $\Sigma_{\mathbf{XX}}$ and the factor by which A changes the length of the corresponding eigenvectors. More formally, (4.13) can be justified by a generating model with large d, e in which $\Sigma_{\mathbf{XX}}$ and A are independently chosen at random according to an appropriate (rotation invariant) prior probability. Then they satisfy (4.13) approximately with high probability [Besserve et al., in preparation].

For deterministic invertible relations, the causal direction is identifiable.

Theorem 4.12 (Identifiability via the trace condition) *Let both variables* $\mathbf{X}$ *and* $\mathbf{Y}$ *be* d*-dimensional with* $\mathbf{Y} = A\mathbf{X}$*, where* A *is invertible. If the trace condition* (4.13) *from* $\mathbf{X}$ *to* $\mathbf{Y}$ *is fulfilled, then the backward model*

$$\mathbf{X} = A^{-1}\mathbf{Y}$$

satisfies

$$\tau_d(A^{-1}\Sigma_{\mathbf{YY}}A^{-T}) \leq \tau_d(\Sigma_{\mathbf{YY}})\tau_d(A^{-1}A^{-T}),$$

with equality if and only if all singular values of A *have the same absolute value.*

Proof. The proof follows by applying Theorem 2 in Janzing et al. [2010] to the case $n := m := d$ and observing that $\mathrm{cov}[\mathbf{Z}, 1/\mathbf{Z}]$ is negative whenever $\mathbf{Z}$ is a strictly positive random variable that is almost surely not constant. □

Hence, in the generic case, the trace condition is violated in backward direction and the violation of the equality has always the same sign.

For noisy relations, no statement like Theorem 4.12 is known. One can still check whether (4.13) approximately holds in one of the directions and infer this to be the causal one. Then the structure matrix for the causal model from **Y** to **X** is no longer given by A^{-1}. In this case, we introduce the notation $A_{\mathbf{X}}$ for the model from **X** to **Y** and $A_{\mathbf{Y}}$ for the model from **Y** to **X**. What makes the deterministic case particularly nice is the fact that the quotient

$$\frac{\tau(A_{\mathbf{X}}\Sigma_{\mathbf{YY}}A_{\mathbf{X}}^T)}{\tau(A_{\mathbf{X}}A_{\mathbf{X}}^T)\tau(\Sigma_{\mathbf{YY}})}$$

is known to be *smaller* than 1 because $A_{\mathbf{X}} = A_{\mathbf{Y}}^{-1}$.

The theoretical justification of independence conditions like (4.10), (4.13), and others mentioned in this book rely on highly idealized generating models (for instance, (4.13) has been justified by a model where the covariance matrix of the cause is generated from a rotation invariant prior [Janzing et al., 2010]). There is some hope, however, that violations of the idealized assumptions do not necessarily spoil the causal inference methods. The metaphor with the Beuchet chair may help to make this point. First, consider a scenario where the observational vantage point is chosen uniformly on a sphere. Clearly, this would contain no information about the orientation of the object. In this sense, the uniform prior formalizes an "independence" assumption. Then the chair illusion only happens for a negligible fraction of angles. It is easy to see that strict uniformity for the choice of the vantage point is not needed to come to this conclusion. Instead, any random choice from a prior that is not concentrated within this small fraction of special angles will yield the same result. In other words, the conclusion about what a *typical* subject would see is robust with respect to violations of the underlying independence assumption. For this reason, discussions about the idealized assumptions of causal inference should focus on the question to what extent violations spoil the inference methods rather than explaining why they are too idealized.

4.1.9 Algorithmic Information Theory as Possible Foundation

This section describes an independence principle of which it is unclear how to apply it in practice although it relies on a well-defined mathematical formalism. It thus plays an intermediate role between the informal philosophical discussion about foundations of causal inference in Section 2.1 on the one hand and the concrete results of Sections 4.1.3 to 4.1.8 on possible asymmetries between cause and effect that rely on rather specific model assumptions on the other hand.

To formalize that P_E and $P_{C|E}$ contain no information about each other for more general models than the ones considered in Sections 4.1.7 and 4.1.8 is challenging. It requires a notion of information that refers to objects other than random variables. This is because P_E and $P_{C|E}$ are not random variables themselves but they describe distributions of random variables. One interesting notion of information is given by Kolmogorov complexity, which we briefly explain now.

Notions of Algorithmic Information Theory We first introduce **Kolmogorov complexity**: Consider a universal Turing machine T, that is, an abstraction of a computer that is ideal in the sense of having access to infinite memory space. For any binary string s, we define $K_T(s)$ as the length of the shortest program,[7] denoted by s^*, for which T outputs s and then stops [Solomonoff, 1964, Kolmogorov, 1965, Chaitin, 1966, Li and Vitányi, 1997]. One may call s^* the shortest compression of s, but keep in mind that s^* contains all the information that T needs for running the decompression. Hence,

$$K_T(s) := |s^*|,$$

where $|\cdot|$ denotes the number of digits of a binary word. This defines a probability-free notion of information content with respect to the given Turing machine T. In the following, we will refer to some fixed T and therefore drop the index. Although $K(s)$ is uncomputable, that is, there is no algorithm that computes $K(s)$ from s [Li and Vitányi, 1997], it can be useful to formalize conceptual ideas as it is done in this section.

The **conditional algorithmic information** of s, given t, is denoted by $K(s|t)$ and defined as the length of the shortest program that generates the output s from the input string t and then stops. One can then define the mutual information as[8]

$$I(s:t) := K(s) - K(s|t^*).$$

In particular, we have [Chaitin, 1966]:

$$I(s:t) \stackrel{+}{=} K(s) + K(t) - K(s,t), \tag{4.14}$$

[7]The program is given by a binary word using prefix-free encoding; that is, no program code is the prefix of another one. Otherwise one would need an extra symbol indicating the end of the code.

[8]Note that conditioning on t^* instead of t makes a difference since there is no algorithm that computes t^* from t (but vice versa); t^* can thus be more valuable as input than t. It turns out that $K(s|t^*)$ shows closer analogies to conditional Shannon entropy than $K(s|t)$.

where the symbol $\stackrel{+}{=}$ indicates that the equation only holds up to constants; that is, there is an error term whose length can be bounded independently of the lengths of s and t. To define Kolmogorov complexity $K(s,t)$ for the *pair* (s,t), one constructs a simple bijection between strings and pairs of strings by first using some enumeration of strings and then using a standard bijection between $\mathbb{N}$ and $\mathbb{N} \times \mathbb{N}$.

A simple interpretation of (4.14) is that algorithmic mutual information thus quantifies the amount of memory space saved when compressing s,t jointly instead of compressing them independently. Janzing and Schölkopf [2010] argue that two objects whose binary descriptions s,t have a significant amount of mutual information are likely to be causally related. In other words, in the same way as statistical dependences between *random variables* indicate causal relations (see Principle 1.1), algorithmic dependences between objects indicate causal relations between *objects*. Observing, for instance, two T-shirts with similar designs produced by different companies may indicate that one company copied from the other. Indeed, similarity of patterns in real life may be described by algorithmic mutual information provided that one has first agreed on an "appropriate" way to encode the pattern into a binary word and then on an "appropriate" Turing machine. For the difficult question of what "appropriate" means, see also the brief discussion of "relative causality" in the introduction of Janzing et al. [2016].

Algorithmic Independence of Conditionals The principle of algorithmically independent conditionals has been stated by Janzing and Schölkopf [2010] and Lemeire and Janzing [2013] for multivariate causal structures, but it yields nontrivial implications already for the bivariate case.

For two variables C and E being cause and effect, we assume that P_C and $P_{E|C}$ admit finite descriptions by binary strings s and t, respectively. In a parametric setting, s and t may describe points in the corresponding parameter spaces. Alternatively, one may think of s and t as being programs that compute $p(c)$ and $p(e|c)$ for all values c,e having finite description length. Then we use $I(P_C : P_{E|C})$ for $I(s:t)$ and postulate:

Principle 4.13 (Algorithmically independent conditionals) *P_C and $P_{E|C}$ are algorithmically independent, that is,*

$$I(P_C : P_{E|C}) \stackrel{+}{=} 0, \tag{4.15}$$

or, equivalently,

$$K(P_{C,E}) \stackrel{+}{=} K(P_C) + K(P_{E|C}). \tag{4.16}$$

The equivalence of (4.15) and (4.16) is immediate because describing the pair $(P_C, P_{E|C})$ is equivalent to describing the joint $P_{C,E}$. The idea of Principle 4.13 is that P_C and $P_{E|C}$ are causally unrelated objects of nature. This is certainly an idealized assumption, but for a setting where X causes Y or Y causes X it suggests to infer $X \to Y$ whenever the algorithmic dependences between P_X and $P_{Y|X}$ are weaker than for $P_{X|Y}$ and P_Y. To apply this to empirical data, however, raises the problem that $P_{X,Y}$ cannot be determined from finite data on top of the problem that algorithmic mutual information is uncomputable.

Despite these issues, Principle 4.13 is helpful to justify practical causal inference methods as we describe now for the example of ANMs. Janzing and Steudel [2010] argue that the SCM $Y := f_Y(X) + N_Y$ implies that the second derivative of $y \mapsto \log p(y)$ is determined by partial derivatives of $(x,y) \mapsto \log p(x|y)$. Hence, knowing $P_{X|Y}$ admits a short description of P_Y (up to some accuracy). Whenever $K(P_Y)$ is larger than this small amount of information, Janzing and Steudel [2010] conclude that $Y \to X$ should be rejected because P_Y and $P_{X|Y}$ are algorithmically dependent. For any given data set we cannot guarantee that $K(P_Y)$ is large enough to reject $Y \to X$ just because there is an ANM from Y to X. However, when applying inference that is based on the principle of ANMs to a large set of different distributions, we know that most of the distributions P_Y are complex enough (since the set of distributions with low complexity is small) to justify rejecting causal models that induce ANMs in the opposite direction. Moreover, Figure 5.4, left and right, shows two simple toy examples where looking at P_X alone suggests a simple guess for the joint distribution $P_{X,Y}$. Indeed, one can show that this amounts to algorithmic dependence between P_X and $P_{Y|X}$, as shown for the left case by Janzing and Schölkopf [2010, remarks after Equation (27)].

We should also point out that (4.15) implies

$$K(P_C) + K(P_{E|C}) \stackrel{+}{=} K(P_{C,E}) \stackrel{+}{\leq} K(P_E) + K(P_{C|E}). \tag{4.17}$$

The equality follows because describing $P_{C,E}$ is equivalent to describing the pair $(P_C, P_{E|C})$, which is not shorter than describing marginal and conditional separately. The inequality follows because P_E and $P_{C|E}$ also determine $P_{C,E}$. In other words, independence of conditionals implies that the joint distribution has a shorter description in the causal direction than in the anticausal direction.[9]

[9]Checking whether the left-hand side of inequality (4.17) is smaller than the right-hand side is not the only option to test independence: whenever two strings are algorithmically independent, applying functions of complexity $\mathcal{O}(1)$ to each of them generates again two (possibly simpler) algorithmically

This implication also sounds natural from the perspective of the minimum description length principle [Grünwald, 2007] and in the spirit of Occam's razor. Note, however, that the condition $K(P_C) + K(P_{E|C}) \stackrel{+}{\leq} K(P_E) + K(P_{C|E})$ is strictly weaker than (4.15) since the shortest description of $P_{C,E}$ may not use either of the two possible factorizations, which can happen, for instance, when there is a hidden common cause [Janzing and Schölkopf, 2010, p. 16].

Principle 6.53 generalizes Principle 4.13 to the multivariate setting.

4.2 Methods for Structure Identification

We now present different ideas about how the identifiability results obtained in Section 4.1 can be exploited for causal discovery. That is, the methods estimate a graph from a finite data set. These are challenging statistical problems, which can be approached in many different ways. We try to focus on methodological ideas and do not claim that the methods we present make the most efficient use of the data. It is very well possible that future research will yield novel and successful methods. We restrict the attention to a few examples, mainly to those for which we have reasonable experience regarding their performance.

4.2.1 Additive Noise Models

For causal learning methods based on the identifiability of ANMs according to Theorem 4.5, we mainly refer to the multivariate chapter (Section 7.2). Here, we sketch two methods without claiming their optimality. The first method tests the **independence of residuals** and is a special case of the regression with subsequent independence test (RESIT) algorithm (see Section 7.2).

1. Regress Y on X; that is, use some regression technique to write Y as a function $\hat{f}_Y$ of X plus some noise.
2. Test whether $Y - \hat{f}_Y(X)$ is independent of X.
3. Repeat the procedure with exchanging the roles of X and Y.
4. If the independence is accepted for one direction and rejected for the other, infer the former one as the causal direction.

Figure 4.5 shows the procedure on a simulated data set; see Figure 4.1 for the underlying distribution. At least in the continuous setting, the first two steps are stan-

independent strings [Janzing and Schölkopf, 2010, Lemma 6]. This way, one can in principle reject algorithmic independence without knowing the complexities of the strings to start with.

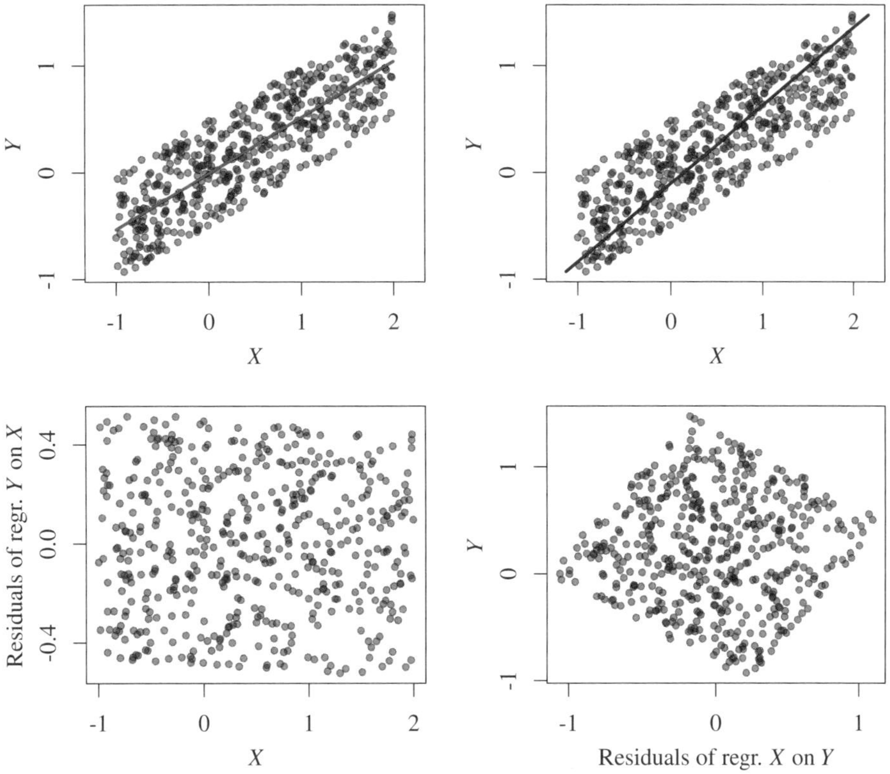

Figure 4.5: We are given a sample from the underlying distribution and perform a linear regression in the directions $X \to Y$ (left) and $Y \to X$ (right). The fitted functions are shown in the top row, the corresponding residuals are shown in the bottom row. Only the direction $X \to Y$ yields independent residuals; see also Figure 4.1.

dard problems of machine learning and statistics (see Appendices A.1 and A.2), with the additional challenge that they are coupled: $\hat{f}_Y$ deviating from f_Y may hide or create dependences between noise and input variable. In general, any test based on the *estimated* residuals may lose its type I error control. As a possible solution one may use sample splitting [Kpotufe et al., 2014]. Moreover, it is important to choose an independence test that accounts for higher order statistics rather than testing correlations only. Any regression technique minimizing quadratic error that includes linear components and an intercept yields uncorrelated noise.[10] In practice, one may use the Hilbert-Schmidt Independence Criterion (HSIC) [Gretton et al., 2008], for example, which we briefly introduce in Appendix A.2. Mooij et al. [2016, Theorem 20] use a continuity property of HSIC to show that even without sample splitting, one obtains the correct value of HSIC in the limit of infinite data (there are no claims about the p-values of the test, however). Finally, the last step deserves our particular attention because it refers to the relation between probability and causality. Depending on the significance levels for rejecting and accepting independence, one may get an ANM in both directions, in no direction, or in one direction. To enforce decisions, one just infers the direction to be the causal one, for which the p-value for rejecting independence is higher.

Recent studies provide some evidence that this procedure yields success rates on real data above chance level [Mooij et al., 2016]. Figure 4.6 shows the scatter plot of real-world data[11] for which an ANM holds reasonably well only in the causal direction. For modifications regarding discrete data, we refer to the corresponding literature [Peters et al., 2011a]. Note that the post-nonlinear model (4.9) is considerably harder to fit in practice than the more standard nonlinear regression model (4.3).

As an alternative to the preceding approach, one may also use a **maximum likelihood**-based approach. Consider a nonlinear SCM with additive Gaussian error terms, for example. One may then distinguish between $X \to Y$ and $X \leftarrow Y$ by comparing the likelihood scores of both models. To do so, we first perform a nonlinear regression from Y on X to obtain residuals $R_Y := Y - \hat{f}_Y(X)$. We then compare

$$L_{X \to Y} = -\log \widehat{\mathrm{var}}[X] - \log \widehat{\mathrm{var}}[R_Y] \tag{4.18}$$

with the analogous version

$$L_{X \leftarrow Y} = -\log \widehat{\mathrm{var}}[R_X] - \log \widehat{\mathrm{var}}[Y] \tag{4.19}$$

that we obtain when interchanging the roles of X and Y. It is not difficult to show (see Problem 4.16) that this indeed corresponds to a comparison of likelihoods when instead of performing the regression, we use the true conditional mean

[10] This can easily be seen using the following standard geometric picture: cov[.,.] defines an inner product in the space of centred random variables with finite variance. Then the length of the vector $Y - \alpha X$ is minimal when it is orthogonal to X.

[11] This is pair001 in the database of cause-effect pairs `https://webdav.tuebingen.mpg.de/cause-effect/`; see also [Mooij et al., 2016].

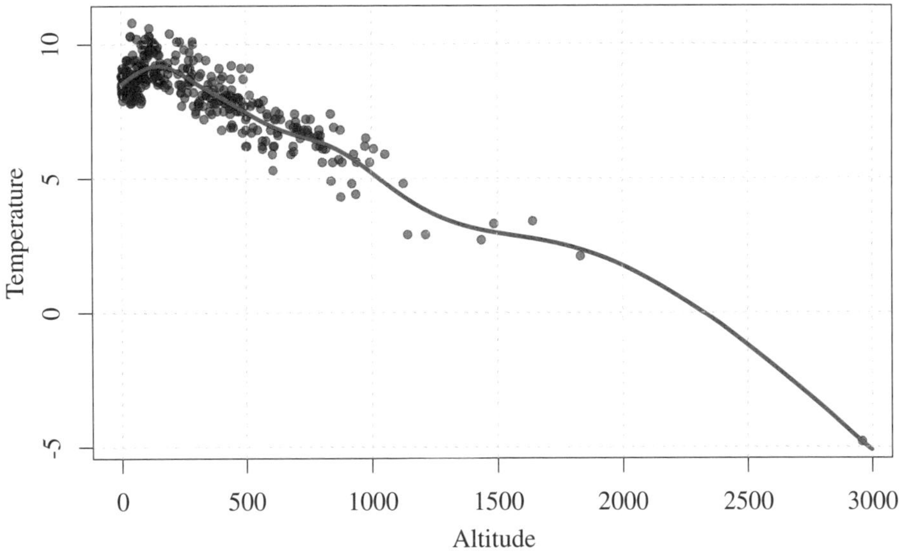

Figure 4.6: Relation between average temperature in degrees Celsius (Y) and altitude in meters (X) of places in Germany. The data are taken from "Deutscher Wetterdienst," see also Mooij et al. [2016]. A nonlinear function (which is close to linear in the regime far away from sea level) with additive noise fits these empirical observations reasonably well.

$\hat{f}_Y(x) = \mathbb{E}[Y \,|\, X = x]$ (and similarly for $\hat{f}_X$). As before, however, this two-step procedure of first performing regression and then computing sample variances requires justification. Bühlmann et al. [2014] use empirical process theory [van de Geer, 2009] to prove consistency. If the noise does not necessarily follow a Gaussian distribution, we have to adapt the score functions by replacing the logarithm of the empirical variance of the residuals with an estimate of the differential entropy of the error term [Nowzohour and Bühlmann, 2016].

Code Snippet 4.14 The following code shows an example with a finite data set. It makes use of the code packages `dHSIC` [Pfister et al., 2017] and `mgcv` [Wood, 2006]. The former package contains the function `dhsic.test`, an implementation of the independence test proposed by [Gretton et al., 2008], and the latter package contains the function `gam` that we use as a nonlinear regression method in lines 10 and 11 (see Section A.1). Only in the backward direction is the independence between residuals and input rejected, see lines 15 and 17. In lines 21 and 23, we see that a Gaussian likelihood score favors the forward direction, too; see also Equations (4.18) and (4.19).

```
library(dHSIC)
library(mgcv)
#
# generate data set
set.seed(1)
X <- rnorm(200)
Y <- X^3 + rnorm(200)
#
# fit models
modelforw <- gam(Y ~ s(X))
modelbackw <- gam(X ~ s(Y))
#
# independence tests
dhsic.test(modelforw$residuals, X)$p.value
# [1] 0.7628932
dhsic.test(modelbackw$residuals, Y)$p.value
# [1] 0.004221031
#
# computing likelihoods
- log(var(X)) - log(var(modelforw$residuals))
# [1] 0.1420063
- log(var(modelbackw$residuals)) - log(var(Y))
# [1] -1.014013
```

4.2.2 Information-Geometric Causal Inference

We sketch the implementation of IGCI briefly and refer to Mooij et al. [2016] for details. The theoretical basis is given by the identifiability result in Theorem 4.10 and some simple conclusions thereof. One can show that the independence condition (4.10) implies

$$C_{X \to Y} \leq C_{Y \to X}$$

if one defines

$$C_{X \to Y} := \int_0^1 \log f'(x) p(x) dx,$$

and $C_{Y \to X}$ similarly. Here, the following straightforward estimators are used:

$$\hat{C}_{X \to Y} := \frac{1}{N-1} \sum_{j=1}^{N-1} \log \frac{|y_{j+1} - y_j|}{|x_{j+1} - x_j|},$$

where the $x_1 < x_2 < \cdots < x_N$ are the observed x-values in increasing order. If Y is an increasing function of X, the y-values are also ordered, but for real data this will usually not be the case. The estimator $\hat{C}_{Y \to X}$ is defined accordingly and $X \to Y$ is inferred whenever $\hat{C}_{X \to Y} < \hat{C}_{Y \to X}$. Apart from the so-called *slope-based* approach, there is also an entropy-based approach. One can show that (4.10) also implies

$$H(X) \leq H(Y),$$

where H denotes the differential Shannon entropy

$$H(X) := -\int_0^1 p(x)\log p(x)dx.$$

Intuitively, the reason is that applying a nonlinear function f to p_X generates additional irregularities (unless the nonlinearity of f is tuned relative to p_X) and thus makes p_Y even less uniform than p_X. Accordingly, the variable with the larger entropy is assumed to be the cause. To estimate H, one can use any standard entropy estimator from the literature.

4.2.3 Trace Method

Recall that this method relies on linear relations between high-dimensional variables $\mathbf{X}$ and $\mathbf{Y}$. First assume that the sample size is sufficiently large (compared to the dimensions of $\mathbf{X}$ and $\mathbf{Y}$) to estimate the covariance matrices $\Sigma_{\mathbf{XX}}$ and $\Sigma_{\mathbf{YY}}$ and the structure matrices $A_{\mathbf{Y}}$ and $A_{\mathbf{X}}$ by standard linear regression. To employ the identifiability result in Theorem 4.12, one can compute the tracial dependency ratio

$$r_{X\to Y} := \frac{\tau(A_{\mathbf{Y}}\Sigma_{\mathbf{XX}}A_{\mathbf{Y}}^T)}{\tau(A_{\mathbf{Y}}A_{\mathbf{Y}}^T)\tau(\Sigma_{\mathbf{XX}})},$$

and likewise $r_{Y\to X}$ (via swapping the roles of $\mathbf{X}$ and $\mathbf{Y}$) and infer that the one that is closer to 1 corresponds to the causal direction [Janzing et al., 2010].

Zscheischler et al. [2011] describe a method to assess whether the deviation from 1 is significant, subject to a generating model where independence of the two matrices A and $\Sigma_{\mathbf{XX}}$ is simulated by some random orthogonal map rotating them against each other. Using ideas from **free probability theory** [Voiculescu, 1997], a mathematical framework that describes asymptotic behavior of large random matrices, Zscheischler et al. [2011] construct an implementation of the trace condition for the regime where the dimension is larger than the sample size. They show that, in the noiseless case, $r_{X\to Y}$ can still be estimated (although there is not enough data to estimate $\Sigma_{\mathbf{XX}}$ and A) subject to an additional independence assumption for A and the empirical covariance matrix of $\mathbf{X}$. Therefore, one can reject the hypothesis $\mathbf{X}\to\mathbf{Y}$ whenever the estimator deviates significantly from 1. Then, either the additional independence assumption is wrong or $r_{X\to Y}$ deviates significantly from 1.

4.2.4 Supervised Learning Methods

Finally, we describe a method that approaches causal learning from a more machine learning point of view. It has, in principle, the ability to make use of either restricted function classes or an independence condition. Suppose, we are given labeled training data of the form $(\mathcal{D}_1, A_1), \ldots, (\mathcal{D}_n, A_n)$. Here, each $\mathcal{D}_i$ is a data set

$$\mathcal{D}_i = \{(X_1, Y_1), \ldots, (X_{n_i}, Y_{n_i})\}$$

containing realizations $(X_1, Y_1), \ldots, (X_{n_i}, Y_{n_i}) \overset{\text{iid}}{\sim} P^i_{X,Y}$, and each label $A_i \in \{\rightarrow, \leftarrow\}$ describes whether data set $\mathcal{D}_i$ corresponds to $X \rightarrow Y$ or $X \leftarrow Y$. Then, causal learning becomes a classical prediction problem, and one may train classifiers hoping that they generalize well from the data set with known ground-truth to unseen test data sets.

To the best of our knowledge, Guyon [2013] was the first one who systematically investigated such an approach in the form of a challenge (providing a mix of synthetic and real data sets as known ground truth data). It is clear that the method will not succeed by exploiting symmetric features as correlation or covariance.

Many of the competitive classifiers in the challenge were based on hand-crafted features; examples include entropy estimates of the marginal distributions or entropy estimates of the distribution of the residuals that resulted from regressing either X on Y or Y from X. Interestingly, such features can be related to the concept of ANMs. For Gaussian distributed variables, for example, the entropy is a linear function of the logarithm of the variance and, therefore, the features are expressive enough to reconstruct the scores (4.18) and (4.19). Considering entropies instead of logarithm of variances corresponds to relaxing the Gaussianity assumption [Nowzohour and Bühlmann, 2016].

Lopez-Paz et al. [2015] aims at an automatic construction of such features. The idea is to map the joint distributions $P^i_{X,Y}$, $i = 1, \ldots, n$ into a reproducing kernel Hilbert space (see Appendix A.2) and perform a classification in this space. In practice, one does not have access to the full distribution $P^i_{X,Y}$ and rather uses the empirical distribution as an approximation. (A similar approach has been used to distinguish time series that are reversed in time from their original version [Peters et al., 2009a].) Because the classification into cause and effect seems to rely on relatively complex properties of the joint distribution, one requires a large sample size n for the training set. To add useful simulated data sets, these must be generated from identifiable cases. Lopez-Paz et al. [2015] use additional samples from ANMs, for example.

Supervised learning methods do not yet work as stand-alone methods for causal learning. They may prove to be useful, however, as statistical tools that can make efficient use of known identifiability properties or combinations of those.

4.3 Problems

Problem 4.15 (ANMs) *a) Consider the SCM*

$$\begin{aligned} X &:= N_X \\ Y &:= 2X + N_Y \end{aligned}$$

with N_X uniformly distributed between 1 and 3 and N_Y uniformly distributed between -0.5 and 0.5 and independent of N_X. The distribution $P_{X,Y}$ admits an ANM from X to Y. Draw the support of the joint distribution of X,Y and convince yourself that $P_{X,Y}$ does not admit an ANM from Y to X, that is there is no function g and independent noise variables M_X and M_Y such that

$$\begin{aligned} X &= g(Y) + M_X \\ Y &= M_Y \end{aligned}$$

with M_X independent of M_Y.

b) Similarly as in part a), consider the SCM

$$\begin{aligned} X &:= N_X \\ Y &:= X^2 + N_Y \end{aligned}$$

with N_X uniformly distributed between 1 and 3 and N_Y uniformly distributed between -0.5 and 0.5 and independent of N_X. Again, draw the support of $P_{X,Y}$ and convince yourself that there is no ANM from Y to X.

Problem 4.16 (Maximum likelihood) *Assume that we are given an i.i.d. data set $(X_1,Y_1),\ldots,(X_n,Y_n)$ from the model*

$$Y = f(X) + N_Y, \text{ with } X \sim \mathcal{N}(\mu_X, \sigma_X^2), \text{ and } N_Y \sim \mathcal{N}(\mu_{N_Y}, \sigma_{N_Y}^2) \text{ independent,}$$

where the function f is supposed to be known.

a) Prove that $f(x) = \mathbb{E}[Y \mid X = x]$.

b) *Write* $\mathbf{x} := (x_1, \ldots, x_n)$, $\mathbf{y} := (y_1, \ldots, y_n)$ *and consider the log-likelihood function*

$$\ell_\theta(\mathbf{x}, \mathbf{y}) = \ell_\theta\left((x_1, y_1), \ldots, (x_n, y_n)\right) = \sum_{i=1}^{n} \log p_\theta(x_i, y_i),$$

where p_θ *is the joint density over* (X, Y) *and* $\theta := (\mu_X, \mu_{N_Y}, \sigma_X^2, \sigma_{N_Y}^2)$. *Prove that for some* $c_1, c_2 \in \mathbb{R}$ *with* $c_2 > 0$

$$\max_\theta \ell_\theta(\mathbf{x}, \mathbf{y}) = c_2 \cdot \left(c_1 - \log \widehat{\mathrm{var}}[\mathbf{x}] - \log \widehat{\mathrm{var}}\left[\mathbf{y} - f(\mathbf{x})\right]\right), \tag{4.20}$$

where $\widehat{\mathrm{var}}[\mathbf{z}] := \frac{1}{n}\sum_{i=1}^{n}(z_i - \frac{1}{n}\sum_{k=1}^{n} z_k)^2$ *estimates the variance.*

Equation (4.20) *motivates the comparison of expressions* (4.18) *and* (4.19). *The main difference is that in this exercise, we have used the conditional mean and not the outcome of the regression method. One can show that, asymptotically, the latter still produces correct results [Bühlmann et al., 2014].*

5

Connections to Machine Learning, I

As argued in Chapter 1, standard machine learning rests on the same basis as statistics: we use data sampled i.i.d. from some unknown underlying distribution, and seek to infer properties of that distribution. In contrast, causal inference assumes a stronger underlying structure, including directed dependences. This makes it harder to learn about the structure from data, but it also allows novel statements once this is done, including statements about the effect of distribution shifts and interventions. If we view machine learning as the process of inferring regularities (or "laws of nature") that go beyond pure statistical associations, then causality plays a crucial role. The present chapter presents some thoughts on this, focusing on the case of two variables only. Chapter 8 will revisit this topic and look at the multivariate case.

5.1 Semi-Supervised Learning

Let us consider a regression task, in which our goal is to predict a target variable Y from a d-dimensional predictor variable $\mathbf{X}$. For many loss functions, knowing the conditional distribution $P_{Y|\mathbf{X}}$ suffices to solve the problem. For instance, the regression function

$$f^0(\mathbf{x}) := \mathbb{E}[Y \,|\, \mathbf{X} = \mathbf{x}]$$

minimizes the L_2 loss,

$$f^0 \in \operatorname*{argmin}_{f:\mathbb{R}^d \to \mathbb{R}} \mathbb{E}\left[(Y - f(\mathbf{X}))^2\right].$$

In **supervised learning** , we receive n i.i.d. data points from the joint distribution: $(\mathbf{X}_1, Y_1), \ldots, (\mathbf{X}_n, Y_n) \overset{\text{iid}}{\sim} P_{\mathbf{X},Y}$. Regression estimation (with L_2 loss) thus amounts to estimating the conditional mean from n data points of the joint distribution. In (inductive) **semi-supervised learning** (SSL), however, we receive m additional unlabeled data points $\mathbf{X}_{n+1}, \ldots, \mathbf{X}_{n+m} \overset{\text{iid}}{\sim} P_{\mathbf{X}}$. The hope is that these additional data points provide information about $P_{\mathbf{X}}$, which itself tells us something about $\mathbb{E}[Y \mid \mathbf{X}]$ or more generally about $P_{Y|\mathbf{X}}$.[1] Many assumptions underlying SSL techniques [see Chapelle et al., 2006, for an overview] concern relations between $P_{\mathbf{X}}$ and $P_{Y|\mathbf{X}}$. The *cluster assumption*, for instance, stipulates that points lying in the same cluster of $P_{\mathbf{X}}$ have the same or a similar Y; this is similar to the *low-density separation* assumption that states that the decision boundary of a classifier (i.e., points $\mathbf{x}$ where $P(Y = 1|\mathbf{X} = \mathbf{x})$ crosses 0.5) should lie in a region where $P_{\mathbf{X}}$ is small. The *semi-supervised smoothness* assumption says that the conditional mean $\mathbf{x} \mapsto \mathbb{E}[Y \mid \mathbf{X} = \mathbf{x}]$ should be smooth in areas where $P_{\mathbf{X}}$ is large.

5.1.1 SSL and Causal Direction

In the simplest setting, where the causal graph has only two variables (cause and effect), a machine learning problem can either be **causal** (if we predict effect from cause) or **anticausal** (if we predict cause from effect). Practitioners usually do not care about the causal structure underlying a given learning problem (see Figure 5.1). However, as we argue herein, the structure has implications for machine learning.

In Section 2.1, we have hypothesized that causal conditionals are *independent* of each other (Principle 2.1 and subsequent discussion). Schölkopf et al. [2012] realize that this principle has a direct implication for SSL. Since the latter relies on the relation between $P_{\mathbf{X}}$ and $P_{Y|\mathbf{X}}$ and the principle claims that P_{cause} and $P_{\text{effect}|\text{cause}}$ do not contain information about one another, we can conclude that SSL will not work if $\mathbf{X}$ corresponds to the cause and Y corresponds to the effect (i.e., for a *causal* learning problem). In this case, additional $\mathbf{x}$-values only tell us more about $P_{\mathbf{X}}$ — which is irrelevant because the prediction requires information about the independent object $P_{Y|\mathbf{X}}$. On the other hand, if $\mathbf{X}$ is the effect and $\mathbf{Y}$ is the cause, information on $P_{\mathbf{X}}$ may tell us something about $P_{Y|\mathbf{X}}$.

A meta-study that analyzed results in SSL supports our hypothesis. All cases

[1] Again, we use the notation $P_{Y|\mathbf{X}}$ as a shorthand for the collection $(P_{Y|\mathbf{X}=\mathbf{x}})_{\mathbf{x}}$ of conditional distributions.

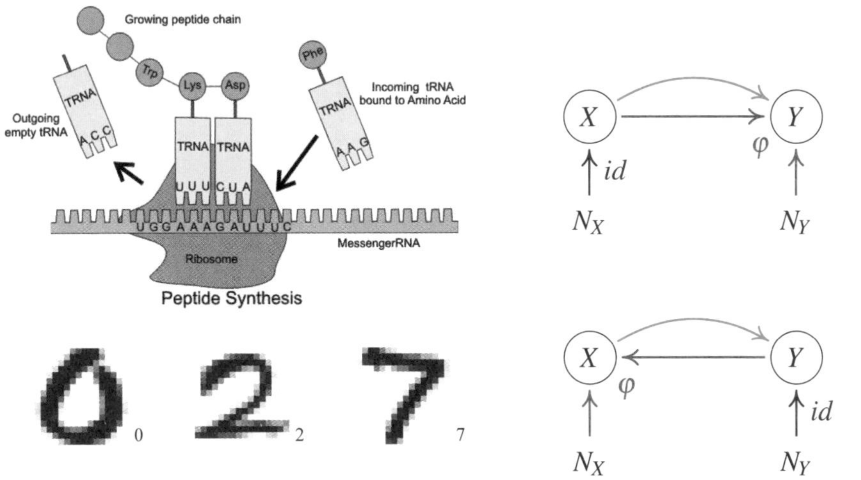

Figure 5.1: *Top:* a complicated mechanism φ called the ribosome translates mRNA information X into a protein chain Y.[2] Predicting the protein from the mRNA is an example of a *causal* learning problem, where the direction of prediction (green arrow) is aligned with the direction of causation (red). *Bottom:* In handwritten digit recognition, we try to infer the class label Y (i.e., the writer's intention) from an image X produced by a writer. This is an *anticausal* problem.

where SSL helped were anticausal, or confounded, or examples where the causal structure was unclear (see Figure 5.2).

Within the toy scenario of a bijective deterministic causal relation (see Section 4.1.7), Janzing and Schölkopf [2015] prove that whenever P_{cause} and $P_{\text{effect}|\text{cause}}$ are independent in the sense of (4.10), then SSL indeed outperforms supervised learning in the anticausal direction but not in the causal direction. The idea is that SSL employs the dependence (4.11) for an improved interpolation algorithm.

Sgouritsa et al. [2015] have developed a causal learning method that exploits the fact that SSL can only work in the anti-causal direction.

Finally, note that SSL contains some versions of unsupervised learning as a special case (with no labeled data). In clustering, for example, Y is often a discrete value indicating the cluster index. Similarly to the preceding reasoning, we can argue that if X is the cause and Y the effect, clustering should not work well. In

[2]By user "Boumphreyfr", https://commons.wikimedia.org/wiki/File:Peptide_syn.png, [CC BY-SA 3.0 (http://creativecommons.org/licenses/by-sa/3.0) or GFDL (http://www.gnu.org/copyleft/fdl.html)]

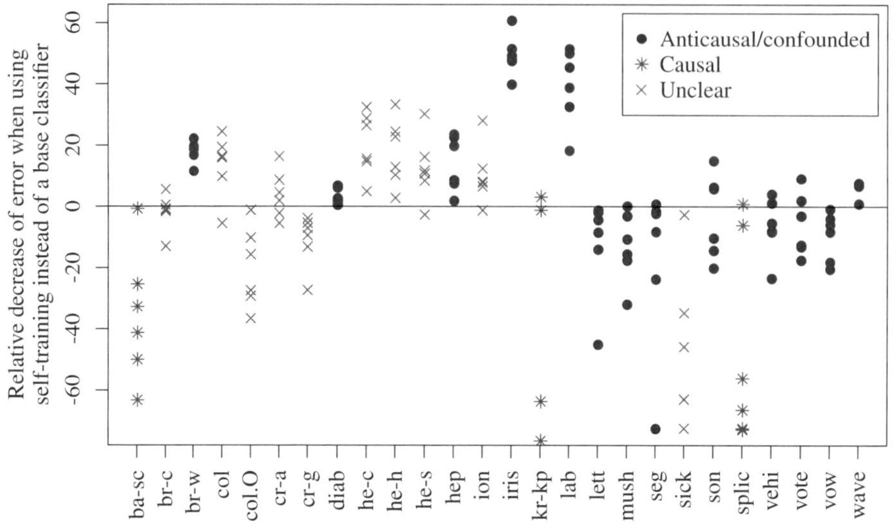

Figure 5.2: The benefit of SSL depends on the causal structure. Each column of points corresponds to a benchmark data set from the UCI repository and shows the performance of six different base classifiers augmented with self-training, a generic method for SSL. Performance is measured by percentage decrease of error relative to the base classifier, that is, (error(base) – error(self-train))/error(base). Self-training overall does not help for the causal data sets, but it does help for some of the anticausal/confounded data sets [from Schölkopf et al., 2012].

many applications of clustering on real data, however, the cluster index is rather the cause than the effect of the features.

While the empirical results in Figure 5.2 are promising, the statement that SSL does not work in the causal direction (always assuming independence of cause and mechanism, cf. Principle 2.1) needs to be made more precise. This will be done in the following section; it may be of interest to readers interested in SSL and covariate shift, but could be skipped at first reading by others.

5.1.2 A Remark on SSL in the Causal Direction

A more precise form of our prediction regarding SSL reads as follows: if the task is to predict y for some specific x, knowledge of P_X does not help when $X \to Y$ is the causal direction. However, even if P_X does not tell us anything about $P_{Y|X}$ (due to $X \to Y$), knowing P_X can still help us for better estimating Y in the sense that we

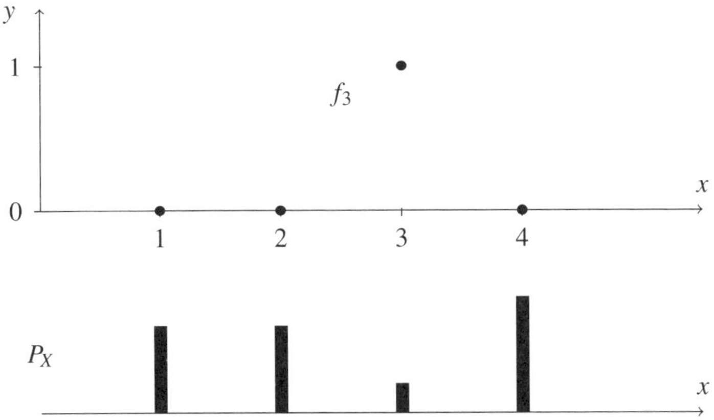

Figure 5.3: In this example, SSL reduces the loss even in the causal direction. Since for every x, the label zero is a priori more likely than the label one, the expected number of errors is minimized when a function is chosen that attains one at a point x where $p(x)$ is minimal (here: $x = 3$).

obtain lower risk in a learning scenario.

To see this, consider a toy example where the relation between X and Y is given by a deterministic function, that is, $Y = f(X)$, where f is known to be from some class $\mathcal{F}$ of functions. Let X take values in $\{1, \ldots, m\}$ with $m \geq 3$ and let Y be a binary label attaining values in $\{0, 1\}$. We define the function class $\mathcal{F} := \{f_1, \ldots, f_m\}$ by $f_j(j) = 1$ and $f_j(k) = 0$ for $k \neq j$. In other words, $\mathcal{F}$ consists of the set of functions that attain the value one at exactly one point. Figure 5.3, top, shows the function f_3 for $m = 4$. Suppose that our learning algorithm infers f_j while the true function is f_i. For $i \neq j$, the risk, that is, the expected number of errors (see Equation (1.2)), equals

$$R_i(f_j) := \sum_{x=1}^{m} |f_j(x) - f_i(x)| p(x) = p(j) + p(i), \tag{5.1}$$

where p denotes the probability mass function for X. We now average $R_i(f_j)$ over the set $\mathcal{F}$ and assume that each f_i is equally likely. This yields the expected risk (where the expectation is taken with respect to a uniform prior over $\mathcal{F}$)

$$\mathbb{E}[R_i(f_j)] = \frac{1}{m} \sum_{i=1}^{m} \sum_{x=1}^{m} |f_j(x) - f_i(x)| p(x) \tag{5.2}$$

$$= \frac{1}{m} \sum_{i \neq j} (p(j) + p(i)) = \frac{m-2}{m} p(j) + \frac{1}{m}. \tag{5.3}$$

To minimize (5.3), we should thus choose f_k such that k minimizes the function p. This makes sense because for any point $x = 1, \ldots, m$, the label $y = 0$ is more likely than $y = 1$ (probability $(m-1)/m$ versus $1/m$). Therefore, we would actually like to infer zero everywhere, but since the zero function is not contained in $\mathcal{F}$, we are forced to select one x-value to which we assign the label zero. Hence, we choose one of the least likely x-values to obtain minimal expected loss (which is $x = 3$ for the distribution in Figure 5.3, bottom). Clearly, unlabeled observations help identify the least likely x-values, hence SSL can help. This example does not require any (x, y)-pairs (labeled instances); unlabeled data x suffices. It is thus actually an example of *un*supervised learning rather than being a typical SSL scenario. However, accounting for a small number of labeled instances in addition does not change the essential idea. Generically, these few instances will not contain any instance with $y = 1$ if m is large enough. Hence, the observed (x, y)-pairs only help because they slightly reduce $\mathcal{F}$ to a smaller class $\mathcal{F}'$ for which the analysis remains basically the same, and we still conclude that the unlabeled instances help.

Although we have not specified a supervised learning scenario as baseline (that is, one that does not employ knowledge of P_X), we know that it must be worse than the best semi-supervised scenario because the optimal estimation depends on P_X, as we have just argued.

Here, the independence of mechanisms is not violated (and thus, X can be considered as a cause for Y): f is assumed to be chosen uniformly among $\mathcal{F}$, and knowing P_X does not tell us anything about f. Knowing P_X is only helpful for minimizing the loss because $p(x)$ appears in (5.2) as a weighting factor.

The preceding example is close in spirit to a Bayesian analysis because it involved an average over functions in $\mathcal{F}$. It can be modified, however, to apply to a worst case analysis, in which the true function f is chosen by an adversarial to maximize (5.1) [see also Kääriäinen, 2005]. Given a function f_j, the adversarial chooses f_i with i an x-value different from j with maximal probability mass. The worst case risk thus reads $\max_{x \neq j}\{p(x)\} + p(j)$, which is, again, minimized when j is chosen to be an x-value that minimizes the probability mass function $p(x)$. Therefore, we conclude that optimal performance is attained only when P_X is taken into account.

Another example can be constructed on the basis of an argument that is given in a non-causality context by Urner et al. [2011, proof of Theorem 4]. They construct a case of model misspecification; where the true function f_0 is not contained in the class $\mathcal{F}$ that is optimized over. In their example, additional information about the marginal P_X helps for reducing the risk, even though the conditional $P_{Y|X}$ can be considered as being independent of the marginal. Our example above is not based on the same kind of model misspecification. Each possible (unknown) ground truth f_i is indeed contained in the class of functions; however, we would like to minimize the *expectation* of the risk over a prior, and our function class does not contain a function that has zero expected risk. Therefore, for the expected risk, this is akin to a situation of model misspecification.

Finally, we try to give some further intuition about the example by Urner et al. [2011]. Since f_0 is not contained in the function class $\mathcal{F}$, we need to find a function $\hat{f} \in \mathcal{F}$ that minimizes the distance $d(f, f_0)$, defined as the risk of f, over $f \in \mathcal{F}$; we say f_0 is projected onto $\mathcal{F}$. Roughly speaking, additional information about P_X provides us with a better understanding of this projection.[3]

5.2 Covariate Shift

As explained in Section 2.1, the independence between P_{cause} and $P_{\text{effect}|\text{cause}}$ (Principle 2.1) can be interpreted in two different ways: in Section 5.1 above, we argued that given a fixed joint distribution, these two objects contain no information about each other (see the middle box in Figure 2.2). Alternatively, suppose the joint distribution $P_{\text{cause,effect}}$ changes across different data sets; then the change of P_{cause} does not tell us anything about the change of $P_{\text{effect}|\text{cause}}$ (this corresponds to the left box in Figure 2.2). Knowing that X is the cause and Y the effect thus has important consequences for a prediction scenario where Y is predicted from X. Assume we have learned the statistical relation between X and Y using examples from one data set and we are supposed to employ this knowledge for predicting Y from X for a second data set. Further, assume that we observe that the x-values in the second data set follow a distribution P'_X that differs from the distribution P_X of the first data set. How would we make use of this information? By the independence of mechanisms, the fact that P'_X differs from P_X does not tell us anything about whether $P_{Y|X}$ also changed across the data sets. Therefore, it might be the case that the conditional $P_{Y|X}$ still holds true for the second data set. Second, even if the conditional did change to $P'_{Y|X} \neq P_{Y|X}$, it is natural to still use $P_{Y|X}$ for our prediction. After all, the independence principle states that the new change of the marginal distribution from P_X to P'_X does not tell us anything about *how* the conditional has changed. Therefore, we use $P_{Y|X}$ in absence of any better candidate. Using the same conditional $P_{Y|X}$ although P_X has changed is usually referred to as

[3] We are grateful to several people who contributed to this discussion: Sebastian Nowozin, Ilya Tolstikhin, and Ruth Urner.

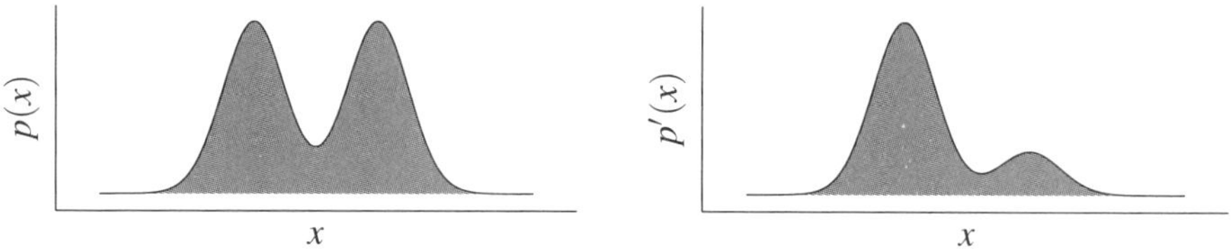

Figure 5.4: Example where P_X changes to P'_X in a way that suggests that P_Y has changed and $P_{X|Y}$ remained the same. When Y is binary and known to be the cause of X, observing that P_X is a mixture of two Gaussians makes it plausible that the two modes correspond to the two different labels $y = 0, 1$. Then, the influence of Y on X consists just in shifting the mean of the Gaussian (which amounts to an ANM — see Section 4.1.4), which is certainly a simple explanation for the joint distribution. Observing furthermore that the weights of the mixture changed from one data set to another one makes it likely that this change is due to the change of P_Y.

covariate shift. Meanwhile, this is a well-studied assumption in machine learning [Sugiyama and Kawanabe, 2012]. The argument that this is only justified in the *causal* scenario, in other words, if X is the cause and Y the effect, has been made by Schölkopf et al. [2012].

To further illustrate this point, consider the following toy example of an *anticausal* scenario where X is the effect. Let Y be a binary variable influencing the real-valued variable X in an additive way:

$$X = Y + N_X, \tag{5.4}$$

where we assume N_X to be Gaussian noise, independent of Y. Figure 5.4, left, shows the corresponding probability density p_X.

If its width is sufficiently small, the distribution P_X is bimodal. Even if one does not know anything about the generating model, P_X can be recognized as a mixture of two Gaussian distributions with equal width. In this case, one can therefore guess the joint distribution $P_{X,Y}$ from P_X alone because it is natural to assume that the influence of Y consists only in shifting the mean of X. Under this assumption, we do not need any (x,y)-pairs to learn the relation between X and Y. Assume now that in a second data set we observe the same mixture of two Gaussian distributions but with different weights (see Figure 5.4, right). Then, the most natural conclusion reads that the weights have changed because the same equation (5.4) still holds but only P_Y has changed. Accordingly, we would no longer use the same $P_{Y|X}$ for our prediction and reconstruct $P'_{Y|X}$ from P'_X. The example illustrates that in the anticausal scenario the changes of P_X and $P_{Y|X}$ may be related and that this relation may be due to the fact that P_Y has changed and $P_{X|Y}$ remained the same. In other

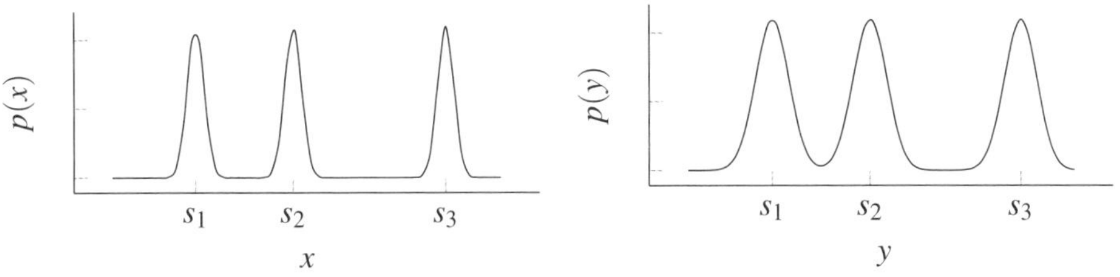

Figure 5.5: Example where X causes Y and, as a result, P_Y and $P_{X|Y}$ contain information about each other. Left: P_X is a mixture of sharp peaks at the positions s_1, s_2, s_3. Right: P_Y is obtained from P_X by convolution with Gaussian noise with zero mean and thus consists of less sharp peaks at the same positions s_1, s_2, s_3. Then $P_{X|Y}$ also contains information about s_1, s_2, s_3 (see Problem 5.1).

words, P_{effect} and $P_{\text{cause}|\text{effect}}$ often change in a dependent way because P_{cause} and $P_{\text{effect}|\text{cause}}$ change independently.

The previous example elicits a specific scenario. Conceiving of general methods exploiting the fact that P_{effect} and $P_{\text{cause}|\text{effect}}$ change in a dependent way is a hard problem. This may be an interesting avenue for further research, and we believe that causality could play a major role in domain adaptation and transfer problems; see also Bareinboim and Pearl [2016], Rojas-Carulla et al. [2016], Zhang et al. [2013], and Zhang et al. [2015].

5.3 Problems

Problem 5.1 (Independence of mechanisms) *Let P_X be the mixture of k sharp Gaussian peaks at positions $s_1, \ldots, s_k$ as shown in Figure 5.5, left. Let Y be obtained from X by adding some Gaussian noise N with zero mean and a width σ_N such that the separate peaks remain visible as in Figure 5.5, right.*

a) Argue intuitively why $P_{X|Y}$ also contains information about the positions $s_1, \ldots, s_k$ of the peaks and thus $P_{X|Y}$ and P_Y share this information.

b) The transition between P_X and P_Y can be described by convolution (from P_X to P_Y) and deconvolution (from P_Y to P_X). If $P_{Y|X}$ is considered as the linear map converting the input P_X to the output P_Y then $P_{Y|X}$ coincides with the convolution map. Argue why $P_{X|Y}$ does not coincide with the deconvolution map (as one may think at first glance).

6

Multivariate Causal Models

In Chapter 3, we discussed causal models for two variables. While some of the basic notions can be more easily explained in the bivariate case, a lot of the structure of causal inference derives from multivariate relations, which involve at least three variables. We now consider causal models in the more general case of $d \geq 2$ variables.

Many of the concepts carry over directly and we hope that the reader, equipped with the intuition gained in Chapter 3, can easily follow the definitions of SCMs (Section 6.2), interventions (Section 6.3), and counterfactuals (Section 6.4). But there are fundamental differences to the bivariate case, too. In Section 6.5, we will see that the graph structure implies conditional independence statements that have been trivial in the bivariate case. Also, computing intervention distributions requires more thought in the multivariate setting: We will discuss adjustment formulas and do-calculus [Pearl, 2009] in Section 6.6.

We first introduce some graphical terminology. Most of the definitions are self-explanatory and can be found in Spirtes et al. [2000], Koller and Friedman [2009], and Lauritzen [1996], for example. The reader who is already familiar with graphical models may want to skip this section. The most important terms for this book are directed acyclic graphs (DAGs), v-structures, and d-separation.

6.1 Graph Terminology

Consider finitely many random variables $\mathbf{X} = (X_1, \ldots, X_d)$ with index set $\mathbf{V} := \{1, \ldots, d\}$, joint distribution $P_{\mathbf{X}}$, and density $p(\mathbf{x})$. A **graph** $\mathcal{G} = (\mathbf{V}, \mathcal{E})$ consists of (finitely many) **nodes** or **vertices** $\mathbf{V}$ and **edges** $\mathcal{E} \subseteq \mathbf{V}^2$ with $(v, v) \notin \mathcal{E}$ for any $v \in \mathbf{V}$. We further have the following definitions:

Let $\mathcal{G} = (\mathbf{V}, \mathcal{E})$ be a graph with $\mathbf{V} := \{1, \ldots, d\}$ and corresponding random variables $\mathbf{X} = (X_1, \ldots, X_d)$. A graph $\mathcal{G}_1 = (\mathbf{V}_1, \mathcal{E}_1)$ is called a **subgraph** of $\mathcal{G}$ if $\mathbf{V}_1 = \mathbf{V}$ and $\mathcal{E}_1 \subseteq \mathcal{E}$; we then write $\mathcal{G}_1 \leq \mathcal{G}$. If additionally, $\mathcal{E}_1 \neq \mathcal{E}$, then $\mathcal{G}_1$ is a **proper subgraph** of $\mathcal{G}$.

A node i is called a **parent** of j if $(i, j) \in \mathcal{E}$ and $(j, i) \notin \mathcal{E}$ and a **child** if $(j, i) \in \mathcal{E}$ and $(i, j) \notin \mathcal{E}$. The set of parents of j is denoted by $\mathbf{PA}_j^{\mathcal{G}}$, and the set of its children by $\mathbf{CH}_j^{\mathcal{G}}$. Two nodes i and j are **adjacent** if either $(i, j) \in \mathcal{E}$ or $(j, i) \in \mathcal{E}$. We call $\mathcal{G}$ **fully connected** if all pairs of nodes are adjacent. We say that there is an **undirected edge** between two adjacent nodes i and j if $(i, j) \in \mathcal{E}$ and $(j, i) \in \mathcal{E}$. An edge between two adjacent nodes is **directed** if it is not undirected. We then write $i \to j$ for $(i, j) \in \mathcal{E}$. We call $\mathcal{G}$ **directed** if all its edges are directed.[1] Three nodes are called an **immorality** or a **v-structure** if one node is a child of the two others that themselves are not adjacent. The **skeleton** of $\mathcal{G}$ does not take the directions of the edges into account. It is the graph $(\mathbf{V}, \tilde{\mathcal{E}})$ with $(i, j) \in \tilde{\mathcal{E}}$, if $(i, j) \in \mathcal{E}$ or $(j, i) \in \mathcal{E}$.

A **path** in $\mathcal{G}$ is a sequence of (at least two) distinct vertices $i_1, \ldots, i_m$, such that there is an edge between i_k and i_{k+1} for all $k = 1, \ldots, m-1$. If $i_{k-1} \to i_k$ and $i_{k+1} \to i_k$, i_k is called a **collider relative to this path**. If $i_k \to i_{k+1}$ for all k, we speak of a **directed path** from i_1 to i_m and call i_1 an **ancestor** of i_m and i_m a **descendant** of i_1. In this work, all ancestors of i are denoted by $\mathbf{AN}_i^{\mathcal{G}}$ and i is not an ancestor of itself. Furthermore, i is neither a descendant nor a non-descendant of itself. We denote all descendants of i by $\mathbf{DE}_i^{\mathcal{G}}$ and all non-descendants of i, excluding i, by $\mathbf{ND}_i^{\mathcal{G}}$. In this book, $\mathbf{ND}_i^{\mathcal{G}}$ include the parents of i in graph $\mathcal{G}$. A node without parents is called a **source node**, a node without children a **sink node**. A permutation π, that is a bijective function $\pi : \{1, \ldots, d\} \to \{1, \ldots, d\}$ is called a **topological** or **causal ordering** if it satisfies $\pi(i) < \pi(j)$ if $j \in \mathbf{DE}_i^{\mathcal{G}}$ (see also Appendix B).

A graph $\mathcal{G}$ is called a **partially directed acyclic graph (PDAG)** if there is no directed cycle, that is, if there is no pair (j, k) with directed paths from j to k and from k to j. $\mathcal{G}$ is called a **directed acyclic graph (DAG)** if it is a PDAG and all edges are directed.

Since we will use it at many places herein, we formulate the graphical concept of d-separation [Pearl, 1985, 1988] as a definition.

[1] Note that this excludes cycles of length 2, but it does not excludes longer cycles.

Definition 6.1 (Pearl's d-separation) *In a DAG $\mathcal{G}$, a path between nodes i_1 and i_m is* ***blocked by a set*** $\mathbf{S}$ *(with neither i_1 nor i_m in $\mathbf{S}$) whenever there is a node i_k, such that one of the following two possibilities holds:*

(i) $i_k \in \mathbf{S}$ *and*

$$\begin{aligned} & i_{k-1} \to i_k \to i_{k+1} \\ \text{or } & i_{k-1} \leftarrow i_k \leftarrow i_{k+1} \\ \text{or } & i_{k-1} \leftarrow i_k \to i_{k+1} \end{aligned}$$

(ii) neither i_k nor any of its descendants is in $\mathbf{S}$ *and*

$$i_{k-1} \to i_k \leftarrow i_{k+1}.$$

Furthermore, in a DAG $\mathcal{G}$, we say that two disjoint subsets of vertices $\mathbf{A}$ *and* $\mathbf{B}$ *are* ***d-separated*** *by a third (also disjoint) subset* $\mathbf{S}$ *if every path between nodes in* $\mathbf{A}$ *and* $\mathbf{B}$ *is blocked by* $\mathbf{S}$. *We then write*

$$\mathbf{A} \perp\!\!\!\perp_{\mathcal{G}} \mathbf{B} \,|\, \mathbf{S}.$$

The reader may have a look at Figure 6.5 and be convinced that for this DAG, we have $C \perp\!\!\!\perp_{\mathcal{G}} G \,|\, X$ but $C \not\!\perp\!\!\!\perp_{\mathcal{G}} G \,|\, (X,H)$.

6.2 Structural Causal Models

SCMs have been used for a long time in fields such as agriculture, social sciences, and econometrics [Wright, 1921, Haavelmo, 1944, Bollen, 1989]; see also Chapter 2. Model selection, for example, was done by fitting different structures that were considered as reasonable given the prior knowledge about the system. These candidate structures were then compared using goodness of fit tests. In this chapter, we introduce the semantics of SCMs and learn how to use them for computing intervention distributions, for example. Throughout the whole chapter we will assume that the SCM or at least its structure is given. We discuss the question of identifying the structure in Chapter 7.

Definition 6.2 (Structural causal models) *A* ***structural causal model (SCM)*** $\mathfrak{C} := (\mathbf{S}, P_{\mathbf{N}})$ *consists of a collection* $\mathbf{S}$ *of d* ***(structural) assignments***

$$X_j := f_j(\mathbf{PA}_j, N_j), \qquad j = 1, \ldots, d, \tag{6.1}$$

$$
\begin{aligned}
X_1 &:= f_1(X_3, N_1)\\
X_2 &:= f_2(X_1, N_2)\\
X_3 &:= f_3(N_3)\\
X_4 &:= f_4(X_2, X_3, N_4)
\end{aligned}
$$

- $N_1, \ldots, N_4$ jointly independent
- $\mathcal{G}$ is acyclic

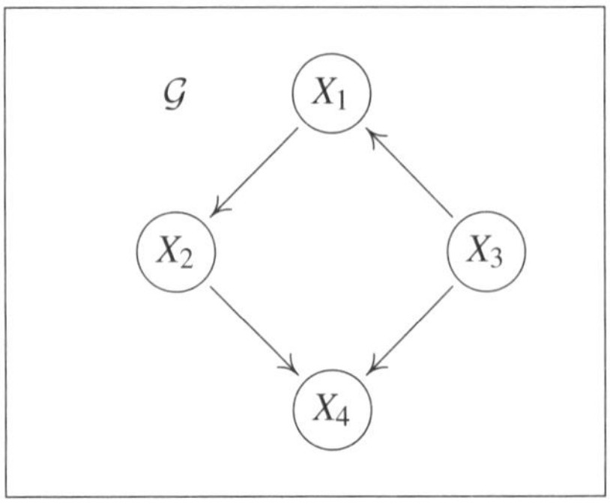

Figure 6.1: Example of an SCM (left) with corresponding graph (right). There is only one causal ordering π (that satisfies $3 \mapsto 1$, $1 \mapsto 2$, $2 \mapsto 3$, $4 \mapsto 4$).

where $\mathbf{PA}_j \subseteq \{X_1, \ldots, X_d\} \setminus \{X_j\}$ *are called* ***parents of*** X_j*; and a joint distribution* $P_{\mathbf{N}} = P_{N_1,\ldots,N_d}$ *over the noise variables, which we require to be jointly independent; that is,* $P_{\mathbf{N}}$ *is a product distribution.*

The graph $\mathcal{G}$ *of an SCM is obtained by creating one vertex for each* X_j *and drawing directed edges from each parent in* $\mathbf{PA}_j$ *to* X_j*, that is, from each variable* X_k *occurring on the right-hand side of equation* (6.1) *to* X_j *(see Figure 6.1). We henceforth assume this graph to be acyclic.*

We sometimes call the elements of $\mathbf{PA}_j$ *not only parents but also* ***direct causes of*** X_j*, and we call* X_j *a* ***direct effect*** *of each of its direct causes. SCMs are also called (nonlinear) SEMs.*

Although some of the terminology is causal ("direct cause" and "direct effect"), Definition 6.2 is purely mathematical. We discuss its role as a model for a real system in Section 6.8.

SCMs are the key for formalizing causal reasoning and causal learning. We first show that an SCM entails an observational distribution. But unlike usual probabilistic models, they additionally entail intervention distributions (Section 6.3) and counterfactuals (Section 6.4); see Figure 6.2.

Proposition 6.3 (Entailed distributions) *An SCM* $\mathfrak{C}$ *defines a unique distribution over the variables* $\mathbf{X} = (X_1, \ldots, X_d)$ *such that* $X_j = f_j(\mathbf{PA}_j, N_j)$*, in distribution, for* $j = 1, \ldots, d$*. We refer to it as the entailed distribution* $P_{\mathbf{X}}^{\mathfrak{C}}$ *and sometimes write* $P_{\mathbf{X}}$*.*

The proof can be found in Appendix C.2. It formalizes the procedure for how we sample n data points from the joint distribution ("ancestral sampling"): We first generate an i.i.d. sample $\mathbf{N}^1, \ldots, \mathbf{N}^n \sim P_{\mathbf{N}}$ and then subsequently use the structural

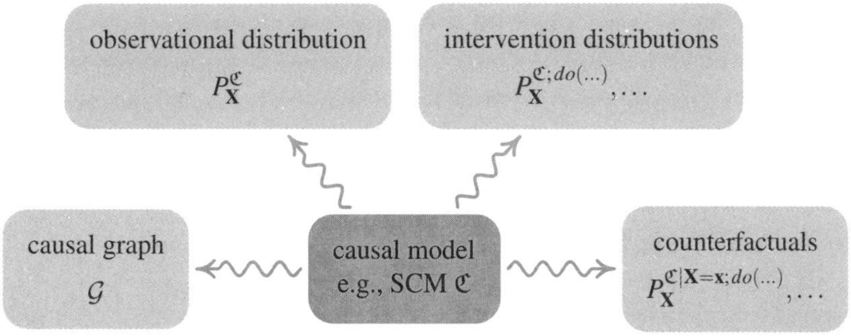

Figure 6.2: Causal models as SCMs do not only model an observational distribution P (Proposition 6.3) but also intervention distributions (Section 6.3) and counterfactuals (Section 6.4).

assignments (starting from source nodes, then nodes with at most one parent and so on) to generate i.i.d data points $\mathbf{X}^1, \ldots, \mathbf{X}^n \sim P_{\mathbf{X}}$. Structural assignments (6.1) should be thought of as a set of assignments or functions (rather than a set of mathematical equations) that tells us how certain variables determine others. This is the reason why we prefer to avoid the term **structural equations**, which is commonly used in the literature.

Code Snippet 6.4 The following code generates an i.i.d. sample from an SCM with the form shown in Figure 6.1: structural assignments $f_1(x_3, n) = 2x_3 + n$, $f_2(x_1, n) = (0.5x_1)^2 + n$, $f_3(n) = n$, and $f_4(x_2, x_3, n) = x_2 + 2\sin(x_3 + n)$, and jointly independent noise variables with a normal, chi squared, uniform, and normal distribution, respectively.

```
# generate a sample from the distribution entailed by the SCM
set.seed(1)
X3 <- runif(100)-0.5
X1 <- 2*X3 + rnorm(100)
X2 <- (0.5*X1)^2 + rnorm(100)^2
X4 <- X2 + 2*sin(X3 + rnorm(100))
```

Remark 6.5 (Linear cyclic assignments) In this book we focus mainly on acyclic structures. We now briefly discuss linear SCMs with assignments that lead to a cyclic structure; these are well understood [Lauritzen and Richardson, 2002, Lacerda et al., 2008, Hyttinen et al., 2012]. We focus on the intuition and do not provide a formal treatment. More details for the linear case are provided by Hyttinen et al. [2012], and the nonlinear case is discussed by Mooij et al. [2011] and Bongers et al. [2016].

Let us denote $\mathbf{X} = (X_1, \ldots, X_d)$ and consider the assignment

$$\mathbf{X} := B\mathbf{X} + \mathbf{N},$$

with a $d \times d$ matrix B that allows for a cyclic structure and some noise vector $\mathbf{N} = (N_1, \ldots, N_d) \sim P_{\mathbf{N}}$. Formally, if $I - B$ is invertible, for each value of $\mathbf{N}$, the preceding equation induces a unique solution for $\mathbf{X}$, namely

$$\mathbf{X} = (I - B)^{-1}\mathbf{N} \tag{6.2}$$

(see also Problem 3.8). Equation (6.2) clearly defines a joint distribution over $\mathbf{X}$. But what is its (causal) interpretation?

One possibility is to interpret it as a result of an equilibration process. Consider a sequence of random variables $\mathbf{X}^t$ that occur as solutions to the iteration

$$\mathbf{X}^t := B\mathbf{X}^{t-1} + \mathbf{N},\ t = 1, 2, \ldots. \tag{6.3}$$

The sequence $\mathbf{X}^t$ converges if $B^t \to 0$ as $t \to \infty$, which is equivalent to the eigenvalues of B lying within the unit circle. This is a strictly stronger condition than the invertibility of $I - B$ (see Problem 6.60). If satisfied, the distribution of the limit is identical to the distribution induced by Equation (6.2); see Problem 6.61.

In (6.3), we have added the same noise realization in each time step. The limiting distribution of $\mathbf{X}^t$ changes if we instead update the noise in each step:

$$\mathbf{X}^t := B\mathbf{X}^{t-1} + \mathbf{N}^{t-1},\ t = 1, 2, \ldots \tag{6.4}$$

with $\mathbf{N}^1, \mathbf{N}^2, \ldots$ being i.i.d. copies of $\mathbf{N}^t$. This can be regarded as a time series setting and will be discussed in Section 10.2. □

Proposition 6.3 shows that each SCM entails a distribution. What about the other direction? Is any distribution entailed by an SCM? Indeed, we will see later (Proposition 7.1) that each distribution can be induced by any SCM whose graph structure is a complete DAG (a DAG is called complete if any pair of vertices is connected). This means that the (observational) model class of SCMs, that is, the set of distributions that can be induced by an SCM, is the set of *all* distributions.

The definition of SCMs allows for the possibility that a variable appears on the right-hand side of the structural assignment without affecting the variable on the left-hand side. Even though such a parent-child relation is in some sense "inactive," it still appears as an edge in the corresponding graph. Formally, we exclude this by the following remark:

Remark 6.6 (Structural minimality of SCMs) Definition 6.2 can be read such that one distinguishes between the two SCMs

$$\mathbf{S}_1 : X := N_X,\ Y := 0 \cdot X + N_Y \quad \text{and}$$
$$\mathbf{S}_2 : X := N_X,\ Y := N_Y,$$

even though clearly $0 \cdot X = 0$. This contradicts our intuition. We therefore add the requirement that the functions f_j depend on all of their input arguments. Mathematically speaking, whenever there is a $k \in \{1, \ldots, d\}$ and a function g such that

$$f_k(\mathbf{pa}_k, n_k) = g(\mathbf{pa}_k^*, n_k), \qquad \forall \mathbf{pa}_k, \forall n_k \text{ with } p(n_k) > 0, \tag{6.5}$$

where $\mathbf{PA}_k^* \subsetneq \mathbf{PA}_k$, we choose the latter representation. In the preceding example, we would therefore choose the representation $\mathbf{S}_2$ over $\mathbf{S}_1$. We will see later that these two SCMs can indeed be identified in that they entail the same observational distribution, intervention distribution,[2] and counterfactuals (see Section 6.8).

Furthermore, there is a unique representation in which each function has a minimal number of inputs. Although this statement seems plausible, we formally prove it in Appendix C.3. We say that such an (least) SCM satisfies **structural minimality**.[3] From now on, we assume that structural minimality holds. As opposed to faithfulness (Section 6.5), for example, this is not an assumption about the underlying world. It is a convention to avoid redundant descriptions. □

Remark 6.7 (Relationship to ordinary differential equations) In Remark 6.5, we have already seen a relation between SCMs and discrete time models, and we would now like to comment on continuous time models. In physical systems, we would often expect that causal relationships are governed by sets of coupled differential equations. A differential equation system $\dot{\mathbf{X}} = f(\mathbf{X})$ can be represented approximately as an assignment $\mathbf{X}_{t+\Delta t} := \mathbf{X}_t + \Delta t \cdot f(\mathbf{X}_t)$ with small $\Delta t > 0$, and it thus contains information about the causal structure at a fine-grained time scale. An intervention can be implemented physically as a forcing term pulling a variable toward a desired value. Under certain stability assumptions, we can assay the effect of interventions in a time-independent manner by analyzing the behavior of the equilibrium state. This entails an SCM that describes how the equilibrium states

[2] We do not allow for interventions that keep the function in the structural assignment fixed and change only the noise distribution; see (6.5).

[3] This term does not coincide with causal minimality (Definition 6.33). Causal minimality implies structural minimality (Proposition 6.49) but not vice versa; see Problem 6.57.

of such a dynamical system will react to physical interventions on the observables [Mooij et al., 2013]. In the SCM, the variables no longer describe measurements at specific points in time. On this phenomenological level, the original time structure disappears. The framework is in principle also applicable to cyclic structures, but it does not yet address the stochastic case; the theory is restricted to deterministic relations. This shortcoming is significant, since uncertainty can arise from a number of sources, including incomplete knowledge of the parameters of the differential equations or of initial conditions, and — as always — confounding. We will not discuss further details on deriving phenomenological structural equations from differential equations and refer to some literature instead [see, e.g., Dash, 2005, Hansen and Sokol, 2014].

Our main motivation for this remark is to avoid a common misconception. It is sometimes argued that part of the task of causal inference becomes obsolete by specifying the exact time to which a variable refers. This view is particularly supported by physics where it is common that every measurement can be uniquely assigned to a point in space-time where it has been performed. These arguments show, however, that even variables in physics do not always refer to observations that are well-defined in time — for example, because they arise from an equilibrium scenario. □

6.3 Interventions

We are now ready to model interventions in a system. Intuitively, when we intervene on variable X_2, say, and set it to the binary outcome of a coin flip, we expect that this intervention changes the distribution of the system compared to its earlier behavior without intervention. Furthermore, even if the variable X_2 was causally influenced by other variables before, it is now influenced by nothing else than the coin flip: its causal parents have changed.

Formally, we construct intervention distributions from an SCM $\mathfrak{C}$. They are obtained by making modifications to $\mathfrak{C}$ and considering the new entailed distribution. In general, intervention distributions differ from the observational distribution.

Definition 6.8 (Intervention distribution) *Consider an SCM $\mathfrak{C} := (\mathbf{S}, P_{\mathbf{N}})$ and its entailed distribution $P_{\mathbf{X}}^{\mathfrak{C}}$. We replace one (or several) of the structural assignments to obtain a new SCM $\tilde{\mathfrak{C}}$. Assume that we replace the assignment for X_k by*

$$X_k := \tilde{f}(\widetilde{\mathbf{PA}}_k, \tilde{N}_k).$$

We then call the entailed distribution of the new SCM an intervention distribution and say that the variables whose structural assignment we have replaced have been ***intervened*** *on. We denote the new distribution by*[4]

$$P_{\mathbf{X}}^{\tilde{\mathfrak{C}}} =: P_{\mathbf{X}}^{\mathfrak{C}; do\left(X_k := \tilde{f}(\widetilde{\mathbf{PA}}_k, \tilde{N}_k)\right)}.$$

The set of noise variables in $\tilde{\mathfrak{C}}$ *now contains both some "new"* $\tilde{N}$*'s and some "old"* N*'s, all of which are required to be jointly independent.*

When $\tilde{f}(\widetilde{\mathbf{PA}}_k, \tilde{N}_k)$ *puts a point mass on a real value* a*, we simply write* $P_{\mathbf{X}}^{\mathfrak{C}; do(X_k := a)}$ *and call this an* ***atomic*** *intervention.*[5] *An intervention with* $\widetilde{\mathbf{PA}}_k = \mathbf{PA}_k$*, that is, where direct causes remain direct causes, is called* ***imperfect****.*[6] *This is a special case of a* ***stochastic*** *intervention [Korb et al., 2004], in which the marginal distribution of the intervened variable has positive variance.*

We require that the new SCM $\tilde{\mathfrak{C}}$ *have an acyclic graph; the set of allowed interventions thus depends on the graph induced by* $\mathfrak{C}$*.*

Code Snippet 6.9 The following code samples from an intervention distribution. We consider the SCM $\mathfrak{C}$ from Code Snippet 6.4 and perform the intervention $do(X_2 := 3)$; that is, we generate an i.i.d. sample from the distribution $P_{\mathbf{X}}^{\mathfrak{C}; do(X_2 := 3)}$.

```
# generate a sample from the intervention distribution
set.seed(1)
X3 <- runif(100)-0.5
X1 <- 2*X3 + rnorm(100)
# old:
# X2 <- (0.5*X1)^2 + rnorm(100)^2
X2 <- rep(3,100)
X4 <- X2 + 2*sin(X3 + rnorm(100))
```

It turns out that the concept of interventions is a powerful tool to model differences in distributions and to understand causal relationships. We try to illustrate this with some examples.

---

[4] Although the set of parents can change arbitrarily as long as they are not introducing cycles, we mainly consider interventions, for which the new set of parents $\widetilde{\mathbf{PA}}_k$ is either empty or equals $\mathbf{PA}_k$.

[5] This is also referred to as an **ideal**, **structural** [Eberhardt and Scheines, 2007], **surgical** [Pearl, 2009], **independent**, or **deterministic** [Korb et al., 2004] intervention.

[6] This is also referred to as a **parametric** [Eberhardt and Scheines, 2007] or **dependent** intervention [Korb et al., 2004] or simply as a **mechanism change** [Tian and Pearl, 2001]. For the term **soft** intervention, see Eberhardt and Scheines [2007] , Eaton and Murphy [2007], and Markowetz et al. [2005].

Example 6.10 (Predictors and intervention targets) This example considers prediction. It shows that even though some variables may be good predictors for a target variable Y, intervening on them may leave the target variable unaffected. Consider the SCM $\mathfrak{C}$

$$\begin{aligned} X_1 &:= N_{X_1} \\ Y &:= X_1 + N_Y \\ X_2 &:= Y + N_{X_2} \end{aligned}$$

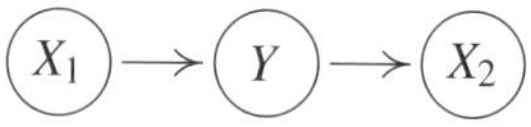

with $N_{X_1}, N_Y \overset{\text{iid}}{\sim} \mathcal{N}(0,1)$ and $N_{X_2} \sim \mathcal{N}(0, 0.1)$ being jointly independent. Assume that we are interested in *predicting* Y from X_1 and X_2. Clearly, X_2 is a better predictor for Y than X_1 is; for example, a linear model without X_2 leads to a (significantly) larger mean squared error than a linear model without X_1 would. If we want to *change* Y, however, interventions on X_2 are useless:

$$P_Y^{\mathfrak{C};do(X_2:=\tilde{N})} = P_Y^{\mathfrak{C}} \quad \text{for all variables } \tilde{N};$$

in other words, no matter how strongly we intervene on X_2, the distribution of Y remains unaffected. An intervention on X_1, however, does change the distribution of Y:

$$P_Y^{\mathfrak{C};do(X_1:=\tilde{N})} = \mathcal{N}\left(\mathbb{E}[N_Y] + \mathbb{E}[\tilde{N}], \mathrm{var}[N_Y] + \mathrm{var}[\tilde{N}]\right) \neq P_Y^{\mathfrak{C}}$$

if $P_{\tilde{N}} \neq P_{N_{X_1}}$. □

This example can also be used to show that intervening is usually different from conditioning:

$$p_Y^{\mathfrak{C};do(X_2:=x)}(y) = p_Y^{\mathfrak{C}}(y) \neq p_Y^{\mathfrak{C}}(y|X_2 = x).$$

Example 6.11 (Myopia) The following case study is one example (out of many), in which a statistical dependence is mistakenly interpreted as a direct causal relationship. Humans seem to be particularly susceptible for such a false causal conclusion when little background knowledge is available. A study established a dependence between the usage of a night light in a child's room and the occurrence of myopia [Quinn et al., 1999, page 113]. While the authors are cautious enough to say that the study "does not establish a causal link," they add that "the statistical strength of the association ...does suggest that the absence of a daily period of darkness during early childhood is a potential precipitating factor in the development of myopia." Based on these findings, a patent was filed [Peterson, 2005]. It suggests that if we intervene on the variable *night light*, this changes the probability to develop myopia.

Subsequently, Gwiazda et al. [2000] and Zadnik et al. [2000] found that the correlation is due to whether the child's parents have myopia. They argue that myopic parents are more likely to put a night light in their child's room, and at the same time, the child has an increased risk of inheriting the condition. Therefore, assume that the underlying ("correct") SCM is of the form

$$\mathbf{S}: \quad \begin{array}{rcl} PM & := & N_{PM} \\ NL & := & f(PM, N_{NL}) \\ CM & := & g(PM, N_{CM}) \end{array}$$

where PM stands for parent myopia, NL for night light, and CM for child myopia. The corresponding graph is

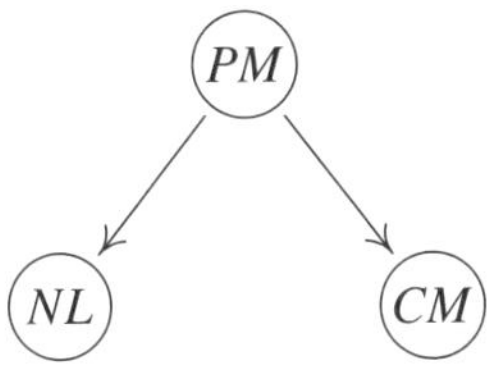

In their paper, Quinn et al. [1999] found that $NL \not\perp\!\!\!\perp CM$, consistent with the model (assuming faithfulness — see Definition 6.33). Now we replace the structural assignment of NL with $NL := \tilde{N}_{NL}$, where $\tilde{N}_{NL}$ could randomly assign one out of the three night light conditions ("darkness," "night light," "room light") with equal probability. In the corresponding intervention distribution

$$P_{NL,CM}^{\mathfrak{C};do\left(NL:=\tilde{N}_{NL}\right)},$$

we would find $NL \perp\!\!\!\perp CM$ since $CM := g(N_{PM}, N_{CM})$. This holds independently of the distribution of $\tilde{N}_{NL}$. We say there is no causal effect from NL to CM. □

Motivated by the last statement in Example 6.11, we define the existence of a total causal effect [cf. Pearl, 2009, "total causal effect"].

Definition 6.12 (Total causal effect) *Given an SCM $\mathfrak{C}$, there is a total causal effect from X to Y if and only if*

$$X \not\perp\!\!\!\perp Y \quad \text{in } P_{\mathbf{X}}^{\mathfrak{C};do\left(X:=\tilde{N}_X\right)}$$

for some random variable $\tilde{N}_X$.

There are concepts other than the one from Definition 6.12 that intuitively describe the existence of a total causal effect. It turns out, however, that most of the statements one may have thought about are equivalent. The following proposition is proved in Appendix C.4.

Proposition 6.13 (Total causal effects) *Given an SCM $\mathfrak{C}$, the following statements are equivalent:*

(i) There is a total causal effect from X to Y.

(ii) There are $x^{\triangle}$ and $x^{\square}$ such that $P_Y^{\mathfrak{C};do(X:=x^{\triangle})} \neq P_Y^{\mathfrak{C};do(X:=x^{\square})}$.

(iii) There is $x^{\triangle}$ such that $P_Y^{\mathfrak{C};do(X:=x^{\triangle})} \neq P_Y^{\mathfrak{C}}$.

(iv) $X \not\perp\!\!\!\perp Y$ in $P_{X,Y}^{\mathfrak{C};do(X:=\tilde{N}_X)}$ for any $\tilde{N}_X$ whose distribution has full support.

Not surprisingly, the existence of a total causal effect is related to the existence of a directed path in the corresponding graph. The correspondence, however, is not one-to-one. While a directed path is necessary for a total causal effect, it is not sufficient.

Proposition 6.14 (Graphical criteria for total causal effects) *Assume we are given an SCM $\mathfrak{C}$ with corresponding graph $\mathcal{G}$.*

(i) If there is no directed path from X to Y, then there is no total causal effect.

(ii) Sometimes there is a directed path but no total causal effect.

The proof can be found in Appendix C.5.

Example 6.15 (Randomized trials) The definition of a causal effect is implemented in randomized trials. In those studies, one randomly assigns the treatment T according to $\tilde{N}_T$ to a patient and, for example, observes the (binary) recovery variable R. Assume that T takes three possible values ($T = 0$: no medication, $T = 1$: placebo, and $T = 2$: drug of interest) and that $\tilde{N}_T$ randomly chooses one of these three possibilities: $P(\tilde{N}_T = 0) = P(\tilde{N}_T = 1) = P(\tilde{N}_T = 2) = 1/3$. In the SCM, such a randomization is modeled with observing data from the distribution

$$P_{\mathbf{X}}^{\mathfrak{C};do(T:=\tilde{N}_T)}.$$

(Here, $\mathfrak{C}$ denotes the original SCM without randomization.) If we then still find a dependence between the treatment and recovery, we conclude that T has a total

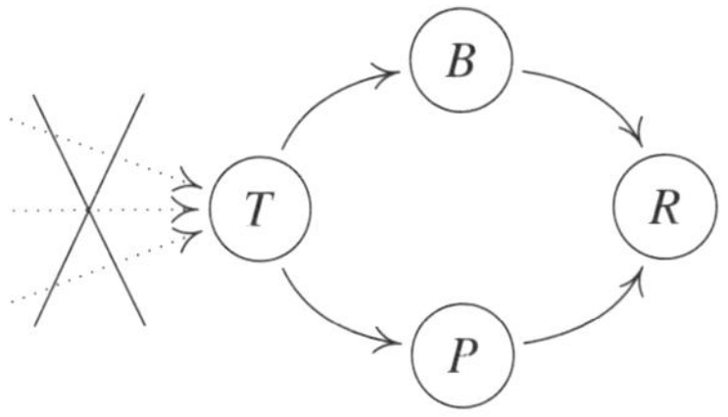

Figure 6.3: Simplified description of randomized studies. T denotes the treatment, P and B the patient's psychology and some biochemical state, and R indicates whether the patient recovers. The randomization over T removes the influence of any other variable on T, and thus there cannot be any hidden common cause between T and R. We distinguish between two different effects: the placebo effect via P and the biochemical effect via B.

causal effect on the recovery. It may turn out, however, that there is a total causal effect independently of the type of drug. A simplified description can be found in Figure 6.3. A patient's psychology (P) changes, when taking a pill independently of its content, which then affects the recovery. Let us assume that this **placebo effect** is the same for the placebo and the drug of interest. That is, the structural assignment for P satisfies

$$f_P(T=0,N_P) \neq f_P(T=1,N_P) = f_P(T=2,N_P).$$

In pharmaceutical studies, we are more interested in the biochemical effect than the placebo effect. We therefore restrict the randomization to be supported on placebo and drug of interest, that is, $P(\tilde{N}_T = 0) = 0$. If we then still see a dependence between treatment T and recovery R, this must be due to a biochemical effect.

The idea of using randomized trials for causal learning was described (using different mathematical language) by Peirce [1883] and Peirce and Jastrow [1885], and later by Neyman [see Splawa-Neyman et al., 1990, for a translated and edited version of the original article] and Fisher [1925]. Most of this work dealt with applications in agriculture.

An early example of a randomized trial was performed by James Lind. During the eighteenth century, Great Britain lost more soldiers from scurvy than from enemy action; vitamin C and its relation to scurvy was still unknown. The Scottish physician James Lind (1716–1794) worked as a surgeon on a ship and reports the trial as follows [cited after Bhatt, 2010]:

> On the 20th of May 1747, I selected twelve patients in the scurvy, on board the Salisbury at sea. Their cases were as similar as I could

> have them. They all in general had putrid gums, the spots and lassitude, with weakness of the knees.... Two were ordered each a quart of cyder a day. Two others took twenty-five drops of elixir vitriol three times a day.... Two others took two spoonfuls of vinegar three times a day.... Two of the worst patients were put on a course of sea-water.... Two others had each two oranges and one lemon given them every day.... The two remaining patients, took ... an electary recommended by a hospital surgeon.... The consequence was, that the most sudden and visible good effects were perceived from the use of oranges and lemons; one of those who had taken them, being at the end of six days fit for duty.

The reader will notice that the trial was not fully randomized, but the historical curiosity makes up for it. □

Example 6.16 (Kidney stones) Table 6.1 shows a famous data set from kidney stone recovery [Charig et al., 1986]. Out of 700 patients, one half was treated with open surgery (treatment $T = a$, 78% recovery rate) and the other half with percutaneous nephrolithotomy ($T = b$, 83% recovery rate), a surgical procedure to remove kidney stones by a small puncture wound. If we do not know anything else than the overall recovery rates, and neglect side effects, for example, many people would prefer treatment b if they had to decide. Observing the data in more detail, we can categorize kidney stones into small and large stones. We realize that the open surgery performs better in both categories. How do we deal with this inversion of conclusion?

We first give an intuitive explanation. Larger stones are more severe than small stones (see Table 6.1), and treatment a had to deal with many more of these difficult cases (even though the total number of patients assigned to a and b are equal). This is why treatment a can look worse than b on the full population but better in both subgroups. The imbalance in assignment could, for example, arise if the medical doctors expect treatment a to be better than treatment b and therefore assign the difficult cases to treatment a with higher probability.

As an alternative point of view, we propose to use the language of interventions to formulate the precise question we are interested in. And this is not whether treatment $T = a$ or treatment $T = b$ was more successful in this particular study but how the treatments compare when we force all patients to take treatment a or treatment b, respectively, or we compare the recovery rates, when each patient is assigned randomly to one of the treatments. These three situations concern an intervention distribution that is different from the observational distribution $P_{\mathbf{X}}$. In

	Overall	Patients with small stones	Patients with large stones
Treatment a: Open surgery	78% (273/350)	**93%** (81/87)	**73%** (192/263)
Treatment b: Percutaneous nephrolithotomy	**83%** (289/350)	87% (234/270)	69% (55/80)

Table 6.1: A classic example of Simpson's paradox. The table reports the success rates of two treatments for kidney stones [Bottou et al., 2013, Charig et al., 1986, tables I and II]. Although the overall success rate of treatment b seems better (any bold number is largest in its column), treatment b performs worse than treatment a on both patients with small kidney stones and patients with large kidney stones (see Examples 6.37 and Section 9.2).

particular, they correspond to $P^{\mathfrak{C};do(T:=a)}$, $P^{\mathfrak{C};do(T:=b)}$, or $P^{\mathfrak{C};do(T:=\tilde{N}_T)}$. We will compute these intervention distributions in Example 6.37, and we will see why we should prefer treatment a over treatment b. This data set is a famous example of Simpson's paradox [Simpson, 1951] (Section 9.2). In fact, it is much less a paradox than the result of the influence of confounding, that is, a hidden common cause.

If you perform a significance test on the data (e.g., using a proportion test or χ^2 independence test), it turns out that the difference in methods is not significant at 5% significance level. Note, however, this is not the point of this example. By multiplying each entry in Table 6.1 by a factor of 10, the results would become statistically significant. Also, we concentrate on the recovery R and ignore possible side effects that might influence our decision of treatment, too. □

Intervention variables We now describe an alternative approach to formalize interventions; see, for example, Dawid [2015] or Pearl [2009, Chapter 3.2.2]. One augments the SCM $\mathfrak{C}$ and therefore its DAG with parentless nodes $I_1, I_2, \ldots, I_d$, called "intervention variables," pointing at $X_1, \ldots, X_d$, respectively. For simplicity, we only discuss interventions on single nodes here. Every I_j attains either the value `idle` or one of the possible values x_j that X_j can attain. Then $I_j = x_j$ means that X_j is set to the value x_j, while $I_j = \texttt{idle}$ denotes that X_j has not been intervened on. Accordingly, one replaces the structural assignments

$$X_j := f_j(\mathbf{PA}_j, N_j)$$

with

$$X_j := \begin{cases} f_j(\mathbf{PA}_j, N_j) & \text{if } I_j = \texttt{idle} \\ I_j & \text{otherwise} \end{cases}$$

and adds assignments for $I_1, \ldots, I_d$, all of which are determined only by noise variables. After assigning non-zero probability (or probability density) to all possible values of I_j, the intervention probabilities entailed by the original SCM $\mathfrak{C}$ turn into usual conditional probabilities in the augmented SCM $\mathfrak{C}^*$:

$$P_Y^{\mathfrak{C};do(X_j:=x_j)} = P_{Y\,|\,I_j=x_j}^{\mathfrak{C}^*},$$

see Remark 6.40. Moreover, the statement on whether an intervention on a variable changes the distribution of a certain target variable turns into a usual statistical independence statement.

6.4 Counterfactuals

The definition and interpretation of counterfactuals has received a lot of attention in the literature. They deal with the following situation: Assume you are playing poker and as a starting hand you have ♣J and ♣3 (sometimes called a "lumberjack" — tree and a jack); you stop playing ("fold") because you estimate the probability of winning to be too small and you do not want to lose even more money. Three more cards are dealt face-up to the board ("flop"). They are ♣4, ♣Q, and ♣2. The reaction is a typical counterfactual statement: "If I had stayed in the game, my chances would have been good." (Five cards of the same suit is the fifth-highest hand and is called a "flush," there are even chances for a "straight flush," the second-highest hand.) This statement incorporates the observed data (cards in hand and flop) into the model and then analyzes an intervention distribution (stay in the game), in which the rest of the environment remains unchanged (same cards). Formally, this corresponds to updating the noise distributions of an SCM (by conditioning) and then performing an intervention.

Definition 6.17 (Counterfactuals) *Consider an SCM* $\mathfrak{C} := (\mathbf{S}, P_{\mathbf{N}})$ *over nodes* $\mathbf{X}$. *Given some observations* $\mathbf{x}$, *we define a* counterfactual SCM *by replacing the distribution of noise variables:*

$$\mathfrak{C}_{\mathbf{X}=\mathbf{x}} := \left(\mathbf{S}, P_{\mathbf{N}}^{\mathfrak{C}|\mathbf{X}=\mathbf{x}}\right),$$

where $P_{\mathbf{N}}^{\mathfrak{C}|\mathbf{X}=\mathbf{x}} := P_{\mathbf{N}\,|\,\mathbf{X}=\mathbf{x}}$.[7] *The new set of noise variables need not be jointly independent anymore. Counterfactual statements can now be seen as do-statements in the new counterfactual SCM.*

[7] In the continuous case, this definition comes with measure theoretic problems since usually the

This definition can be generalized such that we observe not the full vector $\mathbf{X} = \mathbf{x}$ but only some of the variables.

Example 6.18 (Computing counterfactuals) Consider the following SCM:

$$X := N_X$$
$$Y := X^2 + N_Y$$
$$Z := 2 \cdot Y + X + N_Z$$

with $N_X, N_Y, N_Z \overset{\text{iid}}{\sim} \mathrm{U}(\{-5, -4, \ldots, 4, 5\})$ that are uniformly distributed on the integers between -5 and 5. Now, assume that we observe $(X,Y,Z) = (1,2,4)$. Then $P_{\mathbf{N}}^{\mathfrak{C}|\mathbf{X}=\mathbf{x}}$ puts a point mass on $(N_X, N_Y, N_Z) = (1,1,-1)$ because here all noise terms can be uniquely reconstructed from the observations. We therefore have the counterfactual statement (in the context of $(X,Y,Z) = (1,2,4)$): "Z would have been 11 had X been 2." In this book, such a sentence is interpreted as: "Z would have been 11 had X been *set to* 2." Mathematically, this means that $P_Z^{\mathfrak{C}|\mathbf{X}=\mathbf{x};do(X:=2)}$ has a point mass on 11. In the same way, we obtain "Y would have been 5, had X been 2," and "Z would have been 10, had Y been 5." □

Since the construction of counterfactuals involves several steps, its notation looks quite complicated.[8] We hope that the following image provides further clarification.

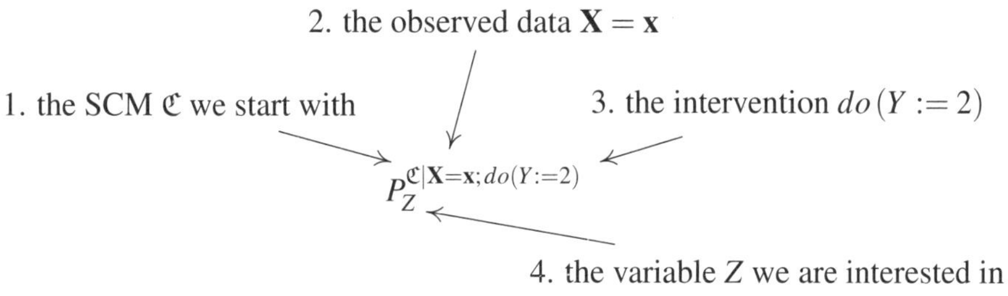

conditional distribution is only defined up to null sets. To make our life easier, we restrict counterfactuals to the discrete case, that is, when the noise distribution has a probability mass function. In the case of continuous variables with density, we condition not on $\mathbf{X} = \mathbf{x}$ but on $\mathbf{X} \in A$ with $P(\mathbf{X} \in A) > 0$ instead.

[8] Pearl [2009] uses the somewhat simpler notation $Z_y(\mathbf{u})$, where the subscript y denotes the intervention $do(Y := y)$ and $\mathbf{u}$ represents the additional information about the error terms, which he calls $\mathbf{u}$, that may be implied by $\mathbf{X} = \mathbf{x}$, for example.

Counterfactual statements depend strongly on the structure of the SCM. Example 6.19 shows two SCMs that induce the same graph, observational distributions, and intervention distributions but entail different counterfactual statements. Later, we will call those SCMs "probabilistically and interventionally equivalent" but not "counterfactually equivalent" (see Definition 6.47).

Example 6.19 Let $N_1, N_2 \sim \text{Ber}(0.5)$, and $N_3 \sim \text{U}(\{0,1,2\})$, such that the three variables are jointly independent. That is, N_1, N_2 have a Bernoulli distribution with parameter 0.5 and N_3 is uniformly distributed on $\{0,1,2\}$. We define two different SCMs. First consider $\mathfrak{C}_A$:

$$\begin{aligned} X_1 &:= N_1 \\ X_2 &:= N_2 \\ X_3 &:= (1_{N_3>0} \cdot X_1 + 1_{N_3=0} \cdot X_2) \cdot 1_{X_1 \neq X_2} + N_3 \cdot 1_{X_1 = X_2}. \end{aligned}$$

If X_1 and X_2 have different values, depending on N_3 we either choose $X_3 = X_1$ or $X_3 = X_2$. Otherwise $X_3 = N_3$. Now, $\mathfrak{C}_B$ differs from $\mathfrak{C}_A$ only in the latter case:

$$\begin{aligned} X_1 &:= N_1 \\ X_2 &:= N_2 \\ X_3 &:= (1_{N_3>0} \cdot X_1 + 1_{N_3=0} \cdot X_2) \cdot 1_{X_1 \neq X_2} + (2 - N_3) \cdot 1_{X_1 = X_2}. \end{aligned}$$

Both SCMs entail the same observational distribution; and for any possible intervention they entail the same intervention distributions, too.[9] But the two models differ in a counterfactual statement. Suppose, we have made an observation $(X_1, X_2, X_3) = (1,0,0)$ and we are interested in the counterfactual question "what would X_3 have been if X_1 had been 0?" From both SCMs, it follows that $N_3 = 0$, and thus the two SCMs $\mathfrak{C}_A$ and $\mathfrak{C}_B$ "predict" different values for X_3 under a counterfactual change of X_1 (namely 0 and 2, respectively). □

The implications from the preceding example are twofold: (1) Both SCMs correspond to the same causal graphical model (see Section 6.5.2), and in this sense, causal graphical models are not rich enough to predict counterfactuals. (2) In Section 6.8, we relate intervention distributions to real-world randomized experiments.

[9] In this example, the observational distribution satisfies causal minimality with respect to the underlying graph (here $X_1 \rightarrow X_3 \leftarrow X_2$); see Definition 6.33. Another example can be found in Section 3.4; it is less complex but violates causal minimality.

For this example, we cannot use randomized trials or observational data to distinguish between $\mathfrak{C}_A$ or $\mathfrak{C}_B$. Thus, if we are interested in counterfactual statements, we require additional assumptions that let us distinguish between $\mathfrak{C}_A$ or $\mathfrak{C}_B$.

We now summarize some properties of counterfactuals.

Remark 6.20 (i) Counterfactual statements are not transitive. In Example 6.18 we found that given the observation $(X,Y,Z) = (1,2,4)$,

"Y would have been 5, had X been 2,"
"Z would have been 10, had Y been 5," and
"Z would have not been 10, had X been 2."

Therefore, we cannot simply introduce new variables $\tilde{X}$ and $\tilde{Y}$, say, and interpret the statement "Y would have been 5, had X been 2" as a logical implication of the form "$\tilde{X} = 2 \Rightarrow \tilde{Y} = 5$." In the preceding example, the non-transitivity is due to the direct link from X to Z, that is, the existence of a path from X to Z that does not pass Y. A similar counterexample holds for intervention distributions.

(ii) Humans often think in counterfactuals: "I should have taken the train.", "Do you remember our flight to New York on September 11, 2000? Imagine if we would have taken the flight one year later!" or "We should have invested in CHF in December 2014!" are only a few examples. Interestingly, this sometimes even concerns situations in which we made optimal decisions — based on the available information. Assume someone offers you $10,000 if you predict the result of a coin flip; you guess "heads" and lose. Some people may then think, "Why did I not say 'tails'?" even though there was no way they could have possibly known the outcome. Roese [1997], Byrne [2007], and others provide the psychological implications of counterfactual thinking. Discussing whether counterfactual statements contain any information that can help us make better decisions in the future is interesting but lies beyond this work; see also Pearl [2009, Chapter 4].

(iii) We do not discuss the role of counterfactuals in our legal system either; it is an interesting question whether and how counterfactuals should be taken as a basis of verdicts (see Example 3.4).

(iv) People have been thinking about counterfactuals for a long time; it is a popular tool of historians. Titus Livius, for example, discusses in 25 BC what would have happened if Alexander the Great had not died in Asia and had attacked Rome [Geradin and Girgenson, 2011]. Paul's First Epistle to the Corinthians (7:29–7:31) states: "But I say this, brothers: the time is short, that from now on, both those who have wives may be as though they had none; / and those who weep, as though they didn't weep; and those who rejoice, as though they didn't rejoice; and those who buy, as though they didn't possess; / and those who use the world, as not using it to the fullest."

(v) We can think of interventional statements as a mathematical construct for (randomized) experiments. For counterfactual statements, there is no comparable correspondence in the real world. One may speculate that many counterfactual statements cannot be falsified and should therefore not be used in scientific inquiry [cf. Popper, 2002]. Note, however, that sometimes we can make falsifiable counterfactual statements (for example, when the actual value of the noise terms for the respective instance in the sample becomes apparent in retrospect; see Example 3.4). Moreover, the counterfactuals we described above are consequences of positing an SCM. Another target of falsification can therefore also be the SCM rather than a given counterfactual statement. This may or may not be possible, for example, using methods from a scientific domain that the SCM refers to.[10]

□

These remarks can be considered as food for thought. We do not go into further depth regarding the interpretation of counterfactual statements and how they should or can be used in court cases, for example. Many of these deliberations lie outside our field of expertise. Instead, we refer to Halpern [2016] who discusses what it means that some event was an "actual cause" of some other event.

6.5 Markov Property, Faithfulness, and Causal Minimality

6.5.1 Markov Property

The Markov property is a commonly used assumption that forms the basis of graphical models. When a distribution is Markovian with respect to a graph, this graph encodes certain independences in the distribution that we can exploit for efficient computation or data storage. The Markov property exists for both directed and undirected graphs, and the two classes encode different sets of independences

[10]Note that the freedom of reparametrization, as described in Section 3.4, always remains.

[Koller and Friedman, 2009]. In causal inference, however, we are mainly interested in directed graphs. Many introductions to causal inference start by postulating the Markov property. Instead, in this book, we assume the existence of an underlying SCM. We will see in Proposition 6.31 that this is sufficient for proving the Markov property. But first, let us define it.

Definition 6.21 (Markov property) *Given a DAG $\mathcal{G}$ and a joint distribution $P_{\mathbf{X}}$, this distribution is said to satisfy*

(i) *the **global Markov property** with respect to the DAG $\mathcal{G}$ if*

$$\mathbf{A} \perp\!\!\!\perp_{\mathcal{G}} \mathbf{B} \,|\, \mathbf{C} \;\Rightarrow\; \mathbf{A} \perp\!\!\!\perp \mathbf{B} \,|\, \mathbf{C}$$

for all disjoint vertex sets $\mathbf{A}, \mathbf{B}, \mathbf{C}$ (the symbol $\perp\!\!\!\perp_{\mathcal{G}}$ denotes d-separation — see Definition 6.1),

(ii) *the **local Markov property** with respect to the DAG $\mathcal{G}$ if each variable is independent of its non-descendants given its parents, and*

(iii) *the **Markov factorization property** with respect to the DAG $\mathcal{G}$ if*

$$p(\mathbf{x}) = p(x_1, \ldots, x_d) = \prod_{j=1}^{d} p(x_j \,|\, \mathbf{pa}_j^{\mathcal{G}}).$$

*For this last property, we have to assume that $P_{\mathbf{X}}$ has a density p; the factors in the product are referred to as **causal Markov kernels** describing the conditional distributions $P_{X_j|\mathbf{PA}_j^{\mathcal{G}}}$.*

It turns out that as long as the joint distribution has a density,[11] these three definitions are equivalent.

Theorem 6.22 (Equivalence of Markov properties) *If $P_{\mathbf{X}}$ has a density p, then all Markov properties in Definition 6.21 are equivalent.*

The proof can be found as Theorem 3.27 in Lauritzen [1996], for example.

Example 6.23 A distribution P_{X_1,X_2,X_3,X_4} is Markovian with respect to the graph $\mathcal{G}$ shown in Figure 6.1 on page 84 if, according to (i) or (ii),

$$X_2 \perp\!\!\!\perp X_3 \,|\, X_1 \quad \text{and} \quad X_1 \perp\!\!\!\perp X_4 \,|\, X_2, X_3,$$

[11] In this book, we always consider densities with respect to a product measure.

or, according to (iii),

$$p(x_1,x_2,x_3,x_4) = p(x_3)p(x_1\,|\,x_3)p(x_2\,|\,x_1)p(x_4\,|\,x_2,x_3).$$

We will see later in Proposition 6.31 that a distribution entailed from an SCM is Markovian with respect to the graph of the SCM. Therefore, these conditions are indeed satisfied for a distribution P_{X_1,X_2,X_3,X_4} entailed by the SCM as in Figure 6.1, left. Intuitively, the statement $X_2 \perp\!\!\!\perp X_3\,|\,X_1$ is reasonable. Considering the path $X_2 \leftarrow X_1 \leftarrow X_3$, we have that X_3 does not provide any new information about X_2 if we already know X_1. In this sense, the graph structure of an SCM leaves some "traces" in the joint distribution. □

The Markov condition relates statements about graph separation to conditional independences. It is possible, however, that different graphs encode the exact same set of conditional independences.

Definition 6.24 (Markov equivalence of graphs) *We denote by $\mathcal{M}(\mathcal{G})$ the set of distributions that are Markovian with respect to $\mathcal{G}$:*

$$\mathcal{M}(\mathcal{G}) := \{P : P \text{ satisfies the global (or local) Markov property with respect to } \mathcal{G}\}.$$

Two DAGs $\mathcal{G}_1$ and $\mathcal{G}_2$ are Markov equivalent if $\mathcal{M}(\mathcal{G}_1) = \mathcal{M}(\mathcal{G}_2)$. This is the case if and only if $\mathcal{G}_1$ and $\mathcal{G}_2$ satisfy the same set of d-separations, which means the Markov condition entails the same set of (conditional) independence conditions.

The set of all DAGs that are Markov equivalent to some DAG is called ***Markov equivalence class*** *of $\mathcal{G}$. It can be represented by a completed PDAG that is denoted by CPDAG($\mathcal{G}$) $= (V, \mathcal{E})$; it contains the (directed) edge $(i, j) \in \mathcal{E}$ if and only if one member of the Markov equivalence class does; see Figure 6.4.*

From this definition, determining whether two DAGs are Markov equivalent appears a non-trivial problem. Fortunately, Verma and Pearl [1991] provide a concise characterization, see also Frydenberg [1990].

Lemma 6.25 (Graphical criteria for Markov equivalence) *Two DAGs $\mathcal{G}_1$ and $\mathcal{G}_2$ are Markov equivalent if and only if they have the same skeleton and the same immoralities.*

Here, three nodes A, B, and C in a DAG form an **immorality** or **v-structure** if $A \rightarrow B \leftarrow C$ and A and C are not directly connected (see Section 6.1).

Figure 6.4 shows an example of two Markov equivalent graphs (center and left). The graphs share the same skeleton and both of them have only one immorality:

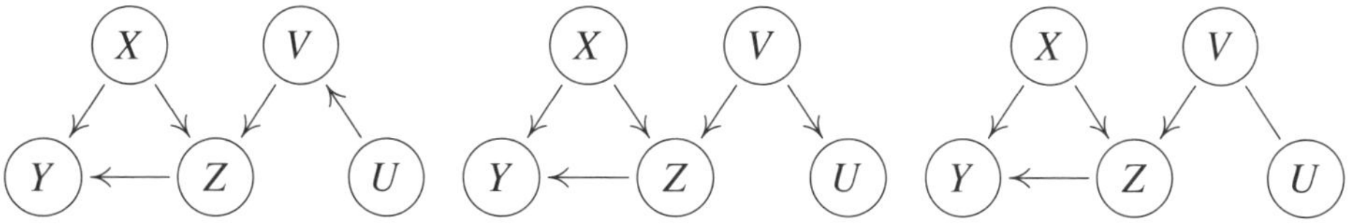

Figure 6.4: Two Markov equivalent DAGs (left and center); these are the only two DAGs in the corresponding Markov equivalence class that can be represented by the CPDAG on the right-hand side.

$X \to Z \leftarrow V$. In the corresponding CPDAG (see Figure 6.4, right), not all directed edges are part of an immorality. The edge $Z \to Y$, for example, is required to avoid a v-structure $Y \to Z \leftarrow V$. Furthermore, $X \to Y$ prevents the existence of a directed cycle.

We now introduce the graphical concept of a Markov blanket [Pearl, 1988] that becomes relevant when one tries to predict the value of a target variable Y from the observed values of all the other variables. One may then wonder what would be the smallest set of variables whose knowledge renders the remaining ones irrelevant for the prediction task.

Definition 6.26 (Markov blanket) *Consider a DAG $\mathcal{G} = (\mathbf{V}, \mathcal{E})$ and a target node Y. The Markov blanket of Y is the smallest set M such that*

$$Y \perp\!\!\!\perp_{\mathcal{G}} \mathbf{V} \setminus (\{Y\} \cup M) \textit{ given } M.$$

If $P_{\mathbf{X}}$ is Markovian with respect to $\mathcal{G}$, then

$$Y \perp\!\!\!\perp \mathbf{V} \setminus (\{Y\} \cup M) \text{ given } M.$$

In other words, given M, the other variables do not provide any further information about Y. In an idealized regression setting, we thus only need to include the variables in M for predicting Y. This does not imply that in a finite sample setting, the other variables are useless. If the dependence from Y on its Markov blanket M is not well aligned with the prior or function class used by the given regression method, adding variables outside M may improve the prediction of Y.

For DAGs, we know what the Markov blanket looks like. It contains not only the parents, but also children and parents of children [Pearl, 1988].

Proposition 6.27 (Markov blanket) *Consider a DAG $\mathcal{G}$ and a target node Y. Then, the Markov blanket M of Y includes its parents, its children, and the parents of its children*

$$M = \mathbf{PA}_Y \cup \mathbf{CH}_Y \cup \mathbf{PA}_{\mathbf{CH}_Y}.$$

So far, we have discussed the Markov property as relating distributions and graphs. Now, we would like to discuss some of its causal implications. The Markov property can be used to justify **Reichenbach's common cause principle** (Principle 1.1). Recall that it states that when the random variables X and Y are dependent, there must be a "causal explanation" for this dependence:

(i) X is (possibly indirectly) causing Y, or

(ii) Y is (possibly indirectly) causing X, or

(iii) there is a (possibly unobserved) common cause Z that (possibly indirectly) causes both X and Y.

Here, we have not further specified the meaning of the word "causing." The following proposition justifies Reichenbach's principle with respect to a weak notion of "causing," namely the existence of a directed path.

Proposition 6.28 (Reichenbach's common cause principle) *Assume that any pair of variables X and Y can be embedded into a larger system in the following sense. There exists a correct SCM over the collection $\mathbf{X}$ of random variables that contains X and Y with graph $\mathcal{G}$. Then Reichenbach's common cause principle follows from the Markov property. If X and Y are (unconditionally) dependent, then there is*

(i) either a directed path from X to Y, or

(ii) from Y to X, or

(iii) there is a node Z with a directed path from Z to X and from Z to Y.

Proof. Due to the Markov property, the dependence implies that $\mathcal{G}$ contains an unblocked path between X and Y. This path cannot contain a collider, for otherwise it would be blocked by the empty set. The statement follows since any path between X and Y without collider must be of the form $X \to \ldots \to Y$, $X \leftarrow \ldots \leftarrow Y$, or $X \leftarrow \ldots \leftarrow Z \to \ldots \to Y$. □

Remark 6.29 (Selection bias) In Reichenbach's principle, we start with two dependent random variables and obtain a valid statement. In real applications, however, it might be that we have implicitly conditioned on a third variable (selection bias). As Example 6.30 shows, this may lead to a dependence between X and Y, although none of the three conditions hold (see also the discussion in the last paragraph of Section 1.3). □

Example 6.30 (Berkson's paradox) The following example "Why are handsome men such jerks?" is taken from Ellenberg [2014] and is an instance of Berkson's paradox [Berkson, 1946]. Let us assume that whether men are in a relationship

($R = 1$) is determined only by whether they are handsome ($H = 1$) and whether they are friendly ($F = 1$). More precisely, assume that the correct SCM has the form:

$$H := N_H,$$
$$F := N_F,$$
$$R := \min(H,F) \oplus N_R,$$

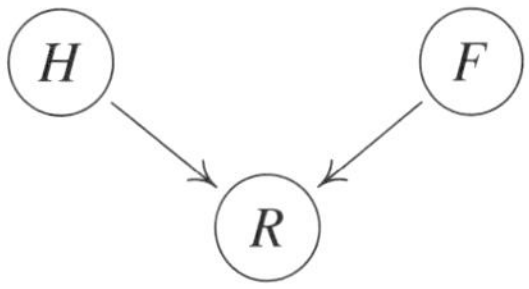

where $N_H, N_F \overset{\text{iid}}{\sim} \text{Ber}(0.5)$ and $N_R \sim \text{Ber}(0.1)$. The symbol $\oplus$ denotes addition modulo 2. In this model, a man is very likely to be in a relationship if he is handsome and friendly. Otherwise, he is likely to be single. As we can see from the SCM, H and F are assumed to be independent. If you consider men, however, that are *not in a relationship*, that is, you condition on $R = 0$, the characteristics, whether a man is friendly or handsome, become anti-correlated. If someone is handsome, he is more likely to be unfriendly (otherwise he would be in a relationship). We have that

$$F \not\perp\!\!\!\perp H \,|\, R = 0$$

and therefore F is not independent of H given R. □

As we have mentioned before, Pearl [2009] shows in Theorem 1.4.1 that the law $P_{\mathbf{X}}$ induced by an SCM is Markovian with respect to its graph [see also Verma and Pearl, 1988].

Proposition 6.31 (SCMs imply Markov property) *Assume that $P_{\mathbf{X}}$ is induced by an SCM with graph $\mathcal{G}$. Then, $P_{\mathbf{X}}$ is Markovian with respect to $\mathcal{G}$.*

The assumption that a distribution is Markovian with respect to the causal graph is sometimes called the causal Markov condition; this requires the notion of a causal graph. For us, causal graphs are induced by the underlying SCM. The concept of causal graphical models, on the other hand, uses them as a starting point for causal inference.

6.5.2 Causal Graphical Models

We will see in Section 6.6 that for defining intervention distributions, it usually suffices to have knowledge of the observational distribution and the graph structure. We therefore define a causal graphical model as a pair that consists of a graph and an observational distribution such that the distribution is Markovian with respect to the graph (causal Markov condition). There is a subtle technicality, however. Formally, we need to have access to the full conditionals. If $p(x_2|x_1 = 3)$ is not defined, for example, because $p(x_1 = 3) = 0$, we may not be able to define $p^{do(X_1:=3)}(x_2)$. This motivates the following definition:

Definition 6.32 (Causal graphical model) *A causal graphical model over random variables $\mathbf{X} = (X_1, \ldots, X_d)$ contains a graph $\mathcal{G}$ and a collection of functions $f_j(x_j, x_{\mathbf{PA}_j^{\mathcal{G}}})$ that integrate to* 1*:*

$$\int f_j(x_j, x_{\mathbf{PA}_j^{\mathcal{G}}})\, dx_j = 1.$$

These functions induce a distribution $P_{\mathbf{X}}$ over $\mathbf{X}$ via

$$p(x_1, \ldots, x_d) = \prod_{j=1}^{d} f_j(x_j, x_{\mathbf{PA}_j^{\mathcal{G}}}),$$

and thus play the role of conditionals: $f_j(x_j, x_{\mathbf{PA}_j^{\mathcal{G}}}) = p(x_j|x_{\mathbf{PA}_j^{\mathcal{G}}})$. A causal graphical model induces intervention distribution according to Equations (6.8) *and* (6.9) *in Section 6.6. In the most general form, we can define*

$$p^{do\left(X_k := q(\cdot\,|\,x_{\widetilde{\mathbf{PA}}_k})\right)}(x_1, \ldots, x_d) = \prod_{j \neq k} f_j(x_j, x_{\mathbf{PA}_j^{\mathcal{G}}})\, q(\cdot\,|\,x_{\widetilde{\mathbf{PA}}_k}),$$

with $q(\cdot\,|\,x_{\widetilde{\mathbf{PA}}_k})$ integrating to 1 *and the new parents not leading to a cycle.*

If a distribution $P_{\mathbf{X}}$ over $\mathbf{X}$ is Markovian with respect to a graph $\mathcal{G}$ and allows for a strictly positive, continuous density p, the pair $(P_{\mathbf{X}}, \mathcal{G})$ defines a causal graphical model by $f_j(x_j, x_{\mathbf{PA}_j^{\mathcal{G}}}) := p(x_j|x_{\mathbf{PA}_j^{\mathcal{G}}})$.

Why do we primarily work with SCMs and not just with graphs and the Markov condition, that is, causal graphical models? Formally, SCMs contain strictly more information than their corresponding graph and law (e.g., counterfactual statements) and hence also more information than the family of all intervention distributions together with the observational distribution. It is debatable, though, whether this additional information is useful. Maybe more importantly, restricting the function class in SCMs can lead to identifiability of the causal structure (see Sections 4.1.3–4.1.6 and 7.1.2). Those assumptions are easier to phrase in the language of SCMs than in the language of graphical models.

6.5.3 Faithfulness and Causal Minimality

In the previous subsection, we discussed the Markov assumption, which enables us to read off independences from the graph structure. Faithfulness allows us to infer dependences from the graph structure.

Definition 6.33 (Faithfulness and causal minimality) *Consider a distribution $P_{\mathbf{X}}$ and a DAG $\mathcal{G}$.*

(i) $P_{\mathbf{X}}$ is faithful to the DAG $\mathcal{G}$ if

$$\mathbf{A} \perp\!\!\!\perp \mathbf{B} \,|\, \mathbf{C} \;\Rightarrow\; \mathbf{A} \perp\!\!\!\perp_{\mathcal{G}} \mathbf{B} \,|\, \mathbf{C}$$

for all disjoint vertex sets $\mathbf{A}, \mathbf{B}, \mathbf{C}$.

(ii) A distribution satisfies causal minimality with respect to $\mathcal{G}$ if it is Markovian with respect to $\mathcal{G}$, but not to any proper subgraph of $\mathcal{G}$.

Part (i) posits an implication that is the opposite of the global Markov condition

$$\mathbf{A} \perp\!\!\!\perp_{\mathcal{G}} \mathbf{B} \,|\, \mathbf{C} \;\Rightarrow\; \mathbf{A} \perp\!\!\!\perp \mathbf{B} \,|\, \mathbf{C},$$

see Definition 6.21. Faithfulness is not very intuitive at first glance. We now give an example of a distribution that is Markovian but not faithful with respect to a given DAG $\mathcal{G}_1$. This is achieved by making two paths cancel each other and creating an independence that is not implied by the graph structure.

Example 6.34 (Violation of faithfulness) Consider the following figure.

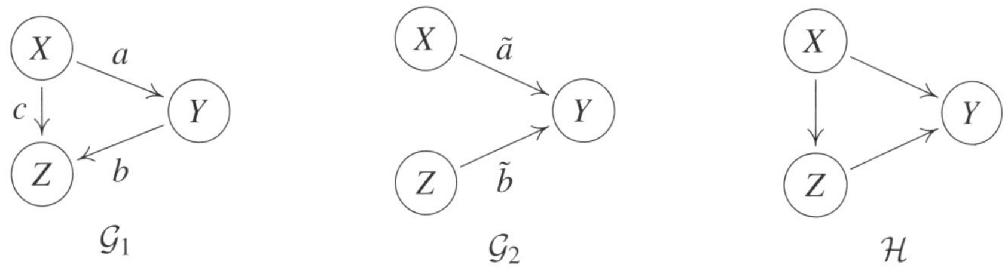

We first look at a linear Gaussian SCM that corresponds to the left graph $\mathcal{G}_1$.

$$\begin{aligned} X &:= N_X, \\ Y &:= aX + N_Y, \\ Z &:= bY + cX + N_Z, \end{aligned}$$

with normally distributed noise variables $N_X \sim \mathcal{N}(0, \sigma_X^2)$, $N_Y \sim \mathcal{N}(0, \sigma_Y^2)$, and $N_Z \sim \mathcal{N}(0, \sigma_Z^2)$ that are jointly independent. This is an example of a linear Gaussian SCM with graph $\mathcal{G}_1$ (see Definition 6.2). Now, if

$$a \cdot b + c = 0, \tag{6.6}$$

the distribution is not faithful with respect to $\mathcal{G}_1$ since we obtain $X \perp\!\!\!\perp Z$, which is not implied by the graph structure.[12] The reader can easily verify that there is an SCM with DAG $\mathcal{G}_2$ inducing the same distribution. □

To obtain the extra independence in the preceding example, we had to "tune" the coefficients such that the two paths cancel each other out in (6.6). Spirtes et al. [2000, Theorem 3.2] show for linear models that this happens with zero probability if we assume that the coefficients are drawn randomly from positive densities.

The distribution from Example 6.34 is faithful with respect to $\mathcal{G}_2$, but not with respect to $\mathcal{G}_1$. Nevertheless, for both models, causal minimality is satisfied if none of the parameters vanishes. In other words, the distribution is not Markovian to any proper subgraph of $\mathcal{G}_1$ or $\mathcal{G}_2$ since removing any edge would correspond to a new (conditional) independence that does not hold in the distribution; note that $\mathcal{G}_2$ is not a proper subgraph of $\mathcal{G}_1$. It is a proper subgraph of $\mathcal{H}$, however, and therefore, the distribution does not satisfy causal minimality with respect to $\mathcal{H}$. In general, causal minimality is weaker than faithfulness.

Proposition 6.35 (Faithfulness implies causal minimality) *If $P_{\mathbf{X}}$ is faithful and Markovian with respect to $\mathcal{G}$, then causal minimality is satisfied.*

Proof. The argument is as follows: If $P_{\mathbf{X}}$ is Markovian with respect to a proper subgraph $\tilde{\mathcal{G}}$ of $\mathcal{G}$, there are two nodes that are directly connected in $\mathcal{G}$ but not in $\tilde{\mathcal{G}}$. Thus, they can be d-separated in $\tilde{\mathcal{G}}$ but not in $\mathcal{G}$ (see Problem 6.62). The Markov condition implies the corresponding conditional independence statement in $P_{\mathbf{X}}$, and thus $P_{\mathbf{X}}$ cannot be faithful with respect to $\mathcal{G}$. □

The following formulation is equivalent to causal minimality and hopefully is of further help to understand the condition. A distribution is minimal with respect to $\mathcal{G}$ if and only if there is no node that is conditionally independent of any of its parents, given the remaining parents. In some sense, all the parents are "active."

[12] More precisely, it is not triangle-faithful [Zhang and Spirtes, 2008].

Proposition 6.36 (Equivalence of causal minimality) *Consider the random vector $\mathbf{X} = (X_1, \ldots, X_d)$ and assume that the joint distribution has a density with respect to a product measure. Suppose that $P_{\mathbf{X}}$ is Markovian with respect to $\mathcal{G}$. Then $P_{\mathbf{X}}$ satisfies causal minimality with respect to $\mathcal{G}$ if and only if $\forall X_j \; \forall Y \in \mathbf{PA}_j^{\mathcal{G}}$ we have that $X_j \not\perp\!\!\!\perp Y \,|\, \mathbf{PA}_j^{\mathcal{G}} \setminus \{Y\}$.*

Proof. See Appendix C.6. □

We have seen that while faithfulness is a strong assumption that links conditional independence statements with causal semantics, causal minimality is a much weaker condition. Suppose we are given a causal graphical model, for example, in which causal minimality is violated. Then, one of the edges is "inactive" in the notion of Proposition 6.36. If we remove this edge, the two models do not need to be counterfactually or interventionally equivalent in the sense of Definition 6.47. They are interventionally equivalent, however, if all densities are strictly positive (or if we only allow for interventions on X_k that are supported on a subset of the support of X_k); see Problem 6.58. Then, causal minimality could be interpreted as the convention to avoid redundancies in the description of an interventional model. In most model classes, identifiability from observational data is impossible to obtain without causal minimality. We cannot distinguish between $Y := f(X) + N_Y$ and $Y := c + N_Y$, for example, if f is allowed to differ from c only outside the support of X; see also Remark 6.6 and Proposition 6.49.

6.6 Calculating Intervention Distributions by Covariate Adjustment

In this section we will make use of a somewhat trivial but very powerful invariance statement. Given an SCM $\mathfrak{C}$, and writing $pa(j) := \mathbf{PA}_j^{\mathcal{G}}$, we have

$$p^{\tilde{\mathfrak{C}}}(x_j \,|\, x_{pa(j)}) = p^{\mathfrak{C}}(x_j \,|\, x_{pa(j)}) \tag{6.7}$$

for any SCM $\tilde{\mathfrak{C}}$ that is constructed from $\mathfrak{C}$ by intervening on (some) X_k but not on X_j. Equation (6.7) shows that causal relationships are autonomous under interventions; this property is therefore sometimes called "autonomy." If we intervene on a variable, then the other mechanisms remain invariant (see the left box in Figure 2.2).

We deduce a formula from (6.7) that became known under three different names: **truncated factorization** [Pearl, 1993], G-**computation formula** [Robins, 1986], and **manipulation theorem** [Spirtes et al., 2000]. Its importance stems from the fact that it allows us to compute statements about intervention distributions even though we have never seen data from it.

Consider an SCM $\mathfrak{C}$ with structural assignments

$$X_j := f_j(X_{pa(j)}, N_j), \qquad j = 1, \ldots, d,$$

and density $p^{\mathfrak{C}}$. Because of the Markov property, we have[13]

$$p^{\mathfrak{C}}(x_1, \ldots, x_d) = \prod_{j=1}^{d} p^{\mathfrak{C}}(x_j \,|\, x_{pa(j)}).$$

Now consider the SCM $\tilde{\mathfrak{C}}$ that evolves from $\mathfrak{C}$ after $do\left(X_k := \tilde{N}_k\right)$, where $\tilde{N}_k$ allows for the density $\tilde{p}$. Again, it follows from the Markov assumption that

$$\begin{aligned} p^{\mathfrak{C};do\left(X_k:=\tilde{N}_k\right)}(x_1, \ldots, x_d) &= \prod_{j \neq k} p^{\mathfrak{C};do\left(X_k:=\tilde{N}_k\right)}(x_j \,|\, x_{pa(j)}) \cdot p^{\mathfrak{C};do\left(X_k:=\tilde{N}_k\right)}(x_k) \\ &= \prod_{j \neq k} p^{\mathfrak{C}}(x_j \,|\, x_{pa(j)}) \tilde{p}(x_k). \end{aligned} \tag{6.8}$$

In the last step, we make use of the powerful invariance (6.7). Equation (6.8) allows us to compute an interventional statement (left-hand side) from observational quantities (right-hand side). As a special case, we obtain

$$p^{\mathfrak{C};do(X_k:=a)}(x_1, \ldots, x_d) = \begin{cases} \prod_{j \neq k} p^{\mathfrak{C}}(x_j \,|\, x_{pa(j)}) & \text{if } x_k = a \\ 0 & \text{otherwise.} \end{cases} \tag{6.9}$$

Usually, conditioning and intervening with $do()$ are different operations (see the discussion after Example 6.10). We are now able to show that these operations become identical for variables that do not have any parents. Without loss of generality, let us assume that X_1 is such a source node. We then have

$$\begin{aligned} p^{\mathfrak{C}}(x_2, \ldots, x_d \,|\, x_1 = a) &= \frac{p(x_1 = a) \prod_{j=2}^{d} p^{\mathfrak{C}}(x_j \,|\, x_{pa(j)})}{p(x_1 = a)} \\ &= p^{\mathfrak{C};do(X_1:=a)}(x_2, \ldots, x_d). \end{aligned} \tag{6.10}$$

Equations (6.8) and (6.9) are widely applicable but sometimes a bit cumbersome to use. We will now learn about some practical alternatives. Therefore, we first recall Example 6.16 (kidney stones) that we will then be able to generalize.

---

[13]Note that the conditionals $p^{\mathfrak{C}}(x_j \,|\, x_{pa(j)})$ can be defined even for values $x_{pa(j)}$ s.t. $p^{\mathfrak{C}}(x_{pa(j)}) = 0$.

Example 6.37 (Kidney stones, continued) Assume that the true underlying SCM allows for the graph

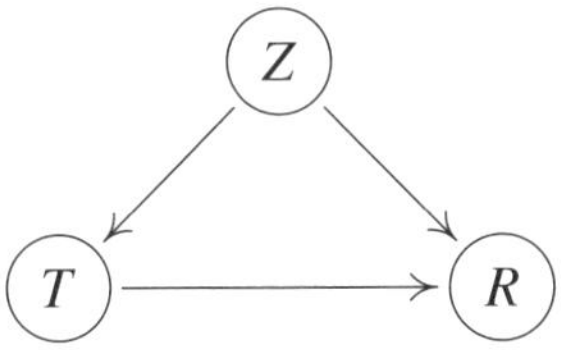

Here, Z is the size of the stone, T the treatment, and R the recovery (all binary). We see that the recovery is influenced by the treatment and the size of the stone. The treatment itself depends on the size, too. A large proportion of difficult cases was assigned to treatment A. Consider further the two SCMs $\mathfrak{C}_A$ and $\mathfrak{C}_B$ that we obtain after replacing the structural assignment for T with $T := A$ and $T := B$, respectively. Let us call the corresponding resulting probability distributions $P^{\mathfrak{C}_A}$ and $P^{\mathfrak{C}_B}$. Given that we are diagnosed with a kidney stone *without knowing its size*, we should base our choice of treatment on a comparison between

$$\mathbb{E}^{\mathfrak{C}_A} R = P^{\mathfrak{C}_A}(R=1) = P^{\mathfrak{C};do(T:=A)}(R=1)$$

and

$$\mathbb{E}^{\mathfrak{C}_B} R = P^{\mathfrak{C}_B}(R=1) = P^{\mathfrak{C};do(T:=B)}(R=1).$$

Given that we have observed data from $\mathfrak{C}$, how can we estimate these quantities? Consider the following computation:

$$\begin{aligned} P^{\mathfrak{C}_A}(R=1) &= \sum_{z=0}^{1} P^{\mathfrak{C}_A}(R=1, T=A, Z=z) \\ &= \sum_{z=0}^{1} P^{\mathfrak{C}_A}(R=1 \mid T=A, Z=z)\, P^{\mathfrak{C}_A}(T=A, Z=z) \\ &= \sum_{z=0}^{1} P^{\mathfrak{C}_A}(R=1 \mid T=A, Z=z)\, P^{\mathfrak{C}_A}(Z=z) \\ &\overset{(6.7)}{=} \sum_{z=0}^{1} P^{\mathfrak{C}}(R=1 \mid T=A, Z=z)\, P^{\mathfrak{C}}(Z=z). \end{aligned} \tag{6.11}$$

The last step contains the key idea. Again, we have made use of the invariance (6.7). We can estimate $P^{\mathfrak{C}_A}(R=1)$ from the empirical data shown in Table 6.1 and obtain

$$P^{\mathfrak{C}_A}(R=1) \approx 0.93 \cdot \frac{357}{700} + 0.73 \cdot \frac{343}{700} = 0.832.$$

Analogously, we obtain

$$P^{\mathfrak{C}_B}(R=1) \approx 0.87 \cdot \frac{357}{700} + 0.69 \cdot \frac{343}{700} \approx 0.782,$$

and we conclude that we would rather go for treatment A. (As stated before, we ignore the question of statistical significance, which seems justified if we need to decide between A and B.) The quantity

$$P^{\mathfrak{C}_A}(R=1) - P^{\mathfrak{C}_B}(R=1) \approx 0.832 - 0.782 \tag{6.12}$$

is sometimes called the **average causal effect (ACE)** for binary treatments. It is important to realize that this is different from simple conditioning:

$$P^{\mathfrak{C}}(R=1 \mid T=A) - P^{\mathfrak{C}}(R=1 \mid T=B) = 0.78 - 0.83,$$

which, in this example, has even the opposite sign of the ACE. □

This three-node example nicely highlights the difference between intervening and conditioning. In terms of densities, it reads:

$$p^{\mathfrak{C};do(T:=t)}(r) = \sum_z p^{\mathfrak{C}}(r|z,t)p^{\mathfrak{C}}(z) \neq \sum_z p^{\mathfrak{C}}(r|z,t)p^{\mathfrak{C}}(z|t) = p^{\mathfrak{C}}(r|t).$$

Equation (6.11) is called "adjusting" for the variable Z. It denotes an important concept that is often used in practice and that we formally define in Definition 6.38. It once more allows us to compute intervention statements from observed quantities. Note that the derivation of the adjustment formula (6.11) is sometimes based on the truncated factorization (6.9), but we will see in Proposition 6.41 that the alternative computation using the invariance (6.11) nicely carries over to more complicated settings.

Definition 6.38 (Valid adjustment set) *Consider an SCM $\mathfrak{C}$ over nodes $\mathbf{V}$ and let $Y \notin \mathbf{PA}_X$ (otherwise we have $p^{\mathfrak{C};do(X:=x)}(y) = p^{\mathfrak{C}}(y)$). We call a set $\mathbf{Z} \subseteq \mathbf{V} \setminus \{X,Y\}$ a valid adjustment set for the ordered pair (X,Y) if*

$$p^{\mathfrak{C};do(X:=x)}(y) = \sum_{\mathbf{z}} p^{\mathfrak{C}}(y \mid x, \mathbf{z})\, p^{\mathfrak{C}}(\mathbf{z}). \tag{6.13}$$

Here, the sum (could also be an integral) is over the range of $\mathbf{Z}$, that is, over all values $\mathbf{z}$ that $\mathbf{Z}$ can take.

In Example 6.37, $\mathbf{Z} = \{Z\}$ is a valid adjustment set for (T,R). Adjusting for Z was necessary to compute the average causal effect. We have seen that simple conditioning led to false conclusions. In other words, the empty set was not a valid adjustment set. In such a case, we say that the causal effect from T to R is confounded.

Definition 6.39 (Confounding) *Consider an SCM $\mathfrak{C}$ over nodes $\mathbf{V}$ with a directed path from X to Y, $X,Y \in \mathbf{V}$. The causal effect from X to Y is called confounded if*

$$p^{\mathfrak{C};do(X:=x)}(y) \neq p^{\mathfrak{C}}(y\,|\,x). \tag{6.14}$$

Otherwise, the causal effect is called "unconfounded."

It is sometimes believed that one should make the adjustment set as large as possible to reduce the influence of potential confounders. This is, however, not always a good idea as demonstrated by Berkson's paradox [Berkson, 1946] in Example 6.30. It shows that not all sets are valid adjustment sets and that sometimes it is better to not include a covariate in the adjustment set. Let us try to investigate which sets we can use for adjusting. We use the same idea as in Example 6.37 and write (for any set $\mathbf{Z}$)

$$\begin{aligned} p^{\mathfrak{C};do(X:=x)}(y) &= \sum_{\mathbf{z}} p^{\mathfrak{C};do(X:=x)}(y,\mathbf{z}) \\ &= \sum_{\mathbf{z}} p^{\mathfrak{C};do(X:=x)}(y\,|\,x,\mathbf{z})\, p^{\mathfrak{C};do(X:=x)}(\mathbf{z}). \end{aligned}$$

If we have

$$p^{\mathfrak{C};do(X:=x)}(y\,|\,x,\mathbf{z}) = p^{\mathfrak{C}}(y\,|\,x,\mathbf{z}) \text{ and } p^{\mathfrak{C};do(X:=x)}(\mathbf{z}) = p^{\mathfrak{C}}(\mathbf{z}), \tag{6.15}$$

it follows (as before) that $\mathbf{Z}$ is a valid adjustment set. Property (6.15) states that the conditionals remain the same even after intervening on X; we say that they are **invariant**. We thus need to address the question of which conditionals remain invariant under the intervention $do\,(X := x)$.

Remark 6.40 (Characterization of invariant conditionals) Consider an SCM $\mathfrak{C}$ with structural assignments

$$X_j := f_j(\mathbf{PA}_j, N_j)$$

and an intervention $do\,(X_k := x_k)$. Analogously to what is done in Pearl [2009, Chapter 3.2.2], for example, we can now construct a new SCM $\mathfrak{C}^*$ that equals $\mathfrak{C}$

but has one more variable I that indicates whether the intervention took place or not (see also the paragraph "Intervention Variables" in Section 6.3 on page 95). More precisely, I is a parent of X_k and does not have any other neighbors. The corresponding structural assignments are

$$\begin{aligned} I &:= N_I \\ X_j &:= f_j(\mathbf{PA}_j, N_j) \quad \text{for } j \neq k \\ X_k &:= \begin{cases} f_k(\mathbf{PA}_k, N_k) & \text{if } I = 0 \\ x_k & \text{otherwise} \end{cases}, \end{aligned}$$

where N_I has a Bernoulli distribution with $P(I=0) = P(I=1) = 0.5$, for example (other distributions work, too). Thus, $I = 0$ corresponds to the observational setting and $I = 1$ to the interventional setting. More precisely, using Equation (6.10), we obtain

$$\begin{aligned} p^{\mathfrak{C}^*}(x_1, \ldots, x_d \,|\, I=0) &= p^{\mathfrak{C}^*; do(I:=0)}(x_1, \ldots, x_d) \\ &= p^{\mathfrak{C}}(x_1, \ldots, x_d) \end{aligned}$$

and similarly

$$p^{\mathfrak{C}^*}(x_1, \ldots, x_d \,|\, I=1) = p^{\mathfrak{C}; do(X_k:=x_k)}(x_1, \ldots, x_d). \tag{6.16}$$

Using the Markov condition for $\mathfrak{C}^*$, it thus follows for variables A and a set of variables $\mathbf{B}$ that

$$\begin{aligned} A \perp\!\!\!\perp_{\mathcal{G}^*} I \,|\, \mathbf{B} \quad &\Longrightarrow \quad p^{\mathfrak{C}^*}(a \,|\, \mathbf{b}, I=0) = p^{\mathfrak{C}^*}(a \,|\, \mathbf{b}, I=1) \\ &\Longrightarrow \quad p^{\mathfrak{C}}(a \,|\, \mathbf{b}) = p^{\mathfrak{C}; do(X_k:=x_k)}(a \,|\, \mathbf{b}). \end{aligned}$$

The right-hand side states that the distribution $P_{A|\mathbf{B}}$ of the conditional A given $\mathbf{B}$ remains invariant under an intervention on X_k. □

We are now able to continue the argument from before. Equation (6.15) is satisfied for sets $\mathbf{Z}$, for which we have

$$Y \perp\!\!\!\perp_{\mathcal{G}^*} I \,|\, X, \mathbf{Z} \qquad \text{and} \qquad \mathbf{Z} \perp\!\!\!\perp_{\mathcal{G}^*} I. \tag{6.17}$$

The subscript $\mathcal{G}^*$ means that the d-separation statement is required to hold in $\mathcal{G}^*$. Our deliberation immediately implies the first two statements of the following proposition:

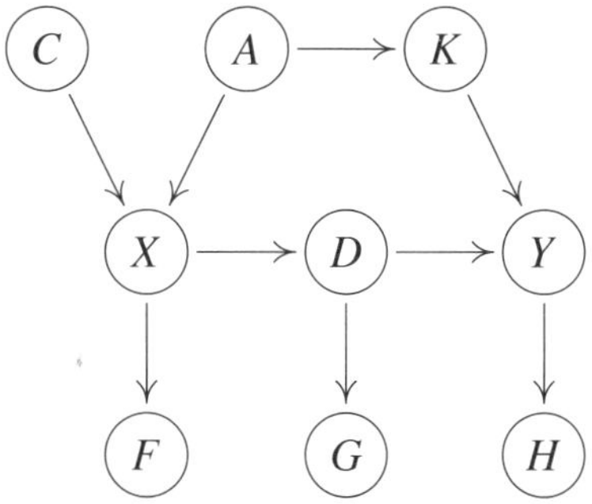

Figure 6.5: Only the path $X \leftarrow A \rightarrow K \rightarrow Y$ is a "backdoor path" from X to Y. The set $\mathbf{Z} = \{K\}$ satisfies the backdoor criterion (see Proposition 6.41 (ii)); but $\mathbf{Z} = \{F, C, K\}$ is also a valid adjustment set for (X, Y); see Proposition 6.41 (iii).

Proposition 6.41 (Valid adjustment sets) *Consider an SCM over variables* $\mathbf{X}$ *with* $X, Y \in \mathbf{X}$ *and* $Y \notin \mathbf{PA}_X$. *Then, the following three statements are true.*

(i) ***"parent adjustment":***

$$\mathbf{Z} := \mathbf{PA}_X$$

is a valid adjustment set for (X, Y).

(ii) ***"backdoor criterion":*** *Any* $\mathbf{Z} \subseteq \mathbf{X} \setminus \{X, Y\}$ *with*

- $\mathbf{Z}$ *contains no descendant of* X *AND*
- $\mathbf{Z}$ *blocks all paths from* X *to* Y *entering* X *through the backdoor* ($X \leftarrow \ldots$, *see Figure 6.5*)

is a valid adjustment set for (X, Y).

(iii) ***"toward necessity":*** *Any* $\mathbf{Z} \subseteq \mathbf{X} \setminus \{X, Y\}$ *with*

- $\mathbf{Z}$ *contains no descendant of any node on a directed path from* X *to* Y *(except for descendants of* X *that are not on a directed path from* X *to* Y*) AND*
- $\mathbf{Z}$ *blocks all non-directed paths from* X *to* Y

is a valid adjustment set for (X, Y).

Only the third statement [Shpitser et al., 2010, Perkovic et al., 2015] requires some explanation. Let us start with a valid adjustment set $\mathbf{Z}$, for example, obtained via the backdoor criterion. We can then add any node Z_0 to $\mathbf{Z}$ that satisfies

$Z_0 \perp\!\!\!\perp Y \,|\, X, \mathbf{Z}$ because then

$$\sum_{\mathbf{z}, z_0} p(y \,|\, x, \mathbf{z}, z_0) p(\mathbf{z}, z_0) = \sum_{\mathbf{z}} p(y \,|\, x, \mathbf{z}) \sum_{z_0} p(\mathbf{z}, z_0)$$
$$= \sum_{\mathbf{z}} p(y \,|\, x, \mathbf{z}) p(\mathbf{z}).$$

In fact, Proposition 6.41 (iii) characterizes *all* valid adjustment sets [Shpitser et al., 2010].

Example 6.42 (Adjustment in linear Gaussian systems) Consider an SCM $\mathfrak{C}$ over variables $\mathbf{V}$ with $\{X, Y\}, \mathbf{Z} \subseteq \mathbf{V}$. Sometimes, we want to summarize a causal effect from X to Y by a single real number instead of looking at $p^{\mathfrak{C}; do(X:=x)}(y)$ for all x. We have seen an example in the case of binary treatments X (see Equation (6.12)). But what can be done in the case of continuous random variables? As a first approximation we may look at the expectation of this distribution and then take the derivative with respect to x:

$$\frac{\partial}{\partial x} \mathbb{E}^{\mathfrak{C}; do(X:=x)}[Y]. \tag{6.18}$$

In general, this is still a function of x. In linear Gaussian systems, however, this function turns out to be constant. Assume that $\mathbf{Z}$ is a valid adjustment set for (X, Y). If $\mathbf{V}$ has a Gaussian distribution, then the conditional $Y \,|\, X = x, \mathbf{Z} = \mathbf{z}$ follows a Gaussian distribution, too; its mean is

$$\mathbb{E}[Y \,|\, X = x, \mathbf{Z} = \mathbf{z}] = ax + \mathbf{b}^t \mathbf{z} \tag{6.19}$$

for some a and $\mathbf{b}$. It follows from (6.13) (see Problem 6.63) that

$$\frac{\partial}{\partial x} \mathbb{E}^{\mathfrak{C}; do(X:=x)}[Y] \;=\; a. \tag{6.20}$$

It is possible to obtain the value of a in (6.19) in two different ways. (1) One can use the method of path coefficients: if there is exactly one directed path from X to Y, then a equals the product of the path coefficients. If there is no directed path, then $a = 0$ and if there are different paths, a can be computed using Wright's formula [Wright, 1934]. (2) One can directly compute the conditional mean (6.19). If we are not given the joint distribution but rather a sample from it, we can estimate (6.20) by regressing Y on X and $\mathbf{Z}$ and then reading off the regression coefficient for X (see also Code Snippet 6.43). □

Code Snippet 6.43 The following code generates an i.i.d. sample of size $n = 100$ from an SCM with the structure shown in Figure 6.5 (see the code for the coefficients). Since we know the underlying SCM, the true value of quantity (6.20) can be obtained by multiplying the path coefficients of the path $X \to D \to Y$; in our example, it equals $(-2) \cdot (-1) = 2$ (see lines 8 and 10 in the code). We can now pretend that the precise form of the structural assignments; that is, the set of coefficients is unknown but we are given the data sample and the graph structure of the SCM (see Figure 6.5) instead. We can then estimate the value (6.20) by regressing Y on X and an adjustment set $\mathbf{Z}$. If $\mathbf{Z}$ is a valid adjustment set, we obtain an unbiased estimator. In the code, the adjustment set $\mathbf{Z} = \emptyset$ leads to a biased estimator (see line 15); only the adjustment sets $\mathbf{Z} = \{K\}$ and $\mathbf{Z} = \{F, C, K\}$ are valid (see lines 19 and 23, respectively).

```
1  # generate a sample from the distribution entailed by the SCM
2  set.seed(1); n <- 100
3  C <- rnorm(n)
4  A <- 0.8*rnorm(n)
5  K <- A + 0.1*rnorm(n)
6  X <- C - 2*A + 0.2*rnorm(n)
7  F <- 3*X + 0.8*rnorm(n)
8  D <- -2*X + 0.5*rnorm(n)
9  G <- D + 0.5*rnorm(n)
10 Y <- 2*K - D + 0.2*rnorm(n)
11 H <- 0.5*Y + 0.1*rnorm(n)
12 #
13 lm(Y~X)$coefficients
14 # (Intercept)---------X
15 # 0.09724282 1.27941073
16 #
17 lm(Y~X+K)$coefficients
18 # (Intercept)---------X----------K
19 # 0.01428974 2.07038809 2.16964827
20 #
21 lm(Y~X+F+C+K)$coefficients
22 # (Intercept)---------X----------F-----------C----------K
23 # 0.01687018 1.90495456 0.05901385 -0.02260164 2.18276488
```

We now briefly comment on propensity score matching [Rosenbaum and Rubin, 1983]. The following remark repeats the argument given by Pearl [2009, 11.3.5].

Remark 6.44 (Propensity score matching) Consider an SCM over variables $\mathbf{X} = (X, Y, \mathbf{Z})$, with $\mathbf{Z} = (Z_1, Z_2, Z_3)$ and the following graph.

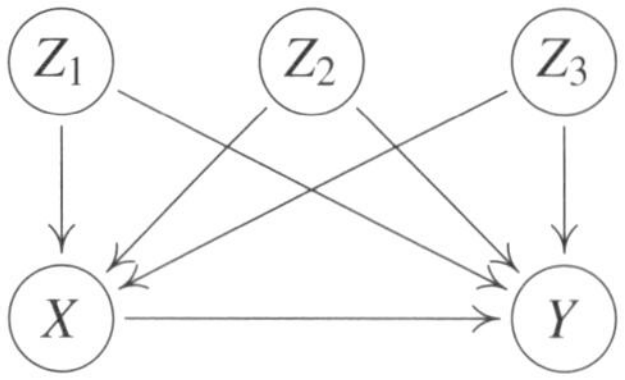

One can see that the set $\{Z_1, Z_2, Z_3\}$ is a valid adjustment set, for example, by parent adjustment (see Proposition 6.41). That is,

$$p^{\mathfrak{C};do(X:=x)}(y) = \sum_{z_1,z_2,z_3} p^{\mathfrak{C}}(y\,|\,x,z_1,z_2,z_3)\, p^{\mathfrak{C}}(z_1,z_2,z_3). \tag{6.21}$$

Sometimes, however, the value of X does not depend on $\mathbf{Z}$ "directly" but only through a (real-valued) **propensity score** $L := L(\mathbf{Z}) = L(Z_1, Z_2, Z_3)$. This means "$X \perp\!\!\!\perp \mathbf{Z}\,|\,L(\mathbf{Z})$," or, more formally, s we have for all $\mathbf{z}, x$ and $\ell = L(\mathbf{z})$ that

$$p(\mathbf{z}\,|\,\ell, x) = p(\mathbf{z}\,|\,\ell).$$

If X is a binary choice that indicates treatment or no treatment, one may choose $L(\mathbf{z}) = p(x = 1\,|\,\mathbf{Z} = \mathbf{z})$, for example. But then, it follows with (6.21)

$$\begin{aligned} p^{\mathfrak{C};do(X:=x)}(y) &= \sum_{\mathbf{z}} p^{\mathfrak{C}}(y\,|\,x,\mathbf{z})\, p^{\mathfrak{C}}(\mathbf{z}) = \sum_{\mathbf{z}}\sum_{\ell} p^{\mathfrak{C}}(y\,|\,x,\mathbf{z})\, p^{\mathfrak{C}}(\ell) p^{\mathfrak{C}}(\mathbf{z}\,|\,\ell) \\ &= \sum_{\mathbf{z}}\sum_{\ell} p^{\mathfrak{C}}(y\,|\,\ell,x,\mathbf{z})\, p^{\mathfrak{C}}(\ell) p^{\mathfrak{C}}(\mathbf{z}\,|\,\ell,x) \\ &= \sum_{\ell} p^{\mathfrak{C}}(y\,|\,\ell,x)\, p^{\mathfrak{C}}(\ell). \end{aligned} \tag{6.22}$$

In the population setting, both computations (6.21) and (6.22) of the intervention distribution are correct. The point is, however, that for finite data, (6.22) may lead to a better estimate than (6.21) would: although one needs to estimate the function L, the resulting conditional $p^{\mathfrak{C}}(y\,|\,x,\ell)$ is potentially lower dimensional than $p^{\mathfrak{C}}(y\,|\,x,\mathbf{z})$. In practice, one often matches realizations with a "similar" value of ℓ to compute (6.22). Important practical details include estimating of the function L and the matching procedure. The idea works for any number of covariates.

In this sense, propensity score matching can be a nice and useful trick to gain statistical performance. It is irrelevant for population considerations. □

6.7 Do-Calculus

Again, consider an SCM over variables $\mathbf{V}$. Sometimes, we can compute intervention distributions $p^{\mathfrak{C};do(X:=x)}$ in other ways than the adjustment formula (6.13). Let us therefore call an intervention distribution $p^{\mathfrak{C};do(X:=x)}(y)$ *identifiable* if it can be computed from the observational distribution and the graph structure. If there is a valid adjustment set for (X,Y), for example, $p^{\mathfrak{C};do(X:=x)}(y)$ is certainly identifiable. Pearl [2009, Theorem 3.4.1] has developed the so-called *do*-calculus that consists of three rules. Given a graph $\mathcal{G}$ and disjoint subsets $\mathbf{X}, \mathbf{Y}, \mathbf{Z}$, and $\mathbf{W}$, we have

1. "Insertion/deletion of observations":

$$p^{\mathfrak{C};do(\mathbf{X}:=\mathbf{x})}(\mathbf{y} \,|\, \mathbf{z}, \mathbf{w}) = p^{\mathfrak{C};do(\mathbf{X}:=\mathbf{x})}(\mathbf{y} \,|\, \mathbf{w})$$

   if $\mathbf{Y}$ and $\mathbf{Z}$ are d-separated by $\mathbf{X}, \mathbf{W}$ in a graph where incoming edges in $\mathbf{X}$ have been removed.

2. "Action/observation exchange":

$$p^{\mathfrak{C};do(\mathbf{X}:=\mathbf{x},\mathbf{Z}=\mathbf{z})}(\mathbf{y} \,|\, \mathbf{w}) = p^{\mathfrak{C};do(\mathbf{X}:=\mathbf{x})}(\mathbf{y} \,|\, \mathbf{z}, \mathbf{w})$$

   if $\mathbf{Y}$ and $\mathbf{Z}$ are d-separated by $\mathbf{X}, \mathbf{W}$ in a graph where incoming edges in $\mathbf{X}$ and outgoing edges from $\mathbf{Z}$ have been removed.

3. "Insertion/deletion of actions":

$$p^{\mathfrak{C};do(\mathbf{X}:=\mathbf{x},\mathbf{Z}=\mathbf{z})}(\mathbf{y} \,|\, \mathbf{w}) = p^{\mathfrak{C};do(\mathbf{X}:=\mathbf{x})}(\mathbf{y} \,|\, \mathbf{w})$$

   if $\mathbf{Y}$ and $\mathbf{Z}$ are d-separated by $\mathbf{X}, \mathbf{W}$ in a graph where incoming edges in $\mathbf{X}$ and $\mathbf{Z}(\mathbf{W})$ have been removed. Here, $\mathbf{Z}(\mathbf{W})$ is the subset of nodes in $\mathbf{Z}$ that are not ancestors of any node in $\mathbf{W}$ in a graph that is obtained from $\mathcal{G}$ after removing all edges into $\mathbf{X}$.

Theorem 6.45 (Do-calculus) *The following statements hold.*

(i) The rules are complete; that is, all identifiable intervention distributions can be computed by an iterative application of these three rules [Huang and Valtorta, 2006, Shpitser and Pearl, 2006].

(ii) In fact, there is an algorithm, proposed by Tian [2002] that is guaranteed [Huang and Valtorta, 2006, Shpitser and Pearl, 2006] to find all identifiable intervention distributions.

(iii) There is a necessary and sufficient graphical criterion for identifiability of intervention distributions [Shpitser and Pearl, 2006, Corollary 3], based on so-called hedges [see also Huang and Valtorta, 2006].

As a corollary of the do-calculus, we obtain the front-door adjustment (see Problem 6.65).

Example 6.46 (Front-door adjustment) Let $\mathfrak{C}$ be an SCM with corresponding graph

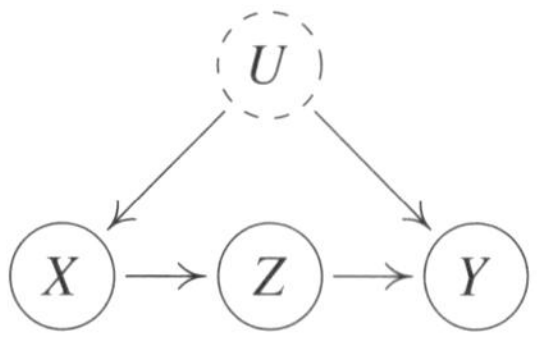

If we do not observe U, we cannot apply the backdoor criterion. In fact, there is no valid adjustment set. But still, provided that $p^{\mathfrak{C}}(x,z) > 0$, the *do*-calculus provides us with

$$p^{\mathfrak{C};do(X:=x)}(y) = \sum_{z} p^{\mathfrak{C}}(z\,|\,x) \sum_{\tilde{x}} p^{\mathfrak{C}}(y\,|\,\tilde{x},z)\; p^{\mathfrak{C}}(\tilde{x}). \tag{6.23}$$

The fact that observing Z in addition to X and Y here reveals causal information nicely shows that causal relations can also be explored by observing the "channel" (here Z) that carries the "signal" from X to Y. □

Bareinboim and Pearl [2014] consider the problem of transportability. They are also interested in intervention distributions, but they allow for the possibility to include knowledge (i.e., observational distributions and intervention distributions) that has been gained in SCMs that coincide with the target SCM in some structural assignments and differ in others.

6.8 Equivalence and Falsifiability of Causal Models

So far, SCMs have been mathematical objects. To link them to reality, we regard them as models for a data-generating process. It can be a complicated class of models, though. Instead of modeling "just" a joint distribution (as we can model a physical process with a Poisson process, for example), we can now model the system in an observational state and under perturbations at the same time. We have seen that it is even possible to regard SCMs as models for counterfactual statements.

More formally, consider a vector $\mathbf{X} = (X_1,\ldots,X_d)$ of random variables. A **probabilistic model** for $\mathbf{X}$ predicts an observational distribution $P_{\mathbf{X}}$. We call such a model an **interventional model** if it additionally predicts intervention distributions in which some variables X_j have been set to (independent) variables $\tilde{N}_j$. Finally, a **counterfactual model** additionally predicts the result of counterfactual statements. Traditional machine learning methods, for example, build probabilistic models;

causal graphical models (Definition 6.32) can be used as interventional models, and SCMs can be used as counterfactual models. We call two models equivalent if they agree on the corresponding predictions [see Bongers et al., 2016] for a similar construction.

Definition 6.47 (Equivalence of causal models) *Two models are called*

$$\{\textbf{\textit{probabilistically}} \,/\, \textbf{\textit{interventionally}} \,/\, \textbf{\textit{counterfactually}}\} \ \textbf{\textit{equivalent}}$$

if they entail the same $\{$*obs.* / *obs. and int.* / *obs., int., and counterf.*$\}$ *distributions.*

It is apparent that the notion of interventional equivalence applies only to interventional and counterfactual models, for example. Proposition 7.1 implies that for each probabilistic model, there is an observationally equivalent SCM.

If $\mathbf{X}$ has a strictly positive density, Proposition 6.48 shows that we can restrict the notion to interventions on single nodes, that is, interventions in which a variable X_j has been set to a variable $\tilde{N}_j$ where the distribution of $\tilde{N}_j$ has full support. If two models agree on this subclass of interventions, they agree on all other interventions, too. The rationale is that interventions on single nodes, correspond to the standard version of randomized experiments.

For a given data-generating process, we can now **falsify** a probabilistic or interventional model if the corresponding distributions do not agree with the data observed from the process. That is, if an interventional model predicts the observational distribution correctly but does not predict what happens in a randomized experiment, the model is still considered to be falsified. This notion includes the assumption that there is an agreement about what a randomized experiment should look like. One should be careful about writing down an SCM when it is unclear how to randomize over the involved variables in reality (or perform interventions on them). The notion of falsifiability further requires the concept of (statistical) significance, which is not discussed here. We do not include counterfactual models, since they are hard to falsify in general. We could falsify them based on their implications on observational distributions and intervention distributions (see Shpitser and Pearl [2008a] and references therein). In some specific experimental setups, it is furthermore possible to construct counterfactual statements that are falsifiable (see Example 3.4). Example 6.19, however, shows two SCMs that entail the same observational and intervention distributions but entail different counterfactual statements.

The above-mentioned restriction to a subclass of interventions (single variables are set to a noise variable) serves a practical purpose. To check the validity of the model we have to compare the outcome of randomized experiments with the model's predictions. For more complex interventions, the corresponding experiments in reality seem more complicated to implement. The following proposition states that this comes without loss of generality: if causal models agree on all single-node interventions, they are interventionally equivalent. The proof can be found in Appendix C.7.

Proposition 6.48 (Interventional equivalence) *Assume that two SCMs (or causal graphical models) $\mathfrak{C}_1$ and $\mathfrak{C}_2$ induce strictly positive, continuous conditional densities $p(x_j|x_{pa(j)})$, where $pa(j) := \mathbf{PA}_{X_j}$, and satisfy causal minimality. Assume further that they entail the same intervention distributions, in which some variable X_j has been set to a variable $\tilde{N}_j$ with full support:*

$$P_{\mathbf{X}}^{\mathfrak{C}_1;do(X_j:=\tilde{N}_j)} = P_{\mathbf{X}}^{\mathfrak{C}_2;do(X_j:=\tilde{N}_j)} \qquad \forall j\, \forall \tilde{N}_j \text{ with full support.}$$

Then, $\mathfrak{C}_1$ and $\mathfrak{C}_2$ are interventionally equivalent; that is, they agree on any possible intervention, including atomic interventions or interventions in which the set of parents is altered (without creating a cycle).

If the density is not strictly positive, this is not necessarily the case. One may then have to consider simultaneous interventions on several nodes (e.g., double knockout gene experiments); see Problem 6.59.

Furthermore, we are now able to justify the notion of structural minimality of SCMs (see Remark 6.6). We have argued that if the function in a structural assignment of an SCM does not depend on one of the inputs, we can choose a sparser representation. The following proposition formalizes in what sense these representations are equivalent.

Proposition 6.49 (Counterfactual equivalence) *Consider two SCMs $\mathfrak{C}$ and $\mathfrak{C}^*$ that share the same noise distribution $P_{\mathbf{N}}$ and that differ only in the kth structural assignment:*

$$f_k(\mathbf{pa}_k, n_k) = f_k^*(\mathbf{pa}_k^*, n_k), \qquad \forall \mathbf{pa}_k, \forall n_k \text{ with } p(n_k) > 0, \tag{6.24}$$

with $\mathbf{PA}_k^* \subsetneq \mathbf{PA}_k$. Then, both SCMs are counterfactually equivalent.

The proof is provided in Appendix C.8.

6.9 Potential Outcomes

We now introduce an alternative approach to causal inference that is not based on SCMs. The framework is often referred to as potential outcomes or the Rubin causal model and is widely used in the social sciences. The ideas date back to Neyman [1923] and Fisher [1925] who mainly discussed randomized experiments. Rubin [1974] extended the ideas to observational studies. Rubin [2005], Morgan and Winship [2007], and Imbens and Rubin [2015] provide more elaborate introductions into the topic.

6.9.1 Definitions and Example

To explain potential outcomes, we revisit Example 3.4 (the eye doctor) and reformulate it in this framework. Rather than with random variables, we now start with a group of n patients (or units) $u = 1, \dots, n$, each of which may or may not receive the treatment. We assign two **potential outcomes** to each patient u: $B_u(t = 1)$ indicates whether the patient would go blind ($B = 1$) or get cured ($B = 0$) if she receives treatment ($T = 1$). Analogously, $B_u(t = 0)$ encodes what happens without treatment ($T = 0$). Both of these potential outcomes are assumed to be deterministic. For each patient the treatment either helps or it does not help: there is no randomness involved. If $B_u(t = 1) = 0$ and $B_u(t = 0) = 1$, we say that the treatment has a positive effect for unit u.

In practice, however, we are not able to check these conditions. The "fundamental problem of causal inference" [Holland, 1986] states that for each unit u we can observe either $B_u(t = 1)$ or $B_u(t = 0)$ and never both of them at the same time. The reason is that after we have chosen to treat a person, we cannot go back in time and undo the treatment. This even holds the other way around. If we decide to not give a treatment, we can still apply the treatment later in time but this cannot be interpreted as an outcome of the variable $B_u(t = 1)$ anymore. The patient might have recovered in the meantime by herself, for example. Thus, we can observe only one of the potential outcomes; the unobserved quantity becomes a counterfactual.

Table 6.2 shows a (hypothetical) data set for the previous example. In fact, the data points are sampled according to the model described in Example 3.4. To justify the presentation in Table 6.2, we often implicitly assume the **stable unit treatment value assumption** (SUTVA) [Rubin, 2005]. It states that the units do not interfere (e.g., the potential outcome of a unit does not depend on which treatment any other unit received) [Cox, 1958]; furthermore it requires that the potential outcomes do not depend on *how* or *why* the treatment has been received. We will see in Section 6.9.2 that SUTVA is satisfied when the data are generated from an SCM (as was done for this example).

The potential outcomes tell us the effect of a treatment on an individual basis; we define the **unit-level causal effect** as $B_u(t = 1) - B_u(t = 0)$ and an average causal

Unit u	Treatment T	Pot. Outcome $B_u(t=0)$	Pot. Outcome $B_u(t=1)$	Unit-Level Causal Effect $B_u(t=1)-B_u(t=0)$
1	1	1	0	-1
2	0	1	0	-1
3	1	1	0	-1
⋮				
43	1	1	0	-1
44	0	0	1	1
45	0	1	0	-1
⋮				
119	1	1	0	-1
120	1	0	1	1
121	0	1	0	-1
⋮				
200	0	1	0	-1

Table 6.2: This table presents Example 3.4 using potential outcomes. For each patient (or unit), we observe only one of the two potential outcomes. The observed information has a gray background. The treatment T is helpful for almost all patients. Only in 2 of 200 cases, the treatment harms the patient and blinds him $B = 1$. Although assigning the treatment ($T = 1$) is a good idea in most cases, for patient $u = 120$ it was exactly the wrong decision.

effect

$$CE = \frac{1}{n}\sum_{u=1}^{n} B_u(t=1) - B_u(t=0). \tag{6.25}$$

The "fundamental problem of causal inference" prevents us from computing (6.25) directly. Assume that in a completely randomized experiment, units $u \in U_0 \subset \{1,\ldots,n\}$ received treatment $T = 0$ and units $u \in U_1 = U_0^C$ treatment $T = 1$. Neyman [1923] shows that

$$\widehat{CE} := \frac{1}{\#U_0}\sum_{u\in U_0} B_u(t=1) \;-\; \frac{1}{\#U_1}\sum_{u\in U_1} B_u(t=0) \tag{6.26}$$

is an unbiased estimator for (6.25). Here, the randomness in $\widehat{CE}$ comes from the random assignments that determine, which of the unit's two potential outcomes we observe; the outcomes themselves are considered hidden, not random. Note that (6.26) contains only observed quantities and can therefore be computed after the study has been conducted.

There is an extensive debate about which of the two approaches is better suited for practical applications [see, e.g., Pearl, 1995, Imbens and Rubin, 1995, Rubin,

2004, Lauritzen, 2004]. We do not plan to take an active part in this discussion but rather mention the following three results: (1) We describe how to represent potential outcomes as counterfactuals [Pearl, 2009, Section 3.6.3]; (2) there is a logical equivalence between both frameworks [Galles and Pearl, 1998, Halpern, 2000]; and (3), we comment on a recently proposed framework [Richardson and Robins, 2013] that brings both worlds closer together.

6.9.2 Relation between Potential Outcomes and SCMs

In SCMs, we can represent potential outcomes using the language of counterfactuals (Section 6.4). In the eye doctor example, the SCM $\mathfrak{C}$ satisfies $T = N_T$ and $B = T \cdot N_B + (1-T) \cdot (1-N_B)$. We can therefore represent each patient by specific values for N_B and N_T. In Table 6.2, for example, patient 43 is characterized by $N_T = 1, N_B = 0$, while patient 44 satisfies $N_T = 0, N_B = 1$. The two terms $t = 0$ and $t = 1$ then correspond to interventions on T. Summarizing, we have that

$$\underbrace{B_u(t=\tilde{t})}_{\text{potential outcome}} \quad = \quad \underbrace{B \text{ in the SCM } \mathfrak{C}|\mathbf{N} = \mathbf{n}_u; do(T := \tilde{t})}_{\text{counterfactual SCM}}, \tag{6.27}$$

where $\mathbf{n}_u$ characterizes unit u [Pearl, 2009, Equation (3.51)]. Since in the counterfactual SCM all noise terms are deterministic, the entailed distribution of B is degenerate, too, and B is deterministic (as required). In the example shown in Table 6.2, we have sampled 200 i.i.d. units using Bernoulli distributions $N_T \sim \text{Ber}(0.6)$ and $N_B \sim \text{Ber}(0.01)$. In this case, SUTVA is satisfied. The i.i.d. assumption implies that the units do not interfere with each other and modularity (intervening on T changes only the structural assignment for T) yields that the way the treatment is taken does not influence the result.

We now discuss a result that shows in what sense both representations in (6.27) are equivalent. For this, we mainly follow the presentation in Pearl [2009, 7.3.1] and Halpern [2000]. The main argumentation is based on the following steps:

1. Define the properties (axioms): (C0)–(C5) and (MP) [Halpern, 2000, Section 3]. Property (C4), for example, states that

   $$T_u(t=\tilde{t}, w=\tilde{w}) = t;$$

   it postulates that setting variable T for unit u to t is "effective."
2. These axioms are satisfied in both representations ("soundness").
3. It can be shown that these properties are complete for counterfactual SCMs. Any counterfactual statement follows from one of these axioms.

4. We can conclude that any theorem that holds for counterfactual SCMs holds in the world of potential outcomes and vice versa.[14] Also, it follows from step 3. that any data set (like that in Table 6.2) satisfying the three axioms could be modeled with a counterfactual SCM.[15]

The two worlds differ, however, in their language. Even if every theorem holds true in both frameworks, some theorems might be "easier" to prove in one world than in the other. Similarly, any assumption that appears in a theorem imposes restrictions on the underlying data-generating process; depending on the application, one formulation might simplify the assessment of these restrictions. Working with settings, in which the average causal effect is zero but the individual causal effects are non-zero, seems to be easier for potential outcomes. The graphical representation of SCMs, on the other hand, might be beneficial to exploit assumptions on the causal relations between random variables.

Richardson and Robins [2013] propose to use **single world intervention graphs**. These graphs allow us to set variables to certain values and therefore construct graphical correspondences to counterfactual variables. These modified graphs allow us to read off conditional independence statements that involve both factual and counterfactual variables. We can therefore see these graphs as a useful tool to translate graphical assumptions into counterfactual statements that are often used by potential outcomes analysts.

6.10 Generalized Structural Causal Models Relating Single Objects

So far, we have studied causal relations among *random variables* $X_1, \dots, X_d$ and focused only on a scenario where the data are i.i.d. observations drawn from $P_{\mathbf{X}}$. We now consider a set $\mathbf{v} = \{x_1, \dots, x_d\}$ of nodes of the causal DAG that consists of any mathematical objects $x_1, \dots, x_d$ formalizing the idea of observations. For instance, after observing similarities among the texts $x_1, \dots, x_d$ written by different authors, one may be interested in the causal relation in the sense of which author has been influenced by which one. Following Steudel et al. [2010], we now de-

[14] Strictly speaking, the "vice versa" requires that the potential outcome framework does not assume more than the axioms mentioned.

[15] If no SCM could possibly generate this data set, this would mean that counterfactuals from SCMs would satisfy another property not implied by the three axioms, namely the property that this data set cannot be generated.

scribe in which sense the underlying DAG also entails conditional independence statements, given an appropriate notion of *information*, without referring to statistical sampling. To this end, we assume that we are given some information function

$$R : 2^{\mathbf{V}} \to \mathbb{R}_0^+,$$

which is monotone in the sense that a set of nodes cannot contain more information than any of its supersets. Then, for any two sets $\mathbf{x}, \mathbf{y} \subseteq \mathbf{v}$ of nodes, the expression $R(\mathbf{x}, \mathbf{y}) - R(\mathbf{y})$ is non-negative and can be interpreted as measuring the conditional information of $\mathbf{x}$, given $\mathbf{y}$. Moreover, we assume that R is such that for any three disjoint sets $\mathbf{x}, \mathbf{y}, \mathbf{z}$ of nodes, the expression

$$I(\mathbf{x} : \mathbf{y} \,|\, \mathbf{z}) := R(\mathbf{x}, \mathbf{z}) + R(\mathbf{y}, \mathbf{z}) - R(\mathbf{x}, \mathbf{y}, \mathbf{z}) - R(\mathbf{z}) \tag{6.28}$$

is non-negative, which is the case if and only if R is submodular (see Section 9.5.2). Then, we can interpret (6.28) as generalized conditional mutual information between $\mathbf{x}$ and $\mathbf{y}$, given $\mathbf{z}$ because $R(\mathbf{x}, \mathbf{z}) - R(\mathbf{z})$ measures the information of $\mathbf{x}$, given $\mathbf{z}$ while $R(\mathbf{x}, \mathbf{y}, \mathbf{z}) - R(\mathbf{y}, \mathbf{z})$ is the information of $\mathbf{x}$, given $\mathbf{y}$ and $\mathbf{z}$. In the same way, conditional mutual information among random variables can be written as a difference of Shannon entropies [Cover and Thomas, 1991]. If (6.28) vanishes, we call $\mathbf{x}$ and $\mathbf{y}$ conditionally independent, given $\mathbf{z}$.

To define generalized SCMs, one introduces unobserved noise objects n_j for each observed node x_j and postulates the following statement.

Principle 6.50 (No additional information) *A node x_j contains no additional information on top of the information contained in its parent nodes $\mathbf{pa}_j$ and the unobserved node n_j, that is,*

$$R(x_j, \mathbf{pa}_j, n_j) = R(\mathbf{pa}_j, n_j).$$

This generalizes the assumption that every random variable X_j is *determined* by its parents and its noise variable, which for discrete random variables amounts to saying that the Shannon entropy of $X_j, \mathbf{PA}_j, N_j$ is the same as the one of $\mathbf{PA}_j, N_j$.

The second crucial assumption of an SCM is the statistical independence of noise terms. The generalized version of this assumption reads as follows:

Principle 6.51 (Independence of unobserved objects) *The unobserved nodes n_j do not contain information about each other, that is,*

$$R(n_1, \ldots, n_d) = \sum_{j=1}^{d} R(n_j).$$

Steudel et al. [2010] prove the following theorem.

Theorem 6.52 (Generalized causal Markov condition) *If both Principles 6.50 and 6.51 hold, then* $\mathbf{x}$ *and* $\mathbf{y}$ *are conditionally independent, given* $\mathbf{z}$ *for any three set of nodes for which* $\mathbf{x}$ *and* $\mathbf{y}$ *are d-separated by* $\mathbf{z}$.

To apply these concepts to the text example, let us consider a text as a collection of its meaningful words and let its information R be the number of different words. Assume that the influence among d texts $x_1, \ldots, x_d$ is given by the following simplified mechanism: the author of x_j takes some of the words from the parent texts of x_j and adds some words from his own ideas. These additional words are given by n_j. Then, Principle 6.50 is satisfied by definition of n_j. According to Principle 6.51, the words added by different authors are assumed to be different. Two texts are conditionally independent, given a third one, if they only have words in common that already appear in the latter. The example shows that reasonable notions of conditional independence can be defined for a much broader class of objects than random variables. To ensure that the causal Markov condition holds with respect to that particular notion of independence, the underlying information measure needs to be appropriate for the respective class of causal mechanisms under consideration in the sense of Principles 6.50 and 6.51.

Janzing and Schölkopf [2010] quantify the information between binary strings using Kolmogorov complexity K with respect to some fixed Turing machine T (see Section 4.1.9). The function K is approximately submodular up to terms of $\mathcal{O}(1)$, that is, an error that does not grow with the size of the considered strings. Then, Janzing and Schölkopf [2010] define an "algorithmic model of causality" where T computes each x_j from its parents and a noise string n_j, which ensures Principle 6.50. Each n_j can also be interpreted as the program that computes x_j from its parents, that is, the mechanism that generates x_j from its direct causes. Then, Principle 6.51 amounts to the independence of the mechanisms (see Principle 2.1).[16] Applying Theorem 6.52 to $R = K$ yields the "algorithmic Markov condition" [Janzing and Schölkopf, 2010]: whenever $\mathbf{x}$ and $\mathbf{y}$ are d-separated by $\mathbf{z}$, knowing $\mathbf{y}$ does not admit a shorter description of $\mathbf{x}$ with respect to a Turing machine that gets $\mathbf{z}$ as free background information.

On a higher level, this addresses a deep problem of causal reasoning: the statement "dependences between observations only occur if they are causally related"

[16]This way, the second and the third branch of Figure 2.2 can be seen to coincide. The string n_j encodes the mechanism (i.e., the program running on the Turing machine), and at the same time it is the analog of the noise term in the statistical setting.

(a generalization of Principle 1.1) only holds if the dependence measure is appropriate for the class of observations and the class of potential causal mechanisms under consideration. For instance, after observing that the height of a child has increased during the past decade, and, at the same time, the value of some stock has increased, one would not infer them to be causally related because growth is a property that many time series share without being causally related. Only if two time series share more sophisticated patterns of different growth (and/or decrease), do we ask for the common reason behind the similarity. Since non-stationary time series are ubiquitous, it would be interesting to find information measures for which we believe dependences to indicate causal relations (after sufficiently accounting for multiple testing issues if the time series were found by searching over large databases). Speaking from a more applied machine learning perspective, the problem leads us to construct appropriate *features* for which similarities in feature space indicate causal relations.

6.11 Algorithmic Independence of Conditionals

Section 6.10 shows that causal structures not only imply statistical (conditional) independences, but also independences with respect to other (non-statistical) information measures. We have further seen that the Markov condition can also be stated for *algorithmic* information. Then the most elementary implication of the algorithmic Markov condition is an analogy of Reichenbach's principle for algorithmic dependences. Two objects can only be algorithmically dependent when they have a common cause or when one of it influences the other [Janzing and Schölkopf, 2010]. This is because they are otherwise d-separated by the empty set and thus independent. Likewise, d objects $x_1, \ldots, x_d$ that are causally unrelated are jointly algorithmically independent, that is,

$$K(x_1, \ldots, x_d) \stackrel{+}{=} \sum_{j=1}^{d} K(x_j). \tag{6.29}$$

One can also call the difference between the left- and right-hand sides multi-information (in analogy to the corresponding terminology in statistical information theory) and write the joint independence as

$$I(x_1, x_2, \cdots, x_d) \stackrel{+}{=} 0. \tag{6.30}$$

Then, joint independence implies also independence of every subset. For instance, if the joint description of x_1, x_2 is shorter than the separate description of x_1 and

x_2, then the joint description of $x_1, \ldots, x_d$ is automatically shorter than the separate descriptions of all x_j and thus (6.30) implies

$$I(x_1 : x_2) \stackrel{+}{=} 0.$$

If we assume now that the conditionals[17] $P_{X_j|\mathbf{PA}_j}$ in a causal graphical model are "independently chosen by nature," then we conclude that they are jointly algorithmically independent [Janzing and Schölkopf, 2010, Lemeire and Janzing, 2013] and state the multivariate version of Principle 4.13.

Principle 6.53 (Algorithmic independence of conditionals (AIC)) *The causal conditionals described by the Markov kernels in a causal Bayesian network as in Definition 6.21 (iii) are algorithmically independent, that is,*

$$I(P_{X_1|\mathbf{PA}_1}, P_{X_2|\mathbf{PA}_2}, \cdots, P_{X_d|\mathbf{PA}_d}) \stackrel{+}{=} 0, \tag{6.31}$$

or equivalently,

$$K(P_{X_1,\ldots,X_d}) \stackrel{+}{=} \sum_{j=1}^{d} K(P_{X_j|PA_j}). \tag{6.32}$$

Note that Principle 6.53 must not be confused with the algorithmic Markov condition discussed in Section 6.10. While the latter refers to causal relations among n single objects without referring to statistical sampling, the former still assumes the traditional i.i.d. setting with n random variables and only states an additional inference principle.

As for the bivariate case, the equivalence of (6.31) and (6.32) is immediate because describing the joint distribution is equivalent to describing all the causal Markov kernels. In other words, AIC states that the shortest description of the joint distribution is given by separate descriptions of the causal Markov kernels.

Causal faithfulness and AIC are related in spirit and often yield similar conclusions. To discuss similarities and differences, we revisit Example 6.34. Since the parameter a describes $P_{Y|X}$ and the parameters (b,c) describe the conditionals $P_{Z|X,Y}$, we have

$$I(P_{Y|X} : P_{Z|X,Y}) \stackrel{+}{\geq} I(a : (b,c)). \tag{6.33}$$

This is because the algorithmic mutual information between two objects cannot be increased by restricting the attention to some of their "aspects"; see, for example,

[17] As stated before, we use the notation $P_{Y|\mathbf{X}}$ as a shorthand for the collection $(P_{Y|\mathbf{X}=\mathbf{x}})_{\mathbf{x}}$ of conditional distributions.

Janzing and Schölkopf [2010, Lemma 6]. The "non-generic" independence $X \perp\!\!\!\perp Z$ occurs when the structure coefficients of the linear model satisfy

$$a \cdot b + c = 0. \tag{6.34}$$

Then $K(a|b,c) \stackrel{+}{=} 0$ because a can be computed from b,c via a program of length $\mathcal{O}(1)$. Thus,

$$I(a:(b,c)) \stackrel{+}{=} K(a) - K(a|(b,c)^*) \stackrel{+}{=} K(a).$$

We conclude that AIC is violated whenever $K(a)$ is significantly larger than 0. For a generic real number a, $K(a)$ grows logarithmically with the desired (relative) accuracy. Then AIC rejects the corresponding causal DAG because (6.34) is considered an unlikely coincidence.

We have to explain the phrase "whenever $K(a)$ is significantly larger than 0" because it amounts to a conceptual difference between AIC and faithfulness. Assume, for instance, that $b = c$ and $a = -1$. Then (6.34) is satisfied, yet the description of a does not get shorter when b and c are known because $K(a)$ is already negligible. Therefore, that AIC is not violated despite (6.34) seems to indicate fine-tuning of parameters. Following Lemeire and Janzing [2013], we now argue why we consider not rejecting *this* kind of tuning as a *feature* of AIC rather than as a flaw. The idea is that structure coefficients ± 1 (up to some given precision) occur much more often in nature than some "more generic" value such as 2.36724.... For instance, spending some money S decreases the amount A of available money by $-S$. The causal relation between S and A is thus described by[18] the structure coefficient -1. Implicitly, AIC and our argument are based on a prior that considers values with short description length as more likely (in agreement with Solomonoff's theory of inductive inference [Solomonoff, 1964]).

Another feature of AIC is that it also rejects *almost* cancellation of different paths: assume, for instance, that a is very close to $-c/b$. To estimate $I(a:(b,c))$ in this case, we observe

$$I(a:(b,c)) \stackrel{+}{\geq} I(a:(c/b))$$

and use the following idea. The algorithmic mutual information of two integers n, m that are close to each other is typically about $\log n/|m-n|$ because describing

[18] The example suggests that structure coefficients being simple is often a result of how we define variables rather than being a property of "nature." In general, one may wonder to what extent we *define* variables in a way that yields *simple* causal relations.

n after m is known requires about $\log|n-m|$ bits, while it requires about $\log n$ bits otherwise. After arbitrarily fine discretization, we may then represent a and c/b by integers and take $\log[a/(a+c/b)]$ as a rough estimation for the algorithmic mutual information between $P_{Y|X}$ and $P_{Z|X,Y}$.

6.12 Problems

Problem 6.54 (DAGs) *Table B.1 on page 223 states that for three nodes there are 25 DAGs. Why is this the case?*

Problem 6.55 (Multivariate SCMs) *Consider the following SCM $\mathfrak{C}$*

$$\begin{aligned}
V &:= N_V \\
W &:= -2V + 3Y + 5Z + N_W \\
X &:= 2V + N_X \\
Y &:= -X + N_Y \\
Z &:= \alpha X + N_Z
\end{aligned}$$

with $N_V, N_W, N_X, N_Y, N_Z \overset{iid}{\sim} \mathcal{N}(0,1)$.

a) *Draw the graph corresponding to the SCM.*

b) *Set $\alpha = 2$ and simulate 200 i.i.d. data points from the joint distribution; plot the values of X and W to visualize the distribution $P^{\mathfrak{C}}_{X,W}$.*

c) *Again, set $\alpha = 2$ and sample 200 i.i.d. data points from the intervention distribution*

$$P^{\mathfrak{C};do(X:=3)}_{X,W}$$

in which we have intervened on X. Again, plot the sample and compare with the plot from part b.

d) *A directed path from one node to another does not necessarily imply that the former node has a causal effect on the latter. Choose a value of α and prove that for this value X, has no causal effect on W.*

e) *For any given α, compute*

$$\frac{\partial}{\partial x}\mathbb{E}^{\mathfrak{C};do(X:=x)}[W].$$

Problem 6.56 (Interventions) *Consider the SCM*

$$\begin{aligned} X &:= N_X \\ Y &:= (X-4)^2 + N_Y \\ Z &:= X^2 + Y^2 + N_Z \end{aligned}$$

with $N_X, N_Y, N_Z \overset{iid}{\sim} \mathcal{N}(0,1)$. *You may intervene on either* X *or* Y. *Which hard intervention yields the smallest expected value of* Z*?*

Problem 6.57 (Minimality) *We have stated in Remark 6.6 that causal minimality (Definition 6.33) implies structural minimality.*

a) Convince yourself that this is shown by Proposition 6.49.

b) Provide an example of an SCM that satisfies structural minimality but violates causal minimality.

Problem 6.58 (Causal Minimality) *Consider a causal graphical model with a distribution that has a strictly positive, continuous density and for which causal minimality is violated. According to Proposition 6.36, we can then remove an "inactive" edge from the graph and obtain a new causal graphical model. Prove that the two models are interventionally equivalent.*

Problem 6.59 (Interventional equivalence) *Consider two SCMs* $\mathfrak{C}_1$ *and* $\mathfrak{C}_2$ *of the form*

$$\begin{aligned} X &:= N_X \\ Y &:= X + N_Y \\ Z &:= f_j(X,Y) + N_Z \end{aligned}$$

with $N_X, N_Y, N_Z \overset{iid}{\sim} \mathcal{U}(-1,1)$*, a continuous uniform distribution between* -1 *and* 1. *Choose the functions* f_1 *and* f_2 *such that* $\mathfrak{C}_1$ *and* $\mathfrak{C}_2$ *are observationally equivalent, and agree on all single node interventions, but disagree on simultaneous interventions on several nodes. This problem shows that Proposition 6.48 does not need to be true if the density is not strictly positive.*

Problem 6.60 (Cyclic SCMs) *Prove that whenever the absolute values of the eigenvalues of a square matrix* B *are strictly smaller than* 1 *(i.e., the spectral radius of* B *is strictly smaller than* 1*), then* $I - B$ *is invertible.*

Problem 6.61 (Cyclic SCMs) *Consider the assignment* $\mathbf{X} := B\mathbf{X} + \mathbf{N}$, *as described in Remark 6.5. Prove that if the spectral radius of B is strictly smaller than* 1, *then* $\mathbf{X}^t$ *defined by* $\mathbf{X}^t := B\mathbf{X}^{t-1} + \mathbf{N}$ *in Equation* (6.3) *converges in distribution against* $\mathbf{X} := (I - B)^{-1}\mathbf{N}$ *as defined in Equation* (6.2).

Problem 6.62 (*d*-separation) *Prove that one can d-separate any two nodes in a DAG* $\mathcal{G}$ *that are not directly connected by an edge. Use this statement to prove Proposition 6.35.*

Problem 6.63 (Covariate adjustment) *Assume that* $\mathbf{Z}$ *is a valid adjustment set for the causal effect from* $\mathbf{X}$ *to* Y *and that* $(Y, \mathbf{X}, \mathbf{Z})$ *has a (zero mean) Gaussian distribution with*

$$\mathbb{E}[Y \,|\, X = x, \mathbf{Z} = \mathbf{z}] = ax + \mathbf{b}^t\mathbf{z}.$$

Prove that

$$\frac{\partial}{\partial x}\,\mathbb{E}^{\mathfrak{C};do(X:=x)}[Y] \;=\; a;$$

in other words, prove Equation (6.20) *using Equations* (6.19) *and* (6.13). *This result allows us to consistently estimate the causal effect a by regressing Y on X and* $\mathbf{Z}$.

Problem 6.64 (Covariate adjustment) *Prove the parent adjustment and the backdoor criterion Proposition 6.41 (i) and (ii) using Equation* (6.17).

Problem 6.65 (Covariate adjustment) *Prove the frontdoor criterion* (6.23) *starting with*

$$p^{\mathfrak{C};do(X:=x)}(y) = \sum_z p^{\mathfrak{C};do(X:=x)}(y \,|\, z, x)\, p^{\mathfrak{C};do(X:=x)}(z)$$

and then using rules 2 and 3 from do-calculus (Section 6.7).

7

Learning Multivariate Causal Models

As in Chapter 4, we now turn to the problem of learning causal models. We first discuss different assumptions under which (parts of) the graph structure can be recovered from the joint distribution in Section 7.1 ("structure identifiability"). Some of these results carry over from the bivariate setting discussed earlier. As in the bivariate case, there is no complete characterization of identifiability assumptions, and future research may reveal promising alternatives. In Section 7.2, we then introduce methods and algorithms, such as independence-based and score-based methods, that estimate the graph from a finite data set ("structure identification").

As in the bivariate setting, we are again facing the problem that the class of SCMs is too flexible. Given a distribution $P_{\mathbf{X}}$ over random variables $\mathbf{X} = (X_1, \ldots, X_d)$, can different SCMs entail this distribution? This question is answered by the following proposition: indeed, usually for many different graph structures, there is an SCM that induces the distribution $P_{\mathbf{X}}$.[1]

Proposition 7.1 (Non-uniqueness of graph structures) *Consider a random vector $\mathbf{X} = (X_1, \ldots, X_d)$ with distribution $P_{\mathbf{X}}$ that has a density with respect to Lebesgue measure and assume it is Markovian with respect to $\mathcal{G}$. Then there exists an SCM $\mathfrak{C} = (\mathbf{S}, P_{\mathbf{N}})$ with graph $\mathcal{G}$ that entails the distribution $P_{\mathbf{X}}$.*

Proof. See Appendix C.9. □

In particular, given any complete DAG, we can find a corresponding SCM that entails the distribution at hand. As in the bivariate case, it is therefore apparent

[1] Statements similar to Proposition 7.1 can be found in Druzdzel and Simon [1993] and Druzdzel and van Leijen [2001].

that we require further assumptions to obtain identifiability results. The following section discusses some of those assumptions.

7.1 Structure Identifiability

7.1.1 Faithfulness

If the distribution $P_{\mathbf{X}}$ is Markovian and faithful with respect to the underlying DAG $\mathcal{G}^0$, we have a one-to-one correspondence between d-separation statements in the graph $\mathcal{G}^0$ and the corresponding conditional independence statements in the distribution. All graphs outside the correct Markov equivalence class of $\mathcal{G}^0$ can therefore be rejected because they impose a set of d-separations that does not equal the set of conditional independences in $P_{\mathbf{X}}$. Since both the Markov condition and faithfulness put restrictions *only* on the conditional independences in the joint distribution, it is also clear that we are not able to distinguish between two Markov equivalent graphs, that is, between two graphs that entail exactly the same set of conditional independences (see for example Figure 6.4 on page 103). Summarizing, under the Markov condition and faithfulness, the Markov equivalence class of $\mathcal{G}^0$, represented by CPDAG($\mathcal{G}^0$), is identifiable from $P_{\mathbf{X}}$ [e.g., Spirtes et al., 2000].

Lemma 7.2 (Identifiability of Markov equivalence class) *Assume that $P_{\mathbf{X}}$ is Markovian and faithful with respect to $\mathcal{G}^0$. Then, for each graph $\mathcal{G} \in CPDAG(\mathcal{G}^0)$, we find an SCM that entails the distribution $P_{\mathbf{X}}$. Furthermore, there is no graph $\mathcal{G}$ with $\mathcal{G} \notin CPDAG(\mathcal{G}^0)$, such that $P_{\mathbf{X}}$ is Markovian and faithful with respect to $\mathcal{G}$.*

Proof. The first statement is a direct implication from Proposition 7.1, and the second statement follows from the definitions of Markov equivalence, seen in Definition 6.24. □

Independence-based methods (also called constraint-based methods) assume that the distribution is Markovian and faithful with respect to the underlying graph and then estimate the correct Markov equivalence class; see Section 7.2.1.

We have seen in Example 6.42 that for Gaussian distributions the causal effect can be summarized by a single number (6.20). If instead of the correct graph, we only know the Markov equivalence class of that graph, this quantity is not identifiable anymore. It is possible, however, to provide bounds [Maathuis et al., 2009].

7.1.2 Additive Noise Models

Proposition 7.1 shows that a given distribution could have been entailed from several SCMs with different graphs. For many of these graph structures, however, the functions f_j appearing in the structural assignments are rather complicated. It turns out that we obtain non-trivial identifiability results if we do not allow for arbitrarily complex functions, that is, if we restrict the function class. As we have already seen in Chapter 4, we will assume in the following Sections 7.1.4 and 7.1.5 that the noise acts in an additive way.

Definition 7.3 (ANMs) *We call an SCM $\mathfrak{C}$ an ANM if the structural assignments are of the form*

$$X_j := f_j(\mathbf{PA}_j) + N_j, \qquad j = 1, \ldots, d, \tag{7.1}$$

that is, if the noise is additive. For simplicity, we further assume that the functions f_j are differentiable and the noise variables N_j have a strictly positive density.[2]

Some of the following identifiability results assume causal minimality (Definition 6.33). For ANMs, this means that each function f_j is not constant in any of its arguments. Intuitively, the function should really "depend" on its arguments. The proof of the following proposition is provided in Appendix C.10.

Proposition 7.4 (Causal minimality and ANMs) *Consider a distribution induced by a model (7.1) and assume that the functions f_j are not constant in any of its arguments, that is, for all j and $i \in \mathbf{PA}_j$ there is some value $\mathbf{pa}_{j,-i}$ of the variables $\mathbf{PA}_j \setminus \{i\}$ and some $x_i \neq x_i'$ such that*

$$f_j(\mathbf{pa}_{j,-i}, x_i) \neq f_j(\mathbf{pa}_{j,-i}, x_i').$$

Then the joint distribution satisfies causal minimality with respect to the corresponding graph. Conversely, if there are nodes j and i such that for all $\mathbf{pa}_{j,-i}$ the function $f_j(\mathbf{pa}_{j,-i}, \cdot)$ is constant, causal minimality is violated.

We have argued in Remark 6.6 that we can restrict ourselves to functions that are not constant in one of their arguments; see Proposition 6.49. We have now seen that for ANMs with fully supported noise, this restriction implies causal minimality.

Given the restricted class of SCMs described in (7.1), do we obtain full structure identifiability? Again, the answer is negative. Theorem 4.2 and Problem 7.13

[2]These two conditions guarantee that the joint distribution over $X_1, \ldots, X_d$ allows for a strictly positive density, for example.

Type of structural assignment		Condition on funct.	DAG identif.	See
(General) SCM:	$X_j := f_j(X_{\mathbf{PA}_j}, N_j)$	—	✗	Prop. 7.1
ANM:	$X_j := f_j(X_{\mathbf{PA}_j}) + N_j$	nonlinear	✓	Thm. 7.7(i)
CAM:	$X_j := \sum_{k \in \mathbf{PA}_j} f_{jk}(X_k) + N_j$	nonlinear	✓	Thm. 7.7(ii)
Linear Gaussian:	$X_j := \sum_{k \in \mathbf{PA}_j} \beta_{jk} X_k + N_j$	linear	✗	Problem 7.13
Lin. G., eq. error var.:	$X_j := \sum_{k \in \mathbf{PA}_j} \beta_{jk} X_k + N_j$	linear	✓	Prop. 7.5

Table 7.1: Summary of some known identifiability results for Gaussian noise. Results for non-Gaussian noise identifiability results are available, too, but they are more technical.

show that if the distribution is induced by a linear Gaussian SCM, for example, we cannot necessarily recover the correct graph. It turns out, however, that this case is exceptional in the following sense. For almost all other combinations of functions and distributions, we obtain identifiability. All the nonidentifiable cases have been characterized [Zhang and Hyvärinen, 2009, Peters et al., 2014]. Another non-identifiable example different from the linear Gaussian case is shown in the right plot in Figure 4.2. Its details can be found in Peters et al. [2014, Example 25]. Table 7.1 shows some of the known identifiability results.

Let us mention again that there are several extensions to the framework of ANMs. For example, Zhang and Hyvärinen [2009] allow for a post-nonlinear transformation of the variables and Peters et al. [2011a] consider ANMs for discrete variables.

In general, nonlinear ANMs are not closed under marginalization. That is, if $P_{X,Y,Z}$ allows for ANMs from X to Y and from Y to Z, $P_{X,Z}$ does not necessarily allow for an ANM from X to Z. This may restrict the applicability of ANMs in practice, since one may not observe intermediate variables on a causal path. For experiments in physics, one could argue that every influence is propagated via infinitely many intermediate variables. Thus, there is no absolute notion of direct or indirect effect (instead, it must always be relative to the observed set). In this sense, ANMs can only be taken as good approximations.

In the following three subsections, we will look at three specific identifiable examples in more detail: the linear Gaussian case with equal error variances (Section 7.1.3), the linear non-Gaussian case (Section 7.1.4), and the nonlinear Gaussian case (Section 7.1.5). Although more general results are available [Peters et al., 2014], we concentrate on those two examples because for them precise conditions can be stated easily. We omit proofs and concentrate on the statements. Most of the proofs can be based on the techniques developed in Peters et al. [2011b]. They allow many of the bivariate identifiability results that we developed in Chapter 4 to carry over to the multivariate setting.

7.1.3 Linear Gaussian Models with Equal Error Variances

There is another deviation from linear Gaussian SEMs that makes the graph identifiable. Peters and Bühlmann [2014] show that restricting the noise variables to have the same variance is sufficient to recover the graph structure. The proof can be found in Peters and Bühlmann [2014].

Proposition 7.5 (Identifiability with equal error variances) *Consider an SCM with graph $\mathcal{G}_0$ and assignments*

$$X_j := \sum_{k \in \mathbf{PA}_j^{\mathcal{G}_0}} \beta_{jk} X_k + N_j, \qquad j = 1, \ldots, d,$$

where all N_j are i.i.d. and follow a Gaussian distribution. In particular, the noise variance σ^2 does not depend on j. Additionally, for each $j \in \{1, \ldots, p\}$ we require $\beta_{jk} \neq 0$ for all $k \in \mathbf{PA}_j^{\mathcal{G}_0}$. Then, the graph $\mathcal{G}_0$ is identifiable from the joint distribution.

For estimating the coefficients β_{jk} (and therefore the graph structure) Peters and Bühlmann [2014] propose to use a penalized maximum likelihood score based on the Bayesian information criterion (BIC); see also Section 7.2.2, and a greedy search algorithm in the space of DAGs. Rescaling the variables changes the variance of the error terms. Therefore, in many applications, model (7.2) cannot be sensibly applied. The BIC, however, allows us to compare the method's score with the score of a linear Gaussian SCM that uses more parameters and does not make the assumption of equal error variances.

7.1.4 Linear Non-Gaussian Acyclic Models

Shimizu et al. [2006] prove the following statement using independent component analysis (ICA) [Comon, 1994, Theorem 11], which itself is proved using the Darmois-Skitovič theorem.

Theorem 7.6 (Identifiability of LiNGAMs) *Consider an SCM with graph $\mathcal{G}_0$ and assignments*

$$X_j := \sum_{k \in \mathbf{PA}_j^{\mathcal{G}_0}} \beta_{jk} X_k + N_j, \qquad j = 1, \ldots, d, \tag{7.2}$$

where all N_j are jointly independent and non-Gaussian distributed with strictly *positive density.*[3] *Additionally, for each* $j \in \{1,\ldots,p\}$, *we require* $\beta_{jk} \neq 0$ *for all* $k \in \mathbf{PA}_j^{\mathcal{G}_0}$. *Then, the graph* $\mathcal{G}_0$ *is identifiable from the joint distribution.*

The authors call this model a LiNGAM. As mentioned in Section 4.1.3, there is an alternative proof for Theorem 7.6: Theorem 28 in Peters et al. [2014] extends bivariate identifiability results such as Theorem 4.2 to the multivariate case. This trick is also used for nonlinear additive models (by extending Theorem 4.5).

7.1.5 Nonlinear Gaussian Additive Noise Models

We have seen that the graph structure of an ANM becomes identifiable if the assignments are linear and the noise variables are non-Gaussian. Alternatively, we can also exploit nonlinearity. The result is easiest to state with Gaussian noise:

Theorem 7.7 (Identifiability of nonlinear Gaussian ANMs)

(i) Let $P_{\mathbf{X}} = P_{X_1,\ldots,X_d}$ *be induced by an SCM with*

$$X_j := f_j(\mathbf{PA}_j) + N_j,$$

with normally distributed noise variables $N_j \sim \mathcal{N}(0,\sigma_j^2)$ *and three times differentiable functions* f_j *that are not linear in any component in the following sense. Denote the parents* $\mathbf{PA}_j$ *of* X_j *by* $X_{k_1},\ldots,X_{k_\ell}$, *then the function* $f_j(x_{k_1},\ldots,x_{k_{a-1}},\cdot,x_{k_{a+1}},\ldots,x_{k_\ell})$ *is assumed to be nonlinear for all a and some* $x_{k_1},\ldots,x_{k_{a-1}},x_{k_{a+1}},\ldots,x_{k_\ell} \in \mathbb{R}^{\ell-1}$.

(ii) As a special case, let $P_{\mathbf{X}} = P_{X_1,\ldots,X_d}$ *be induced by an SCM with*

$$X_j := \sum_{k \in \mathbf{PA}_j} f_{j,k}(X_k) + N_j, \tag{7.3}$$

with normally distributed noise variables $N_j \sim \mathcal{N}(0,\sigma_j^2)$ *and three times differentiable, nonlinear functions* $f_{j,k}$. *This model is known as a causal additive model (CAM).*

In both cases (i) and (ii), we can identify the corresponding graph $\mathcal{G}_0$ *from the distribution* $P_{\mathbf{X}}$. *The statements remain true if the noise distributions for source nodes, that is, nodes without parents, are allowed to have a non-Gaussian density with full support on the real line* $\mathbb{R}$ *(the proof remains identical).*

The proof can be found in Peters et al. [2014, Corollary 31].

[3] The condition of a strictly positive density can be weakened (see details of the proof of ICA), but it is certainly necessary to assume that the noise variables are non-degenerate, for example.

7.1.6 Observational and Experimental Data

We have already seen in Section 6.3 that knowing causal relations can help improve predictions when the underlying distribution changes. We will now turn this idea around and show how observing the system in different environments can be used to learn causal relations. We therefore turn to the following setup, in which we observe data from different environments $e \in \mathcal{E}$. The corresponding model reads

$$\mathbf{X}^e = (X_1^e, \dots, X_d^e) \sim P^e,$$

where each variable X_j^e denotes the same (physical) quantity, measured in environment $e \in \mathcal{E}$. We will talk about a variable X_j in different environments, which is a slight abuse of notation.

Known Intervention Targets A first type of method assumes that the different environments stem from different interventional settings. In the case that the intervention targets $\mathcal{I}^e \subseteq \{1, \dots, d\}$ are known, several methods have been proposed. Tian and Pearl [2001] and Hauser and Bühlmann [2012], for example, assume faithfulness and consider mechanism changes and stochastic interventions, respectively. They define and characterize the interventional equivalence classes of graphs: that is, the class of graphs that can explain the given distributions. For mechanism changes, for example, we can include an intervention node into the model whose children are the variables that are intervened on. This way we increase the number of v-structures and two graphs become intervention equivalent (with respect to the given distributions) if they have the same skeletons and v-structures, and the nodes that are intervened on have the same parents [cf. Tian and Pearl, 2001, Theorem 2]. Eberhardt et al. [2010] allow for hard and stochastic interventions even in the presence of cycles.

Hyttinen et al. [2012] analyze conditions on the interventions under which the graph becomes identifiable. Eberhardt et al. [2005] and Hauser and Bühlmann [2014] investigate how many intervention experiments are necessary in the worst case to identify the graph.

Different Environments Let us now turn to a slightly different setting, in which we do not try to learn the whole causal structure. Instead, we consider a target variable Y with a set of d predictors $\mathbf{X}$ and try to learn which of the predictors are the causal parents of Y. Both $\mathbf{X}$ and Y are observed in different environments $e \in \mathcal{E}$ (which could be intervention settings with unknown targets). That is, we have

$$(\mathbf{X}^e, Y^e) \sim P_{\mathbf{X}^e, Y^e} =: P^e$$

for $e \in \mathcal{E}$. The key assumption is the existence of an unknown set $\mathbf{PA}_Y \subseteq \{1,\ldots,d\}$ (one may think of the direct causes of Y) such that the conditional Y given $\mathbf{PA}_Y$ is invariant over all environments, that is, for all $e, f \in \mathcal{E}$ we have

$$P_{Y^e \,|\, \mathbf{PA}_Y^e} = P_{Y^f \,|\, \mathbf{PA}_Y^f}.$$

This assumption is satisfied if the distributions are induced by an underlying SCM and the different environments correspond to different intervention distributions, for which Y has not been intervened on [Peters et al., 2016] (see Code Snippet 7.11 for an example). Having said that, the setting is more general and the environments do not need to correspond to interventions; one does not even require an underlying SCM. One can consider the collection $\mathcal{S}$ of all sets $S \subseteq \{1,\ldots,d\}$ of variables that lead to "invariant prediction," that is, for all $e, f \in \mathcal{E}$ and for all $S \in \mathcal{S}$, we have

$$P_{Y^e \,|\, S^e} = P_{Y^f \,|\, S^f}. \tag{7.4}$$

Here, $Y^e \,|\, S^e$ is shorthand notation for $Y^e \,|\, \mathbf{X}_S^e$. It is not difficult to see (Problem 7.15) that the variables appearing in *all* those sets $S \in \mathcal{S}$ must be direct causes of Y:

$$\bigcap_{S \in \mathcal{S}} S \subseteq \mathbf{PA}_Y, \tag{7.5}$$

where we define the intersection over an empty index set as the empty set. Peters et al. [2016] consider the left-hand side of (7.5) as an estimate for $\mathbf{PA}_Y$. (7.5) then guarantees that any variable contained in the output of this method is indeed in $\mathbf{PA}_Y$. In the special case of SCMs and interventions, there are sufficient conditions [Peters et al., 2016] under which $\mathbf{PA}_Y$ becomes identifiable, in other words, (7.5) is an equality. Interestingly, the method we present in Section 7.2.5 realizes whether the data come from such an identifiable case, it does not need to assume it.

Tian and Pearl [2001] also address the question of identifiability with unknown intervention targets. They do not specify a target variable and focus on changes in marginal distributions rather than conditionals.

7.2 Methods for Structure Identification

We have seen several assumptions that lead to (partial) identifiability of the causal structure. The purpose of this section is to show how these assumptions can be exploited to provide estimators of the underlying graph from a finite amount of data (see Figure 7.1 for two examples). We provide an overview of methods and try to focus on their ideas. There is a large pool of methods, and we believe that future research needs to show which of these methods will prove to be most useful in practice. We nevertheless try to highlight some of the methods' potential problems and most crucial assumptions. Although some papers study the consistency of the presented methodology, we omit most of those results and present ideas only. Subtleties of algorithmic implementation will not be discussed either, and we would like to refer the interested reader to the references we provide. Kalisch et al. [2012] maintain the software package `pcalg` for R [R Core Team, 2016] that contains code not only for the PC (for the inventors Peter Spirtes and Clark Glymour) algorithm (see Section 7.2.1), but also for many of the described methods.

Before providing more details about the existing methodology, we would like to add two comments first: (1) While there are several simulation studies available, a topic that receives little attention is the question of a loss function. Given the true underlying causal structure, how "good" is an estimated causal graph? In practice, one often uses variants of the structural Hamming distance [Acid and de Campos, 2003, Tsamardinos et al., 2006], which counts the number of misspecified edges. As an alternative, Peters and Bühlmann [2015] suggest evaluating the graph based on its ability to predict intervention distributions. (2) Some of the methods that we present assume that the structural assignments (6.1) and the corresponding functions f_j in particular are simple. Often, those methods do provide estimates not only for the causal structure but also for the corresponding assignments, which can usually be used to compute residuals, too. In principle, and under this model, we can then test the strong assumption of mutually independent noise variables (Definition 3.1), for example, by applying a mutual independence test [e.g., Pfister et al., 2017]; see Section 4.2.1 for statistical subtleties of such a procedure.

7.2.1 Independence-Based Methods

Independence-based methods such as the inductive causation (IC) algorithm, the SGS (for the inventors Spirtes, Glymour, and Scheines) algorithm, and the PC algorithm assume that the distribution is faithful to the underlying DAG. This renders the Markov equivalence class, that is, the corresponding CPDAG, identifiable (see Section 7.1.1). There is a one-to-one correspondence between d-separations in the graph and conditional independences in $P_{\mathbf{X}}$. Any query of a d-separation statement can therefore be answered by checking the corresponding conditional independence test. We first assume that an oracle provides us with the correct answers to the conditional independence questions and discuss some finite sample issues in the paragraph "Conditional Independence Tests."

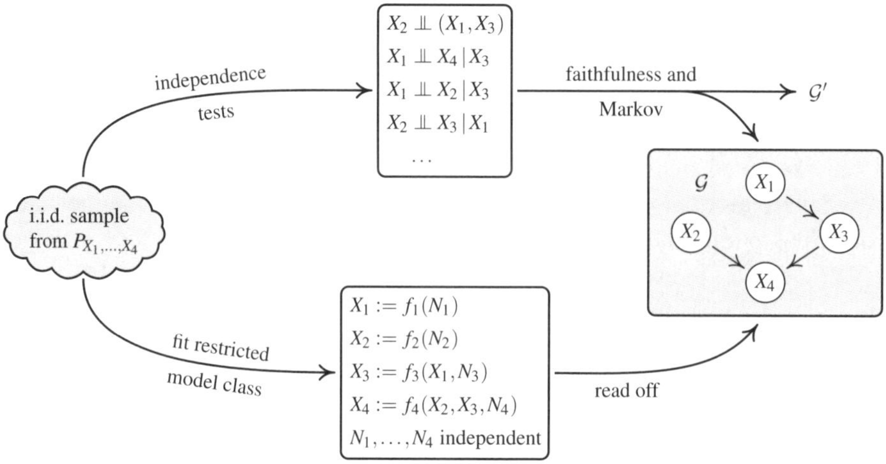

Figure 7.1: The figure summarizes two approaches for the identification of causal structures. Independence-based methods (top) test for conditional independences in the data; these properties are related to the graph structure by the Markov condition and faithfulness. Often, the graph is not uniquely identifiable; the method may therefore output different graphs $\mathcal{G}$ and $\mathcal{G}'$. Alternatively, one may restrict the model class and fit the SCM directly (bottom).

Estimation of Skeleton Most independence-based methods first estimate the skeleton, that is, the undirected edges, and orient as many edges as possible afterward. For the skeleton search, the following lemma is useful to know [see Verma and Pearl, 1991, Lemma 1].

Lemma 7.8 *The following two statements hold.*

(i) Two nodes X, Y in a DAG $(\mathbf{X}, \mathcal{E})$ are adjacent if and only if they cannot be d-separated by any subset $S \subseteq \mathbf{V} \setminus \{X, Y\}$.

(ii) If two nodes X, Y in a DAG $(\mathbf{X}, \mathcal{E})$ are not adjacent, then they are d-separated by either $\mathbf{PA}_X$ or $\mathbf{PA}_Y$.

Using Lemma 7.8(i), we have that if two variables are always dependent, no matter what other variables one conditions on, these two variables must be adjacent. This result is used in the **IC algorithm** [Pearl, 2009] and in the **SGS algorithm** [Spirtes et al., 2000]. For each pair of nodes (X, Y), these methods search through all possible subsets $\mathbf{A} \subseteq \mathbf{X} \setminus \{X, Y\}$ of variables neither containing X nor Y and check whether X and Y are d-separated given $\mathbf{A}$. After all those tests, X and Y are adjacent if and only if no set $\mathbf{A}$ was found that d-separates X and Y.

Searching through all possible subsets $\mathbf{A}$ does not seem optimal, especially if the graph is sparse. The **PC algorithm** [Spirtes et al., 2000] starts with a fully connected undirected graph and step-by-step increases the size of the conditioning set $\mathbf{A}$, starting with $\#\mathbf{A} = 0$. At iteration k, it considers sets $\mathbf{A}$ of size $\#\mathbf{A} = k$, using the following neat trick: to test whether X and Y can be d-separated, one only has to go through sets $\mathbf{A}$ that are subsets either of the neighbors of X or of the neighbors of Y; this idea is based on Lemma 7.8(ii) and clearly improves the computation time, especially for sparse graphs.

Orientation of Edges Lemma 6.25 suggests that we should be able to orient the immoralities (or v-structures) in the graph. If two nodes are not directly connected in the obtained skeleton, there is a set that d-separates these nodes. Suppose that the skeleton contains the structure $X - Z - Y$ with no direct edge between X and Y; further, let $\mathbf{A}$ be a set that d-separates X and Y. The structure $X - Z - Y$ is an immorality and can therefore be oriented as $X \rightarrow Z \leftarrow Y$ if and only if $Z \notin \mathbf{A}$. After the orientation of immoralities, we may be able to orient some further edges in order to avoid cycles, for example. There is a set of such orientation rules that has been shown to be complete and is known as Meek's orientation rules [Meek, 1995].

Satisfiability Methods An alternative to the graphical approach just described is to formulate causal learning as a satisfiability (SAT) problem [Triantafillou et al., 2010]. First, one formulates graphical relations as Boolean variables, such as $A :=$ *"There is a direct edge from X to Y."* The non-trivial part is then to translate the independence statements (we still assume that they are provided by an independence oracle), as d-separation statements into "formulas" that involve Boolean variables and the operators "and" and "or." The SAT question then asks whether we can assign a value "true" or "false" to each of the Boolean variables to make the overall formula true. SAT solvers not only check whether this is the case but also provide us with the information as to whether in all of the assignments that make the overall formula true, certain variables are always assigned to the same value. For example, the d-separation statements may be satisfied by different graph structures that correspond to different assignments, but if in all such assignments the Boolean variable A from above takes the value "true," we can infer that in the underlying graph, X must be a parent of Y. Even though the Boolean SAT problem is known to be nondeterministic polynomial time (NP)-complete [Cook, 1971, Levin, 1973], that is, it is NP and NP-hard, there are heuristic algorithms that can solve instances of large problems, involving millions of variables. SAT methods in causal learning allow us to query specific statements as an ancestral relation rather than estimating the full graph. They let us incorporate different kinds of prior knowledge and furthermore, we can put weights on the independence constraints if we believe that some of the (statistical) findings contradict each other. These approaches have been extended to cycles, latent variables, and overlapping data sets [Hyttinen et al., 2013, Triantafillou and Tsamardinos, 2015].

Conditional Independence Tests In the three preceding paragraphs we have assumed the existence of an independence oracle that tells us whether a specific (conditional) independence is or is not present in the distribution. In practice, however, we have to infer this statement from a finite amount of data. This comes with two major challenges: (1) All causal discovery methods that are based on conditional independence tests draw conclusions both from dependences and independences. In practice, however, one most often uses statistical significance tests, which are inherently asymmetric. One therefore usually forgets about the original meaning of the significance level and treats it as a tuning parameter. Furthermore, due to finite samples, the testing results might even contradict each other in the sense that there is no graph structure that encodes the exact set of inferred conditional independences. (2) Although there is some recent work on kernel-based tests [Fukumizu et al., 2008, Tillman et al., 2009, Zhang et al., 2011], nonparametric conditional independence tests are difficult to perform with a finite amount of data. One therefore often restricts oneself to a subclass of possible dependences, some of which we now briefly review.

If the variables are assumed to follow a Gaussian distribution, we can test for vanishing **partial correlation** (see Appendices A.1 and A.2). Under faithfulness, the Markov equivalence class of the underlying DAG becomes identifiable (Lemma 7.2) and indeed, in the Gaussian setting, the PC algorithm with a test for vanishing partial correlation provides a consistent estimator for the correct CPDAG [Kalisch and Bühlmann, 2007]. Additionally assuming a condition called strong faithfulness [Zhang and Spirtes, 2003, Uhler et al., 2013] even yields uniform consistency [Kalisch and Bühlmann, 2007]; see also the discussion in Robins et al. [2003].

Non-parametric conditional independence testing is a difficult problem in theory and practice. For non-Gaussian distributions, vanishing partial correlation is neither necessary nor sufficient for conditional independence, as shown by the following example.

Example 7.9 (Conditional independence and partial correlation)

(i) If the distribution $P_{X,Y,Z}$ is entailed by the SCM

$$Z := N_Z, \quad X := Z^2 + N_X, \quad Y := Z^2 + N_Y,$$

where $N_X, N_Y, N_Z \overset{\text{iid}}{\sim} \mathcal{N}(0,1)$, it satisfies

$$X \perp\!\!\!\perp Y \,|\, Z \qquad \text{and} \qquad \rho_{X,Y|Z} \neq 0.$$

The partial correlation coefficient $\rho_{X,Y|Z}$ equals the correlation of $X - \alpha Z$ and $Y - \beta Z$ where α and β are the regression coefficients when regressing X and Y on Z, respectively. In this example, $\alpha = \beta = 0$ because X and Y do not correlate with Z.

(ii) The distribution $P_{X,Y,Z}$ entailed by the SCM

$$Z := N_Z, \quad X := Z + N_X, \quad Y := Z + N_Y,$$

where $(N_X, N_Y) \perp\!\!\!\perp N_Z$ and (N_X, N_Y) are uncorrelated but not independent, satisfies

$$X \not\!\perp\!\!\!\perp Y \,|\, Z \qquad \text{and} \qquad \rho_{X,Y|Z} = 0$$

since here, $\rho_{X,Y|Z}$ is the correlation between N_X and N_Y.

Therefore, vanishing partial correlation does not imply and is not implied by conditional independence. □

The following procedure for testing whether X and Y are conditionally independent given Z provides a natural **nonlinear extension of partial correlation** [e.g., Ramsey, 2014]: (1) (nonlinearly) regress X on Z and test whether the residuals are independent of Y; (2) (nonlinearly) regress Y on Z and test whether the residuals are independent of X; (3) if one of those two independences hold, conclude that $X \perp\!\!\!\perp Y \,|\, Z$. This seems to be the correct test in the case of ANMs; see Section 7.1.2. For three variables, for example, we have the following result.

Proposition 7.10 *Consider a distribution $P_{X,Y,Z}$ induced by an ANM (Definition 7.3) with all variables having strictly positive densities. If X and Y are d-separated given Z, then the procedure just described outputs the corresponding conditional independence in the sense that either $X - \mathbb{E}[X|Z]$ is independent of Y or $Y - \mathbb{E}[Y|Z]$ is independent of X.*

Proof. Assume that $X := h(Z) + N_X$ and $Y := f(Z) + N_Y$, with Z, N_X, and N_Y being mutually independent. Then, $X - \mathbb{E}[X|Z] = N_X$ is independent of Y. The statement follows analogously for the other possible structures, for example, $X \to Z \to Y$ or $X \leftarrow Z \leftarrow Y$. □

The proposition shows that (in a population sense) the test described is appropriate for ANMs with three variables. Considering four variables X, Y, Z, V, however, may already lead to problems. Clearly, the graphs $X \leftarrow Z \to W \to Y$ and $X \to Z \to W \to Y$ are Markov equivalent. But while the test outputs $X \perp\!\!\!\perp Y \,|\, Z$ for the first graph, there is no such guarantee for the second graph. Thus, the above-mentioned restriction of the dependence model between random variables that can be used to construct feasible conditional independence tests leads to asymmetric treatment of graphs within a Markov equivalence class. This effect may be the same for many other types of methods for conditional independence testing. This asymmetry does not necessarily need to be a drawback since, as we have seen, restricted function classes may lead to identifiability within the Markov equivalence class (see Section 7.1). It certainly requires consideration, though.

7.2.2 Score-Based Methods

In the preceding section we have directly used the independence statements to infer the graph. Alternatively, we can test different graph structures in their ability to fit the data. The rationale is that graph structures encoding the wrong conditional independences, for example, will yield bad model fits. Although the roots for score-based methods for causal learning may date back even further, we mainly refer to Geiger and Heckerman [1994a], Heckerman et al. [1999], Chickering [2002], and references therein. The Max-Min Hill-Climbing algorithm [Tsamardinos et al., 2006] combines score-based and independence-based techniques.

Best Scoring Graph Given data $\mathcal{D} = (\mathbf{X}^1, \ldots, \mathbf{X}^n)$ from a vector $\mathbf{X}$ of variables, that is, a sample containing n i.i.d. observations, the idea is to assign a score $S(\mathcal{D}, \mathcal{G})$ to each graph $\mathcal{G}$ and search over the space of DAGs to find the graph with the highest score:

$$\hat{\mathcal{G}} := \underset{\mathcal{G} \text{ DAG over } \mathbf{X}}{\operatorname{argmax}} \; S(\mathcal{D}, \mathcal{G}). \tag{7.6}$$

There are several possibilities to define such a scoring function S. Often a parametric model is assumed (e.g., linear Gaussian equations or multinomial distributions), which introduces a set of parameters $\theta \in \Theta$.

(Penalized) Likelihood For each graph we may consider the maximum likelihood estimator $\hat{\theta}$ for θ and then define a score function by the BIC

$$S(\mathcal{D},\mathcal{G}) = \log p(\mathcal{D}|\hat{\theta},\mathcal{G}) - \frac{\#\text{parameters}}{2} \log n, \tag{7.7}$$

where $\log p(\mathcal{D}|\hat{\theta},\mathcal{G})$ is the log likelihood and n is the sample size. Estimators that output the graph with the largest (penalized) likelihood are often consistent. This follows from the consistency of BIC [Haughton, 1988], and identifiability of the model class. To guarantee rates of convergence, however, one usually relies on a "degree of identifiability" [e.g., Bühlmann et al., 2014]. In practice, finding the best scoring graph among all possible graphs may not be feasible and search techniques over the space of graphs are required (e.g., see the paragraph "Greedy Search Techniques"). Regularization different from BIC is possible, too. Roos et al. [2008] base their score on the minimum description length principle [Grünwald, 2007], for example. Using work by Haughton [1988], Chickering [2002] discusses how the BIC approach relates to a Bayesian formulation that we discuss next.

Bayesian Scoring Functions We define priors $p_{pr}(\mathcal{G})$ and $p_{pr}(\theta)$ over DAGs and parameters, respectively, and consider the log posterior as a score function (note that $p(\mathcal{D})$ is constant over all DAGs):

$$S(\mathcal{D},\mathcal{G}) := \log p(\mathcal{G}\,|\,\mathcal{D}) \propto \log p_{pr}(\mathcal{G}) + \log p(\mathcal{D}\,|\,\mathcal{G}),$$

where $p(\mathcal{D}|\mathcal{G})$ is the marginal likelihood

$$p(\mathcal{D}|\mathcal{G}) = \int_{\theta\in\Theta} p(\mathcal{D}|\mathcal{G},\theta)\, p_{pr}(\theta\,|\,\mathcal{G})\, d\theta.$$

Here, the resulting estimator $\hat{\mathcal{G}}$ from Equation (7.6) is the mode of the posterior distribution, which is usually called a maximum a posteriori (MAP) estimator. Alternatively, one may output the full posterior distribution over DAGs, and, in principle, even more detailed information is available. For instance, one can average over all graphs to get a posterior probability of the existence of a specific edge.

As an example, consider random variables that take only finitely many values. For a given structure $\mathcal{G}$, one may then assume that for each parent configuration the probability distribution of a random variable X_j follows a multinomial distribution. If we put a Dirichlet prior on its parameters (together with some further conditions on parameter independence and modularity), this leads to the Bayesian Dirichlet (BD) score [Geiger and Heckerman, 1994b].

In the case of parametric models, we call two graphs $\mathcal{G}_1$ and $\mathcal{G}_2$ **distribution equivalent** if for each parameter θ_1 there is a corresponding parameter θ_2, such that the distribution obtained from $\mathcal{G}_1$ in combination with θ_1 is the same as the distribution obtained from graph $\mathcal{G}_2$ with θ_2, and vice versa. It can be shown (see Problem 7.12) that in the linear Gaussian case, for example, two graphs are distribution equivalent if and only if they are Markov equivalent. It has therefore been argued that $p(\mathcal{D}|\mathcal{G}_1)$ and $p(\mathcal{D}|\mathcal{G}_2)$ should be the same for Markov equivalent graphs $\mathcal{G}_1$ and $\mathcal{G}_2$. The BD score can be adapted to satisfy this property. It is usually referred to as the Bayesian Dirichlet equivalence (BDe) score [Geiger and Heckerman, 1994b]. Buntine [1991] proposes a specific version of this score with even fewer hyperparameters.

Greedy Search Techniques The search space of all DAGs is growing super-exponentially in the number of variables [e.g., Chickering, 2002], the numbers of DAGs for 2, 3, 4, and 10 variables are 3, 25, 543, and 4175098976430598143, respectively (see Table B.1). Therefore, computing a solution to Equation (7.6) by searching over all graphs is often infeasible. Instead, greedy search algorithms can be applied to solve (7.6). At each step there is a candidate graph and a set of neighboring graphs. For all these neighbors, one computes the score and considers the best-scoring graph as the new candidate. If none of the neighbors obtains a better score, the search procedure terminates (not knowing whether one obtained only a local optimum). Clearly, one therefore has to define a neighborhood relation. Starting from a graph $\mathcal{G}$, we may define all graphs as neighbors from $\mathcal{G}$ that can be obtained by removing, adding, or reversing one edge, for example.

In the case of a linear Gaussian SCM, one cannot distinguish between Markov equivalent graphs. It turns out that then it is beneficial to change the search space to Markov equivalence classes instead of DAGs. The greedy equivalence search (GES) [Chickering, 2002] optimizes the BIC criterion (7.7) and starts with the empty graph. It consists of two-phases: in the first phase, edges are added until a local maximum is reached; in the second phase, edges are removed until a local maximum is reached, which is then given as an output of the algorithm.

Exact Methods In general, finding the optimal scoring DAG is NP-hard [Chickering, 1996] but still there is a lot of interesting research that tries to scale up exact methods. Here, "exact" means that they aim at finding (one of) the best scoring graphs for a given finite data set. Greedy search techniques are often heuristic and have guarantees — if at all — only in the limit of infinite data.

One line of research is based on dynamic programming [Silander and Myllymak, 2006, Koivisto and Sood, 2004, Koivisto, 2006]. These approaches exploit the decomposability of many scores that are used in practice: due to the Markov factorization, we have for $\mathcal{D} = (\mathbf{X}^1, \ldots, \mathbf{X}^n)$ that

$$\log p(\mathcal{D}|\hat{\theta}, \mathcal{G}) = \sum_{j=1}^{d} \sum_{i=1}^{n} \log p(X_j^i \,|\, X^i_{\mathbf{PA}_j^{\mathcal{G}}}, \hat{\theta}),$$

which is a sum of d "local" scores. Methods based on dynamic programming exploit this decomposability, and despite their exponential complexity they can find the best scoring graph for ≥ 30 variables, even if one does not restrict the number of parents. This is a remarkable result given the enormous number of different DAGs over this number of variables (see Table B.1).

The integer linear programming (ILP) framework assumes not only decomposability but also that the scoring function gives the same score to Markov equivalent graphs. The idea is then to represent graphical structures as vectors, such that the scoring function becomes an affine function in this vector representation. Studený and Haws [2014] describe how Hemmecke et al. [2012] base their representation on characteristic imsets, while Jaakkola et al. [2010] and Cussens [2011] use (exponentially long) zero-one codes instead that indicate parent-child-relationships between nodes and reduce the search space exploiting work by De Campos and Ji [2011]. Having formulated the problem as an ILP problem, the problem is still NP-hard, but one may now use off-the-shelf methods for ILP. Restricting the number of parents leads to further advances, for example, in "pedigree learning" each node has at most two parents [Sheehan et al., 2014].

7.2.3 Additive Noise Models

ANMs can be learned with score-based methods that are combined with a greedy search technique. This has been proposed for linear Gaussian models with equal error variances (Section 7.1.3) or nonlinear Gaussian ANMs (Section 7.1.5) [see Peters and Bühlmann, 2014, Bühlmann et al., 2014]. In the nonlinear Gaussian case, for example, we can proceed analogously to the bivariate case (see Equations (4.18) and (4.19)). For a given graph structure $\mathcal{G}$, we regress each variable on its parents and obtain the score

$$\log p(\mathcal{D}|\mathcal{G}) = \sum_{j=1}^{d} -\log \widehat{\text{var}}[R_j];$$

here, $\widehat{\text{var}}[R_j]$ is the empirical variance of the residuals R_j obtained from the regression of variable X_j on its parents. Intuitively, the better the model fits the data, the smaller the variance of the residuals and thus the larger our score. Formally, the procedure is an instance of maximum likelihood and can be shown to be consistent [Bühlmann et al., 2014]. Computationally, we can again exploit the property that the score decomposes over the different nodes. When computing the score for a neighboring graph that changes the parent set of only one variable, we need to update only the corresponding summand. If the noise cannot be assumed to have a Gaussian distribution, for example, one can estimate the noise distribution [Nowzohour and Bühlmann, 2016] and obtain an entropy-like score.

Alternatively, one can estimate the structure in an iterative way using independence tests. Mooij et al. [2009] and Peters et al. [2014] propose a regression with subsequent independence test (RESIT). The method is based on the property that the noise variables are independent of all preceding variables. For linear non-Gaussian models (Section 7.1.4), Shimizu et al. [2006] provide a practical method based on ICA [Comon, 1994, Hyvärinen et al., 2001] that can be applied to a finite amount of data. Later, an improved version of this method has been proposed in Shimizu et al. [2011].

7.2.4 Known Causal Ordering

It is often difficult to find the causal ordering (see Appendix B) of the underlying causal model. Given the causal ordering, however, estimating the graph reduces to "classical" variable selection. Assume, for example, that

$$
\begin{aligned}
X &:= N_X \\
Y &:= f(X, N_Y) \\
Z &:= g(X, Y, N_Z)
\end{aligned}
$$

with unknown f, g, N_X, N_Y, N_Z. Deciding whether f depends on X, and g depends on X and/or Y (see the assumption of structural minimality in Remark 6.6) is then a well-studied significance problem in "traditional" statistics. Standard methods can be used, especially if further structural assumptions are made, such as linearity [e.g., Hastie et al., 2009, Bühlmann and van de Geer, 2011]. This observation has been made before [e.g., Teyssier and Koller, 2005, Shojaie and Michailidis, 2010] and it has been suggested that instead of searching over the space of directed acyclic graphs, it might be beneficial to search over the causal order first and then perform variable selection [e.g., Teyssier and Koller, 2005, Bühlmann et al., 2014].

7.2.5 Observational and Experimental Data

Section 7.1.6 describes how causal structures may become identifiable when we observe the system under different conditions ("environments"). We now discuss how these results can be exploited in practice, that is, given only finitely many data. Let us therefore assume that we obtain one sample $\mathbf{X}^e_{n_e}$ for each environment $e \in \mathcal{E}$; that is, for each of the environments, we observe n^e i.i.d. data points.

Known Intervention Targets Here, each setting corresponds to an interventional experiment, and we have additional knowledge of the intervention targets $\mathcal{I}^e \subseteq \{1,\ldots,p\}$. Cooper and Yoo [1999] incorporate the intervention effects as mechanism changes into a Bayesian framework. For perfect interventions, Hauser and Bühlmann [2015] consider linear Gaussian SCMs and propose a greedy interventional equivalence search (GIES), a modified version of the GES algorithm that we briefly described in Section 7.2.2.

Sometimes, one is not able to measure all variables in each experiment (this can even be the case when all experiments are observational) but nevertheless wants to combine the information from the available data; this problem has been addressed by SAT-based approaches [see, e.g., Triantafillou and Tsamardinos, 2015, Tillman and Eberhardt, 2014, references therein].

Unknown Intervention Targets Eaton and Murphy [2007] do not assume that the targets of the different interventions are known. Instead, they introduce for each environment $e \in \mathcal{E}$ an intervention node I_e with no incoming edges (see "Intervention Variables" on page 95); for each data point only one intervention node is active. Then, they apply standard methods to the enlarged model with $d + \#\mathcal{E}$ variables, subject to the constraint that intervention nodes do not have any parents.

Tian and Pearl [2001] propose to test whether the marginal distributions change in the different settings and use this information to infer parts of the graph structure. They even combine this method with an independence-based method.

Different Environments In Section 7.1.6, we have also considered the problem of estimating the causal parents of a target variable Y among the set $\mathbf{X}$ of d predictors. Therefore, we have defined the set $\mathcal{S}$ as the collection of all sets $S \subseteq \{1,\ldots,d\}$ that satisfy invariant prediction, that is, for which $P_{Y^e \mid S^e}$ remains invariant over all environments $e \in \mathcal{E}$; see (7.4). In practice, we can test the hypothesis of invariant prediction at level α and collect all sets S that pass the test as an estimate $\hat{\mathcal{S}}$ for the set $\mathcal{S}$. Because the true set of parents $\mathbf{PA}_Y \subseteq \mathbf{X}$ is a member of $\hat{\mathcal{S}}$ with high probability $(1-\alpha)$, we obtain the coverage statement

$$\bigcap_{S \in \hat{\mathcal{S}}} S \subseteq \mathbf{PA}_Y \tag{7.8}$$

with high probability $(1-\alpha)$. The left-hand side of (7.8) is the output of a method called "invariant causal prediction" [Peters et al., 2016]. Code Snippet 7.11 shows an example for which the environments correspond to different interventions (this is not required by the method). To obtain correct coverage in the sense of (7.8), one only needs to model the conditional Y given $\mathbf{PA}_Y$; in particular, one does not assume anything on the distribution of the d predictors $\mathbf{X}$. This is different for the method proposed by Eaton and Murphy [2007] (see the paragraph "Unknown Intervention Targets"), which additionally tries to estimate the full causal structure.

Code Snippet 7.11 The following code shows an example of a causal system in two environments. In the true underlying structure we have that X_1 and X_2 are causing Y, which itself is causing X_3. In a linear model on the pooled data (line 13), all variables X_1, X_2, and X_3 are highly significant since all of them are good predictors for Y. Such a model is not invariant, however. In the two environments a regression from Y on X_1, X_2, X_3 yields coefficients -0.15, 1.09, -0.39, and -0.32, 1.62, -0.54, respectively. The method of invariant causal prediction outputs only the causal parents of Y, that is, X_1 and X_2. In this example, $\{1,2\}$ is the only set yielding an invariant model, that is, $\hat{\mathcal{S}} = \{\{1,2\}\}$.

```
1  library(InvariantCausalPrediction)
2  #
3  # generate data from two environments
4  env <- c(rep(1,400),rep(2,700))
5  n <- length(env)
6  set.seed(1)
7  X1 <- rnorm(n)
8  X2 <- 1*X1 + c(rep(0.1,400), rep(1.0,700))*rnorm(n)
9  Y <- -0.7*X1 + 0.6*X2 + 0.1*rnorm(n)
10 X3 <- c(rep(-2,400),rep(-1,700))*Y + 2.5*X2 + 0.1*rnorm(n)
11 #
12 summary(lm(Y~-1+X1+X2+X3))
13 # Coefficients:
14 # ----Estimate Std.Error t.val. Pr(>|t|)
15 # X1 -0.396212 0.008667 -45.71 <2e-16 ***
16 # X2 +1.381497 0.021377 +64.63 <2e-16 ***
17 # X3 -0.410647 0.011152 -36.82 <2e-16 ***
18 #
19 ICP(cbind(X1,X2,X3),Y,env)
20 #lower bd upper bd p-value
21 # X1 -0.71 -0.68 3.7e-06 ***
22 # X2 +0.59 +0.61 0.0092 **
23 # X3 -0.00 +0.00 0.2972
```

7.3 Problems

Problem 7.12 (Gaussian SCMs) *Prove that for linear Gaussian SCMs, two graphs $\mathcal{G}_1$ and $\mathcal{G}_2$ are distribution equivalent if and only if they are Markov equivalent. Here, we allow for zero coefficients.*

Problem 7.13 (Gaussian SCMs) *Consider a distribution $P_{\mathbf{X}}$ of $\mathbf{X} = (X_1, \ldots, X_d)$ with density p induced from a linear Gaussian SCM $\mathfrak{C}$. Prove that for any DAG $\mathcal{G}$ such that $P_{\mathbf{X}}$ is Markovian with respect to $\mathcal{G}$, there is a corresponding linear Gaussian SCM $\mathfrak{C}_{\mathcal{G}}$ entailing $P_{\mathbf{X}}$.*

Problem 7.14 (ANMs) *Prove that ANMs over $\mathbf{X} = (X_1, \ldots, X_d)$ with differentiable functions f_j and noise variables that have a strictly positive density entail a distribution over $\mathbf{X}$ that has a strictly positive density, too (see Definition 7.3).*

Problem 7.15 (Invariant causal prediction) *Prove Equation* (7.5).

8

Connections to Machine Learning, II

As argued in Chapter 5, the causal structure that underlies a statistical model can have strong implications for machine learning tasks such as semi-supervised learning or domain adaptation. We now revisit this general topic, focusing on the multivariate case. We begin with a method that uses machine learning to model systematic errors for a given causal structure, followed by some thoughts on reinforcement learning (with an application in computational advertising), and finally we comment on the topic of domain adaptation.

8.1 Half-Sibling Regression

This method exploits a given causal structure (see Figure 8.1) to reduce systematic noise in a prediction task. The goal is to reconstruct the unobserved signal Q. Schölkopf et al. [2015] suggest that we can denoise the signal Y by removing all information that can be explained by other measurements X that have been corrupted with the same source of noise. Here, X are measurements of some signals R that are independent of Q. Intuitively, everything in Y that can be explained by X must be due to the systematic noise N and should therefore be removed. More precisely, we consider

$$\hat{Q} := Y - \mathbb{E}[Y \,|\, X]$$

as an estimate for Q. Here, $\mathbb{E}[Y \,|\, X]$ is the *regression* of Y on its *half-siblings* X (note that X and Y share the parent N; see Figure 8.1).

One can show that for any random variables Q, X, Y that satisfy $Q \perp\!\!\!\perp X$, we have

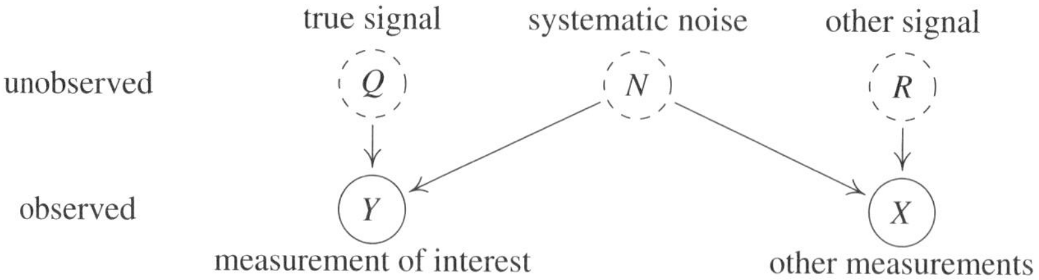

Figure 8.1: The causal structure that applies to the exoplanet search problem. The underlying signal of interest Q can only be measured as a noisy version Y. If the same noise source also corrupts measurements of other signals that are independent of Q, those measurements can be used for denoising. In our example, the telescope N constitutes systematic noise that affects measurements X and Y of independent light curves.

[Schölkopf et al., 2016, Proposition 1]:

$$\mathbb{E}\left[(Q - E[Q] - \hat{Q})^2\right] \leq \mathbb{E}\left[(Q - E[Q] - (Y - E[Y]))^2\right],$$

that is, the method is never worse than taking the measurement Y. If, moreover, the systematic noise acts in an additive manner, that is, $Y = Q + f(N)$ for some (unknown) function f, we have [Schölkopf et al., 2016, Proposition 3]:

$$\mathbb{E}\left[(Q - E[Q] - \hat{Q})^2\right] = \mathbb{E}[\text{var}[f(N)|X]]. \tag{8.1}$$

If the additive noise is a function of X, that is, $f(N) = \psi(X)$ for some (unknown) function ψ, then the right-hand side of (8.1) vanishes and hence $\hat{Q}$ recovers Q up to an additive shift; see Schölkopf et al. [2016] for other sufficient conditions.

As an example, consider the search for exoplanets. The Kepler space observatory, launched in 2009, observed a small fraction of the Milky Way during its search for exoplanets, monitoring the brightness of approximately 150,000 stars.[1] Those stars that are surrounded by a planet with a suitable orbit to allow for partial occlusions of the star will exhibit light curves that show a periodic decrease of light intensity; see Figure 8.2. These measurements are corrupted with systematic noise that is due to the telescope and that makes the signal from possible planets hard to detect.

Fortunately, the telescope measures many stars at the same time. These stars can be assumed to be causally and therefore statistically independent since they are light-years apart from each other. Thus, the causal structure depicted in Figure 8.1 fits very well to this problem and we may apply the half-sibling regression. This simple method performs surprisingly well [Schölkopf et al., 2015].

[1] `https://en.wikipedia.org/wiki/Kepler_(spacecraft)`, accessed 13.07.2016.

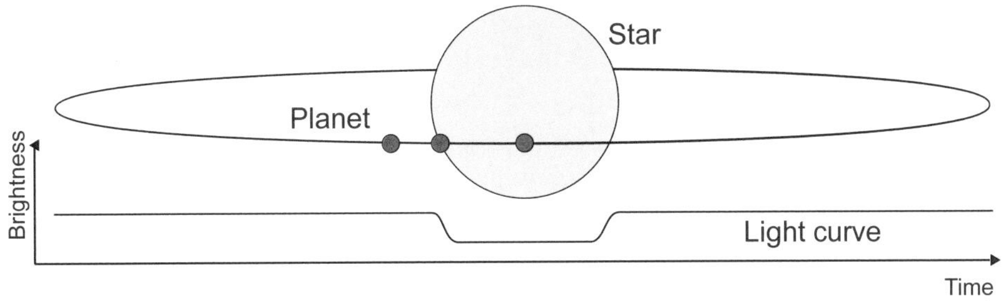

Figure 8.2: Every time a planet occludes a part of the star, the light intensity decreases. If the planet orbits the star, this phenomenon occurs periodically. (Image courtesy of Nikola Smolenski, `https://en.wikipedia.org/wiki/File:Planetary_transit.svg`, [CC BY-SA 3.0]. Image has been edited for clarity and style.)

Related approaches have been used in other application fields without reference to causal modeling [Gagnon-Bartsch and Speed, 2012, Jacob et al., 2016]. Considering the causal structure of the problem (Figure 8.1) immediately suggests the proposed methodology and leads to theoretical arguments justifying the approach.

8.2 Causal Inference and Episodic Reinforcement Learning

We now describe a class of problems in reinforcement learning from a causal perspective. Roughly speaking, in reinforcement learning, an agent is embedded in a world and chooses among a set of different actions. Depending on the current state of the world, these actions yield some reward and change the state of the world. The goal of the agent is to maximize the expected cumulated reward (see Section 8.2.2 for more details). We first introduce the concept of inverse probability weighting that has been applied in different contexts throughout machine learning and statistics and then relate it to episodic reinforcement learning. Drawing this connection is a first small step toward relating causality and reinforcement learning. The causal point of view enables us to exploit conditional independences that directly follow from the causal structure. We briefly mention two applications — blackjack and the placement of advertisement — and show how they benefit from causal knowledge. The causal formulation leads to these improvements of methodology very naturally but it is certainly possible to formulate these problems and corresponding algorithms without causal language. This section does not prove that reinforcement learning benefits from causality. Instead, we regard it as a step toward establishing a formal link between these two fields that may lead to fruitful research in future [see also Bareinboim et al., 2015, for example]. More concretely, we believe that causality could play a role when transferring knowledge between different tasks in reinforcement learning (e.g., when progressing to the next level in a computer game or when changing the opponent in table tennis); however, we are not aware of any such result.

8.2.1 Inverse Probability Weighting

Inverse probability weighting is a well-known technique that is used to estimate properties of a distribution from a sample that follows a different distribution. It therefore naturally relates to causal inference. Consider the kidney stone example (Example 6.37). We defined the binary variables size S, treatment T, and recovery R, and after obtaining observational data, we were interested in the expected recovery rate $\tilde{\mathbb{E}}[R]$ in a hypothetical study in which everyone received treatment A, that is under a different distribution. Formally, consider an SCM $\mathfrak{C}$ entailing the distribution $P_{\mathbf{X}}^{\mathfrak{C}}$ over variables $\mathbf{X} = (X_1, \ldots, X_d)$. We have argued that one often observes a sample from the observational distribution $P_{\mathbf{X}}^{\mathfrak{C}}$, but one is interested in some intervention distribution $P_{\mathbf{X}}^{\tilde{\mathfrak{C}}}$. Here, the new SCM $\tilde{\mathfrak{C}}$ is constructed from the original $\mathfrak{C}$ by intervening on a node X_k, say,

$$do\left(X_k := \tilde{f}(X_{\widetilde{\mathbf{PA}}_k}, \tilde{N}_k)\right);$$

see Section 6.3. In particular, we might want to estimate a certain property

$$\tilde{\mathbb{E}}\, \ell(\mathbf{X}) := \mathbb{E}_{P_{\mathbf{X}}^{\tilde{\mathfrak{C}}}}\, \ell(\mathbf{X})$$

of the new distribution $P_{\mathbf{X}}^{\tilde{\mathfrak{C}}}$ (in the kidney stone example, this is $\tilde{\mathbb{E}}[R]$). If densities exist, we have seen in Section 6.3 that the densities of $\mathfrak{C}$ and $\tilde{\mathfrak{C}}$ factorize in a similar way:

$$p(x_1, \ldots, x_d) := p^{\mathfrak{C}}(x_1, \ldots, x_d) = \prod_{j=1}^{d} p^{\mathfrak{C}}\left(x_j \,|\, x_{pa(j)}\right) \quad \text{and}$$

$$\tilde{p}(x_1, \ldots, x_d) := p^{\tilde{\mathfrak{C}}}(x_1, \ldots, x_d) = \prod_{j \neq k} p^{\mathfrak{C}}\left(x_j \,|\, x_{pa(j)}\right)\, \tilde{p}\left(x_k \,|\, x_{\widetilde{pa}(k)}\right).$$

The factorizations agree except for the term of the intervened variable. We therefore have

$$\xi := \tilde{\mathbb{E}}\,\ell(\mathbf{X}) = \int \ell(\mathbf{x})\,\tilde{p}(\mathbf{x})\,d\mathbf{x} = \int \ell(\mathbf{x})\,\frac{\tilde{p}(\mathbf{x})}{p(\mathbf{x})}\,p(\mathbf{x})\,d\mathbf{x}$$
$$= \int \ell(\mathbf{x})\,\frac{\tilde{p}\left(x_k\,|\,x_{\widetilde{pa}(k)}\right)}{p\left(x_k\,|\,x_{pa(k)}\right)}\,p(\mathbf{x})\,d\mathbf{x}.$$

(For simplicity, we assume throughout the whole section that the densities are strictly positive.) Given a sample $\mathbf{X}^1,\dots,\mathbf{X}^n$ drawn from the distribution $P_{\mathbf{X}}^{\mathfrak{C}}$, we can thus construct an estimator

$$\hat{\xi}_n := \frac{1}{n}\sum_{i=1}^{n}\ell(\mathbf{X}^i)\,\frac{\tilde{p}\left(X_k^i\,|\,\mathbf{X}^i_{\widetilde{pa}(k)}\right)}{p\left(X_k^i\,|\,\mathbf{X}^i_{pa(k)}\right)} = \frac{1}{n}\sum_{i=1}^{n}\ell(\mathbf{X}^i)\,w_i \tag{8.2}$$

for $\xi = \tilde{\mathbb{E}}\,\ell(\mathbf{X})$ by *reweighting* the observations; here, the weights w_i are defined as the ratio of the conditional densities. The data points, that have a high likelihood under $P_{\mathbf{X}}^{\tilde{\mathfrak{C}}}$ (they "could have been drawn" from the new distribution of interest) receive a large weight and contribute more to the estimate $\hat{\xi}_n$ than those with a small weight. This kind of estimator appears in the following three situations, for example.

(i) Suppose that $\mathbf{X} = (Y,Z)$ contains only a target variable Y and a *causal* covariate Z, that is, $Z \to Y$. Let us consider an intervention in Z and the function $\ell(\mathbf{X}) = \ell((Z,Y)) = Y$. Then, the estimator (8.2) reduces to

$$\hat{\xi}_n := \frac{1}{n}\sum_{i=1}^{n} Y^i\,\frac{\tilde{p}(Z^i)}{p(Z^i)}, \tag{8.3}$$

which is known as the **Horvitz-Thompson estimator** [Horvitz and Thompson, 1952]. This setting corresponds to the assumption of covariate shift [e.g., Shimodaira, 2000, Quionero-Candela et al., 2009, Ben-David et al., 2010]; see also Sections 5.2 and 8.3. The estimator (8.3) is an example of a weighted likelihood estimator.

(ii) For $\mathbf{X} = Z$, we may estimate the expectation $\tilde{\mathbb{E}}\,[\ell(Z)]$ under $\tilde{p}$ using data sampled from p. Thus, Equation (8.2) reduces to

$$\hat{\xi}_n := \frac{1}{n}\sum_{i=1}^{n}\ell(Z^i)\,\frac{\tilde{p}(Z^i)}{p(Z^i)},$$

a formula that is known as **importance sampling** [e.g., MacKay, 2002, Chapter 29.2]. The formula can be adapted if p and $\tilde{p}$ are known only up to constants.

(iii) We will make use of Equation (8.2) in the context of episodic reinforcement learning. We describe this application in a bit more detail next.

8.2.2 Episodic Reinforcement Learning

Reinforcement learning [e.g Sutton and Barto, 2015] models the behavior of agents taking actions in a world. Depending on the current state S_t of the world and the action A_t, the state of the world changes according to a **Markov decision process**, for example [e.g., Bellman, 1957]; that is, the probability $P(S_{t+1} = s)$ of entering a new state s depends only on the current state S_t and action A_t. Furthermore, the agent will receive some reward R_{t+1} that depends on S_t, A_t, and S_{t+1}; the sum over all rewards is sometimes called the return, which we write as $Y := \sum_t R_t$. The way the return Y depends on states and action is unknown to the agent who tries to improve his **strategy** $(a,s) \mapsto \pi(a\,|\,s) := P(A_t = a\,|\,S_t = s)$, that is, the conditional of the action he chooses depending on the observational part of the state of the world. In **episodic reinforcement learning**, the state is reset after a finite number of actions (see Figure 8.3). In Section 8.2.3, we consider the example of

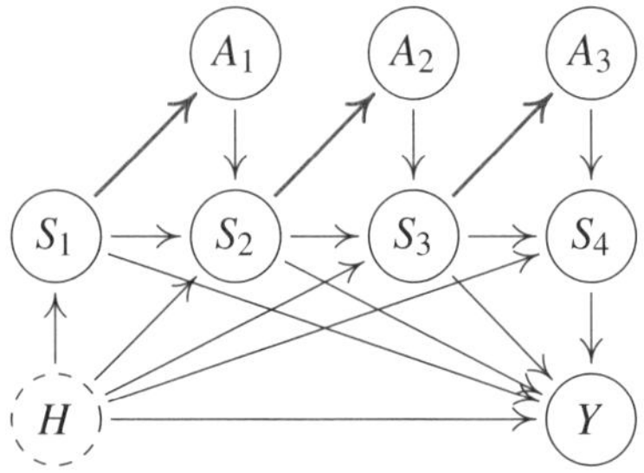

Figure 8.3: The graph describes an episodic reinforcement learning problem. The action variables A_i influence the system's next state S_{i+1}. The variable Y describes the output or return that we receive after one episode. This return Y may depend on the actions, too (edges omitted for clarity); it is often modelled as the (possibly weighted) sum of rewards that are received after each decision; see Section 8.2.3. The whole system can be confounded by an unobserved variable H. The bold, red edges indicate the conditionals that the player can influence, that is, the strategy. Equation (8.4) estimates the expected outcome $\tilde{\mathbb{E}}[Y]$ under a strategy $\tilde{\pi}$ from data obtained using strategy π. The equation still holds, when there are additional edges from the actions A to H and/or Y.

blackjack. In the example of Figure 8.3, the player makes $K = 3$ decisions, after which the cards are reshuffled. Then, a new episode starts.

Suppose that we play n games under a certain strategy $(a,s) \mapsto \pi(a \,|\, s)$, and each game is an episode. This function π does not depend on the number of "moves" we have played so far but just on the value of the state. As long as this strategy assigns a positive probability to any action, Equation (8.2) allows us to estimate the performance of a different strategy $(a,s) \mapsto \tilde{\pi}(a \,|\, s)$.

$$\hat{\xi}_{n,\mathrm{ERL}} := \frac{1}{n} \sum_{i=1}^{n} Y^i \frac{\prod_{j=1}^{K} \tilde{\pi}(A_j^i \,|\, S_j^i)}{\prod_{j=1}^{K} \pi(A_j^i \,|\, S_j^i)}. \tag{8.4}$$

This can be seen as a Monte Carlo method for off-policy evaluation [Sutton and Barto, 2015, Chapter 5.5]. In practice, the estimator (8.4) often has large variance; in continuous settings the variance may even be infinite. It has been suggested to reweight [Sutton and Barto, 2015] or to disregard the (five) largest weights [Bottou et al., 2013] to trade off variance for bias. Bottou et al. [2013] additionally compute confidence intervals and gradients in the case of parametrized densities. The latter are important if one wants to search for optimal strategies.

We now briefly discuss two examples, in which exploiting the causal structure leads to an improved *statistical* performance of the learning procedure. We regard them as interesting examples that shed some light on the relationship between reinforcement learning and causality.

8.2.3 State Simplification in Blackjack

The methodology proposed in Section 8.2.2 can be used to learn how to play blackjack (a card game). We pretend that a player enters a casino and starts playing blackjack knowing neither the objective of the game nor the optimal strategy; instead, he applies a random strategy. At each point in the game, the player is asked which of the legal actions he wants to take, and after the game has finished the dealer reveals how much money the player won or lost. After a while the player may update his strategy toward decisions that proved to be successful and continue playing. From a mathematical point of view, blackjack is solved. The optimal strategy (for infinitely many decks) was discovered by Baldwin et al. [1956] and leads to an expectation of $\mathbb{E}[Y] \approx -0.006$€ for a player betting 1€.

How does causality come into play? We have assumed that the player is unaware of the precise rules of blackjack; maybe he knows, however, that the win or loss is determined only by the values of the cards and not their suits; that is, the rules do not distinguish between a queen of clubs and a queen of hearts. The player can

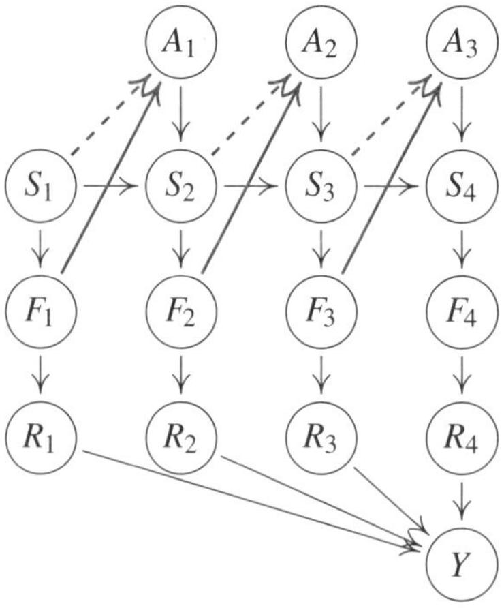

Figure 8.4: Here, there exist variables $F_1, \ldots, F_4$ that contain all relevant information about the states $S_1, \ldots, S_4$ in the sense that Equations (8.5) and (8.6) hold. Equation (8.6) is not represented in the graph. Then, it suffices if the actions A_j depend on F_{j-1} (red, solid lines) rather than S_{j-1} (red, dashed lines). In the blackjack example, the S_j's encode the dealer's hand and player's hand including suits, while the F_j encode the same information except for suits (suits do not have an influence on the outcome of blackjack). Since F_j take fewer values than S_j, the optimal strategy becomes easier to learn.

then immediately conclude that the optimal strategy does not depend on the suit. This comes with an obvious advantage when searching for the optimal strategy: the number of relevant state spaces and therefore the space of possible strategies reduces significantly. Figure 8.4 depicts this argument: the variables S_t contain all information, whereas the variables F_t do not contain suits. For example,

$$
\begin{aligned}
S_3 &= (\text{Player: } \heartsuit K, \spadesuit 5, \diamondsuit 4; \quad \text{Dealer: } \diamondsuit K) \\
F_3 &= (\text{Player: } \quad K, \quad 5, \quad 4; \quad \text{Dealer: } \quad K).
\end{aligned}
$$

Since the final result Y depends only on $(F_1, \ldots, F_4)$ and not on the "full state" $(S_1, \ldots, S_4)$, the actions may be chosen to depend on the F variables. Similarly, one may exploit that the order of the cards does not matter either. More formally, we have the following result:

Proposition 8.1 (State simplification) *Suppose that we are interested in the return $Y := \sum_j R_j$, and all variables are discrete. Assume that there is a function f such that for all j and for $F_j := f(S_j)$, we have*

$$R_j \perp\!\!\!\perp S_j \,|\, F_j, A_j, \tag{8.5}$$

and the full states do not matter for the change of states in the following sense: for all s_j and for all s_{j-1}, s°_{j-1} with $f(s_{j-1}) = f(s^\circ_{j-1})$

$$p(f(s_j) \,|\, s_{j-1}) = p(f(s_j) \,|\, s^\circ_{j-1}). \tag{8.6}$$

Then the optimal strategy $(a,s) \mapsto \pi_{opt}(a \,|\, s)$ depends only on F_j and not on S_j. There exists

$$\pi_{opt} \in \operatorname*{argmax}_{\pi} \mathbb{E}[Y],$$

such that

$$\pi_{opt}(a_j \,|\, s_{j-1}) = \pi_{opt}(a_j \,|\, s^\circ_{j-1}) \quad \forall s_{j-1}, s^\circ_{j-1} : f(s_{j-1}) = f(s^\circ_{j-1}).$$

This result is particularly helpful if F_j takes fewer values than S_j. The proof is provided in Appendix C.11. In the blackjack example, Equation (8.6) states that the probability of drawing another king depends only on the values of the cards drawn before (the number of kings in particular), not their suits.

8.2.4 Improved Weighting in Advertisement Placement

A related argument is used by Bottou et al. [2013] for the optimal placement of advertisements. Consider the following simplified description of the system. A company, which we will refer to as the publisher, runs a search engine and may want to display advertisements in the space above the search results, the mainline. Only if a user clicks on an ad does the publisher receive money from the corresponding company. Before displaying the ads, the publisher sets the mainline reserve A, a real-valued parameter that determines how many ads are shown in the mainline. In most systems, the number of mainline ads F varies between 0 and 4, that is, $F \in \{0,1,2,3,4\}$. The mainline reserve A usually depends on many variables (e.g., search query, date and time of the query, location), that we call the state S. If the search query indicates that the user intends to buy new shoes, for example, one may want to show more ads compared to when a user is looking for the time of the next service at church. We can model the system as episodic reinforcement learning with episodes of length 1.[2] The return Y equals the number of clicks per episode; its value is either 0 or 1. The question how to choose an optimal mainline reserve A then corresponds to finding the optimal strategy $(a,s) \mapsto \pi_{\text{opt}}(a|s)$. Figure 8.5 shows a picture of the simplified problem. The state S contains information

[2] In reality, the systems are usually more complicated. For example, in an auction-like procedure, the advertisers place bids on certain search queries, which then influence the price for a click.

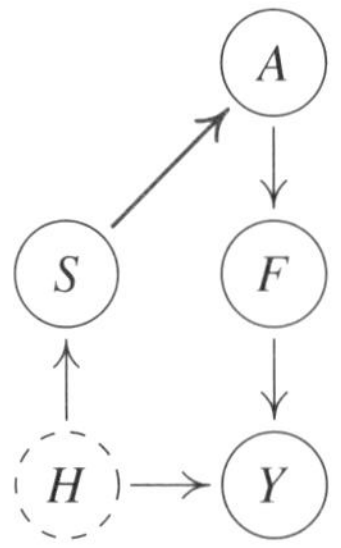

Figure 8.5: Example for the placement of advertisements. The target variable Y indicates whether a user has clicked on one of the shown ads. H (unknown) and S (known) are state variables and the action A corresponds to the mainline reserve, a real-valued parameter that determines how many ads are shown in the mainline. F is a discrete variable indicating the (known) number of ads placed in the mainline. Although the conditional $p(a \mid s)$ is randomized over, we may use $p(f \mid s)$ for the reweighting (see Proposition 8.2).

about the user that is available to the publisher. The hidden variable H contains unknown user information (e.g., his intention), the action A is the mainline reserve, and Y is the event whether or not a person clicks on one of the ads. Finally, F is the discrete variable that says, how many ads are shown. Evaluating new strategies $(a,s) \mapsto \tilde{p}(a \mid s)$, corresponds to applying Equation (8.4):

$$\hat{\xi}_{n,\mathrm{ERL}} := \frac{1}{n}\sum_{i=1}^{n} Y^i \, \frac{\tilde{p}(A^i \mid S^i)}{p(A^i \mid S^i)}.$$

(Here, we write $p(a \mid s)$ rather than $\pi(a \mid s)$ for notational convenience.) We can now benefit from the following key insight. Whether a person clicks on an ad depends on the mainline reserve A but only via the value of F. The user never sees the real-valued parameter A. This is a somewhat trivial observation, when we think about the causal structure of the system (see Figure 8.5). Exploiting this fact, however, we can use a different estimator

$$\frac{1}{n}\sum_{i=1}^{n} Y^i \, \frac{\tilde{p}(F^i \mid S^i)}{p(F^i \mid S^i)};$$

see Proposition 8.2. And since F is a discrete variable taking values between 0 and 4, say, this usually leads to weights that are much better behaved. In practice, the modification may reduce the size of confidence intervals considerably [Bottou et al., 2013, Section 5.1]. As in Section 8.1, we can exploit our knowledge of the causal structure to improve statistical performance. More formally, the procedure is justified by the following proposition:

Method	Training data from	Test domain
Domain generalization	$(\mathbf{X}^1, Y^1), \ldots, (\mathbf{X}^D, Y^D)$	$T := D+1$
Multi-task learning	$(\mathbf{X}^1, Y^1), \ldots, (\mathbf{X}^D, Y^D)$	$T \in \{1, \ldots, D\}$
Asymmetric multi-task learning	$(\mathbf{X}^1, Y^1), \ldots, (\mathbf{X}^D, Y^D)$	$T := D$

Table 8.1: In domain generalization, the test data come from an unseen domain, whereas in multi-task learning, some data in the test domain(s) are available.

Proposition 8.2 (Improved weighting) *Suppose there is a density p over $\mathbf{X} = (A, F, H, S, Y)$ that is entailed by an SCM $\mathfrak{C}$ with graph shown in Figure 8.5. Assume further that the density $\tilde{p}$ is entailed by an SCM $\tilde{\mathfrak{C}}$ that corresponds to an intervention in A of the form $do\big(A := \tilde{f}(S, \tilde{N}_A)\big)$ and satisfies $\tilde{p}(f \,|\, s) = 0$ if $p(f \,|\, s) = 0$ and $\tilde{p}(a \,|\, s) = 0$ if $p(a \,|\, s) = 0$. We then have*

$$\tilde{\mathbb{E}} Y = \int y \, \frac{\tilde{p}(a \,|\, s)}{p(a \,|\, s)} \, p(\mathbf{x}) \, d\mathbf{x} = \int y \, \frac{\tilde{p}(f \,|\, s)}{p(f \,|\, s)} \, p(\mathbf{x}) \, d\mathbf{x}.$$

The proof can be found in Appendix C.12. In general, the condition of the non-vanishing densities is indeed necessary: if there is a set of a and s values (with non-vanishing Lebesgue measure) that belong to the support of $\tilde{p}$ and contribute to the expectation of Y, there must be a non-vanishing probability under p to sample data in this area.

8.3 Domain Adaptation

Domain adaptation is another machine learning problem that is naturally related to causality [Schölkopf et al., 2012]. Here, we will relate domain adapation to what we called invariant prediction in "Different Environments" in Section 7.2.5. We do not claim that this connection, in its current form, yields major improvements, but we believe that it could prove to be useful for developing a novel methodology in domain adaptation.

Let us assume that we obtain data from a target variable Y^e and d possible predictors $\mathbf{X}^e = (X_1^e, \ldots, X_d^e)$ in different domains $e \in \mathcal{E} = \{1, \ldots, D\}$ and that we are interested in predicting Y. Adapting to widely used notation, we use the terms "domain" or "task." Table 8.1 describes a taxonomy of three problems in domain adaptation that we consider here.

Our main assumption is that there exists a set $S^* \subseteq \{1, \ldots, d\}$ such that the conditional $Y^e \,|\, \mathbf{X}^e_{S^*}$ is the same for all domains $e \in \mathcal{E}$, including the test domain, that is, for all $e, f \in \mathcal{E}$ and for all $\mathbf{x}_{S^*}$

$$Y^e \,|\, \mathbf{X}^e_{S^*} = \mathbf{x}_{S^*} \quad \text{and} \quad Y^f \,|\, \mathbf{X}^f_{S^*} = \mathbf{x}_{S^*} \quad \text{have the same distribution.} \tag{8.7}$$

In Sections 7.1.6 and 7.2.5 we have considered a similar setup, where we used the term "environments" rather than "domains" and called the property (8.7) "invariant prediction." We have argued that if there is an underlying SCM and if the environments correspond to interventions on nodes other than the target Y, property (8.7) is satisfied for $S^* = \mathbf{PA}_Y$ (cf. also our discussion of Simon's invariance criterion in Section 2.2). Property (8.7) may also hold, however, for sets other than the causal parents. Since our goal is prediction, we are most interested in sets S^* that satisfy (8.7) and additionally predict Y as accurately as possible. Let us for now assume, that we are given such a set S^* (we will return to this issue later) and point at how the assumption (8.7) relates to domain adaptation.

In settings of covariate shift [e.g., Shimodaira, 2000, Quionero-Candela et al., 2009, Ben-David et al., 2010], one usually assumes that the conditional $Y^e \,|\, \mathbf{X}^e = \mathbf{x}$ remains invariant over all tasks e. Assumption (8.7) means that covariate shift holds for some subset S^* of the variables and thus constitutes a generalization of the covariate shift assumption.

For domain generalization, and if the set S^* is known, we can then apply traditional methods for covariate shift for this subset S^*. For example, if the supports of the data in input space are overlapping (or the system is linear), we may use the estimator $f_{S^*}(\mathbf{X}^T_{S^*})$ with $f_{S^*}(\mathbf{x}) := \mathbb{E}\left[Y^1 \,|\, \mathbf{X}^1_{S^*} = \mathbf{x}\right]$ in test domain T. One can prove that this approach is optimal in an adversarial setting, where the distributions in the test domain may be arbitrarily different from the training domains, except for the conditional distribution (8.7) that we require to remain invariant [Rojas-Carulla et al., 2016, Theorem 1]. In multi-task learning, it is less obvious how to exploit the knowledge of such a set S^*. In practice, one needs to combine information gained from pooling the tasks and regressing Y on S^* with knowledge obtained from considering the test task separately [Rojas-Carulla et al., 2016].

If the set S^* is unknown, we again propose to search for sets S that satisfy (8.7) over available domains. When learning the causal predictors, one prefers to stay conservative, and the method of invariant causal prediction [Peters et al., 2016] therefore outputs the intersection of all sets S satisfying (8.7); see Equation (7.5). Here, we are interested in prediction instead. Among all sets that lead to invariant prediction, one may therefore choose the set S that leads to the best predictive performance, which is usually one of the larger of those sets. The same applies if there are different known sets S that all satisfy (8.7). If the data are generated by an SCM and the domains correspond to different interventions, the set S with the best predictive power that satisfies (8.7) can, in the limit of infinite data, be shown to be a subset of the Markov blanket of Y (see Problem 8.5).

8.4 Problems

Problem 8.3 (Half-sibling regression) *Consider the DAG in Figure 8.1. The fact that X provides additional information about Q on top of the one provided by Y follows from causal faithfulness. Why?*

Problem 8.4 (Inverse probability weighting) *Consider an SCM $\mathfrak{C}$ of the form*

$$\begin{aligned} Z &:= N_Z \\ Y &:= Z^2 + N_Y, \end{aligned}$$

with $N_Y, N_Z \overset{iid}{\sim} \mathcal{N}(0,1)$ and an intervened version $\tilde{\mathfrak{C}}$ with

$$do\left(Z := \tilde{N}_Z\right),$$

where $\tilde{N}_Z \sim \mathcal{N}(2,1)$.

a) (optional) Compute $\mathbb{E}[Y] := \mathbb{E}_{P^{\mathfrak{C}}}[Y]$ and $\tilde{\mathbb{E}}[Y] := \mathbb{E}_{P^{\tilde{\mathfrak{C}}}}[Y]$.

b) Draw $n = 200$ i.i.d. data points from the SCM $\mathfrak{C}$ and implement the estimator (8.3) for estimating $\tilde{\mathbb{E}}[Y]$.

c) Compute the estimate in b) and the empirical variance of the weights appearing in (8.3) for increasing sample size n between $n = 5$ and $n = 50,000$. What do you conclude?

Problem 8.5 (Invariant predictors) *We want to justify the last sentence in Section 8.3. Consider a DAG over variables Y, E, and $X_1, \ldots, X_d$, in which E (for "environment") is not a parent of Y and does not have any parents itself. Denote the Markov blanket of Y by M. Prove that for any set $S \subseteq \{X_1, \ldots, X_d\}$ with*

$$Y \perp\!\!\!\perp E \,|\, S$$

there is another set $S_{new} \subseteq M$ such that

$$Y \perp\!\!\!\perp E \,|\, S_{new} \quad \text{and} \quad Y \perp\!\!\!\perp (S \setminus S_{new}) \,|\, S_{new}.$$

9

Hidden Variables

So far, we assumed that all variables from the model have been measured (except for the noises). Since in practice, we are choosing the set of random variables ourselves, we need to define a concept of "causally relevant" variables. In Section 9.1 we therefore introduce the terms "causal sufficiency" and "interventional sufficiency." But even if we leave aside the details of the precise definition, it is apparent that in most practical applications many causally relevant variables will be unobserved. Simpson's paradox (Section 9.2) describes how ignoring hidden confounding can lead to wrong causal conclusions. In linear settings, a structure that is often referred to as an instrumental variable can make the regression coefficient, which corresponds to the causal effect (see Example 6.42), identifiable (Section 9.3). It is an active field of research to find good graphical representations for SCMs with hidden variables, in particular those that encode the conditional independence structure; we will present some of the solutions in Section 9.4. Finally, hidden variables lead to constraints appearing in the observed distribution that go beyond conditional independences (Section 9.5). We briefly discuss how these constraints could be used for structure learning but do not provide any methodological details. For more historical notes on the treatment of hidden variables, we refer to Spirtes et al. [2000, Section 6.1].

9.1 Interventional Sufficiency

A set of variables $\mathbf{X}$ is usually said to be **causally sufficient** if there is no hidden common cause $C \notin \mathbf{X}$ that is causing more than one variable in $\mathbf{X}$ [e.g., Spirtes, 2010]. While this definition matches the intuitive meaning of the set of "relevant" variables, it uses the concept of a "common cause" and should therefore be understood relative to a larger set of variables $\tilde{\mathbf{X}} \supseteq \mathbf{X}$ (for which, again, we might want to define causal sufficiency). In the structural causal model corresponding to this larger set $\tilde{\mathbf{X}}$, a variable C is a **common cause** of X and Y if there is a directed path from C to X and Y that does not include Y and X, respectively. Common causes are also called **confounders** and we use these terms interchangeably.

We propose a small modification of causal sufficiency that we call interventional sufficiency, a concept that is based on falsifiability of SCMs; see Section 6.8.

Definition 9.1 (Interventional sufficiency) *We call a set* $\mathbf{X}$ *of variables interventionally sufficient if there exists an SCM over* $\mathbf{X}$ *that cannot be falsified as an interventional model; that is, it induces observational and intervention distributions that coincide with what we observe in practice.*

We believe that this concept is intuitively appealing since it describes when a set of variables is large enough to perform causal reasoning, in the sense of computing observational and intervention distributions.

It should be intuitive that considering two variables is usually not sufficient if there exists a latent common cause. The two variables are causally insufficient by definition, and Simpson's paradox in Section 9.2 (see also Example 6.37) shows that in general these two variables are not interventionally sufficient either. In fact, the paradox drives the statement to an extreme: an SCM over the two observed variables that ignores confounding does not only entail the wrong intervention distributions, it can even reverse the sign of the causal effect: a treatment can look beneficial although it is harmful; see (9.2).

Sometimes, however, we can still compute the correct intervention distributions even in the presence of latent confounding. The set of variables in the following example is interventionally sufficient but causally insufficient.

Example 9.2 Consider the following SCM

$$
\begin{aligned}
Z &:= N_Z \\
X &:= \mathbf{1}_{Z \geq 2} + N_X \\
Y &:= Z \bmod 2 + X + N_Y
\end{aligned}
$$

with $N_Z \sim \mathcal{U}(\{0,1,2,3\})$ being uniformly distributed over $\{0,1,2,3\}$ and $N_X, N_Y \overset{\text{iid}}{\sim} \mathcal{N}(0,1)$; see Figure 9.1 (left). While variables X and Y are clearly causally insuffi-

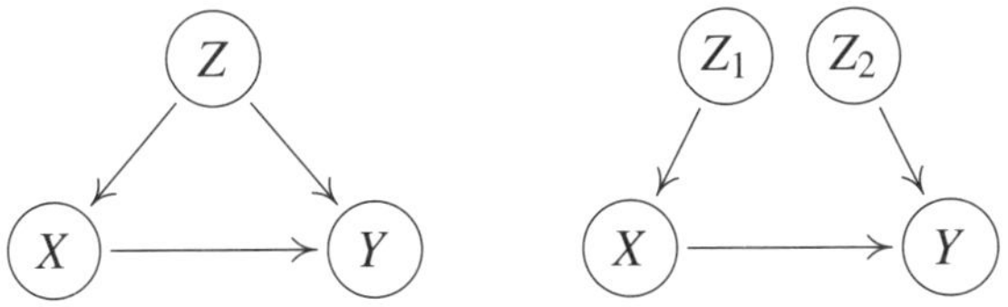

Figure 9.1: Both graphs represent interventionally equivalent SCMs for the model described in Example 9.2. While only the second representation renders X and Y causally sufficient, X and Y are interventionally sufficient independently of the representation.

cient,[1] one can show that the two variables X and Y are interventionally sufficient. The reason is that the "confounder" Z consists of two independent parts: $Z_1 := \mathbf{1}_{Z\geq 2}$ is the first bit of the binary representation of Z, and $Z_2 := Z \bmod 2$ is the second bit. In this sense, we can separate the "confounder" into the independent variables Z_1 and Z_2, with Z_1 influencing X, and Z_2 influencing Y; see Figure 9.1. □

In general, we have the following relationship between causal and interventional sufficiency (see Appendix C.13 for a proof):

Proposition 9.3 (Interventional sufficiency and causal sufficiency) *Let $\mathfrak{C}$ be an SCM for the variables $\mathbf{X}$ that cannot be falsified as an interventional model.*

(i) If a subset $\mathbf{O} \subseteq \mathbf{X}$ is causally sufficient, then it is interventionally sufficient.

(ii) In general, the converse is false; that is, there are examples of interventionally sufficient sets $\mathbf{O} \subseteq \mathbf{X}$ that are not causally sufficient.

Furthermore, Example 9.2 shows that there cannot be a solely graphical criterion for determining whether a subset of the variables are interventionally sufficient. For many SCMs with a structure similar to Figure 9.1 (left), X and Y are interventionally insufficient. However, the following remark shows that omitting an "intermediate" variable preserves interventional sufficiency.

Remark 9.4 We have the following three statements.

(i) Assume that there is an SCM over X, Y, Z with graph $X \to Y \to Z$ and $X \not\perp\!\!\!\perp Z$ that induces the correct interventions. Then X and Z are interventionally sufficient due to the SCM over X, Z satisfying $X \to Z$.

[1] Here, the hidden common cause Z not only points into X and Y but also has a total causal effect on both of them; see Definition 6.12.

(ii) Assume that there is an SCM $\mathfrak{C}$ over X, Y, Z that induces the correct interventions with graph $X \to Y \to Z$ and additional $X \to Z$ and assume further that $P^{\mathfrak{C}}_{X,Y,Z}$ is faithful with respect to this graph; see also (iii). Then, again, X and Z are interventionally sufficient due to the SCM over X, Z satisfying $X \to Z$.

(iii) If the situation is the same as in (ii) with the difference that

$$P^{\mathfrak{C}}_{Z|X=x} = P^{\mathfrak{C};do(X:=x)}_{Z} = P^{\mathfrak{C}}_{Z}$$

for all x (in particular, $P^{\mathfrak{C}}_{X,Y,Z}$ is not faithful with respect to the graph). Then, X and Z are interventionally sufficient due to the SCM over X, Z with the empty graph. Note that the counterfactuals may not be represented correctly.

The proof of these statements is left to the reader (see Problem 9.10). □

Whenever we find an SCM over the observed variables that is interventionally equivalent to the original SCM over all variables, we may want to call the former one a marginalized SCM. We have seen that there is no solely graphical criteria for determining the structure of a marginalized SCM. Instead, some information about the causal mechanisms, that is, the specific form of the assignments, is needed. Bongers et al. [2016] studies **marginalizations of SCMs** in more detail. The key idea is to start with the original SCM and to consider only the structural assignments of the observed variables. One then repeatedly plugs in the assignments of the hidden variables whenever they appear on the right-hand side. This yields an SCM with multivariate, possibly dependent noise variables. In some cases, it is then possible to choose an interventionally equivalent SCM with univariate noise variables.

9.2 Simpson's Paradox

The kidney stone data set in Example 6.16 is well known for the following reason. We have

$$\begin{aligned} P^{\mathfrak{C}}(R=1 \mid T=A) &< P^{\mathfrak{C}}(R=1 \mid T=B) \qquad \text{but} \\ P^{\mathfrak{C};do(T:=A)}(R=1) &> P^{\mathfrak{C};do(T:=B)}(R=1); \end{aligned} \tag{9.1}$$

see Example 6.37. Suppose that we have not measured the variable Z (size of the stone) and furthermore that we do not even know about its existence. We might then hypothesize that $T \to R$ is the correct graph. If we denote this (wrong) SCM by $\tilde{\mathfrak{C}}$, we can rewrite (9.1) as

$$P^{\tilde{\mathfrak{C}};do(T:=A)}(R=1) < P^{\tilde{\mathfrak{C}};do(T:=B)}(R=1) \text{ but}$$
$$P^{\mathfrak{C};do(T:=A)}(R=1) > P^{\mathfrak{C};do(T:=B)}(R=1). \tag{9.2}$$

Due to the model misspecification, the causal statement gets reversed. Although A is the more effective drug, we propose to use B. But even if we knew about the common cause Z, is it possible that there is yet another confounding variable that we did not correct for? If we are unlucky, this is indeed the case and we have to reverse the conclusion once more if we include this variable. In principle, this could lead to an arbitrarily long sequence of reversed causal conclusions (see Problem 9.11).

This example shows how careful we have to be when writing down the underlying causal graph. In some situations, we can infer the DAG from the protocol describing the acquisition of the data. If the medical doctors assigning the treatments, for example, did not have any knowledge about the patient other than the size of the kidney stone, there cannot be any confounding factor other than the size of the stone.

Summarizing, the Simpson's paradox is not so much of a paradox but rather a warning of how sensitive causal reasoning can be with respect to model misspecifications. Although we have phrased the example in a setting with confounding, it can also occur as a result of selection bias (Example 6.30) that has not been accounted for.

9.3 Instrumental Variables

Instrumental variables date back to the 1920s [Wright, 1928] and are widely used in practice [see, e.g., Imbens and Angrist, 1994, Bowden and Turkington, 1990, Didelez et al., 2010]. There exist numerous extensions and alternative methods; we focus on the essential idea. Consider a linear Gaussian SCM with the graph shown in Figure 9.2 (left). Here, the coefficient α in the structural assignment

$$Y := \alpha X + \delta H + N_Y$$

is the quantity of interest (see Equation (6.18) in Example 6.42); it is sometimes called the **average causal effect (ACE)**. It is not directly accessible, however, because of the hidden common cause H. Simply regressing Y on X and taking the regression coefficient generally results in a biased estimator for α:

$$\frac{\mathrm{cov}[X,Y]}{\mathrm{var}[X]} = \frac{\alpha\,\mathrm{var}[X] + \delta\gamma\mathrm{var}[H]}{\mathrm{var}[X]} = \alpha + \frac{\delta\gamma\mathrm{var}[H]}{\mathrm{var}[X]}.$$

Instead, we may be able to exploit an instrumental variable — if it exists. Formally, we call a variable Z in an SCM an **instrumental variable** for (X,Y) if (a) Z is independent of H, (b) Z is not independent of X ("relevance"), and (c) Z effects Y only through X ("exclusion restriction"). For our purposes, it suffices to consider the example graph shown in Figure 9.2 (left) that satisfies all of these assumptions. Note, however, that other structures do, too. For example, one can allow for a hidden common cause between Z and X. In practice, one usually uses domain knowledge to argue why conditions (a), (b), and (c) hold.

In the linear case, we can exploit the existence of Z in the following way. Because (H,N_X) is independent of Z, we can regard $\gamma H + N_X$ in

$$X := \beta Z + \gamma H + N_X$$

as noise. It becomes apparent that we can therefore consistently estimate the coefficient β and therefore have access to βZ (which, in the case of finitely many data, is approximated by fitted values of Z). Because of

$$Y := \alpha X + \delta H + N_Y = \alpha\,(\beta Z) + (\alpha\gamma + \delta)H + N_Y,$$

we can then consistently estimate α by regressing Y on βZ. Summarizing, we first regress X on Z and then regress Y on the predicted values $\hat{\beta}Z$ (predicted from the first regression). The average causal effect α becomes identifiable in the limit of infinite data. This method is commonly referred to as "two-stage least squares." It makes use of linear SCMs, and the above-mentioned assumptions: (a) independence between H and Z, (b) non-zero β (in the case of small or vanishing β, Z is called a "weak instrument"), and (c) the absence of a direct influence from Z to Y.

Identifiability is not restricted to the linear setting, however. We now mention only four such results, even though there are many more [e.g., Hernán and Robins, 2006].

(i) It is not difficult to see that the method of two-stage least squares still works if X depends on Z and H in a nonlinear but additive way; see Problem 9.12.

(ii) If the variables Z, X, and Y are binary, the ACE is defined as

$$P^{\mathfrak{C};do(X:=1)}(Y=1) - P^{\mathfrak{C};do(X:=0)}(Y=1).$$

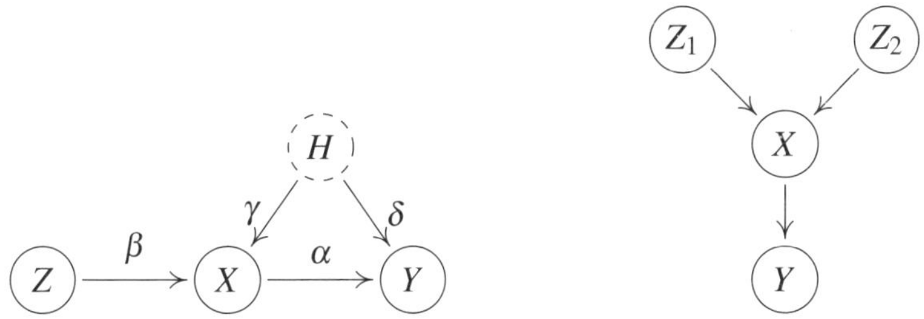

Figure 9.2: Left: setting of an instrumental variable (Section 9.3). A famous example is a randomized clinical trial with non-compliance: Z is the treatment assignment, X the treatment and Y the outcome. Right: Y-structure; see Section 9.4.1.

Balke and Pearl [1997] provide (tight) lower and upper bounds for the ACE without further assumptions on the relation between Y on X and H, for example. These bounds can be rather uninformative or they can collapse to a single point. In the latter case, we call the ACE identifiable.

(iii) Wang and Tchetgen Tchetgen [2016] show that, still in the case of binary treatment, the ACE becomes identifiable if the structural assignment for Y is additive in X and H [Wang and Tchetgen Tchetgen, 2016, Theorem 1].

(iv) For identifiability in the continuous case, see Newey [2013] and references therein.

Most concepts involving instrumental variables, such as the linear setting described previously, extend to situations, in which observed covariates W cause some (or all) relevant variables. For example, in Figure 9.2 (left) we can allow for a variable W pointing at Z, X, and Y. The assumptions (a), (b), and (c), as well as the procedures, are then modified and always include conditioning on W. Brito and Pearl [2002b] extend the idea to multivariate Z and X ("generalized instrumental variables").

9.4 Conditional Independences and Graphical Representations

In causal learning, we are trying to reconstruct the causal model from observational data. We have seen several identifiability results that allow us to identify the graph structure of an SCM over variables $\mathbf{X}$ from the observational distribution $P_{\mathbf{X}}$. Let us now turn to an SCM $\mathfrak{C}$ over variables $\mathbf{X} = (\mathbf{O}, \mathbf{H})$ that includes observed variables $\mathbf{O}$ and hidden variables $\mathbf{H}$. We may then still ask whether the graph structure of $\mathfrak{C}$ becomes identifiable from the distribution $P_{\mathbf{O}}$ over the observed variables, and if so, how we can identify it.

In the case without hidden variables, we discussed in Section 7.2.1 how one can learn (parts of) the causal structure under the Markov condition and faithfulness. These assumptions guarantee a one-to-one correspondence between d-separation and conditional independence, and we can therefore test for conditional independence in $P_{\mathbf{X}}$ and reconstruct properties of the underlying graph. Recall that independence-based methods, in principle, search over the space of DAGs and output a graph (or an equivalence class of graphs) representing exactly the set of conditional independences found in the data.

For causal learning with hidden variables, we would in principle like to search over the space of DAGs with latent variables. This comes with additional difficulties, however. We do not know the size of $\mathbf{H}$ and if we therefore do not restrict the number of hidden variables, there is an infinite number of graphical candidates that we have to search over. Furthermore, there is a statistical argument against this approach: the set of distributions that are Markovian and faithful with respect to a DAG forms a curved exponential family, which justifies the use of the BIC, for example [Haughton, 1988]; the set of distributions that are Markovian and faithful with respect to a DAG with latent variables, however, does not [Geiger and Meek, 1998]. If searching over DAGs with latent variables is infeasible, can we instead represent each DAG with latent variables by a marginalized graph over the observed variables, possibly using more than one type of edge, and then search over those structures? We have seen in Section 9.1 that such an approach also comes with a difficulty: the marginalized graph should depend on the original underlying SCM, and it is not sufficient to consider the information contained in the original graph. As mentioned previously, Bongers et al. [2016] studies marginalizations of SCMs in more detail.

For these reasons, we consider in the remainder of this section a slightly shifted problem: instead of checking whether a full distribution could have been induced by a certain DAG structure with latent variables, we restrict ourselves on certain types of constraints. For example, we consider all distributions that satisfy the same set of conditional independence statements over the observed variables $\mathbf{O}$ (implicitly assuming the Markov condition and faithfulness). We then ask how we can represent this set of conditional independences.

A straightforward solution would be to assume that the entailed distribution $P_{\mathbf{O}}$ is Markovian and faithful with respect to a DAG without hidden variables, and, similarly as before, then output a class of DAGs that represents the conditional independence in the distribution of the observed variables. Representing the con-

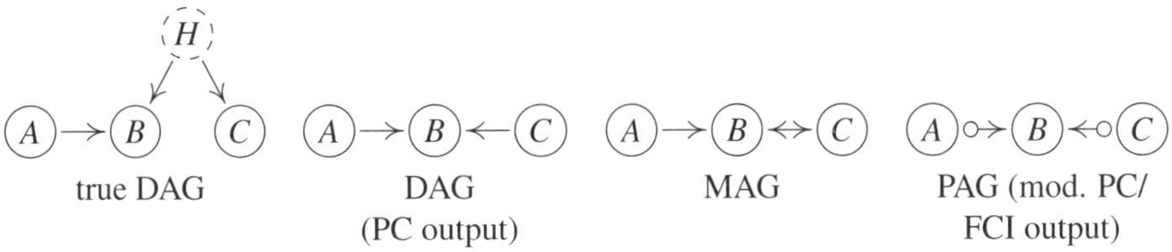

Figure 9.3: Starting with an SCM on the left-hand side, the three graphs on the right encode the set of conditional independences ($A \perp\!\!\!\perp C$). Due to an erroneous causal interpretation, the DAG is not desirable as an output of a causal learning method. In this example, the IPG and the latent projection (ADMG) are equal to the MAG.

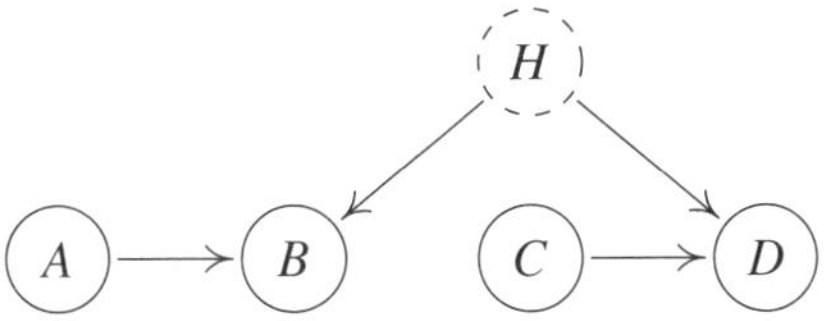

Figure 9.4: This example is taken from Richardson and Spirtes [2002, Figure 2(i)]. It shows that DAGs are not closed under marginalization. There is no DAG over nodes $\mathbf{O} = \{A, B, C, D\}$ that encodes all conditional independences from the graph including H.

ditional independence structure $P_{\mathbf{O}}$ with a DAG has two well-known drawbacks: (1) Representing the set of conditional independences with a DAG over the observed variables can lead to causal misinterpretations, and (2), the set of distributions whose pattern of independences correspond to the d-separation statements in a DAG is not closed under marginalization [Richardson and Spirtes, 2002].

For (1), consider an SCM that entails a distribution $P_{A,B,C,H}$ that is Markovian and faithful with respect to the corresponding DAG shown in Figure 9.3 (left). The only (conditional) independence relation that can be found in the observed distribution $P_{A,B,C}$ is $A \perp\!\!\!\perp C$ and therefore the DAG in Figure 9.3 (second from left) represents this conditional independence perfectly; in this sense, it could be seen as the output of PC. The causal interpretation, however, is erroneous. While in the original SCM an intervention on C does not have any effect on B, the output of PC suggests that there is a causal effect from C to B. Regarding (2), Figure 9.4 (it shows a graph that is taken from Richardson and Spirtes [2002]) shows the structure of an SCM over variables $\mathbf{X} = (\mathbf{O}, \mathbf{H})$ whose distribution is Markovian and faithful with respect to a DAG $\mathcal{G}$ ($\mathcal{G}$ represents all conditional independences in $\mathbf{X}$), that satisfies the following property. There are no DAGs over $\mathbf{O}$ representing the conditional independences that can be found in $P_{\mathbf{O}}$. In this sense, DAGs are not closed under marginalization.

The following subsection discusses some ideas that suggest graphs (over $\mathbf{O}$) for representing conditional independences. Note, however, that they do not necessarily come with an intuitive causal meaning. It may be difficult to infer properties of the structure of the underlying SCM over $\mathbf{X} = (\mathbf{O}, \mathbf{H})$ from the graphical objects. Graphical criteria for adjustment, as in Section 6.6, for example, need to be developed and proved for each type of graph again.

9.4.1 Graphs

Before, we have used graphs to represent the structural relationships of SCMs; see Definitions 3.1 and 6.2. The goal of this section is different: here, the aim is to use graphs to represent constraints in the distribution induced by the SCM. In this Section 9.4, we mainly consider conditional independence relations and discuss other constraints in more detail in Section 9.5. We have seen that in the presence of hidden variables, DAGs are a poor choice for representing conditional independences. These shortcomings of DAGs initiated the development of new graphical representations in causal inference. Richardson and Spirtes [2002] introduce **maximal ancestral graphs** (MAGs), for example, and show that they form the smallest superclass of DAGs that is closed under marginalization (see the preceding discussion). These are mixed graphs and contain directed and bidirected edges.[2] MAGs come with a slightly different separation criterion: instead of d-separation, one now looks at m-separation [Richardson and Spirtes, 2002]. Then, for each DAG with hidden variables there is a unique MAG over the observed variables that represents the same set of conditional independences (by m-separation); a simple construction protocol is provided in Richardson and Spirtes [2002, Section 4.2.1], for an example see Figure 9.3. This mapping is not one-to-one. Each MAG can be constructed by infinitely many different DAGs (containing an arbitrary number of hidden variables). As for DAGs, the Markov condition relates graphical separation statements in a MAG with conditional independences. Different MAGs representing the same set of m-separation, are summarized within a Markov equivalence class [Zhang, 2008b]; this equivalence class itself is often represented by a **partially ancestral graph** (PAG); see Table 9.1 for an overview. In PAGs, edges can end with a circle, which represents both possibilities of an arrow's head and tail; see Figure 9.3. Ali et al. [2009] provide graphical criteria that determine whether two MAGs are Markov equivalent.

[2] In fact, they may even contain undirected edges and can therefore model selection bias. We refer to Richardson and Spirtes [2002] for details.

Graphical object	DAG (without hiddens)	MAG	IPG	ADMG (with nested Markov)
Type of edges directed / undir. / bidir. / combination	✓/ - / - / -	✓/ ✓/ ✓/ -	✓/ - / ✓/ -	✓/ - / ✓/ ✓
Correct causal interpretation	✗	✓	✓	✓
Graphical separation for global Markov	d-seperation	m-seperation	m-seperation	m-seperation
Criterion for valid adjustment sets	✓	✓	?	✓
Algorithm for identification of intervention distribution	✓	?	?	✓
Representation of equivalence class	CPDAG (Markov)	PAG (Markov)	POIPG (Markov)	? (nested Markov)
Independence-based method for learning	PC, IC, SGS	FCI	FCI	-
Score-based method for learning	GDS, GES	for linear/binary/ discrete SCMs	?	for binary/ discrete SCMs
Can encode all equality constraints	✗	✗	✗	✓ (if obs. var. are discrete)
Can encode all constraints	✗	✗	✗	✗

Table 9.1: Consider an SCM over (observed) variables $\mathbf{O}$ and (hidden) variables $\mathbf{H}$ that induces a distribution $P_{\mathbf{O},\mathbf{V}}$. How do we model the observed distribution $P_{\mathbf{O}}$? We would like to use an SCM with (arbitrarily many) latent variables. This model class, however, has bad properties for causal learning. This table summarizes some alternative model classes (current research focuses especially on MAGs and ADMGs).

Example 9.5 (Y-structure) Given that even a single MAG can represent an arbitrary number of hidden variables, one may be wondering, whether a PAG, constructed from a DAG with hidden variables, ever contains non-trivial causal information. In Figure 9.3, for example, the PAG does not specify whether there is a directed path between C and B or a hidden variable with directed path both into C and B. Figure 9.2 (right) shows the example of a Y-structure (Z_1, Z_2, and Y are not directly connected). Consider now an SCM over an arbitrary number of variables that contains four variables X, Z_1, Z_2, and Y over which it induces the same conditional independences as the Y-structure does. We can then conclude that the corresponding PAG contains a directed edge from $X \to Y$. In addition, the causal relation between X and Y has to be unconfounded [e.g., Mani et al., 2006, Spirtes et al., 2000, Figure 7.23]. Any SCM, in which X and Y are confounded or in which X is not an ancestor of Y, leads to a different set of conditional independences. □

We have mentioned that graphical objects such as MAGs are primarily constructed to represent conditional independences and not to visualize SCMs (this is how we have introduced graphs in Definition 3.1). Thus, causal semantics becomes more complicated. In a MAG, for example, an edge $A \to B$ means that in the underlying DAG (including the hidden variables), A is an ancestor of B and B is not an ancestor of A; that is, the ancestral relationships are preserved. The PAG in Figure 9.3, for example, should be interpreted as follows: "In the underlying DAG, there could be a directed path from C to B, a hidden common cause, or a combination of both." As a consequence, causal reasoning in such graphs, that is, computing intervention distribution, becomes more involved, too [e.g., Spirtes et al., 2000, Zhang, 2008b]. Perkovic et al. [2015] characterize valid adjustment sets (Section 6.6) that work not only for DAGs but also for MAGs.

As an alternative to MAGs and PAGs, one may consider **induced path graphs** (IPGs) and (completed) **partially oriented induced path graphs** (POIPGs) that can be used for representing sets of IPGs [Spirtes et al., 2000, Section 6.6]. These graphs have initially been used to represent the output of the fast causal inference (FCI) algorithm; see Section 9.4.2. Consider a distribution that is Markovian and faithful with respect to a MAG. Since every MAG is an IPG but not vice versa, the Markov equivalence class of the MAG is contained in the Markov equivalence class of the corresponding IPG, and thus a PAG usually contains more causal information than a POIPG [Zhang, 2008b, Appendix A].

Even yet another possibility is to start with the original DAG containing hidden variables and then apply a **latent projection** [see Pearl, 2009, Verma and Pearl, 1991, Definition 2.6.1 and "embedded patterns", respectively]. This operation takes a graph $\mathcal{G}$ with observed and hidden variables and constructs a new graphical object $\tilde{\mathcal{G}}$ over the observed variables. The precise definition can be found in Shpitser et al. [2014, Definition 4], for example. The resulting graph structure is called an **acyclic directed mixed graph (ADMG)** and contains both directed and bidirected edges. Again, the m-separation leads to a Markov property [Richardson, 2003]. Instead of searching over DAGs with latent variables, we may now search over ADMGs.

We will see in Section 9.5 that distributions over the observed variables from a DAG with latent variables satisfy constraints other than conditional independences. ADMGs obey the possibility to take some of those constraints into account in the following way. The idea is to define a **nested Markov property** [Richardson et al., 2012, 2017, Shpitser et al., 2014], such that a distribution is nested Markovian with respect to an ADMG if not only some conditional independences hold that are implied by the graph structure but also other constraints; see Section 9.5.1, for example. It turns out that even the nested Markov property does not encode all constraints (in the discrete case they do encode all equality constraints, though [Evans, 2015]). We therefore have [Shpitser et al., 2014]:

$$
\begin{aligned}
&\{P_{\mathbf{O}} : P_{\mathbf{O},\mathbf{V}} \text{ induced by a DAG } \mathcal{G} \text{ with latent variables}\}\\
\subseteq\ &\{P_{\mathbf{O}} : P_{\mathbf{O}} \text{ is nested Markovian with respect to corresponding ADMG}\}\\
\subseteq\ &\{P_{\mathbf{O}} : P_{\mathbf{O}} \text{ is Markovian with respect to corresponding ADMG}\}.
\end{aligned}
$$

For ADMGs with discrete data and the ordinary Markov property, Evans and Richardson [2014] provide a parametrization. This parametrization can be extended to nested Markov models and it can be used to compute (constraint) maximum likelihood estimators [Shpitser et al., 2012]. ADMGs are called **bow-free** if between each pair of nodes there is only one kind of edge. For linear Gaussian models, this subclass of models allows for parameter identifiability [Brito and Pearl, 2002a]; additionally, there are algorithms that compute maximum likelihood estimates [Drton et al., 2009a] or perform causal learning [Nowzohour et al., 2015].

Chain graphs consist of directed and undirected edges and do not allow for partially directed cycles [Lauritzen, 1996, Section 2.1.1]. There is an extensive body of work on chain graphs; see, for example, Lauritzen [1996] for an overview and Lauritzen and Richardson [2002] for a causal interpretation. Note that for chain graphs, different Markov properties have been suggested [Lauritzen and Wermuth, 1989, Frydenberg, 1990, Andersson et al., 2001].

Summarizing, the representation of constraints (so far, we have mainly talked about conditional independences) using graphs, in particular in the case of hidden variables, is a non-trivial task that is still an active field of research; Sadeghi and Lauritzen [2014] relate several types of mixed graphs and discuss their Markov properties. Usually, the graphical objects and their corresponding separation criteria are complicated, and it is not trivial to relate the edges to the existence of causal effects (one may argue that nested Markov models are a step toward simplification though). It is surprising that despite all the difficulties in some situations (see the Y-structure in Example 9.5) we are still able to learn causal ancestral relationships.

9.4.2 Fast Causal Inference

We have seen that for structure learning a PAG might be a more sensible output than a CPDAG. Indeed, it is possible to modify the PC algorithm such that it outputs a PAG [Spirtes et al., 2000, Section 6.2]. While this simple modification of PC works fine for many examples, it is not correct in general. At each iteration, the PC algorithm considers a pair of (currently) adjacent nodes A and B, say, and searches for a set that d-separates them. To achieve considerable speedups, it searches only through subsets of the current neighbors of nodes A and B, based on Lemma 7.8(ii) in Section 7.2.1. In the presence of hidden variables, however, restricting the search space to subsets of the set of neighbors is not sufficient anymore [Verma and Pearl, 1991, Lemma 3]; Spirtes et al. [2000, Section 6.3] provide an example, for which the modified PC algorithm fails to find a d-separating set.

The FCI algorithm [Spirtes et al., 2000] resolves this issue. It outputs a PAG representing several MAGs. Zhang and Spirtes [2005] and Zhang [2008a] prove that a slight modification of the original FCI algorithm is complete. That is, its output is maximally informative. If the conditional independences originate from a DAG with hidden variables, the output indeed represents the correct corresponding PAG.

Several modifications of FCI lead to significant speedups. Spirtes [2001] suggests to restrict the size of the conditioning set (anytime FCI), and Colombo et al. [2012] reduce both the number of conditional independence tests and the size of the conditioning sets (really fast causal inference). Both algorithms can be slightly less informative than FCI. They are succeeded by FCI+, which is fast and complete [Claassen et al., 2013].

As an alternative, one might consider to score MAGs or equivalence classes of MAGs. Such scoring functions exist only for some classes of SCMs, such as linear SCMs [Richardson and Spirtes, 2002]; also, we are not aware of any efficient way of searching over this space of MAGs [Mani et al., 2006]. Silva and Ghahramani [2009] discuss a Bayesian approach for learning mixed graphs.

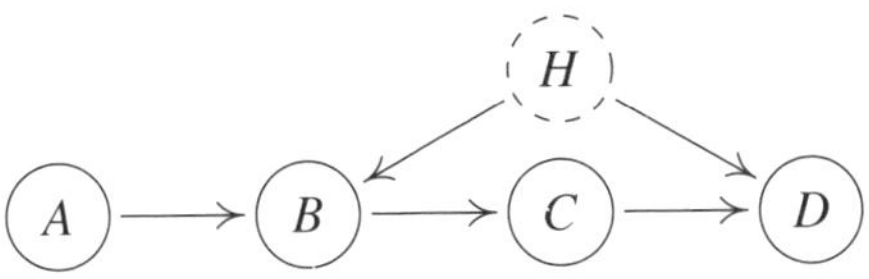

Figure 9.5: Any distribution that is Markovian with respect to this graph satisfies the Verma constraint (9.3), a non-independence constraint that appears in the marginal distribution over A, B, C, and D; the dashed variable H is unobserved [Verma and Pearl, 1991].

9.5 Constraints beyond Conditional Independence

We have mentioned that models with hidden variables can lead to constraints that are different from conditional independence constraints. We will mention a few of them to develop an intuition what kind of constraints we can expect, but we mainly point to the literature for details; see also Kela et al. [2017] for recent work and references to much of the earlier work.

9.5.1 Verma Constraints

Verma and Pearl [1991] provide the example shown in Figure 9.5. Any distribution that is Markovian with respect to the corresponding graph allows for the following Verma constraint [e.g., Spirtes et al., 2000, Chapter 6.9]. For some function f we have

$$\sum_b p(b \,|\, a) p(d \,|\, a, b, c) = f(c, d). \qquad (9.3)$$

Unlike conditional independence constraints, (9.3) lets us decide whether or not there is a directed edge from A to D (note that in Figure 9.5 A and D cannot be d-separated). Although many open questions regarding those algebraic constraints remain, there has been progress in understanding when such constraints appear [Tian and Pearl, 2002]. Shpitser and Pearl [2008b] investigate the special subclass of dormant independences; these are constraints that appear as indepedendence constraints in intervention distributions.

The question remains how one can exploit those constraints for causal learning. In the case of binary variables, for example, Richardson et al. [2012, 2017] and Shpitser et al. [2012] use nested Markov models for the parametrization of such models and provide a method for computing (constraint) maximum likelihood estimators; see also Section 9.4.1. However, nested Markov models do not include all inequality constraints, which we discuss in the following section.

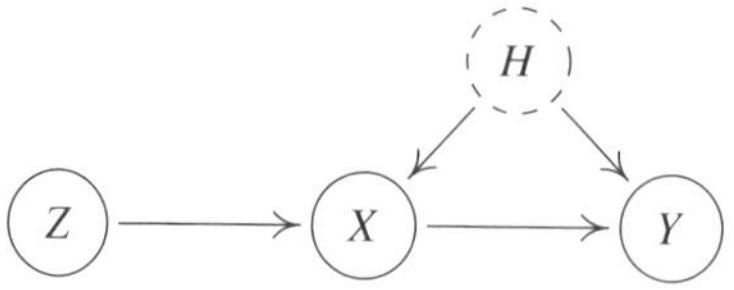

(a) Causal structure where Z is called an instrument for X and enables some causal statements about the effect of X on Y.

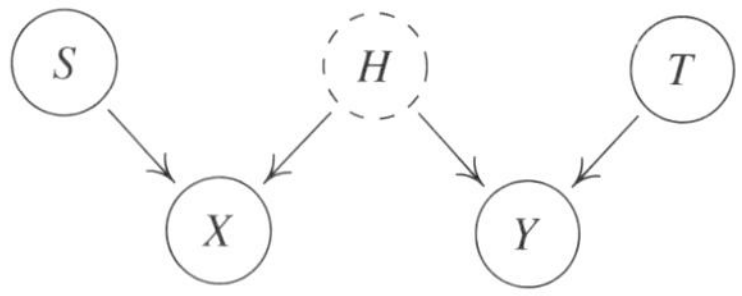

(b) Causal structure of a famous experiment used by quantum physicists to falsify assumptions of classical physics; see Section 9.5.2.

Figure 9.6: Two important examples of latent structures that entail inequality constraints.

9.5.2 Inequality Constraints

Marginalizing a graphical model over some of its variables induces a large set of inequality constraints [see, e.g., Kang and Tian, 2006, Evans, 2012, and references therein]. It would go beyond the scope of this book to mention all the known ones. Instead, we would like to point out the diversity of fields in which they have been applied. To this end, we consider two example DAGs containing observed and unobserved variables that appear in completely different contexts. Note that this section discusses only inequalities that refer to the *observational* distributions of observable variables while the literature contains also inequalities that relate observational and intervention distribution of observable variables [see, e.g., Balke, 1995, Pearl, 2009, Chapter 8], sometimes also under additional assumptions [Silva and Evans, 2014, Geiger et al., 2014]. While the former task aims at falsifying a hypothetical latent structure, the latter one admits statements about interventions given that the respective DAG is true. To show some inequalities concerning only observational probabilities, the causal structure in Figure 9.6(a) with binary variables entails, for instance, that

$$P(X=0, Y=0|Z=0) + P(X=1, Y=1|Z=1) \leq 1. \tag{9.4}$$

Inequalities like this have been provided in the literature [Bonet, 2001, eq. (3)] to test whether a variable is instrumental. This DAG plays a crucial role in analyzing randomized clinical trials with imperfect compliance, where Z is the instruction to take a medical drug, X describes whether the patient takes the drug (assume this can be inferred from a blood test, for example), and Y whether the patient recovers [see, e.g., Pearl, 2009].

The causal structure shown in Figure 9.6(b) is known to entail, for instance, the

Clauser-Horne-Shimony-Holt (CHSH) inequality [Clauser et al., 1969]:

$$\begin{aligned}\mathbb{E}[XY|S=-1,T=-1]+\mathbb{E}[XY|S=-1,T=1]\\+\mathbb{E}[XY|S=1,T=-1]+\mathbb{E}[XY|S=1,T=1]\leq 2\end{aligned} \tag{9.5}$$

if X,Y,S,T take values in $\{-1,1\}$. Equation (9.5) is a generalization of **Bell's inequality** [Bell, 1964]. The latent common cause may attain arbitrarily many values, just as the existence of a variable that d-separates $\{X,S\}$ from $\{Y,T\}$ implies (9.5). Remarkably, the CHSH inequality is violated in quantum physics in a scenario where one would intuitively agree that the underlying causal structure is the one in Figure 9.6(b). Two physicists A and B at different locations receive particles from a common source described by H. Variables X and Y describe the results of dichotomous measurements performed on the particles received by A and B, respectively. S is a coin flip that determines which measurement out of two possible options is performed by A. Likewise, T is a coin flip determining the measurement performed by B. The unobserved common cause of X and Y is the common source of the particles received by A and B. According to a widely accepted interpretation, the violation of (9.5) observed in experiments [Aspect et al., 1981], shows that there is no classical random variable H describing the joint state of the incoming particles such that $\{S,X\}$ and $\{T,Y\}$ are conditionally independent, given H. This is because the state of quantum physical systems cannot be described by values of random variables. Instead, they are density operators on a Hilbert space.

Information-theoretic inequalities for latent structures have gained interest since they are sometimes easier to handle than inequalities that refer directly to probabilities [see, e.g., Steudel and Ay, 2015]. Chaves et al. [2014] describe a family of inequalities for the case of discrete variables that is not complete but can be generated by the following systematic approach.

First, one starts with a distribution entailed by an SCM over d discrete variables $\mathbf{X} := (X_1,\dots,X_d)$. For a given joint distribution $P_{X_1,\dots,X_d}$ we can define a function

$$H : 2^{\mathbf{X}} \to \mathbb{R}_0^+$$

such that $H(X_{j_1},\dots,X_{j_k})$ is the Shannon entropy[3] of $(X_{j_1},\dots,X_{j_k})$. Well-known

[3]We write $H(X_{j_1},\dots,X_{j_k})$ instead of $H\big((X_{j_1},\dots,X_{j_k})\big)$ for notational convenience and again perform set operations on vectors.

properties of H are the **elementary inequalities**

$$H(S\cup\{X_j\}) \geq H(S) \tag{9.6}$$

$$H(S\cup\{X_j,X_k\}) \leq H(S\cup\{X_j\})+H(S\cup\{X_k\}) \tag{9.7}$$

$$H(\emptyset) = 0, \tag{9.8}$$

where S denotes a subset of $\mathbf{X}$. Inequalities (9.6) and (9.7) are known as monotonicity and submodularity conditions, respectively; see also Section 6.10. Furthermore, inequalities (9.6)–(9.8) are known as polymatroid axioms in combinatorial optimization, too.

To employ the causal structure, we now recall that $S \perp\!\!\!\perp T \,|\, R$ for all three disjoint subsets S, T, and R of nodes, for which S and T are d-separated by R. This can be rephrased in terms of Shannon mutual information [Cover and Thomas, 1991] by

$$I(S:T\,|\,R) = 0, \tag{9.9}$$

which is equivalent to

$$H(S\cup R)+H(T\cup R) = H(S\cup T\cup R)+H(R). \tag{9.10}$$

Remarkably, (9.10) is a linear equation. Since conditional independences define *nonlinear* constraints on the space of probability vectors, it is more convenient to consider the constraints on the space of entropy vectors.

These elementary inequalities together with Equation (9.9) imply further inequalities. To derive them in an algorithmic way, Chaves et al. [2014] use a technique from linear programing, the Fourier-Motzkin elimination [Williams, 1986]. Given some subset $\mathbf{O} \subset \mathbf{X}$ of observed variables, this procedure often yields inequalities containing only entropies of variables in $\mathbf{O}$ although there may be no conditional independence constraints that contain only the observed ones. One example is given in Figure 9.7, for which Chaves et al. [2014, Theorem 1] obtain

$$I(X:Z)+I(Y:Z) \leq H(Z), \tag{9.11}$$

and likewise for cyclic permutations of the variable names. A joint distribution violating (9.11) is, for instance, the one where all observed variables are 0 or all variables are 1 with probability $1/2$ each because then $H(Z) = 1$ bit and $I(X:Z) = I(Y:Z) = 1$ bit. To understand this intuitively, note that in this example, we require for each observed node, say Z, a deterministic relationship with both X and Y and therefore with U and V. But there is a trade-off between the extent to which Z can be determined by its unobserved cause U or by V. Z cannot perfectly follow the "instructions" of both U and V simultaneously (which, themselves, are independent).

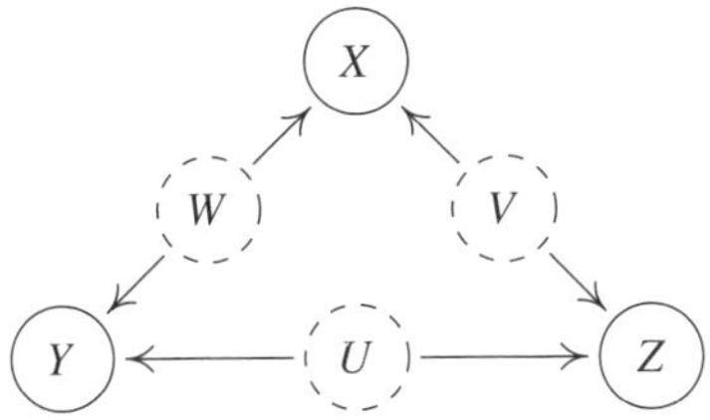

Figure 9.7: DAG that is not able to generate a joint distribution over X, Y, and Z, for which all three observed variables attain simultaneously 0 or 1 with probability $1/2$ each.

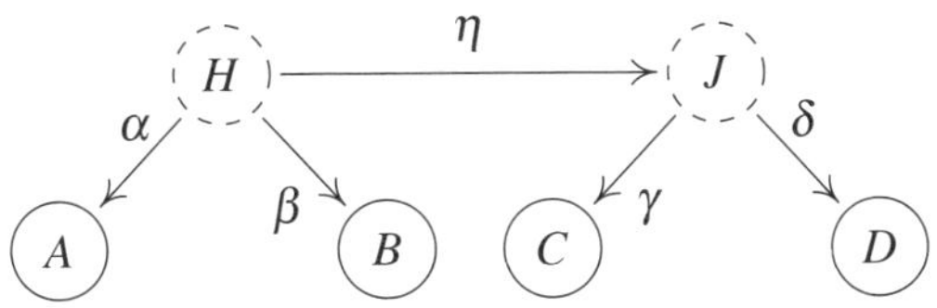

Figure 9.8: If the graph corresponds to a linear SCM, the entailed distribution will satisfy the tetrad constraints (9.12)–(9.14).

9.5.3 Covariance-Based Constraints

Another type of constraint appears in linear models with hidden variables. For example, in Figure 9.8 we obtain the **tetrad constraints** [Spirtes et al., 2000, Spearman, 1904]:

$$\rho_{AC}\rho_{BD} - \rho_{AD}\rho_{BC} = 0 \tag{9.12}$$

$$\rho_{AB}\rho_{CD} - \rho_{AD}\rho_{BC} = 0 \tag{9.13}$$

$$\rho_{AC}\rho_{BD} - \rho_{AB}\rho_{CD} = 0, \tag{9.14}$$

where ρ_{AC} is the correlation coefficient between variables A and C. The first constraint (9.12), for example, can be verified easily from Figure 9.8:

$$\begin{aligned}\operatorname{cov}[A,C]\cdot\operatorname{cov}[B,D] &= \alpha\gamma\eta\operatorname{var}[H]\cdot\beta\delta\eta\operatorname{var}[H]\\ &= \alpha\delta\eta\operatorname{var}[H]\cdot\beta\gamma\eta\operatorname{var}[H] = \operatorname{cov}[A,D]\cdot\operatorname{cov}[B,C].\end{aligned}$$

It is possible to characterize the occurrence of vanishing tetrad constraints graphically using the language of treks and choke points [Spirtes et al., 2000, Theorem 6.10]. Again, these constraints allow us to distinguish between different causal structures, just from observational data. Bollen [1989] and Wishart [1928] constructed statistical tests to test for vanishing tetrad differences. These can be turned into a score that can be exploited for causal learning; this has been investigated by Spirtes et al. [2000, Chapter 11.2] and Silva et al. [2006], for example.

Kela et al. [2017] consider latent structures where all dependences between observed variables are due to a collection of independent common causes and describe constraints on the possible covariance matrix of the observed variables. They emphasize that resorting to covariance matrices instead of the full distribution is advantageous both regarding statistical feasibility and computational tractability. Using functions of the observed variables (i.e., by mapping them into a feature space like in methods based on reproducing kernel Hilbert spaces), the method is also able to account for higher-order dependences.

9.5.4 Additive Noise Models

We have mentioned in Section 7.2.3 that learning the structure of LiNGAMs can be based on ICA. Hoyer et al. [2008b] show that both identifiability statements and methods can be extended to linear non-Gaussian structures with hidden variables by exploiting what is known under overcomplete ICA.

For nonlinear ANMs (Section 4.1.4), we have seen that in the generic case, we cannot have both $Y = f(X) + N_Y$ with $N_Y \perp\!\!\!\perp X$ and $X = g(Y) + M_X$ with $M_X \perp\!\!\!\perp Y$. We expect that a similar identifiability holds for hidden variables. The following ANM describes the influence of a hidden variable H on the observables X and Y:

$$H := N_H \tag{9.15}$$

$$X := f(H) + N_X \tag{9.16}$$

$$Y := g(H) + N_Y. \tag{9.17}$$

For the regime of sufficiently low noise, Janzing et al. [2009a] prove that the joint distribution $P_{H,X,Y}$ can be reconstructed from $P_{X,Y}$ up to reparametrizations of H. It is plausible that the restriction to low noise is not necessary but just a weakness of the proof. Setting $f(H) = H$ and $N_X = 0$ yields an ANM from X to Y (and likewise, we can obtain an ANM from Y to X); this suggests that the additive noise assumption renders the three cases $X \to Y$, $X \leftarrow Y$, and $X \leftarrow * \to Y$ distinguishable from $P_{X,Y}$ alone. A relation to dimensionality reduction helps us to understand how we can fit the model (9.15)–(9.17) from data: data points (x,y) from the distribution $P_{X,Y}$ can be drawn using the following procedure (see Figure 9.9):

1. Draw h according to P_H.
2. Consider the corresponding point $\big(f(h), g(h)\big)$ on the manifold

$$M := \left\{ \big(f(h), g(h)\big) \in \mathbb{R}^2 : h \in \mathbb{R} \right\}. \tag{9.18}$$

3. Add some independent noise (n_X, n_Y) in each dimension.

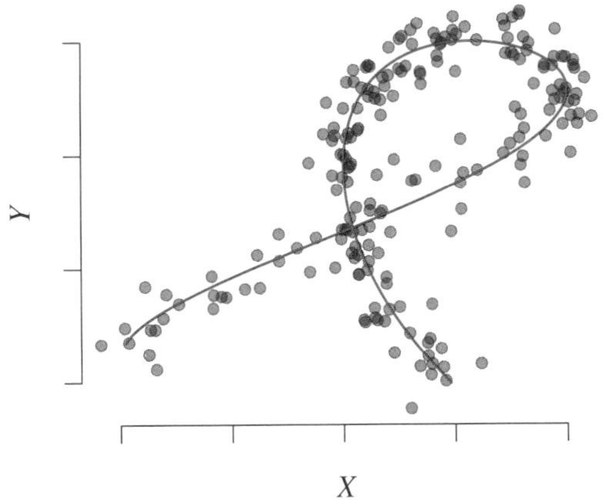

Figure 9.9: The figure shows a scatter plot for $P_{X,Y}$. The red line describes the manifold M; see Equation (9.18).

To fit model (9.15)–(9.17) to a data sample from $P_{X,Y}$, we may therefore apply a dimensionality reduction technique to the sample to obtain the estimate $\hat{M}$. For recovering the corresponding value of h from a given point (x,y), this point (x,y) should not be projected onto the manifold M because this usually leads to residuals that will be dependent on H. Instead of small residuals (n_X, n_Y), we require the residuals to be as independent as possible from H [Janzing et al., 2009a].

There are many remaining open questions regarding the identifiability of ANMs with hidden variables. Such results could have an important implication, however: whenever we find an ANM from X to Y but not from Y to X, these identifiability results would show that the effect is not confounded (within the model class of additive noise).

9.5.5 Detecting Low-Complexity Confounders

Here we explain two methods by Janzing et al. [2011] that infer whether the path between two observed variables X and Y is intermediated by some variable that attains only a few values; see Figure 9.10. The scenario is the following: X is causally linked to Y via a DAG that has an arrowhead at Y. The question is whether the path between X and Y is intermediated by a variable U that has only a few values. Here, the direction of the arrow that connects X and U does not matter, but the typical application of the method would be to detect confounding if the confounding path is intermediated by a variable U of this simple type. Janzing

Figure 9.10: Detecting low-complexity intermediate variables: if the path between X and Y is blocked by some variable U that attains only a few values, $P_{Y|X}$ often shows typically properties as a "fingerprint" of U.

et al. [2011] consider, for instance, two binary variables X and U describing genetic variants (single-nucleotide polymorphisms) of an animal or plant and a variable Y corresponding to some phenotype. Whenever the statistical dependence between X and Y is only due to the fact that U has an influence on Y and U is statistically related to X, then U would play the role of such an intermediate variable. Here, neither U nor X is a cause of the other, but there are variables like "ethnic group" that influence both. Therefore, U is not the common cause itself, but it lies on the confounding path.

The idea of detecting this type of confounding is that U changes the conditional $P_{Y|X}$ in a characteristic way. To discuss this, we first define a class of conditionals of which we will later show that it will usually occur only if the path between X and Y is *not* intermediated by such a U.

Definition 9.6 (Pairwise pure conditionals) *The conditional distribution $P_{Y|X}$ is said to be pairwise pure if for any two $x_1, x_2 \in \mathcal{X}$ the following condition holds. There is no $\lambda < 0$ or $\lambda > 1$ for which*

$$\lambda P_{Y|X=x_1} + (1-\lambda) P_{Y|X=x_2} \tag{9.19}$$

is a probability distribution.

To understand Definition 9.6, note that (9.19) is always a probability distribution for $\lambda \in [0,1]$ because it is then a convex sum of two distributions. On the other hand, for $\lambda \notin [0,1]$, (9.19) may no longer be a non-negative measure: consider the case where Y attains finitely many values $\mathcal{Y} := \{y_1, \ldots, y_k\}$. Then the space of distributions of Y is the simplex whose k vertices are given by the point masses on $y_1, \ldots, y_k$. Figure 9.11 shows this for the case $k = 3$, where the space of probability distributions on $\mathcal{Y}$ is a triangle. Figure 9.11(a) shows an example of a pure conditional: extending the connecting line between $P_{Y|X=x_1}$ and $P_{Y|X=x_2}$ leaves the triangle, while such an extension within the space of distributions is possible in Figure 9.11(b). Figure 9.12 shows, however, that purity is stronger than the condition that the points $P_{Y|X=x}$ lie in the interior of the simplex. Here, they are on the edges of the triangle and yet allow for an extension within the triangle.

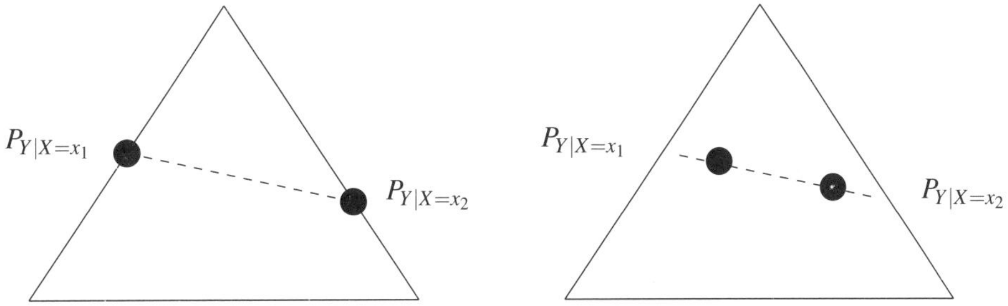

(a) Example of a pure conditional: extending the line connecting the two points $P_{Y|X=x_1}$ and $P_{Y|X=x_2}$ would leave the simplex of probability distributions.

(b) Example of a non-pure conditional: the line connecting $P_{Y|X=x_1}$ and $P_{Y|X=x_2}$ can be slightly extended without leaving the simplex.

Figure 9.11: Visualization of a pure and a non-pure conditional.

If $P_{Y|X}$ has a density $(x,y) \mapsto p(y|x)$ purity can be defined by the following intuitive condition:

$$\inf_{y \in \mathcal{Y}} \frac{p(y|x_1)}{p(y|x_2)} = 0 \quad \forall x_1, x_2 \in \mathcal{X}.$$

To explore to what extent causal conditionals corresponding to $X \to Y$ in nature are pure has to be left to future research. To give an example of an interesting class of pure conditionals, we want to mention that $P_{Y|X}$ is pairwise pure if it admits an ANM with bijective function f_Y [Janzing et al., 2011, Lemma 4] and the density of the noise satisfies a certain decay condition.

The following result shows that a pure conditional strongly suggests that the causal path between X and Y is not intermediated by a variable that attains only a few values.

Theorem 9.7 (Strictly positive conditionals and non-purity) *Assume there is a variable U such that $X \perp\!\!\!\perp Y \,|\, U$. Further, assume that the range $\mathcal{U}$ of U is finite and that the conditional density $p(u|x)$ is strictly positive for all $u \in \mathcal{U}$ and for all x such that $P_{Y|X=x}$ is defined. Then, $P_{Y|X}$ is not pairwise pure.*

Proof. It is easy to see that the conditional $P_{U|X}$ is not pairwise pure because $\inf_{u \in \mathcal{U}} p(u|x_1)/p(u|x_2) \neq 0$ for all x_1, x_2 for which $P_{Y|X=x_i}$ is defined. Due to $p(y|x) = \sum_u p(y|u)p(u|x)$, the conditional $P_{Y|X}$ is a concatenation of $P_{Y|U}$ and $P_{U|X}$ and therefore also not pure because $P_{U|X}$ is not pure [see Janzing et al., 2011, Lemma 8]. □

Although the theorem holds for all finite variables, the second assumption of strict positivity of the conditional $P_{U|X}$ is much more plausible if U attains only a

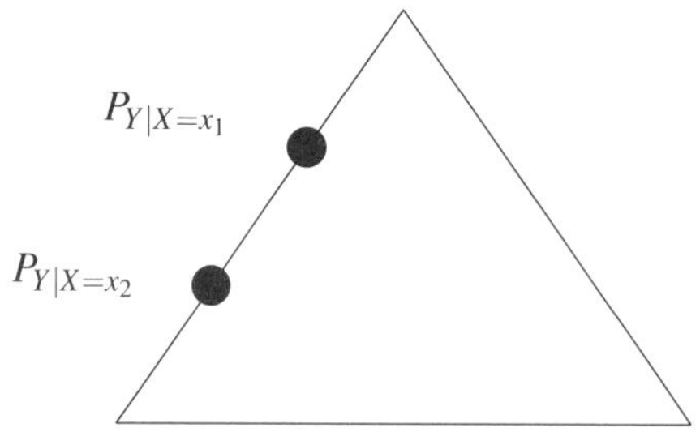

Figure 9.12: Another example of a non-pure conditional: the line connecting $P_{Y|X=x_1}$ and $P_{Y|X=x_2}$ can be extended without leaving the simplex.

few values. Otherwise, it may happen that there exist values u for which $p(u|x)$ is so close to 0 that this may result in $P_{Y|X}$ being *almost* pure.

To see an instructive example showing how the intermediate node typically spoils purity, assume that U and X are binary with $p(u|x) = 1-\varepsilon$ for $u = x$. We then have

$$\begin{aligned} P_{Y|X=0} &= P(U=0|X=0)P_{Y|U=0} + P(U=1|X=0)P_{Y|U=1} \\ &= (1-\varepsilon)P_{Y|U=0} + \varepsilon P_{Y|U=1}. \end{aligned}$$

Hence, $P_{Y|X=0}$ lies on the interior of the line connecting $P_{Y|U=0}$ and $P_{Y|U=1}$ (and likewise for $P_{Y|X=1}$). Thus, $P_{Y|X}$ is not pure.

Another example of how intermediate variables can leave characteristic "fingerprints" in the distribution of $P_{X,Y}$ will be formulated using the following property of a conditional [Allman et al., 2009, Janzing et al., 2011]:

Definition 9.8 (Rank of a conditional) *The rank of $P_{Y|X}$ is the dimension of the vector space spanned by all vectors $P_{Y|X\in\mathcal{A}}$ in the space of measures, where $\mathcal{A}$ runs over all measurable subsets of the range of X with non-zero probability.*

Janzing et al. [2011] does not provide an algorithm for estimating the rank, however. If Y has finite range, $P_{Y|X}$ defines a stochastic matrix whose rank coincides with the rank of $P_{Y|X}$. The following result is a simple observation [Allman et al., 2009]:

Theorem 9.9 (Rank and the range of U) *If $X \perp\!\!\!\perp Y \,|\, U$ and U attains k values, then the rank of $P_{Y|X}$ is at most k.*

It is easy to show that under the conditions of Theorem 9.9, $P_{X,Y}$ can be decomposed into a mixture of k product distributions. This observation generalizes to the multivariate case: whenever there is a variable U attaining k values such that conditioning on U renders $X_1,\ldots,X_d$ jointly independent, then $P_{X_1,\ldots,X_d}$ decomposes into a mixture of d product distributions. Sgouritsa et al. [2013] and Levine et al. [2011] describe methods to find this decomposition with the goal of detecting the "confounder" U via identifying the product distributions.

9.5.6 Different Environments

The invariant causal prediction approach we describe in Sections 7.1.6 and 7.2.5 can be modified to deal with hidden variables [Peters et al., 2016, Section 5.2], as long as the hidden variables are not affected by interventions. Furthermore, Rothenhäusler et al. [2015, "backShift"] consider the special case of linear SCMs. Assume that we observe a vector $\mathbf{X}^e$ of d random variables in different environments $e \in \mathcal{E}$. Here, the environments are generated by (unknown) shift variables $\mathbf{C}^e = (C_1^e, \ldots, C_d^e)$ that are required to be independent of each other and of the noise variables. That is, for each environment e we have

$$\mathbf{X}^e = \mathbf{B}\mathbf{X}^e + \mathbf{C}^e + \mathbf{N}^e,$$

where the distribution of $\mathbf{N}^e$ does not depend on e. We can allow for hidden variables by assuming non-zero covariance between the different components of the noise variables. It still follows that

$$(\mathbf{I} - \mathbf{B})\Sigma_{\mathbf{X},e}(\mathbf{I} - \mathbf{B})^T = \Sigma_{\mathbf{C},e} + \Sigma_{\mathbf{N}}$$

with $\Sigma_{\mathbf{X},e}$, $\Sigma_{\mathbf{C},e}$, and $\Sigma_{\mathbf{N}}$ being the covariance matrices of $\mathbf{X}^e$, $\mathbf{C}^e$, and $\mathbf{N}^e$, respectively. Ergo,

$$(\mathbf{I} - \mathbf{B})\,(\Sigma_{\mathbf{X},e} - \Sigma_{\mathbf{X},f})\,(\mathbf{I} - \mathbf{B})^T = \Sigma_{\mathbf{C},e} - \Sigma_{\mathbf{C},f}. \qquad (9.20)$$

(Note that for each environment e, one may pool all other environments to obtain the "environment" f.) By assumption, for all choices of e and f, the right-hand side of Equation (9.20) is diagonal, which allows us to reconstruct the causal structure $\mathbf{B}$ by joint diagonalization of $\Sigma_{\mathbf{X},e} - \Sigma_{\mathbf{X},f}$. If there are at least three environments, this procedure allows us to identify $\mathbf{B}$ under weak assumptions [Rothenhäusler et al., 2015, Theorem 1].

The latter example shows how imposing regularity conditions (as linear models and independent shift interventions) among different environments, allows us to reconstruct the underlying causal structure even in the presence of hidden variables.

9.6 Problems

Problem 9.10 (Sufficiency) *Prove Remark 9.4.*

Problem 9.11 (Simpson's paradox) *Construct an SCM $\mathfrak{C}$ with binary random variables X, Y and a sequence $Z_1, Z_2, \dots$ of variables, such that for all even $d \geq 0$ and all $z_1, \dots, z_{d+1}$,*

$$\begin{aligned}&P^{\mathfrak{C}}(Y = 1 \mid X = 1, Z_1 = z_1, \dots, Z_d = z_d)\\ &> P^{\mathfrak{C}}(Y = 1 \mid X = 0, Z_1 = z_1, \dots, Z_d = z_d)\end{aligned}$$

but

$$\begin{aligned}&P^{\mathfrak{C}}(Y = 1 \mid X = 1, Z_1 = z_1, \dots, Z_d = z_d, Z_{d+1} = z_{d+1})\\ &< P^{\mathfrak{C}}(Y = 1 \mid X = 0, Z_1 = z_1, \dots, Z_d = z_d, Z_{d+1} = z_{d+1}).\end{aligned}$$

This example drives the Simpson's paradox to an extreme. If X indicates treatment, Y recovery, and $Z_1, Z_2, \dots$ some confounding factors, then, by the adjustment formula (6.13), adjusting for more and more variables always turns around the causal conclusion whether the treatment is helpful or harmful.

Problem 9.12 (Instrumental variables) *Consider the SCM*

$$\begin{aligned}H &:= N_H\\ Z &:= N_Z\\ X &:= f(Z) + g(H) + N_X\\ Y &:= \alpha X + j(H) + N_Y\end{aligned}$$

and assume that we observe the joint distribution over Z, X, and Y. Given the distribution rather than a finite sample, regressing X on Z non-parametrically yields the conditional mean $\mathbb{E}[X \mid Z = z]$ as regression function. Write down the two-stage least square method and prove that it identifies α.

10

Time Series

Reasoning about causal relations among variables that refer to different time instances is easier than causal reasoning without time structure. Causal structures have to be consistent with the time order. We have seen in Section 7.2.4 that, after knowing a causal ordering of nodes and assuming that there are no hidden variables, finding the causal DAG does not require assumptions other than the Markov condition and minimality (more debatable conditions such as faithfulness or restricted function classes, for instance, are not necessary). Given the time order, three main issues remain. First, the set of variables under consideration may not be causally sufficient; second, there may be variables that refer to the same time instant (within the given measurement accuracy) that cannot be causally ordered a priori; third, in practice, we are often given only one repetition of the time series — this differs from the usual i.i.d. setting, in which we observe every variable several times. Accordingly, all these issues play a crucial role for causal reasoning in time series.

10.1 Preliminaries and Terminology

So far, we have considered a setting where samples are i.i.d. drawn from the joint distribution $P_{X_1,\ldots,X_d}$. Here, we discuss causal inference in time series, that is, we have a d-variate time series $(\mathbf{X}_t)_{t\in\mathbb{Z}}$, where each $\mathbf{X}_t$ for fixed t is the vector $(X_t^1,\ldots,X_t^d)$. We assume that it describes a strictly stationary stochastic process [e.g., Brockwell and Davis, 1991]. Each variable X_t^j represents a measurement of the jth observable of some system at time t. Since causal influence can never go

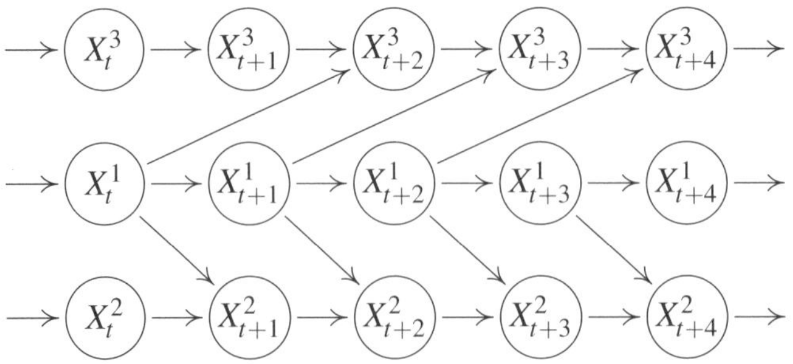

Figure 10.1: Example of a time series with no instantaneous effects.

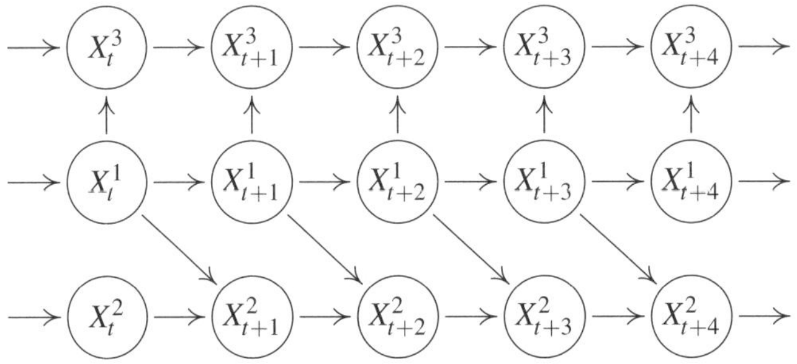

Figure 10.2: Example of a time series with instantaneous effects.

from the future to the past, we distinguish between two types of causal relations in multivariate time series.

First, the causal graph[1] with nodes X_t^j for $(j,t) \in \{1,\ldots,d\} \times \mathbb{Z}$ contains only arrows from X_t^j to X_s^k for $t < s$ but not for $t = s$; see Figure 10.1. Then we say there are no **instantaneous** effects. Second, the causal graph contains instantaneous effects, that is, arrows from X_t^j to X_t^k for some j and k in addition to arrows going from X_t^m to X_s^ℓ for $t < s$ and some m and ℓ, as shown in Figure 10.2. We call the causal structure **purely instantaneous** if for any $j \neq k$ and $h > 0$ the variable X_t^j may influence X_t^k and X_{t+h}^j but not X_{t+h}^k; see Figures 10.5(a) and 10.5(b). The case where each X_t^j is not influenced by any previous variable (including its own past), can be ignored because it need not be described as time series. Instead, the index t may then be considered as labeling indices of independent instances of a statistical sample in the i.i.d. setting of previous chapters.

We define the **full time graph** as the DAG having X_t^i as nodes, as visualized in

[1]Strictly speaking, we have introduced the causal DAG only for finitely many nodes so far. Here, however, we need infinite graphs and neglect this technical subtlety [see, e.g., Peters et al., 2013].

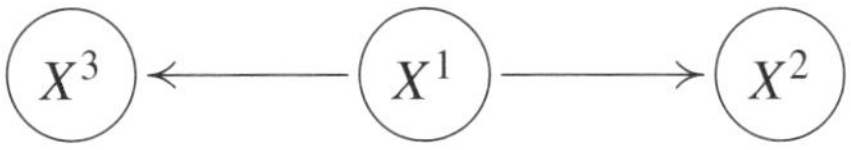

Figure 10.3: Summary graph of the full time graphs shown in Figures 10.1 and 10.2.

Figures 10.1 and 10.2. In contrast to previous chapters, the full time graph is a DAG with infinitely many nodes. The **summary graph** is the directed graph with nodes $X^1, \dots, X^d$ containing an arrow from X^j to X^k for $j \neq k$ whenever there is an arrow from X_t^j to X_s^k for some $t \leq s \in \mathbb{Z}$. Note that the summary graph is a directed graph that may contain cycles, although we will assume that the full time graph is acyclic. Figure 10.3 shows the summary graph corresponding to the full time graphs depicted in Figures 10.1 and 10.2. For any $t \in \mathbb{Z}$, we denote by $\mathbf{X}_{\text{past}(t)}$ the set of of all $\mathbf{X}_s$ with $s < t$ and use $X^j_{\text{past}(t)}$ for the past of a specific component X^j. We also write X^j_{past} if t is some fixed time instant of reference. Moreover, $(\mathbf{X}_t^{-j})_{t \in \mathbb{Z}}$ denotes the collection of time series $(\mathbf{X}_t^k)_{t \in \mathbb{Z}}$ for all $k \neq j$.

10.2 Structural Causal Models and Interventions

We assume that the stochastic process $(\mathbf{X}_t)_{t \in \mathbb{Z}}$ admits a description by an SCM in which at most the past q values (for some q) of all variables occur:

$$X_t^j := f^j\left((\mathbf{PA}_q^j)_{t-q}, \dots, (\mathbf{PA}_1^j)_{t-1}, (\mathbf{PA}_0^j)_t, N_t^j \right), \tag{10.1}$$

where

$$\dots, N_{t-1}^1, \dots, N_{t-1}^d, N_t^1, \dots, N_t^d, N_{t+1}^1, \dots, N_{t+1}^d, \dots$$

are jointly independent noise terms. Here, for each $s \in \mathbb{Z}$, the symbol $(\mathbf{PA}_s^j)_{t-s}$ denotes the set of variables X_{t-s}^k, $k = 1, \dots, d$, that influence X_t^j. Note that $\mathbf{PA}_{t-s}^j$ may contain X_{t-s}^j for all $s > 0$, but not for $s = 0$. We assume the corresponding full time graph to be acyclic.

A popular special case of (10.1) is the class of vector autoregressive models (VAR) [Lütkepohl, 2007]:

$$X_t^j := \sum_{i=1}^{q} A_i^j \mathbf{X}_{t-i} + N_t^j, \tag{10.2}$$

where each A_i^j is a $1 \times d$-matrix; see also Remark 6.5 on linear cyclic models, especially Equation (6.4).

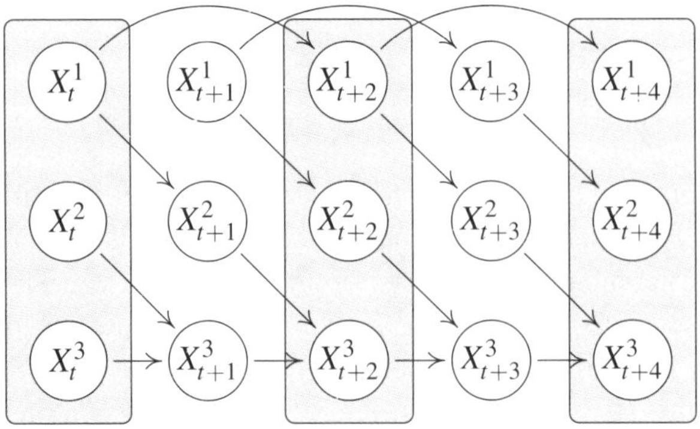

Figure 10.4: Example of a subsampled time series: only the variables in the shaded areas are observed.

As in the i.i.d. setting, SCMs formalize the effect of interventions; more precisely, an intervention corresponds to replacing some of the structural assignments. Interventions may, for instance, consist in setting all values $\{X_t^j\}_{t\in\mathbb{Z}}$ for some j to certain values. Alternatively, one could also intervene on X_t^j only at one specific time instant t.

10.2.1 Subsampling

In many applications, the sampling process may be slower than the time scale of the causal processes. Figure 10.4 shows an example, in which only every second time instance is observed. The summary graph of the original full system contains the edges $X^1 \to X^2 \to X^3$. We may now want to construct a causal model for the observed, subsampled processes. It is therefore important to define which interventions we want to allow for. First, if we constrain ourselves to interventions on observed time points, there should be no causal influence from X^1 to X^2. Intervening on an observed instance of X^1 does not have any effect on the observable part of X^2 (note that the time series X^1 has only lag two effects $X_t^1 \to X_{t+2}^1$). Furthermore, in this setting, subsampling cannot create spurious instantaneous effects if these have not been there before. For the case of an SCM, Bongers et al. [2016, Chapter 3] describe a formal process of how to marginalize the model by substituting the causal mechanisms of the hidden time steps into the other mechanisms. The resulting model describes the effect of interventions correctly if these are restricted to the observed time points. Second, if we do consider interventions on hidden variables, however, we may be interested in recovering the original summary graph, a problem that is addressed by Danks and Plis [2013] and Hyttinen et al. [2016], for example.

There are situations in which subsampling is not a good model for the data-generating process. For many physical measurements, for example, one may want to model the observations as averages of consecutive time points rather than as a sparse subset of those. The former is a useful but also complicated model assumption: the averaging process might change the model class, and one furthermore needs to be careful about modeling interventions.

10.3 Learning Causal Time Series Models

Currently, Granger causality and its variations is among the most popular approaches to causal time series analysis. To provide a better link among the chapters, we nevertheless first explain the conclusions that can be drawn using a conditional independence-based approach. The order should by no means be mistaken as a judgment about the approaches.

Sections 10.3.1 and 10.3.2 contain mostly identifiability results. The remaining three Sections, 10.3.3, 10.3.4, and 10.3.5, contain more concrete causal learning methods for time series. They can be applied if the multivariate time series has been sampled once, at finitely many time points. Most of the ideas, however, transfer to situations, where we receive several i.i.d. repetitions of the same time series.

10.3.1 Markov Condition and Faithfulness

Lemma 6.25 states that two DAGs are Markov equivalent if and only if their skeleton and their set of v-structures coincide. If there are no instantaneous effects, the full time graph is therefore already determined by knowing its skeleton. The arrow can only be directed forward in time. We thus conclude [Peters et al., 2013, Proof of Theorem 1]:

Theorem 10.1 (Identifiabilty in absence of instantaneous effects) *Assume that two full time graphs are induced by SCMs without instantaneous effects. If the full time graphs are Markov equivalent, then they are equal.*

Hence, we can uniquely identify the full time graph from conditional independences provided that Markov condition and faithfulness holds (to deal with infinitely large DAGs, one sometimes assumes that the time series start at $t = 0$).

In the presence of instantaneous effects, Markov equivalent graphs can at most differ by the direction of those effects. However, there are many cases where even

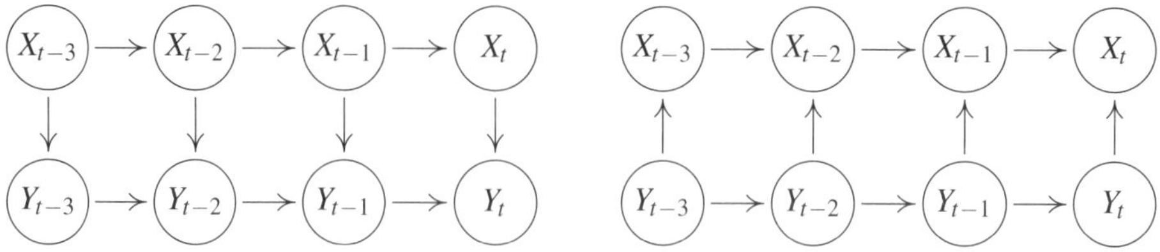

(a) There are v-structures at all nodes of $(Y_t)_{t\in\mathbb{Z}}$.

(b) There are v-structures at all nodes of $(X_t)_{t\in\mathbb{Z}}$.

Figure 10.5: Two DAGs that are not Markov equivalent although they coincide up to instantaneous effects.

that direction can be identified because different directions of instantaneous effects induce different sets of v-structures. A simple example is shown in Figure 10.5. The direction of the instantaneous effect can still be inferred even if arrows from X_t to Y_{t+1} for all $t \in \mathbb{Z}$ are added to Figure 10.5, and likewise if arrows from Y_t to X_{t+1} are added; we cannot add both, however, because this would remove all v-structures. The following sufficient condition for the identifiability of the direction of instantaneous effects has been given by Peters et al. [2013, Theorem 1]:

Theorem 10.2 (Identifiability for acyclic summary graphs) *Assume that two full time graphs are induced by SCMs, and that in both cases for each j, X_t^j is influenced by X_{t-s}^j for some $s \geq 1$. Assume further that the summary graphs are acyclic. If the full time graphs are Markov equivalent, then they are equal.*

The following result shows that the presence of any arrow in the summary graph can in principle be decided from a single conditional independence test.

Theorem 10.3 (Justification of Granger causality) *Consider an SCM without instantaneous effects for the time series $(\mathbf{X}_t)_{t\in\mathbb{Z}}$ such that the induced joint distribution is faithful with respect to the corresponding full time graph. Then the summary graph has an arrow from X^j to X^k if and only if there exists a $t \in \mathbb{Z}$ such that*

$$X_t^k \not\perp\!\!\!\perp X_{past(t)}^j \,|\, \mathbf{X}_{past(t)}^{-j}. \tag{10.3}$$

For completeness, we have included the proof in Appendix C.14. Similar results can be found in White and Lu [2010] and Eichler [2011, 2012]. As already suggested by the headline of Theorem 10.3, this is the basis of Granger causality that we discuss in more detail in Section 10.3.3.

10.3.2 Some Causal Conclusions Do Not Require Faithfulness

Remarkably, interesting causal conclusions can even be made from conditional dependences without using faithfulness. This is in contrast to the i.i.d. case where any distribution is Markovian with respect to the complete DAG for any ordering of nodes. Since there are no arrows backward in time, the Markov condition for time series is sufficient to infer whether the summary graph is $X \to Y$ or $Y \to X$, given that one of the two alternatives is true.

Theorem 10.4 (Detection of arrow $X \to Y$) *Consider an SCM for the bivariate time series $(X_t, Y_t)_{t \in \mathbb{Z}}$.*

(i) If there is a $t \in \mathbb{Z}$ such that

$$Y_t \not\perp\!\!\!\perp X_{past(t)} \,|\, Y_{past(t)}, \tag{10.4}$$

then the summary graph contains an arrow from X to Y.

(ii) Assume further that there are no instantaneous effects and the joint density of any finite subset of variables is strictly positive. If for all $t \in \mathbb{Z}$, we have

$$Y_t \perp\!\!\!\perp X_{past(t)} \,|\, Y_{past(t)}, \tag{10.5}$$

then the summary graph contains no arrow from X to Y.

Again, this proof may have appeared elsewhere, but we include it for completeness in Appendix C.15. Proving (ii) requires causal minimality, which is strictly weaker than faithfulness.

In the next subsection we will see that Theorem 10.4 and various variations [e.g., White and Lu, 2010, Eichler, 2011, 2012] link conditional independence-based approaches to causal discovery to Granger causality.

10.3.3 Granger Causality

For simplicity, we start with the bivariate version of Granger causality.

Bivariate Granger Causality Theorem 10.4 shows (subject to excluding instantaneous effects together with mild technical conditions) that the presence or absence of an arrow in the summary graph can be inferred by testing (10.5) and the analogous statement when exchanging the roles of X and Y. We can then distinguish between the possible summary graphs $X \quad Y$, $X \to Y$, $X \leftarrow Y$, $X \rightleftarrows Y$. One

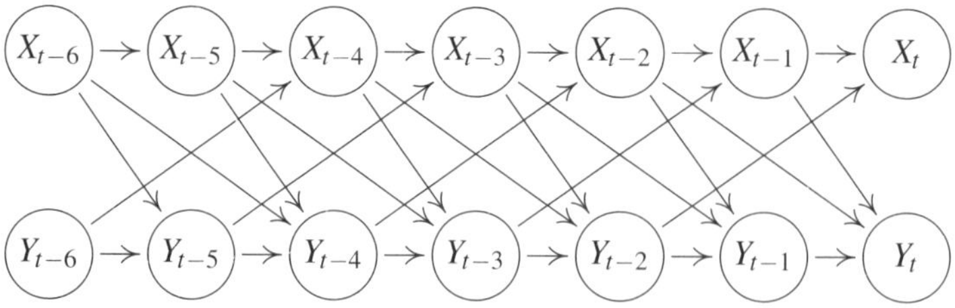

Figure 10.6: Typical scenario, in which Granger causality works: if all arrows from X to Y were missing, Y_t would be conditionally independent of the past values of X, given its own past. Here, Y_t does depend on the past values of X, given its own past. Thus, condition (10.4) proves the existence of an influence from X to Y.

infers that X influences Y whenever the past values of X help in predicting Y from its own past. Formally, we write

$$X \text{ Granger-causes } Y \quad :\Longleftrightarrow \quad Y_t \not\perp\!\!\!\perp X_{\text{past}(t)} \,|\, Y_{\text{past}(t)}. \tag{10.6}$$

This idea already goes back to Wiener [1956, pages 189–190], who argued that X has a causal influence on Y if the prediction of Y from its own past is improved by additionally accounting for X. The typical scenario, in which Theorem 10.4 holds is depicted in Figure 10.6.

Often Granger causality refers to linear prediction. Then, one compares the following two linear regression models:

$$Y_t = \sum_{i=1}^{q} a_i Y_{t-i} + N_t \tag{10.7}$$

$$Y_t = \sum_{i=1}^{q} a_i Y_{t-i} + \sum_{i=1}^{q} b_i X_{t-i} + \tilde{N}_t, \tag{10.8}$$

where $(N_t)_{t\in\mathbb{Z}}$ and $(\tilde{N}_t)_{t\in\mathbb{Z}}$ are assumed to be i.i.d. time series, respectively. X is inferred to Granger-cause Y whenever the noise term $\tilde{N}_t$ (for predictions including X) has significantly smaller variance than the noise term N_t obtained without X. This amounts to saying that Y_t has non-vanishing partial correlations to $X_{\text{past}(t)}$, given $Y_{\text{past}(t)}$. For multivariate Gaussian distributions, this is equivalent to the dependence statement (10.4). Modifications of this idea that use nonlinear regression have been extensively studied, too [e.g., Ancona et al., 2004, Marinazzo et al., 2008]. For non-parametric testing of (10.5) see, for instance, Diks and Panchenko [2006] and references therein.

An information theoretic quantity measuring the dependence between Y_t and the past of X, given the past of Y, is given by **transfer entropy** [Schreiber, 2000]:

$$TE(X \to Y) := I(Y_t : X_{\text{past}(t)} | Y_{\text{past}(t)}), \tag{10.9}$$

where $I(\mathbf{A} : \mathbf{B} \,|\, \mathbf{C})$ denotes the conditional mutual information [Cover and Thomas, 1991] for any three sets $\mathbf{A}$, $\mathbf{B}$, $\mathbf{C}$ of variables; see also Appendix A. Estimating transfer entropy and inferring that X causes Y whenever it is significantly greater than 0 can thus be considered as an information theoretic implementation of Granger causality that accounts for arbitrary nonlinear influences. It is therefore tempting to consider transfer entropy as a measure of the *strength* of the influence of X on Y, but "Limitations of Granger Causality" will explain why this is not appropriate.

Multivariate Granger Causality The assumption of causal sufficiency of a bivariate time series as in Theorem 10.4 is often inappropriate. This has already been addressed by Granger [1980]. We therefore say X^j Granger causes X^k if

$$X_t^k \not\perp\!\!\!\perp X^j_{\text{past}(t)} \,|\, \mathbf{X}^{-j}_{\text{past}(t)}.$$

Granger already emphasized that proper use of Granger causality would actually require to condition on all relevant variables in the world. Nevertheless, Granger causality is often used in its bivariate version or in situations, in which clearly important variables are unobserved. Such a use can yield misleading statements when interpreting the results causally.

Limitations of Granger Causality Violation of causal sufficiency is — as in the i.i.d. scenario of the previous chapters — a serious issue in causal time series analysis. To explain why Granger causality is misleading in a causally insufficient multivariate time series, we restrict the attention to the case where only a bivariate time series $(X_t, Y_t)_{t \in \mathbb{Z}}$ is observed. Assume that both X_t and Y_t are influenced by previous instances of a hidden time series $(Z_t)_{t \in \mathbb{Z}}$. This is depicted in Figure 10.7(a) where Z influences X with a delay of 1, and Y with a delay of 2. Assuming faithfulness, the d-separation criterion tells us

$$Y_t \not\perp\!\!\!\perp X_{\text{past}(t)} \,|\, Y_{\text{past}(t)},$$

while we have

$$X_t \perp\!\!\!\perp Y_{\text{past}(t)} \,|\, X_{\text{past}(t)}.$$

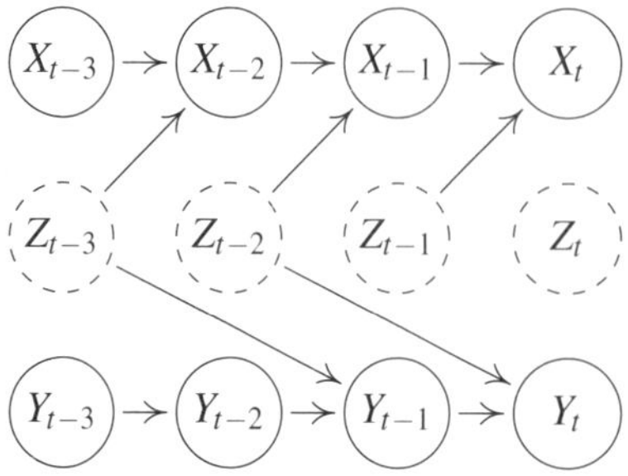

(a) Due to the hidden common cause Z, Granger causality erroneously infers causal influence from X to Y.

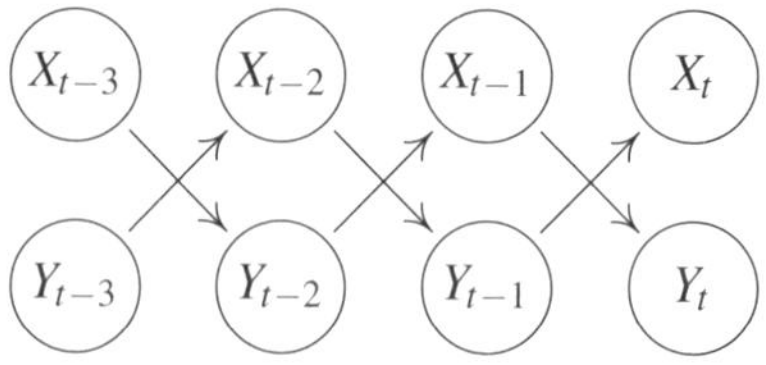

(b) Granger causality erroneously infers neither causal influence from X to Y nor from Y to X if the influence from X_t on Y_{t+1} and the one from Y_t to X_{t+1} are deterministic.

Figure 10.7: In these examples, Granger causality infers an incorrect graph structure.

Thus, naive application of Granger causality infers that X causes Y and Y does not cause X. This effect has been observed, for instance, for the relation between the price of butter and the price of cheese. Both prices are strongly influenced by the price of milk, but the production of cheese takes much longer than the production of butter, which causes a larger delay between the prices of milk and cheese [Peters et al., 2013, Experiment 10]. This failure of Granger causality, however, is only possible because not all relevant variables are observed, which was stated as a requirement by Granger himself.

A second example for a scenario where Granger fails has been provided by Ay and Polani [2008] and is depicted in Figure 10.7(b). Assume that X_{t-1} influences Y_t deterministically via a copy operation, that is, $Y_t := X_{t-1}$. Likewise, the value of Y_{t-1} is copied to X_t. Then it is intuitively obvious that X and Y strongly influence each other in the sense that intervening on the value X_t changes all the values Y_{t+1+2k} for $k \in \mathbb{N}_0$. Likewise, intervening on Y_t changes all values X_{t+1+2k}. Nevertheless, the past of X is useless for predicting Y_t from its past, because Y_t can already be predicted perfectly from its own past. Certainly, deterministic relations are in general problematic for conditional independence-based causal inference since determinism induces additional independences. For instance, if Y is a function of X in the causal chain $X \to Y \to Z$, we get $Y \perp\!\!\!\perp Z \,|\, X$, which is not typical for this causal structure. One may therefore argue that this example is artificial and a more natural version would be a *noisy* copy operation. For the case where X_t and Y_t are binary variables, Janzing et al. [2013, Example 7] show that the transfer entropy converges to 0 when the noise level of the copy operation tends to 0. Then, Granger causality would indeed infer that X causes Y and Y causes X, but for small noise the tiny amount by which the past of X improves the prediction of Y_t does not

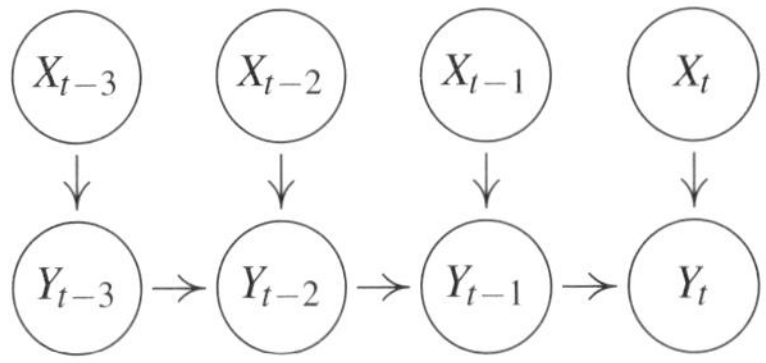

(a) Granger causality cannot detect the influence of X on Y because the past of X influences Y_t only via the past of Y.

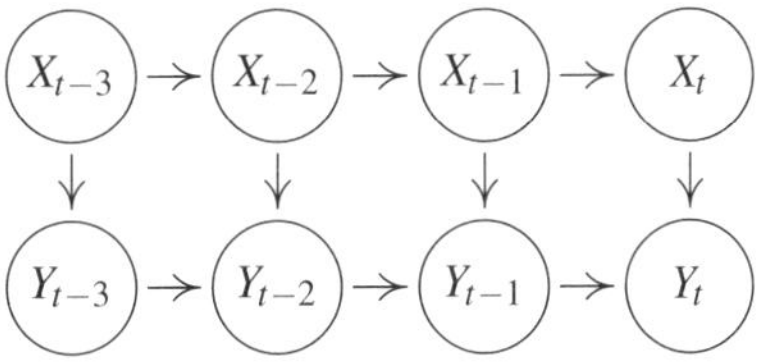

(b) Here, the past of X is still helpful for predicting Y_t since X_{t-1} influences Y_t indirectly via X_t. Thus, Granger causality is still able to detect the influence of X on Y.

Figure 10.8: Two scenarios with instantaneous effects, one where Granger causality fails to detect them (a) and one where it does not (b).

properly account for the mutual influence between the time series (which is still strong in an intuitive sense). In this sense, transfer entropy is not an adequate measure for the strength of causal influence of one time series on another one. Janzing et al. [2013] discuss the limitations of different proposals to quantify causal influence (both for time series and the i.i.d. setting) and propose another information theoretic measure of causal strength. To summarize this paragraph, we emphasize that the *qualitative* statement about presence or absence of causal influence in the case of two causally sufficient time series only fails for a rather artificial scenario, while *quantifying* the causal influence via transfer entropy (which is suggested by interpreting "improvement of prediction" in information theoretic terms) can be problematic also in less artificial scenarios.

There is another scenario where Granger causality is quantitatively misleading but its qualitative statement remains correct unless faithfulness is violated (it uses, however, instantaneous effects, for which one may argue that they disappear for sufficiently fine time resolution [Granger, 1988]). For Figure 10.8(a), d-separation yields

$$Y_t \perp\!\!\!\perp X_{\text{past}(t)} \,|\, Y_{\text{past}(t)}.$$

Intuitively speaking, only the present value X_t would help for better predicting Y_t, but the past values $X_{t-1}, X_{t-2}, \ldots$ are useless and thus, Granger causality does not propose a link from X to Y. In Figure 10.8(b), however, Granger causality does detect the influence of X on Y (if we assume faithfulness) although it is still purely instantaneous, but the slight amount of improvement of the prediction does not properly account for the potentially strong influence of X_t on Y_t. To account for instantaneous effects, modifications of Granger causality have been proposed that add instantaneous terms in the corresponding SCM, but then identifiability may break down [e.g., Lütkepohl, 2007, (2.3.20) and (2.3.21)]. Knowing that a system contains instantaneous effects may suggest modifying Granger causality by regressing Y_t in (10.8) not only on $X_{\text{past}(t)}$ but on $X_t \cup X_{\text{past}(t)}$ instead. However, as already noted by Granger [1988], this may yield wrong conclusions: if X_t helps in predicting Y_t, this could equally well mean that Y_t influences X_t instead of indicating an influence from X_t to Y_t.

Remark 10.5 (Model misspecification may help) There is a paradox message of this insight: even in the case in which variables influence other variables instantaneously, for inferring causal statements it is more conclusive to check whether the past of a variable helps for the prediction rather than to check whether the past *and the present* value help. Condition (i) of Theorem 10.4 does not exclude instantaneous effects. Therefore (subject to causal sufficiency), we can still conclude that every benefit of $X_{\text{past}(t)}$ for predicting Y_t from $Y_{\text{past}(t)}$ is due to an influence of X on Y. Moreover, whenever there is any influence of X on Y, no matter whether it is purely instantaneous or not, $X_{\text{past}(t)}$ will in the generic case improve our prediction of Y_t, given $Y_{\text{past}(t)}$. □

10.3.4 Models with Restricted Function Classes

To address the limitations of Granger causality, Hyvärinen et al. [2008] describe linear non-Gaussian autoregressive models that render causal structures with instantaneous effects identifiable. Peters et al. [2013] describe how to address this task using less restrictive function classes f^j in (10.1). One example is given by adapting ANMs to time series, that is, to use the SCM

$$X_t^j := f^j\left((\mathbf{PA}_q^j)_{t-q}, \cdots, (\mathbf{PA}_1^j)_{t-1}, (\mathbf{PA}_0^j)_t\right) + N_t^j,$$

for $j \in \{1, \ldots, d\}$. Apart from identifiability of causal structures within Markov equivalence classes, there is a second motivation using restricted function classes: using simulated time series, Peters et al. [2013] provide some empirical evidence for the belief that time series that admit models from a restricted function class are less likely to be confounded.

10.3.5 Spectral Independence Criterion

The spectral independence criterion (SIC) is a method that is based on the idea of independence between cause and mechanism described in Shajarisales et al. [2015]. Assume we are given a weakly stationary bivariate time series $(X_t, Y_t)_{t \in \mathbb{Z}}$

where either X influences Y or Y influences X via a linear time invariant filter. More explicitly, for the case that X influences Y, Y is then obtained from X by convolution with a function h:

$$Y_t = \sum_{k=1}^{\infty} h(k) X_{t-k}. \tag{10.10}$$

For technical details, such as the decay conditions for h that ensure that (10.10) and expressions below are well-defined, we refer to Shajarisales et al. [2015]. To formalize an independence condition between X and h, we consider the action of the filter in the frequency domain: for all $\nu \in [-1/2, 1/2]$, let $S_{XX}(\nu)$ denote the power spectral density for the frequency ν; the latter is explicitly given by the Fourier transform of the auto-covariance function

$$C_{XX}(\tau) := \mathbb{E}\left[X_t X_{t+\tau}\right], \quad \text{with } \tau \in \mathbb{Z}.$$

Then, (10.10) yields

$$S_{YY}(\nu) = |\tilde{h}(\nu)|^2 \cdot S_{XX}(\nu), \tag{10.11}$$

where $\tilde{h}(\nu) = \sum_{k\in\mathbb{Z}} e^{-i2\pi k\nu} h(k)$ denotes the Fourier transform of h. In other words, multiplying the power spectrum of the input time series with the squared transfer function of the filter yields the power spectrum of the output. Whenever $\tilde{h}$ is invertible, in addition to (10.11) we have

$$S_{XX}(\nu) = \left|\frac{1}{\tilde{h}(\nu)}\right|^2 \cdot S_{YY}(\nu). \tag{10.12}$$

While both equations (10.11) and (10.12) are valid, the question is which one describes the causal model. The idea is that for the causal direction, the power spectrum of the input time series carries no information about the transfer function of the filter. To formalize this, Shajarisales et al. [2015] state the following independence condition:

Definition 10.6 (SIC) *The time series X and the filter h are said to satisfy the SIC if S_{XX} and $\tilde{h}$ are uncorrelated, that is,*

$$\langle S_{XX} \cdot |\tilde{h}|^2 \rangle = \langle S_{XX} \rangle \cdot \langle |\tilde{h}|^2 \rangle, \tag{10.13}$$

where $\langle f \rangle := \int_{-1/2}^{1/2} f(\nu) d\nu$ denote the average of any function on the frequency interval $[-1/2, 1/2]$.

Shajarisales et al. [2015] show that (10.13) implies that the analogue independence condition for the backward direction does not hold, except for the non-generic case where $|\tilde{h}|$ is constant over the whole interval of frequencies.

Theorem 10.7 (Identifiability via SIC) *If* (10.13) *holds and* $|\hat{h}|$ *is not constant in* ν *then* S_{YY} *is negatively correlated with* $1/|\tilde{h}|$, *that is,*

$$\langle S_{YY} \cdot 1/|\tilde{h}|^2 \rangle < \langle S_{YY} \rangle \cdot \langle 1/|\tilde{h}|^2 \rangle. \tag{10.14}$$

Proof. The left-hand sides of (10.13) and (10.14) are given by $\langle S_{YY} \rangle$ and $\langle S_{XX} \rangle$, respectively. Jensen's inequality states $1/\langle |\tilde{h}|^2 \rangle < \langle 1/|\tilde{h}|^2 \rangle$, which implies the statement. □

Shajarisales et al. [2015] propose a simple causal inference algorithm that checks which direction is closer to satisfying SIC. They report some encouraging results using SIC for experiments with various simulated and real-world data sets.

10.4 Dynamic Causal Modeling

Dynamic causal modeling (DCM) is a technique that has been developed particularly for inferring causal relations between the activities of different brain regions [Friston et al., 2003]. If the vector $z \in \mathbb{R}^n$ encodes the activity of n brain regions and $u \in \mathbb{R}^m$ a vector of perturbations, the dynamics of z is given by a differential equation of the form

$$\frac{d}{dt} z = F(z, u, \theta), \tag{10.15}$$

where F is a known function, $u \in \mathbb{R}^m$ is a vector of external stimulations, and θ parametrizes the model class describing the causal links between the different brain regions. One often considers the following bilinear approximation of (10.15):

$$\frac{d}{dt} z = \left(A + \sum_{j=1}^{m} u_j B^j \right) z + Cu, \tag{10.16}$$

where $A, B^1, \dots, B^m$ are $n \times n$ matrices and C has the size $n \times m$. While A describes the mutual influence of the activities z_j in different regions, the matrices B^j describe how u changes their mutual influence. C encodes the direct influence of u on z.

Here, z is not directly observable, but one can detect the *hemodynamic response*. The blood flow provides an increased amount of nutrients (such as oxygen and glucose) to compensate for the increased demand of energy. Functional magnetic resonance imaging (fMRI) is able to detect this increase via the blood-oxygen-level–dependent (BOLD) signal. Defining a state vector x that includes both the brain activity and some hemodynamic state variables, one ends up with a differential equation for x

$$\frac{d}{dt}x = f(x, u, \theta) \tag{10.17}$$

by combining (10.16) with a dynamical model of the hemodynamic response. The high-dimensional parameter θ consists of all free parameters of (10.16) and parameters from modeling the hemodynamic response. Then, one uses a model of how x determines the measured BOLD signal y:

$$y = \lambda(x). \tag{10.18}$$

Finally, as data, we obtain an observed time series of y-vectors. DCM then infers the matrices in (10.16) from these data using various known techniques for learning models with latent variables, for example, expectation maximization (EM).

Lohmann et al. [2012a] criticize DCM mainly because the number of model parameters explodes with growing n and m, which renders their identification impossible from empirical data. According to their experiments with simulated brain connections, a large fraction of wrong models obtained higher evidence by DCM than the true model. These findings triggered a debate about DCM; see also Friston et al. [2013] for a response to Lohmann et al. [2012a] and Lohmann et al. [2012b] for a response to Friston et al. [2013].

10.5 Problems

Problem 10.8 (Acyclic summary graphs) *Prove Theorem 10.2.*

Problem 10.9 (Instantaneous effects) *Consider an SCM over a multivariate time series, in which each variable X_t^j is influenced by all past values of all components X^k. Additionally, assume that the instantaneous effects form a DAG and that the distribution is Markovian and faithful with respect to the full time graph. To which extent can one identify the instantaneous DAG structure from the distribution?*

Problem 10.10 (Granger causality) *Argue why Granger causality results in "X G causes Y" and "Y G causes X" if one adds arrows $Z_t \to Z_{t+1}$ for $t \in \mathbb{Z}$ in Figure 10.7(a).*

A

Some Probability and Statistics

A.1 Basic Definitions

(i) We denote the underlying probability space by $(\Omega, \mathcal{F}, P)$. Here, Ω, $\mathcal{F}$, and P are set, σ-algebra, and probability measure, respectively.

(ii) We use capital letters for real-valued random variables. For example, $X : (\Omega, \mathcal{F}) \to (\mathbb{R}, \mathcal{B}_{\mathbb{R}})$ is a measurable function, with respect to the Borel σ-algebra. Random vectors are measurable functions $\mathbf{X} : (\Omega, \mathcal{F}) \to (\mathbb{R}^d, \mathcal{B}_{\mathbb{R}^d})$. We call $\mathbf{X}$ non-degenerate if there is no value $\mathbf{c} \in \mathbb{R}^d$ such that $P(\mathbf{X} = \mathbf{c}) = 1$. For an introduction to measure theory, see, for example, Dudley [2002].

(iii) We usually denote vectors with bold letters. In a slight abuse of notation, we consider sets of variables $\mathbf{B} \subseteq \mathbf{X}$ as a single multivariate variable.

(iv) $P_{\mathbf{X}}$ is the distribution of the d-dimensional random vector $\mathbf{X}$, that is, a probability measure on $(\mathbb{R}^d, \mathcal{B}_{\mathbb{R}^d})$.

(v) We write $x \mapsto p_X(x)$ or simply $x \mapsto p(x)$ for the density, that is, the Radon-Nikodym derivative of P_X with respect to a product measure. We (sometimes implicitly) assume its existence or continuity.

(vi) We call X **independent** of Y and write $X \perp\!\!\!\perp Y$ if and only if

$$p(x, y) = p(x)p(y) \tag{A.1}$$

for all x, y. Otherwise, X and Y are **dependent**, and we write $X \not\perp\!\!\!\perp Y$.

(vii) We call $X_1, \dots, X_d$ **jointly (or mutually) independent** if and only if

$$p(x_1, \dots, x_d) = p(x_1) \cdot \ldots \cdot p(x_d) \tag{A.2}$$

for all $x_1, \dots, x_d$. If $X_1, \dots, X_d$ are jointly independent, then any pair X_i and X_j with $i \neq j$ are independent, too. The converse does not hold in general: pairwise independence does not imply joint independence.

(viii) We call X **independent** of Y **conditional on** Z and write $X \perp\!\!\!\perp Y \,|\, Z$ if and only if

$$p(x,y\,|\,z) = p(x\,|\,z)p(y\,|\,z) \tag{A.3}$$

for all x, y, z such that $p(z) > 0$. Otherwise, X and Y are dependent conditional on Z and we write $X \not\!\perp\!\!\!\perp Y \,|\, Z$.

(ix) Conditional independence relations obey the following important rules [e.g., Pearl, 2009, Section 1.1.5]:

$$\begin{array}{rcll} X \perp\!\!\!\perp Y \,|\, Z & \Rightarrow & Y \perp\!\!\!\perp X \,|\, Z & \text{(symmetry)} \\ X \perp\!\!\!\perp Y, W \,|\, Z & \Rightarrow & X \perp\!\!\!\perp Y \,|\, Z & \text{(decomposition)} \\ X \perp\!\!\!\perp Y, W \,|\, Z & \Rightarrow & X \perp\!\!\!\perp Y \,|\, W, Z & \text{(weak union)} \\ X \perp\!\!\!\perp Y \,|\, Z \text{ and } X \perp\!\!\!\perp W \,|\, Y, Z & \Rightarrow & X \perp\!\!\!\perp Y, W \,|\, Z & \text{(contraction)} \\ X \perp\!\!\!\perp Y \,|\, W, Z \text{ and } X \perp\!\!\!\perp W \,|\, Y, Z & \Rightarrow & X \perp\!\!\!\perp Y, W \,|\, Z & \text{(intersection).} \end{array}$$

The existence of a strictly positive density suffices for the intersection property to hold. Necessary and sufficient conditions for the discrete case are provided by Drton et al. [2009b, Exercise 6.6] and by Fink [2011]. Peters [2014] covers the continuous case.

(x) The **variance** of a random variable X is defined as

$$\mathrm{var}[X] := \mathbb{E}\left[(X - \mathbb{E}[X])^2\right] = \mathbb{E}\left[X^2\right] - \mathbb{E}[X]^2$$

if $\mathbb{E}[X^2] < \infty$.

(xi) We call X and Y **uncorrelated** if $\mathbb{E}[X^2], \mathbb{E}[Y^2] < \infty$ and

$$\mathbb{E}[XY] = \mathbb{E}[X]\mathbb{E}[Y],$$

that is

$$\rho_{X,Y} := \frac{\mathbb{E}[XY] - \mathbb{E}[X]\mathbb{E}[Y]}{\sqrt{\mathrm{var}[X]\,\mathrm{var}[Y]}} = 0.$$

Otherwise, that is, if $\rho_{X,Y} \neq 0$, X and Y are correlated. $\rho_{X,Y}$ is called the **correlation coefficient** between X and Y.

(xii) If X and Y are independent, then they are uncorrelated:

$$X \perp\!\!\!\perp Y \Rightarrow \rho_{X,Y} = 0.$$

The other direction does not necessarily hold (see Code Snippet A.1). Only in special cases, such as the bivariate Gaussian distribution or binary variables, does the reversed direction hold, too.

(xiii) We say that X and Y are **partially uncorrelated given** Z if

$$\rho_{X,Y\,|\,Z} := \frac{\rho_{X,Y} - \rho_{X,Z}\rho_{Z,Y}}{\sqrt{(1-\rho_{X,Z}^2)(1-\rho_{Z,Y}^2)}} = 0.$$

The following interpretation of partial correlation is important: $\rho_{X,Y\,|\,Z}$ equals the correlation between residuals after linearly regressing X on Z and Y on Z.

(xiv) In general, we have (see Example 7.9)

$$\rho_{X,Y\,|\,Z} = 0 \quad \not\Rightarrow \quad X \perp\!\!\!\perp Y\,|\,Z \qquad \text{and}$$
$$\rho_{X,Y\,|\,Z} = 0 \quad \not\Leftarrow \quad X \perp\!\!\!\perp Y\,|\,Z.$$

(xv) In **regression estimation**, we are usually given an i.i.d. sample $(\mathbf{X}_1, Y_1), \ldots, (\mathbf{X}_n, Y_n)$ from a joint distribution $P_{\mathbf{X},Y}$. Our aim is to predict the target Y from the covariates or predictors $\mathbf{X}$. In least squares regression, for example, we are looking for a function $\hat{f}$ such that

$$\hat{f} = \underset{f\in\mathcal{F}}{\operatorname{argmin}} \sum_{i=1}^{n} (Y_i - f(\mathbf{X}_i))^2 .$$

Here, we optimize over a function class $\mathcal{F}$ (see Section A.3). Different regression techniques use different function classes. In linear regression, we are only considering linear functions f; see Code Snippet 6.43 for an example. Code Snippet 4.14 shows an example for a nonlinear regression technique.

(xvi) Dependence between sets of discrete random variables $\mathbf{X}$ and $\mathbf{Y}$ can be measured by the **Shannon mutual information** [Cover and Thomas, 1991]

$$I(\mathbf{X}:\mathbf{Y}) := \sum_{\mathbf{x},\mathbf{y}} p(\mathbf{x},\mathbf{y}) \log \frac{p(\mathbf{x},\mathbf{y})}{p(\mathbf{x})p(\mathbf{y})}.$$

(xvii) Conditional dependence of sets of discrete random variables $\mathbf{X}$ and $\mathbf{Y}$, given the set $\mathbf{Z}$, is measured via the **conditional Shannon mutual information** [Cover and Thomas, 1991]

$$I(\mathbf{X}:\mathbf{Y}\,|\,\mathbf{Z}) := \sum_{\mathbf{x},\mathbf{y},\mathbf{z}} p(\mathbf{x},\mathbf{y},\mathbf{z}) \log \frac{p(\mathbf{x},\mathbf{y}|\mathbf{z})}{p(\mathbf{x}|\mathbf{z})p(\mathbf{y}|\mathbf{z})}.$$

(xviii) For continuous variables, the sums are replaced with integrals

$$I(\mathbf{X}:\mathbf{Y}) := \int p(\mathbf{x},\mathbf{y}) \log \frac{p(\mathbf{x},\mathbf{y})}{p(\mathbf{x})p(\mathbf{y})}\, d\mathbf{x}\, d\mathbf{y},$$

and

$$I(\mathbf{X}:\mathbf{Y}\,|\,\mathbf{Z}) := \int p(\mathbf{x},\mathbf{y},\mathbf{z}) \log \frac{p(\mathbf{x},\mathbf{y}|\mathbf{z})}{p(\mathbf{x}|\mathbf{z})p(\mathbf{y}|\mathbf{z})}\, d\mathbf{x}\, d\mathbf{y}\, d\mathbf{z}.$$

A.2 Independence and Conditional Independence Testing

In practice, we are given a finite sample $(X_1,Y_1),\dots,(X_n,Y_n) \overset{\text{iid}}{\sim} P_{X,Y}$ and want to decide whether the underlying random variables are independent or not. Since we do not expect the empirical correlation (or any independence measure) to be exactly 0, we need to take into account random fluctuations of the dependence measures. This can be done by statistical hypothesis tests. The idea is to consider the null hypothesis $H_0 : X \perp\!\!\!\perp Y$ and the alternative $H_A : X \not\!\perp\!\!\!\perp Y$. Therefore, one usually constructs a test statistic T_n that maps any finite sample to a real number, and one decides according to

$$(x_1,y_1),\dots,(x_n,y_n) \mapsto \begin{cases} H_0 & \text{if } T_n \le c \\ H_A & \text{if } T_n > c. \end{cases}$$

Here, T_n is shorthand notation for $T_n((x_1,y_1),\dots,(x_n,y_n))$. The threshold $c \in \mathbb{R}$ is chosen such that we can control the **type I error**; that is, for any P satisfying H_0, we have $P(T_n > c) \le \alpha$, where α is the **significance level** of the test, specified by the user. In practice, we are given data and compute the statistic T_n. If $T_n > c$, the null hypothesis is **rejected**, and we can be relatively confident that our decision is correct; otherwise, the null hypothesis is **not rejected**, which does not necessarily mean much (it could be that the sample size n was too small to detect the dependence between X and Y). The p**-value** of a test is the smallest significance level, such that the test is rejected.

We now briefly mention a couple of choices for T_n. There are many more tests, however, and we do not claim that the list contains optimal procedures; see Code Snippet A.1 for a practical example.

(i) To test for **vanishing correlation**, we can use the empirical correlation coefficient and a t-test (for Gaussian variables) or Fisher's z-transform (e.g., `cor.test` in R Core Team [2016]).

(ii) As an independence test, we may use a χ^2-test for **discrete** or **discretized data** (e.g., `chisq.test` in R Core Team [2016]).

(iii) An example for a general non-parametric independent test is the **Hilbert-Schmidt Independence Criterion (HSIC)** [see Gretton et al., 2008]. Its idea is based on an injective mapping into reproducing kernel Hilbert spaces (RKHSs) [Schölkopf and Smola, 2002]. Given a positive definite kernel, we can map probability distributions into the corresponding RKHS $\mathcal{H}$, that is, $P_{X,Y} \mapsto \mu(P_{X,Y}) \in \mathcal{H}$. For so-called characteristic kernels (e.g., the Gaussian kernel), this mapping is injective. In particular, we then have

$$\mu(P_{X,Y}) = \mu(P_X \otimes P_Y) \quad \text{if and only if} \quad P_{X,Y} = P_X \otimes P_Y,$$

and the latter holds if and only if X and Y are independent. The HSIC is defined as the squared RKHS-distance between the joint distribution and the product of marginals:

$$\text{HSIC}(P_{X,Y}) := \|\mu(P_{X,Y}) - \mu(P_X \otimes P_Y)\|^2_{\mathcal{H}}.$$

As test statistic T_n we can now use an estimator for $\text{HSIC}(P_{X,Y})$. If X and Y are independent, $\text{HSIC}(P_{X,Y})$ equals 0, and we expect its estimator T_n to be small. Gretton et al. [2008] provide ways how to choose the threshold c.

Alternatively, we can express HSIC as the Hilbert-Schmidt norm of the covariance operator C_{XY}. The latter is defined such that for all f and g that are members of the corresponding RKHSs

$$\langle f, C_{XY} g \rangle = \mathbb{E}[f(X)g(Y)] - \mathbb{E}[f(X)]\,\mathbb{E}[g(Y)].$$

The cross-covariance operator is therefore an extension of the covariance matrix. If X is d_X-dimensional, Y is d_Y-dimensional, and the corresponding RKHSs are isomorphic to $\mathbb{R}^{d_X}$ and $\mathbb{R}^{d_Y}$, respectively, C_{XY} can be described with the $d_X \times d_Y$-dimensional cross-covariance matrix. Certainly, X and Y do not need to be independent if the covariance matrix vanishes. For characteristic kernels, however, the RKHSs are infinitely dimensional and not isomorphic to $\mathbb{R}^d$. The cross-covariance operator has zero norm if and only if X and Y are independent.

Pfister et al. [2017] extend the procedure to test for joint independence between d variables. This is necessary to test for joint independence of noise variables, for example. They provide code for both the bivariate and the multivariate procedure (see the `R`-package `dHSIC`).

In practice, one usually needs to choose kernel parameters. For the Gaussian kernel, many implementations choose the bandwidth σ according to the commonly named median heuristic [e.g., Gretton et al., 2008].

(iv) **Conditional independence testing** Conditional independence testing is a hard problem, especially if the conditioning set is large. While it is current research to obtain a precise formalization for this statement, we provide an example that indicates the hardness of the problem. If $Z_1, \dots, Z_d$ are binary variables, we have that

$$X \perp\!\!\!\perp Y \,|\, Z_1, \dots, Z_d \\ \Leftrightarrow \quad \forall (z_1, \dots, z_d) \in \{0,1\}^d : \quad X \perp\!\!\!\perp Y \,|\, Z_1 = z_1, \dots, Z_d = z_d.$$

If we cannot assume anything on the way X and Y may depend on the Z's, we need to perform an unconditional independence test for each of the 2^d assignments (e.g., Z_d could be a common child of X and Y with the dependence only detectable for a specific assignment of the other $Z_1, \dots, Z_{d-1}$).

For continuous variables, extensions of the HSIC test have been proposed. Fukumizu et al. [2008] extend the idea to conditional cross-covariance operators to obtain a conditional independence test. This is developed further by Zhang et al. [2011], who additionally provide an approximation of the test statistic's distribution under the null hypothesis.

Code Snippet A.1 The following code generates a sample of a distribution over two variables that are uncorrelated but dependent.

```
library(dHSIC)
#
# generates a sample from two uncorrelated but dependent random variables
set.seed(1)
A <- runif(200)-0.5
B <- runif(200)-0.5
X <- t( c(cos(pi/4), -sin(pi/4)) %*% rbind(A, B) )
Y <- t( c(sin(pi/4), cos(pi/4)) %*% rbind(A, B) )
#
# performs the statistical test
cor.test(X,Y)$p.value
# 0.3979561
dhsic.test(X,Y)$p.value
# 1.970705e-08
```

A.3 Capacity of Function Classes

Here, we address the question whether the sequence of functions minimizing the empirical risk (1.3) converges against a function that also minimizes the risk (1.2); see Section 1.2. By the law of large numbers, we know that for any fixed $f \in \mathcal{F}$ and $\varepsilon > 0$,

$$\lim_{n\to\infty} P\left(\left|R[f] - R^n_{\text{emp}}[f]\right| > \varepsilon\right) = 0, \tag{A.4}$$

with exponentially fast convergence governed by Chernov's bound [e.g., Vapnik, 1998]. However, this does not imply consistency of empirical risk minimization. This is due to the fact that we are choosing the function f by minimizing (1.3). This implies that even though the (x_i, y_i) are independent, the **errors** or **losses** $\frac{1}{2}|f(x_i) - y_i|$ are not. In this case, the law of large numbers in its usual form does not apply. It turns out that to get consistency, we need a **uniform law of large numbers** [Vapnik, 1998]. This amounts to

$$\lim_{n\to\infty} P\left(\sup_{f\in\mathcal{F}}(R[f] - R^n_{\text{emp}}[f]) > \varepsilon\right) = 0 \tag{A.5}$$

for all $\varepsilon > 0$, a property that depends on the function class $\mathcal{F}$.

How about choosing $\mathcal{F} = \mathcal{Y}^{\mathcal{X}}$, in other words, *all* functions from $\mathcal{X}$ to $\mathcal{Y}$? Unfortunately, this does not lead to (A.5), and the reasoning is as follows: Suppose that based on the available sample (1.1), we decide that f^* is a good solution — for instance, since it satisfies $f(x_i) = y_i$ for all i. In this case, let us construct another function f^{**} that agrees with f^* on the sample and disagrees everywhere else. If our distribution $P_{X,Y}$ possesses a density, then the probability of encountering any of the training points *exactly* again in the future is zero. As a consequence, f^* and f^{**} will almost always disagree. Based on the training set alone, however, there is no way to choose one over the other. Similarly, in (A.5) we would find that whenever we have found a function f^* for which $(R[f^*] - R^n_{\text{emp}}[f^*])$ happens to be small, we can construct another function f^{**} for which $(R[f^{**}] - R^n_{\text{emp}}[f^{**}])$ is large, so uniform convergence (A.5) is impossible to achieve in our considered case where $\mathcal{F} = \mathcal{Y}^{\mathcal{X}}$.

On the other hand, the condition (A.5) becomes weaker as we make $\mathcal{F}$ smaller. How one measures the size (or capacity) of $\mathcal{F}$ is beyond the scope of this book, but it turns out that for a summary of the size of $\mathcal{F}$ irrespective of the underlying distribution, a single number is enough. It is referred to as the **VC (Vapnik-Chervonenkis) dimension** of $\mathcal{F}$. It sometimes coincides with the number of free parameters, but it can also be vastly different. If the VC dimension is finite, we get consistency of empirical risk minimization for any $P_{X,Y}$ [Vapnik, 1998]. The VC dimension is related to falsifiability and Popper's notion of the dimension of a theory [Corfield et al., 2009]. A typical risk bound of statistical learning theory states that for all $\delta > 0$, with probability $1-\delta$ and for all $f \in \mathcal{F}$, we have

$$R[f] \leq R^n_{\text{emp}}[f] + \sqrt{\frac{h(\log(2n/h)+1)-\log(\delta/4)}{n}}, \tag{A.6}$$

where h is the VC dimension of the function class $\mathcal{F}$. This means that if we can come up with an $\mathcal{F}$ that has small VC dimension yet contains functions that are sufficiently suitable for the given task to achieve a small $R^n_{\text{emp}}[f]$, then we can guarantee (with high probability) that those functions have small expected error on future data from the same distribution. This formulates a non-trivial trade-off: on the one hand, we would like to work with a large class of functions to allow for a small R^n_{emp}, but on the other hand, we want the class to be small to control h.

B

Causal Orderings and Adjacency Matrices

Definition B.1 *Given a DAG $\mathcal{G}$, we call a permutation, that is, a bijective mapping,*

$$\pi : \{1, \ldots, p\} \to \{1, \ldots, p\},$$

*a **causal ordering** (sometimes one says topological ordering) if it satisfies*

$$\pi(i) < \pi(j) \quad \text{if} \quad j \in \mathbf{DE}_i^{\mathcal{G}}.$$

Because of the acyclic structure of the DAG, there is always a topological ordering (see Proposition B.2). But this order does not have to be unique. The node $\pi^{-1}(1)$ does not have any parents and is therefore a source node, and $\pi^{-1}(p)$ does not have any descendants and is thus a sink node.

Proposition B.2 *For each DAG there is a topological ordering.*

Proof. We proceed by induction. We need to show that in each DAG, there is a node without any ancestors. Start with any node and move to one of its parents (if there are any). You will never visit a parent that you have seen before (if you did there had been a directed cycle). After at most $p-1$ steps you reach a node without any parent. □

Definition B.3 *We can represent a directed graph $\mathcal{G} = (V, \mathcal{E})$ over d nodes with a binary $d \times d$ matrix A (taking values 0 or 1):*

$$A_{i,j} = 1 \quad \Leftrightarrow \quad (i, j) \in \mathcal{E}.$$

*A is called the **adjacency matrix** of $\mathcal{G}$.*

This representation of DAGs is particularly useful for the efficient implementation of algorithms. There are a couple of useful results transforming adjacency matrices, some of which we report here.

Remark B.4 (i) Let A be the adjacency matrix for DAG $\mathcal{G}$. The entry (i, j) of the squared matrix A^2 equals the number of paths of length two from i to j. This is because

$$A^2_{i,j} = \sum_k A_{ik} A_{kj}.$$

(ii) In general, we have

$$A^k_{ij} = \#\text{ paths of length } k \text{ from } i \text{ to } j.$$

(iii) If indices increase on directed paths, that is, $j \in \mathbf{DE}_i^{\mathcal{G}}$ implies $j > i$, then the identity is a causal ordering and the adjacency matrix is upper triangular, that is, only the upper-right half of the matrix contains non-zeros.

(iv) We may want to use sparse matrices when the graph is sparse to save space and/or computation time.

□

The number of DAGs with d nodes have been studied by Robinson [1970, 1973] and independently by Stanley [1973]. The number of such matrices (or DAGs) is growing very quickly in d (see Table B.1).

McKay [2004] proves the following equivalent description of DAGs which had been conjectured by Eric W. Weisstein.

Theorem B.5 *The matrix A is an adjacency matrix of a DAG $\mathcal{G}$ if and only if $A + \mathrm{Id}$ is a* 0-1*-matrix with all eigenvalues being real and strictly greater than zero.*

d	Number of DAGs with d nodes
1	1
2	3
3	25
4	543
5	29281
6	3781503
7	1138779265
8	783702329343
9	1213442454842881
10	4175098976430598143
11	31603459396418917607425
12	521939651343829405020504063
13	18676600744432035186664816926721
14	1439428141044398334941790719839535103
15	237725265553410354992180218286376719253505
16	83756670773733320287699303047996412235223138303
17	62707921196923889899446452602494921906963551482675201
18	99421195322159515895228914592354524516555026878588305014783
19	332771901227107591736177573311261125883583076258421902583546773505

Table B.1: The number of DAGs depending on the number d of nodes, taken from `http://oeis.org/A003024` [OEIS Foundation Inc., 2017]. The length of the numbers grows faster than any linear term.

C

Proofs

C.1 Proof of Theorem 4.2

We first state a lemma; its proof can be found in Peters [2008], for example.

Lemma C.1 *Let X and N be independent variables and assume that N is non-deterministic. Then* $N \not\perp\!\!\!\perp (X+N)$.

Proof of Theorem 4.2. If X and N_Y are normally distributed, we have

$$\beta := \frac{\mathrm{cov}[X,Y]}{\mathrm{cov}[Y,Y]} = \frac{\alpha \mathrm{var}[X]}{\alpha^2 \mathrm{var}[X] + \mathrm{var}[N_Y]}$$

and define $N_X := X - \beta Y$. N_X and Y are uncorrelated by construction and because N_X and Y are jointly Gaussian, it follows that they are independent, too.

To prove the "only if" statement, we assume that

$$\begin{aligned} Y &= \alpha X + N_Y \\ \text{and} \quad N_X &= (1-\alpha\beta)X - \beta N_Y \end{aligned}$$

are independent. Distinguish between the following cases:

(i) $(1-\alpha\beta) \neq 0$ and $\beta \neq 0$.
Here, Theorem 4.3 implies that X, N_Y and thus also Y, N_X are normally distributed. Hence, $P_{X,Y}$ is bivariate Gaussian, too.

(ii) $\beta = 0$.
This implies

$$X \perp\!\!\!\perp \alpha X + N_Y,$$

which is a contradiction to Lemma C.1.

(iii) $(1-\alpha\beta)=0$.
It follows $-\beta N_Y \perp\!\!\!\perp \alpha X + N_Y$. Thus

$$N_Y \perp\!\!\!\perp \alpha X + N_Y,$$

which, again, contradicts Lemma C.1.

This concludes the proof. □

C.2 Proof of Proposition 6.3

Proof. Recall that our definition of an SCM includes the requirement that the underlying graph is acyclic. We can now substitute the structural assignments recursively into each other and can therefore write each node X_j as a unique function of all noise terms $(N_k)_{k\in\mathbf{AN}_j}$ that belong to the ancestors of X_j. That is,

$$X_j := g_j\big((N_k)_{k\in\mathbf{AN}_j}\big).$$

(The function does not necessarily depend on the noise terms of *all* ancestors.) □

C.3 Proof of Remark 6.6

Proof. We will show that whenever we can remove a variable from $\mathbf{PA}_j$, we can still remove it from $\mathbf{PA}_j^*$ in the reduced model.

Consider an input $X_k \in \mathbf{PA}_j \cap \mathbf{PA}_j^*$ that f_j does not depend on. That is, we have $f_j(\mathbf{pa}_{j,-k}, x_k, n_j) = f_j(\mathbf{pa}_{j,-k}, x_k', n_j)$ for all $x_k, x_k', \mathbf{pa}_{j,-k}$ and n_j with $p(n_j) > 0$. Here, $\mathbf{PA}_{j,-k} := \mathbf{PA}_j \setminus \{k\}$ denotes the set of all input variables except for k. Then, g does not depend on this variable x_k either because $g(\mathbf{pa}^*_{j,-k}, x_k, n_j) = f_j(\mathbf{pa}_j, x_k, n_j)$ for all $x_k, \mathbf{pa}^*_{j,-k}$ and n_j with $p(n_j) > 0$. □

C.4 Proof of Proposition 6.13

Proof. To simplify notation we write X_1 instead of X and X_2 instead of Y. First, the truncated factorization formula (6.9) implies

$$
\begin{aligned}
p_{X_2}^{\mathfrak{C};do(X_1:=x_1)}(x_2) &= \int \prod_{j\neq 1} p_j(x_j\,|\,x_{pa(j)})\,dx_3\cdots dx_d \\
&= \int \prod_{j\neq 1} p_j(x_j\,|\,x_{pa(j)})\frac{\tilde{p}(x_1)}{\tilde{p}(x_1)}\,dx_3\cdots dx_d \\
&= p_{X_2\,|\,X_1=x_1}^{\mathfrak{C};do\left(X_1:=\tilde{N}_1\right)}(x_2) \qquad \text{(C.1)}
\end{aligned}
$$

if $\tilde{N}_1$ puts positive mass on x_1, that is, $\tilde{p}(x_1) > 0$. We furthermore require that the following two statements hold for all distributions Q_{X_1,X_2} over (X_1,X_2) with density q:

$$
X_2 \not\perp\!\!\!\perp X_1 \text{ in } Q \iff \exists x_1^{\triangle}, x_1^{\square} \text{ with } q(x_1^{\triangle}), q(x_1^{\square}) > 0 \text{ and } Q_{X_2\,|\,X_1=x_1^{\triangle}} \neq Q_{X_2\,|\,X_1=x_1^{\square}} \qquad \text{(C.2)}
$$

and

$$
X_2 \not\perp\!\!\!\perp X_1 \text{ in } Q \iff \exists x_1^{\triangle} \text{ with } q(x_1^{\triangle}) > 0 \text{ and } Q_{X_2\,|\,X_1=x_1^{\triangle}} \neq Q_{X_2}. \qquad \text{(C.3)}
$$

We then have for any $\hat{N}_1$ with full support

$$
\begin{aligned}
(i) &\overset{\text{(C.2)}}{\Longrightarrow} \exists x_1^{\triangle}, x_1^{\square} \text{ with pos. density under } \tilde{N}_1 \text{ s.t. } P_{X_2\,|\,X_1=x_1^{\triangle}}^{\mathfrak{C};do\left(X_1:=\tilde{N}_1\right)} \neq P_{X_2\,|\,X_1=x_1^{\square}}^{\mathfrak{C};do\left(X_1:=\tilde{N}_1\right)} \\
&\overset{\text{(C.1)}}{\Longrightarrow} (ii) \\
&\overset{\text{(C.1)}}{\Longrightarrow} \exists x_1^{\triangle}, x_1^{\square} \text{ with pos. density under } \hat{N}_1 \text{ s.t. } P_{X_2\,|\,X_1=x_1^{\triangle}}^{\mathfrak{C};do\left(X_1:=\hat{N}_1\right)} \neq P_{X_2\,|\,X_1=x_1^{\square}}^{\mathfrak{C};do\left(X_1:=\hat{N}_1\right)} \\
&\overset{\text{(C.2)}}{\Longrightarrow} (iv) \\
&\overset{\text{(trivial)}}{\Longrightarrow} (i)
\end{aligned}
$$

We further have $(ii) \overset{\text{(trivial)}}{\Longrightarrow} (iii)$ and that $P_{X_2}^{\mathfrak{C}} = P_{X_2}^{\mathfrak{C};do(X_1:=N_1^*)}$ with N_1^* having the distribution $P_{X_1}^{\mathfrak{C}}$. Together with $\neg(i) \Rightarrow \neg(ii)$, the latter implies

$$
\begin{aligned}
\neg(i) &\Longrightarrow X_2 \perp\!\!\!\perp X_1 \text{ in } P_{\mathbf{X}}^{\mathfrak{C};do(X_1:=N_1^*)} \\
&\overset{\text{(C.3)}}{\Longrightarrow} P_{X_2\,|\,X_1=x^{\triangle}}^{\mathfrak{C};do(X_1:=N_1^*)} = P_{X_2}^{\mathfrak{C};do(X_1:=N_1^*)} \text{ for all } x^{\triangle} \text{ with } p_1(x^{\triangle}) > 0 \\
&\overset{\text{(C.1)}}{\Longrightarrow} P_{X_2}^{\mathfrak{C};do\left(X_1:=x^{\triangle}\right)} = P_{X_2}^{\mathfrak{C}} \text{ for all } x^{\triangle} \text{ with } p_1(x^{\triangle}) > 0 \\
&\overset{\neg(ii)}{\Longrightarrow} P_{X_2}^{\mathfrak{C};do\left(X_1:=x^{\triangle}\right)} = P_{X_2}^{\mathfrak{C}} \text{ for all } x^{\triangle} \\
&\Longrightarrow \neg(iii)
\end{aligned}
$$

Here, the symbol "$\neg$" denotes the negation of a statement. $\square$

C.5 Proof of Proposition 6.14

Proof. Statement (i) follows directly from the Markov property of the interventional SCM. The intervention removes the incoming edges into X, and if there is no direct path from X to Y in the original graph, X and Y are d-separated.

Statement (ii) can be proved by a counterexample (see, e.g., Example 6.34). $\square$

C.6 Proof of Proposition 6.36

Proof. "if": Assume that causal minimality is not satisfied. Then, there is an X_j and a $Y \in \mathbf{PA}_j^{\mathcal{G}}$, such that $P_{\mathbf{X}}$ is also Markovian with respect to the graph obtained when removing the edge $Y \to X_j$ from $\mathcal{G}$. This implies $X_j \perp\!\!\!\perp Y \,|\, \mathbf{PA}_j^{\mathcal{G}} \setminus \{Y\}$ by the local Markov property.

"only if": If $P_{\mathbf{X}}$ has a density, the Markov condition is equivalent to the Markov factorization [Lauritzen, 1996, Theorem 3.27]. Assume now that $Y \in \mathbf{PA}_j^{\mathcal{G}}$ and $X_j \perp\!\!\!\perp Y \,|\, \mathbf{PA}_j^{\mathcal{G}} \setminus \{Y\}$, which implies $p(x_j|\mathbf{pa}_j^{\mathcal{G}}) = p(x_j|\mathbf{pa}_{j,-Y}^{\mathcal{G}})$ where $\mathbf{PA}_{j,-Y}^{\mathcal{G}}$ is defined as $\mathbf{PA}_{j,-Y}^{\mathcal{G}} = \mathbf{PA}_j^{\mathcal{G}} \setminus \{Y\}$. Then, $p(\mathbf{x}) = p(x_j|\mathbf{pa}_{j,-Y}^{\mathcal{G}}) \prod_{k \neq j} p(x_k|\mathbf{pa}_k^{\mathcal{G}})$, which implies that $P_{\mathbf{X}}$ is Markovian with respect to $\mathcal{G}$ without $Y \to X_j$. $\square$

C.7 Proof of Proposition 6.48

Proof. We assume that both models satisfy causal minimality and come with graphs $\mathcal{G}$ and $\mathcal{H}$. Intuitively, we can identify the children of a node X since they change after intervening on X. Some of the children, however, may not change their distribution after an intervention due to two canceling paths, for example. We thus introduce the following notation. Given a DAG $\mathcal{G}$, we call X a **youngest parent** of a node Y and write $X \in \mathbf{YPA}_Y$ if $X \in \mathbf{PA}_Y$ and X is not an ancestor of any other parent of Y. A node Y may have several youngest parents. The proof requires two arguments:

(i) If $X \in \mathbf{YPA}_Y^{\mathcal{G}}$, then there is a total causal effect from X to Y, meaning that there are $x^{\triangle}$ and $x^{\square}$, such that $P_Y^{do(X:=x^{\triangle})} \neq P_Y^{do(X:=x^{\square})}$. This follows from causal minimality.

(ii) If $Z \in \mathbf{AN}_Y^{\mathcal{G}}$, then there exist $X_1, \ldots, X_k$, such that $X_1 = Z$, $X_k = Y$, and $X_i \in \mathbf{YPA}_{X_{i+1}}^{\mathcal{G}}$ for $i \in \{1, \ldots, k-1\}$.

Finally, we can combine these two statements and conclude that if $Z \in \mathbf{AN}_Y^{\mathcal{G}}$, then there are $X_1, \ldots, X_k$ such that for $i \in \{1, \ldots, k-1\}$, X_i has a total causal effect on X_{i+1}, which implies that there must be a direct causal path from X_i to X_{i+1} also in $\mathcal{H}$; see Proposition 6.13. But then $Z \in \mathbf{AN}_Y^{\mathcal{H}}$, which implies that both $\mathcal{G}$ and $\mathcal{H}$ have the same ancestor relationships. Since both $\mathcal{G}$ and $\mathcal{H}$ satisfy causal minimality, this implies that $\mathcal{G} = \mathcal{H}$ and therefore the two models are equivalent as causal graphical models. □

C.8 Proof of Proposition 6.49

Proof. According to the proof of Proposition 6.3, we can write for the first SCM $\mathbf{X} = \mathbf{g}(\mathbf{N})$. But since

$$\mathbf{g}(\mathbf{n}) = \mathbf{g}^*(\mathbf{n}) \quad \forall \mathbf{n} \text{ with } p(\mathbf{n}) > 0,$$

we clearly have that both SCMs induce the same observational distributions (and intervention distributions with the same argument). Regarding counterfactuals, we cover both the discrete and the continuous case by conditioning on $\mathbf{X} \in A$ with $P(\mathbf{X} \in A) > 0$; see Definition 6.17. The new density over the noise variables satisfies

$$\begin{aligned}
\tilde{p}(n_1, \ldots, n_d) &= \begin{cases} \frac{p(n_1,\ldots,n_d)}{P(X \in A)} & \text{if } \mathbf{g}(n_1, \ldots, n_d) \in A \\ 0 & \text{else} \end{cases} \\
&= \begin{cases} \frac{p(n_1,\ldots,n_d)}{P(\mathbf{g}(\mathbf{N}) \in A)} & \text{if } \mathbf{g}^*(n_1, \ldots, n_d) \in A \\ 0 & \text{else} \end{cases} \\
&= \begin{cases} \frac{p(n_1,\ldots,n_d)}{P(\mathbf{g}^*(\mathbf{N}) \in A)} & \text{if } \mathbf{g}^*(n_1, \ldots, n_d) \in A \\ 0 & \text{else} \end{cases} \\
&= \tilde{p}^*(n_1, \ldots, n_d).
\end{aligned}$$

We still have

$$\mathbf{g}(\mathbf{n}) = \mathbf{g}^*(\mathbf{n}) \quad \forall \mathbf{n} \text{ with } \tilde{p}(\mathbf{n}) > 0,$$

which implies that all counterfactual statements coincide. □

C.9 Proof of Proposition 7.1

Proof. Let $N_1,\dots,N_d$ be independent and uniformly distributed between 0 and 1. We then define $X_j := f_j(X_{\mathbf{PA}_j}, N_j)$ with

$$f_j(\mathbf{pa}_j, n_j) := F^{-1}_{X_j|\mathbf{PA}_j=\mathbf{pa}_j}(n_j) \tag{C.4}$$

where $F^{-1}_{X_j|\mathbf{PA}_j=\mathbf{pa}_j}$ is the generalized inverse cumulative distribution function from X_j given $\mathbf{PA}_j = \mathbf{pa}_j$. The generalized inverse cumulative distribution function of a random variable Y is defined as $F_Y^{-1}(a) := \inf\{y \in \mathbb{R} : F_Y(y) \geq a\}$. Equation (C.4) guarantees that in the constructed SCM, the conditional $X_j|\mathbf{PA}_j = \mathbf{pa}_j$ has the correct distribution. The statement then follows from the Markov factorization, Definition 6.21(iii). □

C.10 Proof of Proposition 7.4

Proof. Assume causal minimality is not satisfied. We can then find nodes j and $i \in \mathbf{PA}_j$ with $X_j = f_j(\mathbf{PA}_j \setminus \{i\}, X_i) + N_j$ that does not depend on X_i if we condition on all other parents $A := \mathbf{PA}_j \setminus \{i\}$, that is $X_j \perp\!\!\!\perp X_i \,|\, X_A$ (see Proposition 6.36). Here, we denote $\mathbf{PA}_j \setminus \{X_i\}$ by X_A. For the function f_j, we will now show that $f_j(x_A, x_i) = c_{x_A}$ for P_{X_A,X_i}-almost all (x_A, x_i). Indeed, assume without loss of generality that $\mathbb{E}[N_j] = 0$, then the mean of $X_j \,|\, \mathbf{PA}_j = (x_A, x_i)$ equals $f_j(x_A, x_i)$. Equation (2b) from Dawid [1979] states that if $X_j \perp\!\!\!\perp X_i \,|\, X_A$, then the density of $X_j \,|\, X_A, X_i$ does not depend on the argument of X_i. Therefore, also the conditional mean $f_j(x_A, x_i)$ does not depend on x_i. It follows that $f_j(x_A, x_i) = c_{x_A}$. The continuity of f_j implies that f_j is constant in its last argument.

The converse statement follows from Proposition 6.36, too. □

C.11 Proof of Proposition 8.1

Proof. We use the Bellman optimality equation [e.g., Sutton and Barto, 2015,

Chapter 3.8]. For all s° and s with $f(s^\circ) = f(s)$, we have

$$\begin{aligned} Q^*(s,a) &= \sum_{s'} p(s' \,|\, s,a)\Big(\mathbb{E}[R \,|\, s',a] + \max_{a'} Q^*(s',a')\Big) \\ &= \sum_{f'} \sum_{s':f(s')=f'} p(s' \,|\, s,a)\Big(\mathbb{E}[R \,|\, s',a] + \max_{a'} Q^*(s',a')\Big) \\ &= \sum_{f'} p(f' \,|\, s,a)\Big(\mathbb{E}[R \,|\, f',a] + \max_{a'} Q^*(s',a')\Big) \\ &= \sum_{f'} p(f' \,|\, s^\circ,a)\Big(\mathbb{E}[R \,|\, f',a] + \max_{a'} Q^*(s',a')\Big) = Q^*(s^\circ,a). \end{aligned}$$

This conclude the proof. □

C.12 Proof of Proposition 8.2

Proof. The first equation follows from the discussion in Section 8.2.1. The Markov factorization property implies

$$p(\mathbf{x}) = p(a|s)\, p(s|h)\, p(h)\, p(y|f,h)\, p(f|a);$$

see Figure 8.5. It now follows with $F \perp\!\!\!\perp S \,|\, A$ that

$$\begin{aligned} \int y \, \frac{\tilde{p}(a|s)}{p(a|s)} \, p(\mathbf{x}) \, d\mathbf{x} &= \int y \, \tilde{p}(a|s) p(s|h) p(h) p(y|f,h) p(f|a,s) \, da \, df \, dh \, ds \, dy \\ &= \int y \, \tilde{p}(f,a|s) p(s|h) p(h) p(y|f,h) \, da \, df \, dh \, ds \, dy \\ &= \int y \, \frac{\tilde{p}(f|s)}{p(f|s)} p(s\,|\,h) p(h) p(y|f,h) p(f|s) \, df \, dh \, ds \, dy \\ &= \int y \, \frac{\tilde{p}(f|s)}{p(f|s)} p(s\,|\,h) p(h) p(y|f,h) p(f,a|s) \, da \, df \, dh \, ds \, dy \\ &= \int y \, \frac{\tilde{p}(f|s)}{p(f|s)} \, p(\mathbf{x}) \, d\mathbf{x}. \end{aligned}$$

The last equality follows from $p(f,a|s) = p(f|a,s)p(a|s)$. □

C.13 Proof of Proposition 9.3

Proof. To show (i), we start with the SCM $\mathfrak{C}$ over $\mathbf{X}$ and its entailed distribution $P_{\mathbf{X}}$. We then consider the structural assignments for variables $O \in \mathbf{O}$ and repeatedly plug in the assignments for the variables $X \in \mathbf{X} \setminus \mathbf{O}$ whenever these variables appear on the right-hand side. This leads to a new SCM in which each structural assignment for $O \in \mathbf{O}$ contains a multivariate error variable $\tilde{\mathbf{N}}_O$. It is apparent that this smaller SCM entails the same observational distribution $P_{\mathbf{O}}$ and the same intervention distributions when intervening on any $O \in \mathbf{O}$. From causal sufficiency, it follows that the new noise variables $(\tilde{\mathbf{N}}_O)_{O \in \mathbf{O}}$ are jointly independent. As in the case of one-dimensional noise variables (Proposition 6.31), this again implies that the distribution $P_{\mathbf{O}}$ is Markovian with respect to the induced graph structure. The statement now follows from the fact that this new SCM can be transformed to an SCM with one-dimensional error variables that entails the same observational and intervention distributions (exploiting the same construction as in Proposition 7.1). For a more formal description of this procedure, as well as for more details on these arguments, see Bongers et al. [2016].

Statement (ii) follows from Example 9.2. □

C.14 Proof of Theorem 10.3

Proof. If there is an arrow from $X^j_{\text{past}(t)}$ to X^k_t, the dependence (10.3) follows immediately from faithfulness because two directly connected variables cannot be d-separated. Now assume that there is no edge from $X^j_{\text{past}(t)}$ to X^k_t. Then, X^k_t is d-separated from $X^j_{\text{past}(t)}$ given $\mathbf{X}^{-j}_{\text{past}(t)}$. Any path leaving X^k_t with an outgoing edge is blocked because it will have a collider (and no node after with time index larger or equal to t is conditioned on); any path leaving X^k_t with an incoming edge is blocked because the next node is in the conditioning set $\mathbf{X}^{-j}_{\text{past}(t)}$. □

C.15 Proof of Theorem 10.4

Proof. To prove (i), consider a full time graph containing no arrow from X to Y. Then, every path from Y_t to $X_{\text{past}(t)}$ is blocked by $Y_{\text{past}(t)}$. Any path that starts with an outgoing edge from Y_t must contain a collider that is not in the conditioning set (neither is any of its descendants); any path starting with an incoming edge is blocked since the first node on this path is in $Y_{\text{past}(t)}$.

To prove (ii), assume Y_t has parents from X, denoted by $\mathbf{PA}^X_{Y_t}$. Then (10.5) implies

$$Y_t \perp\!\!\!\perp \mathbf{PA}^X_{Y_t} \,|\, Y_{\text{past}(t)}. \tag{C.5}$$

For any $X_s \in \mathbf{PA}^X_{Y_t}$, (C.5) implies by weak union (see Appendix A.1)

$$Y_t \perp\!\!\!\perp X_s \,|\, Y_{\text{past}(t)} \cup (\mathbf{PA}^X_{Y_t} \setminus \{X_s\}). \tag{C.6}$$

Due to Peters et al. [2014, Lemma 38], minimality implies that Y_t is dependent of any parent A of Y_t, given any set of non-descendants of Y_t that includes the other parents of Y_t except A. Hence we have

$$Y_t \not\perp\!\!\!\perp X_s \,|\, Y_{\text{past}(t)} \cup (\mathbf{PA}^X_{Y_t} \setminus \{X_s\}),$$

in contradiction to (C.6). □

Bibliography

S. Acid and L. M. de Campos. Searching for Bayesian network structures in the space of restricted acyclic partially directed graphs. *Journal of Artificial Intelligence Research*, 18:445–490, 2003.

J. Aldrich. Autonomy. *Oxford Economic Papers*, 41:15–34, 1989.

R. A. Ali, T. S. Richardson, and P. Spirtes. Markov equivalence for ancestral graphs. *The Annals of Statistics*, 37:2808–2837, 2009.

E. S. Allman, C. Matias, and J. A. Rhodes. Identifiability of parameters in latent structure models with many observed variables. *The Annals of Statistics*, 37: 3099–3132, 2009.

N. Ancona, D. Marinazzo, and S. Stramaglia. Radial basis function approach to nonlinear Granger causality of time series. *Physical Review E*, 70:056221–1–7, 2004.

S. A. Andersson, D. Madigan, and M. D. Perlman. Alternative Markov property for chain graphs. *Scandinavian Journal of Statistics*, 28:33–86, 2001.

A. Aspect, P. Grangier, and G. Roger. Experimental tests of realistic local theories via Bell's theorem. *Physical Review Letters*, 47:460–467, 1981.

N. Ay and D. Polani. Information flows in causal networks. *Advances in Complex Systems*, 11(1):17–41, 2008.

R. R. Baldwin, W. E. Cantey, H. Maisel, and J. P. McDermott. The optimum strategy in blackjack. *Journal of the American Statistical Association*, 51(275): 429–439, 1956.

A. Balke. *Probabilistic Counterfactuals: Semantics, Computation, Applications*. PhD thesis, University of California, Los Angeles, CA, 1995.

A. Balke and J. Pearl. Bounds on treatment effects from studies with imperfect compliance. *Journal of the American Statistical Association*, 92:1172–1176, 1997.

E. Bareinboim and J. Pearl. Transportability from multiple environments with limited experiments: Completeness results. In *Advances in Neural Information Processing Systems 27 (NIPS)*, pages 280–288, 2014.

E. Bareinboim and J. Pearl. Causal inference from big data: Theoretical foundations and the data-fusion problem. *Proceedings of the National Academy of Sciences*, 113(27):7345–7352, 2016.

E. Bareinboim, A. Forney, and J. Pearl. Bandits with unobserved confounders: A causal approach. In *Advances in Neural Information Processing Systems 28 (NIPS)*, pages 1342–1350, 2015.

S. Bauer, B. Schölkopf, and J. Peters. The arrow of time in multivariate time series. In *Proceedings of the 33rd International Conference on Machine Learning (ICML)*, pages 2043–2051, 2016.

J. Bell. On the Einstein-Podolsky-Rosen paradox. *Physics*, 1:195–200, 1964. *Reprinted in* J. Bell: Speakable and unspeakable in quantum mechanics, Cambridge University Press, Cambridge, UK, 1987.

R. Bellman. A Markovian decision process. *Indiana University Mathematics Journal*, 6:679–684, 1957.

S. Ben-David, T. Lu, T. Luu, and D. Pál. Impossibility theorems for domain adaptation. In *Proceedings of the International Conference on Artificial Intelligence and Statistics 13 (AISTATS)*, pages 129–136, 2010.

C. Bennett. The thermodynamics of computation — a review. *International Journal of Theoretical Physics*, 21:905–940, 1982.

J. O. Berger. *Statistical Decision Theory and Bayesian Analysis*. Springer, New York, NY, 1985.

J. Berkson. Limitations of the application of fourfold table analysis to hospital data. *Biometrics Bulletin*, 2:47–53, 1946.

M. Besserve, N. Shajarisales, D. Janzing, and B. Schölkopf. Causal inference through spectral independence in linear dynamical systems. in preparation.

A. Bhatt. Evolution of clinical research: A history before and beyond James Lind. *Perspectives in Clinical Research*, 1(1):6–10, 2010.

K. A. Bollen. *Structural Equations with Latent Variables*. Wiley, New York, NY, 1989.

B. Bonet. Instrumentality tests revisited. In *Proceedings of the 17th Conference on Uncertainty in Artificial Intelligence (UAI)*, pages 48–55, 2001.

S. Bongers, J. Peters, B. Schölkopf, and J. M. Mooij. Structural causal models: Cycles, marginalizations, exogenous reparametrizations and reductions. *ArXiv e-prints (1611.06221)*, 2016.

L. Bottou, J. Peters, J. Quiñonero-Candela, D. X. Charles, D. M. Chickering, E. Portugualy, D. Ray, P. Simard, and E. Snelson. Counterfactual reasoning and learning systems: The example of computational advertising. *Journal of Machine Learning Research*, 14:3207–3260, 2013.

R. J. Bowden and D. A. Turkington. *Instrumental Variables*. Econometric Society Monographs. Cambridge University Press, New York, NY, 1990.

C. Brito and J. Pearl. A new identification condition for recursive models with correlated errors. *Structural Equation Modeling*, 9:459–474, 2002a.

C. Brito and J. Pearl. Generalized instrumental variables. In *Proceedings of the 18th Conference on Uncertainty in Artificial Intelligence (UAI)*, pages 85–93, 2002b.

P. J. Brockwell and R. A. Davis. *Time Series: Theory and Methods*. Springer, New York, NY, 2nd edition, 1991.

P. Bühlmann and S. A. van de Geer. *Statistics for High-Dimensional Data: Methods, Theory and Applications*. Springer Series in Statistics. Springer, New York, NY, 2011.

P. Bühlmann, J. Peters, and J. Ernest. CAM: Causal additive models, high-dimensional order search and penalized regression. *The Annals of Statistics*, 42(6):2526–2556, 2014.

W. L. Buntine. Theory refinement on Bayesian networks. In *In Proceedings of the 7th Annual Conference on Uncertainty in Artificial Intelligence (UAI)*, pages 52–60, 1991.

R. M. J. Byrne. *The Rational Imagination: How People Create Alternatives to Reality*. MIT Press, Cambridge, MA, 2007.

G. Chaitin. On the length of programs for computing finite binary sequences. *Journal of the Assocation for Computing Machinery*, 13(4):547–569, 1966.

O. Chapelle, B. Schölkopf, and A. Zien. *Semi-Supervised Learning*. MIT Press, Cambridge, MA, 2006.

C. R. Charig, D. R. Webb, S. R. Payne, and J. E. A. Wickham. Comparison of treatment of renal calculi by open surgery, percutaneous nephrolithotomy, and extracorporeal shockwave lithotripsy. *British Medical Journal (Clin Res Ed)*, 292(6254):879–882, 1986.

R. Chaves, L. Luft, T. O. Maciel, D. Gross, D. Janzing, and B. Schölkopf. Inferring latent structures via information inequalities. In *Proceedings of the 30th Annual Conference on Uncertainty in Artificial Intelligence (UAI)*, pages 112–121, 2014.

D. M. Chickering. Learning Bayesian networks is NP-complete. In *Learning from Data: Artificial Intelligence and Statistics V*, pages 121–130. Springer, New York, NY, 1996.

D. M. Chickering. Optimal structure identification with greedy search. *Journal of Machine Learning Research*, 3:507–554, 2002.

T. Claassen, J. M. Mooij, and T. Heskes. Learning sparse causal models is not NP-hard. In *Proceedings of the 29th Annual Conference on Uncertainty in Artificial Intelligence (UAI)*, pages 172–181, 2013.

J. Clauser, M. Horne, A. Shimony, and R. Holt. Proposed experiment to test local hidden-variable theories. *Physical Review Letters*, 23:880–884, 1969.

D. Colombo, M. H. Maathuis, M. Kalisch, and T. S. Richardson. Learning high-dimensional directed acyclic graphs with latent and selection variables. *The Annals of Statistics*, 40:294–321, 2012.

J. Comley and D. Dowe. General Bayesian networks and asymmetric languages. In *Proceedings of the 2nd Hawaii International Conference on Statistics and Related Fields*, 2003.

P. Comon. Independent component analysis — a new concept? *Signal Processing*, 36:287–314, 1994.

S. A. Cook. The complexity of theorem-proving procedures. In *Proceedings of the 3rd Annual ACM Symposium on Theory of Computing*, pages 151–158, 1971.

G. Cooper and C. Yoo. Causal discovery from a mixture of experimental and observational data. In *Proceedings of the 15th Annual Conference on Uncertainty in Artificial Intelligence (UAI)*, pages 116–125, 1999.

D. Corfield, B. Schölkopf, and V. Vapnik. Falsificationism and statistical learning theory: Comparing the Popper and Vapnik-Chervonenkis dimensions. *Journal for General Philosophy of Science*, 40(1):51–58, 2009.

T. Cover and J. Thomas. *Elements of Information Theory*. Wiley Series in Telecommunications and Signal Processing, Wiley, New York, NY, 1991.

D. R. Cox. *Planning of Experiments*. Wiley, New York, NY, 1958.

J. Cussens. Bayesian network learning with cutting planes. In *Proceedings of the 27th Annual Conference on Uncertainty in Artificial Intelligence (UAI)*, pages 153–160, 2011.

P. Daniušis, D. Janzing, J. M. Mooij, J. Zscheischler, B. Steudel, K. Zhang, and B. Schölkopf. Inferring deterministic causal relations. In *Proceedings of the 26th Annual Conference on Uncertainty in Artificial Intelligence (UAI)*, pages 143–150, 2010.

D. Danks and S. Plis. Learning causal structure from undersampled time series, 2013. URL `http://repository.cmu.edu/cgi/viewcontent.cgi?article=1638&context=philosophy`. Results were presented at NIPS 2013 workshop on causality; last visit of website: 31.01.2017.

G. Darmois. Analyse générale des liaisons stochastiques. *Revue de l'Institut International de Statistique*, 21:2–8, 1953.

D. Dash. Restructing dynamic causal systems in equilibrium. In *Proceedings of the 10th International Conference on Artificial Intelligence and Statistics (AISTATS)*, pages 81–88, 2005.

A. P. Dawid. Conditional independence in statistical theory. *Journal of the Royal Statistical Society, Series B: Statistical Methodology (with discussion)*, 41(1): 1–31, 1979.

A. P. Dawid. Statistical causality from a decision-theoretic perspective. *Annual Review of Statistics and Its Application*, 2:273–303, 2015.

C. P. De Campos and Q. Ji. Efficient structure learning of Bayesian networks using constraints. *Journal of Machine Learning Research*, 12:663–689, 2011.

L. Devroye, L. Györfi, and G. Lugosi. *A Probabilistic Theory of Pattern Recognition*, volume 31 of *Applications of Mathematics*. Springer, New York, NY, 1996.

V. Didelez, S. Meng, and N. A. Sheehan. Assumptions of IV methods for observational epidemiology. *Statistical Science*, 25:22–40, 2010.

C. Diks and V. Panchenko. A new statistic and practical guidelines for nonparametric Granger causality testing. *Journal of Economic Dynamics and Control*, 30(9–10):1647–1669, 2006.

D. DiVincenzo. Two-qubit gates are universal for quantum computation. *Physical Review A*, 51:1015–1022, 1995.

M. Drton, M. Eichler, and T. S. Richardson. Computing maximum likelihood estimates in recursive linear models with correlated errors. *Journal of Machine Learning Research*, 10:2329–2348, 2009a.

M. Drton, B. Sturmfels, and S. Sullivant. *Lectures on Algebraic Statistics*, volume 39 of *Oberwolfach Seminars*. Birkhäuser, Basel, 2009b.

M. Druzdzel and H. Simon. Causality in Bayesian belief networks. In *In Proceedings of the 9th Annual Conference on Uncertainty in Artificial Intelligence (UAI)*, pages 3–11, 1993.

M. J. Druzdzel and H. van Leijen. Causal reversibility in Bayesian networks. *Journal of Experimental and Theoretical Artificial Intelligence*, 13(1):45–62, 2001.

R. M. Dudley. *Real Analysis and Probability*. Cambridge University Press, New York, NY, 2002.

D. Eaton and K. P. Murphy. Exact Bayesian structure learning from uncertain interventions. In *Proceedings of the 11th International Conference on Artificial Intelligence and Statistics (AISTATS)*, pages 107–114, 2007.

F. Eberhardt and R. Scheines. Interventions and causal inference. *Philosophy of Science*, 74(5):981–995, 2007.

F. Eberhardt, C. Glymour, and R. Scheines. On the number of experiments sufficient and in the worst case necessary to identify all causal relations among n variables. In *Proceedings of the 21st Annual Conference on Uncertainty in Artificial Intelligence (UAI)*, pages 178–184, 2005.

F. Eberhardt, P. O. Hoyer, and R. Scheines. Combining experiments to discover linear cyclic models with latent variables. In *Proceedings of the 13th International Conference on Artificial Intelligence and Statistics (AISTATS)*, pages 185–192, 2010.

M. Eichler. Graphical modelling of multivariate time series. *Probability Theory and Related Fields*, pages 1–36, 2011.

M. Eichler. Causal inference in time series analysis. In C. Berzuini, P. Dawid, and L. Bernardinelli, editors, *Causality: Statistical Perspectives and Applications*, pages 327–354. Wiley, Chichester, UK, 2012.

J. Ellenberg. *How Not to Be Wrong: The Power of Mathematical Thinking*. Penguin Press, London, UK, 2014.

R. F. Engle, D. F. Hendry, and J.-F. Richard. Exogeneity. *Econometrica*, 51(2): 277–304, 1983.

R. J. Evans. Graphical methods for inequality constraints in marginalized DAGs. In *Proceedings of the 22nd Workshop on Machine Learning and Signal Processing*, pages 1–12, 2012.

R. J. Evans. Margins of discrete Bayesian networks. *ArXiv e-prints (arXiv:1501.02103)*, 2015.

R. J. Evans and T. S. Richardson. Markovian acyclic directed mixed graphs for discrete data. *The Annals of Statistics*, 42(2):1452–1482, 2014.

T. S. Ferguson. *Mathematical Statistics — A Decision Theoretic Approach*. Academic Press, New York, NY and London, UK, 1967.

A. Fink. The binomial ideal of the intersection axiom for conditional probabilities. *Journal of Algebraic Combinatorics*, 33(3):455–463, 2011.

R. A. Fisher. *Statistical Methods for Research Workers*. Oliver & Boyd, Edinburgh, UK, 1925.

W. T. Freeman. The generic viewpoint assumption in a framework for visual perception. *Nature*, 368(6471):542–545, 1994.

R. Frisch and F. V. Waugh. Partial time regressions as compared with individual trends. *Econometrica*, 1(4):387–401, 1933.

R. Frisch, T. Haavelmo, T. C. Koopmans, and J. Tinbergen. *Autonomy of Economic Relations*. Series: Memorandum fra Universitets Socialøkonomiske Institutt. Universitets Socialøkonomiske Institutt, Oslo, Norway, 1948.

K. Friston, L. Harrison, and W. Penny. Dynamic causal modelling. *NeuroImage*, 19:1273–1302, 2003.

K. Friston, J. Daunizeau, and K. Stephan. Model selection and gobbledygook: Response to Lohmann et al. *NeuroImage*, 75:275–278, 2013.

M. Frydenberg. The chain graph Markov property. *Scandinavian Journal of Statistics*, 17(4):333–353, 1990.

K. Fukumizu, A. Gretton, X. Sun, and B. Schölkopf. Kernel measures of conditional dependence. In *Advances in Neural Information Processing Systems 20 (NIPS)*, pages 489–496, 2008.

J. A. Gagnon-Bartsch and T. P. Speed. Using control genes to correct for unwanted variation in microarray data. *Biostatistics*, 13:539–552, 2012.

D. Galles and J. Pearl. An axiomatic characterization of causal counterfactuals. *Foundations of Science*, 3(1):151–182, 1998.

D. Geiger and D. Heckerman. Learning Gaussian networks. In *Proceedings of the 10th Annual Conference on Uncertainty in Artificial Intelligence (UAI)*, pages 235–243, 1994a.

D. Geiger and D. Heckerman. Learning Bayesian networks: The combination of knowledge and statistical data. In *Proceedings of the 10th Annual Conference on Uncertainty in Artificial Intelligence (UAI)*, pages 293–301, 1994b.

D. Geiger and C. Meek. Graphical models and exponential families. In *Proceedings of 14th Annual Conference on Uncertainty in Artificial Intelligence (UAI)*, pages 156–165, 1998.

P. Geiger, D. Janzing, and B. Schölkopf. Estimating causal effects by bounding confounding. In *Proceedings of the 30th Conference on Uncertainty in Artificial Intelligence (UAI)*, pages 240–249, 2014.

D. Geradin and I. Girgenson. The counterfactual method in EU competition law: The cornerstone of the effects-based approach. Available at SSRN: `http://ssrn.com/abstract=1970917`, 2011.

C. W. J. Granger. Testing for causality: A personal viewpoint. *Journal of Economic Dynamics and Control*, 2(1):329–352, 1980.

C. W. J. Granger. Some recent development in a concept of causality. *Journal of Econometrics*, 39(1–2):199–211, 1988.

A. Gretton, K. Fukumizu, C. H. Teo, L. Song, B. Schölkopf, and A. Smola. A kernel statistical test of independence. In *Advances in Neural Information Processing Systems 20 (NIPS)*, pages 585–592, 2008.

P. D. Grünwald. *The Minimum Description Length Principle*. MIT Press, Cambridge, MA, 2007.

I. Guyon. Challenge: Cause-effect pairs, 2013. URL `https://www.kaggle.com/c/cause-effect-pairs/`. Results were presented at NIPS 2013 workshop `http://clopinet.com/isabelle/Projects/NIPS2013/`; last visit of websites: 19.07.2016.

J. Gwiazda, E. Ong, R. Held, and F. Thorn. Vision: Myopia and ambient night-time lighting. *Nature*, 404:144, 2000.

T. Haavelmo. The statistical implications of a system of simultaneous equations. *Econometrica*, 11(1):1–12, 1943.

T. Haavelmo. The probability approach in econometrics. *Econometrica*, 12:S1–S115 (supplement), 1944.

J. Y. Halpern. Axiomatizing causal reasoning. *Journal of Artificial Intelligence Research*, 12:317–337, 2000.

J. Y. Halpern. *Actual Causality*. MIT Press, Cambridge, MA, 2016.

N. R. Hansen and A. Sokol. Causal interpretation of stochastic differential equations. *Electronic Journal of Probability*, 19(100):1–24, 2014.

T. Hastie, R. Tibshirani, and J. Friedman. *The Elements of Statistical Learning: Data Mining, Inference and Prediction*. Springer, New York, NY, 2nd edition, 2009.

D. M. A. Haughton. On the choice of a model to fit data from an exponential family. *The Annals of Statistics*, 16(1):342–355, 1988.

A. Hauser and P. Bühlmann. Characterization and greedy learning of interventional Markov equivalence classes of directed acyclic graphs. *Journal of Machine Learning Research*, 13:2409–2464, 2012.

A. Hauser and P. Bühlmann. Two optimal strategies for active learning of causal models from interventional data. *International Journal of Approximate Reasoning*, 55:926–939, 2014.

A. Hauser and P. Bühlmann. Jointly interventional and observational data: Estimation of interventional Markov equivalence classes of directed acyclic graphs. *Journal of the Royal Statistical Society, Series B: Statistical Methodology*, 77: 291–318, 2015.

D. M. Hausman and J. Woodward. Independence, invariance and the causal Markov condition. *The British Society for the Philosophy of Science*, 50:521–583, 1999.

D. Heckerman, C. Meek, and G. Cooper. A Bayesian approach to causal discovery. In C. Glymour and G. Cooper, editors, *Computation, Causation, and Discovery*, pages 141–165. MIT Press, Cambridge, MA, 1999.

R. Hemmecke, S. Linder, and M. Studený. Characteristic imsets for learning Bayesian network structure. *International Journal of Approximate Reasoning*, 53:1336–1349, 2012.

M. A. Hernán and J. M. Robins. Instruments for causal inference: An epidemiologists dream? *Epidemiology*, 17:360–372, 2006.

P. W. Holland. Statistics and causal inference. *Journal of the American Statistical Association*, 81:968–970, 1986.

K. D. Hoover. Causality in economics and econometrics. In S. N. Durlauf and L. E. Blume, editors, *The New Palgrave Dictionary of Economics*. Palgrave Macmillan, Basingstoke, UK, 2nd edition, 2008.

D. G. Horvitz and D. J. Thompson. A generalization of sampling without replacement from a finite universe. *Journal of the American Statistical Association*, 47 (260):663–685, 1952.

P. O. Hoyer, A. Hyvärinen, R. Scheines, P. Spirtes, J. Ramsey, G. Lacerda, and S. Shimizu. Causal discovery of linear acyclic models with arbitrary distributions. In *Proceedings of the 24th Annual Conference on Uncertainty in Artificial Intelligence (UAI)*, pages 282–289, 2008a.

P. O. Hoyer, S. Shimizu, A. J. Kerminen, and M. Palviainen. Estimation of causal effects using linear non-Gaussian causal models with hidden variables. *International Journal of Approximate Reasoning*, 49(2):362–378, 2008b.

P. O. Hoyer, D. Janzing, J. M. Mooij, J. Peters, and B. Schölkopf. Nonlinear causal discovery with additive noise models. In *Advances in Neural Information Processing Systems 21 (NIPS)*, pages 689–696, 2009.

Y. Huang and M. Valtorta. Pearl's calculus of intervention is complete. In *Proceedings of the 22nd Annual Conference on Uncertainty in Artificial Intelligence (UAI)*, pages 217–224, 2006.

L Hurwicz. On the structural form of interdependent systems. In E. Nagel, P. Suppes, and A. Tarski, editors, *Logic, Methodology and Philosophy of Science, Proceedings of the 1960 International Congress*, pages 232–239. Stanford University Press, Stanford, CA, 1962.

A. Hyttinen, F. Eberhardt, and P. O. Hoyer. Learning linear cyclic causal models with latent variables. *Journal of Machine Learning Research*, 13(1):3387–3439, 2012.

A. Hyttinen, P. O. Hoyer, F. Eberhardt, and M. Järvisalo. Discovering cyclic causal models with latent variables: A general SAT-based procedure. In *Proceedings of the 29th Annual Conference on Uncertainty in Artificial Intelligence (UAI)*, pages 301–310, 2013.

A. Hyttinen, S. Plis, M. Järvisalo, F. Eberhardt, and D. Danks. Causal discovery from subsampled time series data by constraint optimization. In *Proceedings of the 8th International Conference on Probabilistic Graphical Models (PGM)*, pages 216–227, 2016.

A. Hyvärinen, J. Karhunen, and E. Oja. *Independent Component Analysis*. Adaptive and Learning Systems for Signal Processing, Communications, and Control. Wiley, New York, NY, 2001.

A. Hyvärinen, S. Shimizu, and P. Hoyer. Causal modelling combining instantaneous and lagged effects: An identifiable model based on non-Gaussianity. In *Proceedings of the 25th International Conference on Machine Learning (ICML)*, pages 424–431, 2008.

G. W. Imbens and J. Angrist. Identification and estimation of local average treatment effects. *Econometrica*, 62(2):467–75, 1994.

G. W. Imbens and D. B. Rubin. Discussion of: "Causal Diagrams for Empirical Research" by J. Pearl. *Biometrika*, 82(4):694–695, 1995.

G. W. Imbens and D. B. Rubin. *Causal Inference for Statistics, Social, and Biomedical Sciences: An Introduction*. Cambridge University Press, New York, NY, 2015.

T. Jaakkola, D. Sontag, A. Globerson, and M. Meila. Learning Bayesian network structure using LP relaxations. *Proceedings of the 13th International Conference on Artificial Intelligence and Statistics (AISTATS)*, pages 358–365, 2010.

L. Jacob, J. A. Gagnon-Bartsch, and T. P. Speed. Correcting gene expression data when neither the unwanted variation nor the factor of interest are observed. *Biostatistics*, 17(1):16–28, 2016.

D. Janzing. On the entropy production of time series with unidirectional linearity. *Journal of Statistical Physics*, 138:767–779, 2010.

D. Janzing and B. Schölkopf. Causal inference using the algorithmic Markov condition. *IEEE Transactions on Information Theory*, 56(10):5168–5194, 2010.

D. Janzing and B. Schölkopf. Semi-supervised interpolation in an anticausal learning scenario. *Journal of Machine Learning Research*, 16:1923–1948, 2015.

D. Janzing and B. Steudel. Justifying additive-noise-based causal discovery via algorithmic information theory. *Open Systems and Information Dynamics*, 17 (2):189–212, 2010.

D. Janzing, J. Peters, J. M. Mooij, and B. Schölkopf. Identifying confounders using additive noise models. In *Proceedings of the 25th Annual Conference on Uncertainty in Artificial Intelligence (UAI)*, pages 249–257, 2009a.

D. Janzing, X. Sun, and B. Schölkopf. Distinguishing cause and effect via second order exponential models. *ArXiv e-prints (0910.5561)*, 2009b.

D. Janzing, P. O. Hoyer, and B. Schölkopf. Telling cause from effect based on high-dimensional observations. In *Proceedings of the 27th International Conference on Machine Learning (ICML)*, pages 479–486, 2010.

D. Janzing, E. Sgouritsa, O. Stegle, J. Peters, and B. Schölkopf. Detecting low-complexity unobserved causes. In *Proceedings of the 27th Annual Conference on Uncertainty in Artificial Intelligence (UAI)*, pages 383–391, 2011.

D. Janzing, J. M. Mooij, K. Zhang, J. Lemeire, J. Zscheischler, P. Daniušis, B. Steudel, and B. Schölkopf. Information-geometric approach to inferring causal directions. *Artificial Intelligence*, 182–183:1–31, 2012.

D. Janzing, D. Balduzzi, M. Grosse-Wentrup, and B. Schölkopf. Quantifying causal influences. *The Annals of Statistics*, 41(5):2324–2358, 2013.

D. Janzing, B. Steudel, N. Shajarisales, and B. Schölkopf. Justifying information-geometric causal inference. In V. Vovk, H. Papadopolous, and A. Gammerman, editors, *Measures of Complexity*, Festschrift for Alexey Chervonencis, pages 253–265. Springer, Heidelberg, Germany, 2015.

D. Janzing, R. Chaves, and B. Schölkopf. Algorithmic independence of initial condition and dynamical law in thermodynamics and causal inference. *New Journal of Physics*, 18(093052):1–13, 2016.

M. Kääriäinen. Generalization error bounds using unlabeled data. In *Proceedings of the 18th Annual Conference on Learning Theory (COLT)*, pages 127–142, 2005.

M. Kalisch and P. Bühlmann. Estimating high-dimensional directed acyclic graphs with the PC-algorithm. *Journal of Machine Learning Research*, 8:613–636, 2007.

M. Kalisch, M. Mächler, D. Colombo, M. H. Maathuis, and P. Bühlmann. Causal inference using graphical models with the R package pcalg. *Journal of Statistical Software*, 47(11):1–26, 2012.

C. Kang and J. Tian. Inequality constraints in causal models with hidden variables. In *Proceedings of the 22th Annual Conference on Uncertainty in Artificial Intelligence (UAI)*, pages 233–240, 2006.

Y. Kano and S. Shimizu. Causal inference using nonnormality. In *Proceedings of the International Symposium on the Science of Modeling, the 30th Anniversary of the Information Criterion*, pages 261–270, 2003.

A. Kela, K. von Prillwitz, J. Åberg, R. Chaves, and D. Gross. Semidefinite tests for latent causal structures. *ArXiv e-prints (1701.00652)*, 2017.

M. Koivisto. Advances in exact Bayesian structure discovery in Bayesian networks. In *Proceedings of the 22nd Annual Conference on Uncertainty in Artificial Intelligence (UAI)*, pages 241–248, 2006.

M. Koivisto and K. Sood. Exact Bayesian structure discovery in Bayesian networks. *Journal of Machine Learning Research*, 5:549–573, 2004.

D. Koller and N. Friedman. *Probabilistic Graphical Models: Principles and Techniques.* MIT Press, Cambridge, MA, 2009.

A. Kolmogorov. Three approaches to the quantitative definition of information. *Problems of Information Transmission*, 1(1):3–11, 1965.

T. C. Koopmans. When is an equation system complete for statistical purposes? In T. C. Koopmans, editor, *Statistical Inference in Dynamic Economic Models*, pages 393–409. Wiley and Chapman & Hall, New York, NY, and London, UK, 1950.

K. Korb, L. Hope, A. Nicholson, and K. Axnick. Varieties of causal intervention. In *Proceedings of the Pacific Rim Conference on Artifical Intelligence*, pages 322–331, 2004.

S. Kpotufe, E. Sgouritsa, D. Janzing, and B. Schölkopf. Consistency of causal inference under the additive noise model. In *Proceedings of the 31st International Conference on Machine Learning, ICML 2014, Beijing, China*, pages 478–486, 2014.

G. Lacerda, P. Spirtes, J. Ramsey, and P. O. Hoyer. Discovering cyclic causal models by independent components analysis. In *Proceedings of the 24th Annual Conference on Uncertainty in Artificial Intelligence (UAI)*, pages 366–374, 2008.

S. L. Lauritzen. *Graphical Models.* Oxford University Press, New York, NY, 1996.

S. L. Lauritzen. Discussion on causality. *Scandinavian Journal of Statistics*, 31(2): 189–193, 2004.

S. L. Lauritzen and T. S. Richardson. Chain graph models and their causal interpretations. *Journal of the Royal Statistical Society, Series B: Statistical Methodology (with discussion)*, 64(3):321–361, 2002.

S. L. Lauritzen and N. Wermuth. Graphical models for associations between variables, some of which are qualitative and some quantitative. *Annals of Statistics*, 17(1):31–57, 1989.

J. Lemeire and E. Dirkx. Causal models as minimal descriptions of multivariate systems. `http://parallel.vub.ac.be/~jan/`, 2006.

J. Lemeire and D. Janzing. Replacing causal faithfulness with algorithmic independence of conditionals. *Minds and Machines*, 23:227–249, 2013.

L. A. Levin. Universal sequential search problems. *Problems of Information Transmission*, 9(3):115–116, 1973. (Translated into English by B. A. Trakhtenbrot: "A survey of Russian approaches to perebor (brute-force searches) algorithms," *Annals of the History of Computing* 6(4): 384–400, 1984).

M. Levine, D. R. Hunter, and D. Chauveau. Maximum smoothed likelihood for multivariate mixtures. *Biometrika*, 98(2):403–416, 2011.

M. Li and P. Vitányi. *An Introduction to Kolmogorov Complexity and Its Applications*. Springer, New York, NY, 3rd edition, 1997.

G. Lohmann, K. Erfurth, K. Müller, and R. Turner. Critical comments on dynamic causal modelling. *NeuroImage*, 59:2322–2329, 2012a.

G. Lohmann, K. Müller, and R. Turner. Response to commentaries on our paper: Critical comments on dynamic modeling. *NeuroImage*, 75:279–281, 2012b.

D. Lopez-Paz, K. Muandet, B. Schölkopf, and I. Tolstikhin. Towards a learning theory of cause-effect inference. In *Proceedings of the 32nd International Conference on Machine Learning (ICML)*, pages 1452–1461, 2015.

H. Lütkepohl. *New Introduction to Multiple Time Series Analysis*. Springer, Berlin, Germany, 2007.

M. H. Maathuis, D. Colombo, M. Kalisch, and P. Bühlmann. Estimating high-dimensional intervention effects from observational data. *The Annals of Statistics*, 37(6A):3133–3164, 2009.

D. J. C. MacKay. *Information Theory, Inference, and Learning Algorithms*. Cambridge University Press, New York, NY, 2002.

S. Mani, G. F. Cooper, and P. Spirtes. A theoretical study of y structures for causal discovery. In *Proceedings of the 22nd Annual Conference on Uncertainty in Artificial Intelligence (UAI)*, pages 314–323, 2006.

D. Marinazzo, M. Pellicoro, and S. Stramaglia. Kernel method for nonlinear Granger causality. *Physical Review Letters*, 100:144103–1–4, 2008.

F. Markowetz, S. Grossmann, and R. Spang. Probabilistic soft interventions in conditional Gaussian networks. In *Proceedings of the 10th International Conference on Artificial Intelligence and Statistics (AISTATS)*, pages 214–221, 2005.

J. Marschak. Statistical inference in economics: An introduction. In T. C. Koopmans, editor, *Statistical Inference in Dynamic Economic Models*, pages 1–50. Wiley and Chapman & Hall, New York, NY, and London, UK, 1950. Cowles Commission for Research in Economics, Monograph No. 10.

B. D. McKay. Acyclic digraphs and eigenvalues of (0, 1)–matrices. *Journal of Integer Sequences*, 7(2):1–5, 2004.

C. Meek. Causal inference and causal explanation with background knowledge. In *Proceedings of the 11th Annual Conference on Uncertainty in Artificial Intelligence (UAI)*, pages 403–441, 1995.

J. M. Mooij, D. Janzing, J. Peters, and B. Schölkopf. Regression by dependence minimization and its application to causal inference. In *Proceedings of the 26th International Conference on Machine Learning (ICML)*, pages 745–752, 2009.

J. M. Mooij, D. Janzing, T. Heskes, and B. Schölkopf. On causal discovery with cyclic additive noise models. In *Advances in Neural Information Processing Systems 24 (NIPS)*, pages 639–647, 2011.

J. M. Mooij, D. Janzing, and B. Schölkopf. From ordinary differential equations to structural causal models: The deterministic case. In *Proceedings of the 29th Annual Conference on Uncertainty in Artificial Intelligence (UAI)*, pages 440–448, 2013.

J. M. Mooij, J. Peters, D. Janzing, J. Zscheischler, and B. Schölkopf. Distinguishing cause from effect using observational data: methods and benchmarks. *Journal of Machine Learning Research*, 17:1–102, 2016.

S. L. Morgan and C. Winship. *Counterfactuals and Causal Inference: Methods and Principles for Social Research.* Cambridge University Press, New York, NY, 2nd edition, 2007.

W. K. Newey. Nonparametric instrumental variables estimation. *American Economic Review*, 103(3):550–556, 2013.

J. Neyman. On the application of probability theory to agricultural experiments. Essay on principles. Section 9 (translated). *Statistical Science*, 5:465–480, 1923.

M. Nielsen and I. Chuang. *Quantum Computation and Quantum Information.* Cambridge University Press, New York, NY, 2000.

C. Nowzohour and P. Bühlmann. Score-based causal learning in additive noise models. *Statistics*, 50(3):471–485, 2016.

C. Nowzohour, M. Maathuis, and P. Bühlmann. Structure learning with bow-free acyclic path diagrams. *ArXiv e-prints (1508.01717)*, 2015.

OEIS Foundation Inc. The on-line encyclopedia of integer sequences. `http://oeis.org/A003024`, 2017. last visit of website: 05.09.2016.

J. Pearl. A constraint propagation approach to probabilistic reasoning. In *Proceedings of the 4th Annual Conference on Uncertainty in Artificial Intelligence (UAI)*, pages 31–42, 1985.

J. Pearl. *Probabilistic Reasoning in Intelligent Systems: Networks of Plausible Inference.* Morgan Kaufmann Publishers Inc., San Francisco, CA, 1988.

J. Pearl. Belief networks revisited. *Artificial Intelligence*, 59:49–56, 1993.

J. Pearl. Causal diagrams for empirical research. *Biometrika*, 82(4):669–688, 1995.

J. Pearl. *Causality: Models, Reasoning, and Inference.* Cambridge University Press, New York, NY, 2nd edition, 2009.

J. Pearl. Trygve Haavelmo and the emergence of causal calculus. *Econometric Theory*, 31:152–179, 2015.

J. Pearl, M. Glymour, and N. P. Jewell. *Causal Inference in Statistics*. Wiley, New York, NY, 2016.

C. S. Peirce. A theory of probable inference. In C. S. Peirce, editor, *Studies in Logic by Members of the Johns Hopkins University*, pages 126–181. Little, Brown, and Company, Boston, MA, 1883.

C. S. Peirce and J. Jastrow. On small differences in sensation. *Memoirs of the National Academy of Sciences*, 3:73–83, 1885.

E. Perkovic, J. Textor, M. Kalisch, and M. Maathuis. A complete generalized adjustment criterion. In *Proceedings of the 31st Annual Conference on Uncertainty in Artificial Intelligence (UAI)*, pages 682–691, 2015.

J. Peters. Asymmetries of time series under inverting their direction. Diploma Thesis, University of Heidelberg, Heidelberg, Germany, 2008.

J. Peters. *Restricted Structural Equation Models for Causal Inference*. PhD thesis, ETH Zurich and MPI for Intelligent Systems, 2012. `http://dx.doi.org/10.3929/ethz-a-007597940`.

J. Peters. On the intersection property of conditional independence and its application to causal discovery. *Journal of Causal Inference*, 3:97–108, 2014.

J. Peters and P. Bühlmann. Identifiability of Gaussian structural equation models with equal error variances. *Biometrika*, 101(1):219–228, 2014.

J. Peters and P. Bühlmann. Structural intervention distance (SID) for evaluating causal graphs. *Neural Computation*, 27:771–799, 2015.

J. Peters, D. Janzing, A. Gretton, and B. Schölkopf. Kernel methods for detecting the direction of time series. In *Proccedings of the 32nd Annual Conference of the German Classification Society (GfKl 2008)*, pages 1–10, 2009a.

J. Peters, D. Janzing, A. Gretton, and B. Schölkopf. Detecting the direction of causal time series. In *Proceedings of the 26th International Conference on Machine Learning (ICML)*, pages 801–808, 2009b.

J. Peters, D. Janzing, and B. Schölkopf. Identifying cause and effect on discrete data using additive noise models. In *Proceedings of the 13th International Conference on Artificial Intelligence and Statistics (AISTATS)*, pages 597–604, 2010.

J. Peters, D. Janzing, and B. Schölkopf. Causal inference on discrete data using additive noise models. *IEEE Transactions on Pattern Analysis and Machine Intelligence*, 33:2436–2450, 2011a.

J. Peters, J. M. Mooij, D. Janzing, and B. Schölkopf. Identifiability of causal graphs using functional models. In *Proceedings of the 27th Annual Conference on Uncertainty in Artificial Intelligence (UAI)*, pages 589–598, 2011b.

J. Peters, D. Janzing, and B. Schölkopf. Causal inference on time series using restricted structural equation models. In *Advances in Neural Information Processing Systems 26 (NIPS)*, pages 154–162, 2013.

J. Peters, J. M. Mooij, D. Janzing, and B. Schölkopf. Causal discovery with continuous additive noise models. *Journal of Machine Learning Research*, 15:2009–2053, 2014.

J. Peters, P. Bühlmann, and N. Meinshausen. Causal inference using invariant prediction: identification and confidence intervals. *Journal of the Royal Statistical Society, Series B: Statistical Methodology (with discussion)*, 78(5):947–1012, 2016.

K. Peterson. Night light with sleep timer, 2005. URL `http://www.google.com/patents/US20050007889`. US Patent App. 10/614,245; last visit of website: 19.07.2016.

N. Pfister, P. Bühlmann, B. Schölkopf, and J. Peters. Kernel-based tests for joint independence. *Journal of the Royal Statistical Society: Series B (to appear)*, 2017. doi: 10.1111/rssb.12235.

K. R. Popper. *The Logic of Scientific Discovery*. Routledge, London, 2002. 1st English Edition: 1959.

G. E. Quinn, C. H. Shin, M. G. Maguire, and R. A. Stone. Myopia and ambient lighting at night. *Nature*, 399:113–114, 1999.

J. Quionero-Candela, M. Sugiyama, A. Schwaighofer, and N. D. Lawrence. *Dataset Shift in Machine Learning*. MIT Press, Cambridge, MA, 2009.

R Core Team. *R: A Language and Environment for Statistical Computing*. R Foundation for Statistical Computing, Vienna, Austria, 2016. URL `http://www.R-project.org`.

J. Ramsey. A scalable conditional independence test for nonlinear, non-Gaussian data. *ArXiv e-prints (1401.5031)*, 2014.

H. Reichenbach. *The Direction of Time*. University of California Press, Berkeley, CA, 1956.

T. S. Richardson. Markov properties for acyclic directed mixed graphs. *Scandinavian Journal of Statistics*, 30(1):145–157, 2003.

T. S. Richardson and J. M. Robins. Single world intervention graphs (SWIGs): A unification of the counterfactual and graphical approaches to causality, 2013. Working Paper Number 128, Center for Statistics and the Social Sciences, University of Washington.

T. S. Richardson and P. Spirtes. Ancestral graph Markov models. *The Annals of Statistics*, 30(4):962–1030, 2002.

T. S. Richardson, J. M. Robins, and I. Shpitser. Nested Markov properties for acyclic directed mixed graphs (abstract only). In *Proceedings of the 28th Annual Conference on Uncertainty in Artificial Intelligence (UAI)*, 2012.

T. S. Richardson, R. J. Evans, J. M. Robins, and I. Shpitser. Nested Markov properties for acyclic directed mixed graphs. *ArXiv e-prints (1701.06686)*, 2017.

J. M. Robins. A new approach to causal inference in mortality studies with sustained exposure periods — applications to control of the healthy worker survivor effect. *Mathematical Modeling*, 7:1393–1512, 1986.

J. M. Robins, R. Scheines, P. Spirtes, and L. Wasserman. Uniform consistency in causal inference. *Biometrika*, 90(3):491–515, 2003.

R. W. Robinson. Enumeration of acyclic digraphs. In *Proceedings of the 2nd Chapel Hill Conference on Combinatorial Mathematics and its Applications (University of North Carolina)*, pages 391–399, 1970.

R. W. Robinson. Counting labeled acyclic digraphs. In F. Harary, editor, *New Directions in the Theory of Graphs*, pages 239–273. Academic Press, New York, NY, 1973.

N. J. Roese. Counterfactual thinking. *Psychological Bulletin*, 121:133–148, 1997.

M. Rojas-Carulla, B. Schölkopf, R. Turner, and J. Peters. Causal transfer in machine learning. *ArXiv e-prints (1507.05333v3)*, 2016.

T. Roos, T. Silander, P. Kontkanen, and P. Myllymaki. Bayesian network structure learning using factorized nml universal models. In *2008 Information Theory and Applications Workshop*, pages 272–276, 2008.

P. R. Rosenbaum and D. B. Rubin. The central role of the propensity score in observational studies for causal effects. *Biometrika*, 70(1):41–55, 1983.

D. Rothenhäusler, C. Heinze, J. Peters, and N. Meinshausen. backShift: Learning causal cyclic graphs from unknown shift interventions. In *Advances in Neural Information Processing Systems 28 (NIPS)*, pages 1513–1521, 2015.

D. B. Rubin. Estimating causal effects of treatments in randomized and nonrandomized studies. *Journal of Educational Psychology*, 66:688–701, 1974.

D. B. Rubin. Direct and indirect causal effects via potential outcomes. *Scandinavian Journal of Statistics*, 31(2):161–170, 2004.

D. B. Rubin. Causal inference using potential outcomes. *Journal of the American Statistical Association*, 100(469):322–331, 2005.

K. Sadeghi and S. Lauritzen. Markov properties for mixed graphs. *Bernoulli*, 20 (2):676–696, 2014.

B. Schölkopf and A. J. Smola. *Learning with Kernels*. MIT Press, Cambridge, MA, 2002.

B. Schölkopf, D. Janzing, J. Peters, E. Sgouritsa, K. Zhang, and J. M. Mooij. On causal and anticausal learning. In *Proceedings of the 29th International Conference on Machine Learning (ICML)*, pages 1255–1262, 2012.

B. Schölkopf, D. W. Hogg, D. Wang, D. Foreman-Mackey, D. Janzing, C.-J. Simon-Gabriel, and J. Peters. Removing systematic errors for exoplanet search via latent causes. In *Proceedings of the 32nd International Conference on Machine Learning (ICML)*, pages 2218–2226, 2015.

B. Schölkopf, D. W. Hogg, D. Wang, D. Foreman-Mackey, D. Janzing, C.-J. Simon-Gabriel, and J. Peters. Modeling confounding by half-sibling regression. *Proceedings of the National Academy of Sciences*, 113(27):7391–7398, 2016.

T. Schreiber. Measuring information transfer. *Physical Review Letters*, 85:461–464, 2000.

E. Sgouritsa, D. Janzing, J. Peters, and B. Schölkopf. Identifying finite mixtures of nonparametric product distributions and causal inference of confounders. In *Proceedings of the 29th Annual Conference on Uncertainty in Artificial Intelligence (UAI)*, pages 556–565, 2013.

E. Sgouritsa, D. Janzing, P. Hennig, and B. Schölkopf. Inference of cause and effect with unsupervised inverse regression. In *Proceedings of the 18th International Conference on Artificial Intelligence and Statistics (AISTATS)*, pages 847–855, 2015.

N. Shajarisales, D. Janzing, B. Schölkopf, and M. Besserve. Telling cause from effect in deterministic linear dynamical systems. In *Proceedings of the 32nd International Conference on Machine Learning (ICML)*, pages 285–294, 2015.

N. A. Sheehan, M. Bartlett, and J. Cussens. Improved maximum likelihood reconstruction of complex multi-generational pedigrees. *Theoretical Population Biology*, 97:11–19, 2014.

S. Shimizu, P. O. Hoyer, A. Hyvärinen, and A. J. Kerminen. A linear non-Gaussian acyclic model for causal discovery. *Journal of Machine Learning Research*, 7: 2003–2030, 2006.

S. Shimizu, T. Inazumi, Y. Sogawa, A. Hyvärinen, Y. Kawahara, T. Washio, P. O. Hoyer, and K. Bollen. DirectLiNGAM: A direct method for learning a linear non-Gaussian structural equation model. *Journal of Machine Learning Research*, 12:1225–1248, 2011.

H. Shimodaira. Improving predictive inference under covariate shift by weighting the log-likelihood function. *Journal of Statistical Planning and Inference*, 90 (2):227–244, 2000.

A. Shojaie and G. Michailidis. Penalized likelihood methods for estimation of sparse high dimensional directed acyclic graphs. *Biometrika*, 97(3):519–538, 2010.

I. Shpitser and J. Pearl. Identification of joint interventional distributions in recursive semi-Markovian causal models. In *Proceedings of the 21st AAAI Conference on Artificial Intelligence — Volume 2*, pages 1219–1226, 2006.

I. Shpitser and J. Pearl. Complete identification methods for the causal hierarchy. *Journal of Machine Learning Research*, 9:1941–1979, 2008a.

I. Shpitser and J. Pearl. Dormant independence. In *Proceedings of the 23rd AAAI Conference on Artificial Intelligence*, pages 1081–1087, 2008b.

I. Shpitser, T. J. VanderWeele, and J. M. Robins. On the validity of covariate adjustment for estimating causal effects. In *Proceedings of the 26th Annual Conference on Uncertainty in Artificial Intelligence (UAI)*, pages 527–536, 2010.

I. Shpitser, T. S. Richardson, J. M. Robins, and R. Evans. Parameter and structure learning in nested Markov models. *ArXiv e-prints (1207.5058)*, 2012.

I. Shpitser, R. J. Evans, T. S. Richardson, and J. M. Robins. Introduction to nested Markov models. *Behaviormetrika*, 41:3–39, 2014.

T. Silander and P. Myllymak. A simple approach for finding the globally optimal Bayesian network structure. In *Proceedings of the 22nd Annual Conference on Uncertainty in Artificial Intelligence (UAI)*, pages 445–452, 2006.

R. Silva and R. Evans. Causal inference through a witness program. In *Advances in Neural Information Processing Systems 27 (NIPS)*, pages 298–306, 2014.

R. Silva and Z. Ghahramani. The hidden life of latent variables: Bayesian learning with mixed graph models. *Journal of Machine Learning Research*, 10:1187–1238, 2009.

R. Silva, R. Scheines, C. Glymour, and P. Spirtes. Learning the structure of linear latent variable models. *Journal of Machine Learning Research*, 7:191–246, 2006.

H. A. Simon. Causal ordering and identifiability. In W. C. Hood and T. C. Koopmans, editors, *Studies in Econometric Methods*, pages 49–74. Wiley, New York, NY, 1953. Cowles Commission for Research in Economics, Monograph No. 14.

E. H. Simpson. The interpretation of interaction in contingency tables. *Journal of the Royal Statistical Society, Series B: Statistical Methodology*, 13:238–241, 1951.

V. P. Skitovič. Linear forms in independent random variables and the normal distribution law (in Russian). *Izvestiia Akademii Nauk SSSR, Serija Matematiceskie*, 18:185–200, 1954.

V. P. Skitovič. Linear combinations of independent random variables and the normal distribution law. *Selected Translations in Mathematical Statistics and Probability*, 2:211–228, 1962.

R. Solomonoff. A formal theory of inductive inference. *Information and Control, Part II*, 7(2):224–254, 1964.

C. Spearman. General intelligence, objectively determined and measured. *The American Journal of Psychology*, 15(2):201–292, 1904.

P. Spirtes. An anytime algorithm for causal inference. In *Proceedings of the 8th International Conference on Artificial Intelligence and Statistics (AISTATS)*, pages 213–221, 2001.

P. Spirtes. Introduction to causal inference. *Journal of Machine Learning Research*, 11:1643–1662, 2010.

P. Spirtes, C. Glymour, and R. Scheines. *Causation, Prediction, and Search*. MIT Press, Cambridge, MA, 2nd edition, 2000.

J. Splawa-Neyman, D. M. Dabrowska, and T. P. Speed. On the application of probability theory to agricultural experiments. Essay on principles. Section 9. *Statistical Science*, 5(4):465–472, 1990.

W. Spohn. Stochastic independence, causal independence, and shieldability. *Journal of Philosophical Logic*, 9:73–99, 1980.

R. P. Stanley. Acyclic orientations of graphs. *Discrete Mathematics*, 7(5):171–178, 1973.

I. Steinwart and A. Christmann. *Support Vector Machines*. Springer, New York, NY, 2008.

B. Steudel and N. Ay. Information-theoretic inference of common ancestors. *Entropy*, 17(4):2304–2327, 2015.

B. Steudel, D. Janzing, and B. Schölkopf. Causal Markov condition for submodular information measures. In *Proceedings of the 23rd Annual Conference on Learning Theory (COLT)*, pages 464–476, 2010.

M. Studený and D. Haws. Learning Bayesian network structure: Towards the essential graph by integer linear programming tools. *International Journal of Approximate Reasoning*, 55:1043–1071, 2014.

M. Sugiyama and M. Kawanabe. *Machine Learning in Non-Stationary Environment*. MIT Press, Cambridge, MA, 2012.

X. Sun, D. Janzing, and B. Schölkopf. Causal inference by choosing graphs with most plausible Markov kernels. In *Proceedings of the 9th International Symposium on Artificial Intelligence and Mathematics*, pages 1–11, 2006.

R. S. Sutton and A. G. Barto. *Reinforcement Learning: An Introduction.* MIT Press, Cambridge, MA, 2nd edition, 2015.

M. Teyssier and D. Koller. Ordering-based search: A simple and effective algorithm for learning Bayesian networks. In *Proceedings of the 21st Annual Conference on Uncertainty in Artificial Intelligence (UAI)*, pages 584–590, 2005.

J. Tian. *Studies in Causal Reasoning and Learning*. PhD thesis, Department of Computer Science, University of California, Los Angeles, CA, 2002.

J. Tian and J. Pearl. Causal discovery from changes. In *Proceedings of the 17th Annual Conference on Uncertainty in Artificial Intelligence (UAI)*, pages 512–522, 2001.

J. Tian and J. Pearl. On the testable implications of causal models with hidden variables. In *Proceedings of the 18th Annual Conference on Uncertainty in Artificial Intelligence (UAI)*, pages 519–527, 2002.

R. Tillman, A. Gretton, and P. Spirtes. Nonlinear directed acyclic structure learning with weakly additive noise models. In *Advances in Neural Information Processing Systems 22 (NIPS)*, pages 1847–1855, 2009.

R. E. Tillman and F. Eberhardt. Learning causal structure from multiple datasets with similar variable sets. *Behaviormetrika*, 41(1):41–64, 2014.

S. Triantafillou and I. Tsamardinos. Constraint-based causal discovery from multiple interventions over overlapping variable sets. *Journal of Machine Learning Research*, 16:2147–2205, 2015.

S. Triantafillou, I. Tsamardinos, and I. G. Tollis. Learning causal structure from overlapping variable sets. In *Proceedings of the 13th International Conference on Artificial Intelligence and Statistics (AISTATS)*, pages 860–867, 2010.

I. Tsamardinos, L. E. Brown, and C. F. Aliferis. The max-min hill-climbing Bayesian network structure learning algorithm. *Machine Learning*, 65(1):31–78, 2006.

C. Uhler, G. Raskutti, P. Bühlmann, and B. Yu. Geometry of the faithfulness assumption in causal inference. *The Annals of Statistics*, 41(2):436–463, 2013.

S. Ullman. *The Interpretation of Visual Motion*. MIT Press, Cambridge, MA, 1979.

R. Urner, S. Shalev-Shwartz, and S. Ben-David. Access to unlabeled data can speed up prediction time. In *Proceedings of the 28th International Conference on Machine Learning (ICML)*, pages 641–648, 2011.

S. A. van de Geer. *Empirical Processes in M-Estimation*. Cambridge Series in Statistical and Probabilistic Mathematics. Cambridge University Press, Cambridge, UK, 2009.

V. N. Vapnik. *Statistical Learning Theory*. Wiley, New York, NY, 1998.

T. Verma and J. Pearl. Causal networks: Semantics and expressiveness. In *Proceedings of the 4th Annual Conference on Uncertainty in Artificial Intelligence (UAI)*, pages 352–359, 1988.

T. Verma and J. Pearl. Equivalence and synthesis of causal models. In *Proceedings of the 6th Annual Conference on Uncertainty in Artificial Intelligence (UAI)*, pages 255–270, 1991.

D. Voiculescu, editor. *Free Probability Theory*, volume 12 of *Fields Institute Communications*. American Mathematical Society, Providence, RI, 1997.

A. Wald. *Statistical Decision Functions*. Wiley, New York, NY, 1950.

L. Wang and E. Tchetgen Tchetgen. Bounded, efficient and triply robust estimation of average treatment effects using instrumental variables. *ArXiv e-prints (1611.09925)*, 2016.

H. White and X. Lu. Granger causality and dynamic structural systems. *Journal of Financial Econometrics*, 8(2):193–243, 2010.

N. Wiener. The theory of prediction. In E. Beckenbach, editor, *Modern Mathematics for Engineers*. McGraw-Hill, New York, NY, 1956.

H. P. Williams. Fourier's method of linear programming and its dual. *The American Mathematical Monthly*, 93(9):681–695, 1986.

J. Wishart. Sampling errors in the theory of two factors. *British Journal of Psychology*, pages 180–187, 1928.

S. N. Wood. *Generalized Additive Models: An Introduction with R*. Chapman & Hall/CRC, London, UK, 2006.

P. G. Wright. *The Tariff on Animal and Vegetable Oils*. Investigations in International Commercial Policies. Macmillan, New York, NY, 1928.

S. Wright. On the nature of size factors. *Genetics*, 3:367–374, 1918.

S. Wright. The relative importance of heredity and environment in determining the piebald pattern of guinea-pigs. *Proceedings of the National Academy of Sciences*, 6(6):320–332, 1920.

S. Wright. Correlation and causation. *Journal of Agricultural Research*, 20(7): 557–585, 1921.

S. Wright. The method of path coefficients. *Annals of Mathematical Statistics*, 5 (3):161–215, 1934.

K. Zadnik, L. A. Jones, B. C. Irvin, R. N. Kleinstein, R. E. Manny, J. A. Shin, and D. O. Mutti. Vision: Myopia and ambient night-time lighting. *Nature*, 404: 143–144, 2000.

J. Zhang. On the completeness of orientation rules for causal discovery in the presence of latent confounders and selection bias. *Artificial Intelligence*, 172: 1873–1896, 2008a.

J. Zhang. Causal reasoning with ancestral graphs. *Journal of Machine Learning Research*, 9:1437–1474, 2008b.

J. Zhang and P. Spirtes. Strong faithfulness and uniform consistency in causal inference. In *Proceedings of the 19th Annual Conference on Uncertainty in Artificial Intelligence (UAI)*, pages 632–639, 2003.

J. Zhang and P. Spirtes. A characterization of Markov equivalence classes for ancestral graphical models. Technical Report No. CMU-PHIL-168, 2005.

J. Zhang and P. Spirtes. Detection of unfaithfulness and robust causal inference. *Minds and Machines*, 18(2):239–271, 2008.

K. Zhang and L. Chan. Extensions of ICA for causality discovery in the Hong Kong stock market. In *13th International Conference on Neural Information Processing, (ICONIP)*, pages 400–409, 2006.

K. Zhang and A. Hyvärinen. On the identifiability of the post-nonlinear causal model. In *Proceedings of the 25th Annual Conference on Uncertainty in Artificial Intelligence (UAI)*, pages 647–655, 2009.

K. Zhang, J. Peters, D. Janzing, and B. Schölkopf. Kernel-based conditional independence test and application in causal discovery. In *Proceedings of the 27th Annual Conference on Uncertainty in Artificial Intelligence (UAI)*, pages 804–813, 2011.

K. Zhang, B. Schölkopf, K. Muandet, and Z. Wang. Domain adaptation under target and conditional shift. In *Proceedings of the 30th International Conference on Machine Learning (ICML)*, pages 819–827, 2013.

K. Zhang, M. Gong, and B. Schölkopf. Multi-source domain adaptation: A causal view. In *Proceedings of the 29th AAAI Conference on Artificial Intelligence*, pages 3150–3157, 2015.

J. Zscheischler, D. Janzing, and K. Zhang. Testing whether linear equations are causal: A free probability theory approach. In *Proceedings of the 27th Annual Conference on Uncertainty in Artificial Intelligence (UAI)*, pages 839–846, 2011.

W. Zurek. Algorithmic randomness and physical entropy. *Physical Review A*, 40 (8):4731–4751, 1989.

Index

Adaptive Computation and Machine Learning

Francis Bach, Editor

Christopher Bishop, David Heckerman, Michael Jordan, and Michael Kearns, Associate Editors

Bioinformatics: The Machine Learning Approach, Pierre Baldi and Søren Brunak

Reinforcement Learning: An Introduction, Richard S. Sutton and Andrew G. Barto

Graphical Models for Machine Learning and Digital Communication, Brendan J. Frey

Learning in Graphical Models, Michael I. Jordan

Causation, Prediction, and Search, second edition, Peter Spirtes, Clark Glymour, and Richard Scheines

Principles of Data Mining, David Hand, Heikki Mannila, and Padhraic Smyth

Bioinformatics: The Machine Learning Approach, second edition, Pierre Baldi and Søren Brunak

Learning Kernel Classifiers: Theory and Algorithms, Ralf Herbrich

Learning with Kernels: Support Vector Machines, Regularization, Optimization, and Beyond, Bernhard Schölkopf and Alexander J. Smola

Introduction to Machine Learning, Ethem Alpaydin

Gaussian Processes for Machine Learning, Carl Edward Rasmussen and Christopher K.I. Williams

Semi-Supervised Learning, Olivier Chapelle, Bernhard Schölkopf, and Alexander Zien, Eds.

The Minimum Description Length Principle, Peter D. Grünwald

Introduction to Statistical Relational Learning, Lise Getoor and Ben Taskar, Eds.

Probabilistic Graphical Models: Principles and Techniques, Daphne Koller and Nir Friedman

Introduction to Machine Learning, second edition, Ethem Alpaydin

Machine Learning in Non-Stationary Environments: Introduction to Covariate Shift Adaptation, Masashi Sugiyama and Motoaki Kawanabe

Boosting: Foundations and Algorithms, Robert E. Schapire and Yoav Freund

Machine Learning: A Probabilistic Perspective, Kevin P. Murphy

Foundations of Machine Learning, Mehryar Mohri, Afshin Rostami, and Ameet Talwalker

Introduction to Machine Learning, third edition, Ethem Alpaydin

Deep Learning, Ian Goodfellow, Yoshua Bengio, and Aaron Courville

Elements of Causal Inference: Foundations and Learning Algorithms, Jonas Peters, Dominik Janzing, and Bernhard Schölkopf